Analyzing Qualitative Data

Analyzing Qualitative Data

Systematic Approaches

H. Russell Bernard
University of Florida

Gery W. Ryan
RAND Corporation, Santa Monica, CA

Los Angeles | London | New Delhi
Singapore | Washington DC

For information:

SAGE Publications, Inc.
2455 Teller Road
Thousand Oaks, California 91320
E-mail: order@sagepub.com

SAGE Publications Ltd.
1 Oliver's Yard
55 City Road
London EC1Y 1SP
United Kingdom

SAGE Publications India Pvt. Ltd.
B 1/I 1 Mohan Cooperative Industrial Area
Mathura Road, New Delhi 110 044
India

SAGE Publications Asia-Pacific Pte. Ltd.
33 Pekin Street #02-01
Far East Square
Singapore 048763

Printed in the United States of America

Library of Congress Cataloging-in-Publication Data

Bernard, H. Russell (Harvey Russell), 1940-
Analyzing qualitative data : systematic approaches / H. Russell Bernard, Gery Ryan.
   p. cm.
Includes bibliographical references and index.
ISBN 978-0-7619-2490-6 (pbk.)
1. Social sciences—Research—Methodology. 2. Qualitative research. 3. Quantitative research.
I. Ryan, Gery Wayne. II. Title.

H62.B438 2010
001.4′2—dc22

2009017942

This book is printed on acid-free paper.

11 12 13   10 9 8 7 6 5 4 3

Acquisitions Editor:	Vicki Knight
Associate Editor:	Sean Connelly
Editorial Assistant:	Lauren Habib
Production Editor:	Catherine M. Chilton
Copy Editor:	Carole M. Bernard
Typesetter:	C&M Digitals (P) Ltd.
Proofreader:	Doris Hus
Indexer:	Diggs Publication Services
Cover Designer:	Edgar Abarca
Marketing Manager:	Stephanie Adams

Brief Contents

Detailed Contents

Preface

This book is an introduction to systematic methods for analyzing qualitative data. Most qualitative data are written texts, but increasingly, qualitative data include still and moving images and sound recordings of dialogs or narratives. It won't be long before qualitative data include holographic, 3-D images of people and the artifacts that people create. But that's for another edition.

We mean for this book to be useful—useful to students and colleagues who need an introduction to the range of methods available for analyzing qualitative data. There are whole texts devoted to each of the methods we discuss here—discourse analysis, narrative analysis, grounded theory, content analysis, ethnographic decision modeling, and so on. The problem is that, in the short run, methods get developed in disciplines and sub-disciplines and they get type-casted. In the long run, methods leak out across disciplines. Space sampling is used increasingly in the social sciences, but it comes from animal ethology, a biological science. Multidimensional scaling (MDS) was developed in the social sciences, but is now used across all sciences. A few years ago, chemists took MDS the next step and developed software for building three-dimensional images of proteins. Colleagues in sociology saw very quickly how useful *that* would be in visualizing social networks. In the long run, then, methods really do belong to all of us.

Throughout the book, we use real examples from the literature. We've included examples from across the social sciences—from education, criminology, sociology, political sciences, and so on—but you'll notice many examples from health research. This reflects our own background and also the fact that so much research on methods for analyzing qualitative data is done in the social sciences of health.

One of our reviewers emphasized that "research is not a linear process." We could not agree more. We set research up as if it were linear—first design, then data collection, then analysis, then write-up—but it's never that clean. In projects we've worked on over the years, we've redesigned things after finding out that our plans were, well, unrealistic. We've stopped collecting data to do preliminary analysis, and we've stopped analysis to collect additional, fill-in-the-holes data. And we've gone back and reanalyzed our data many, many times while writing up. When we send our research papers to a journal, anonymous reviewers often ask questions that require analyses we hadn't thought of ourselves. In short, the process of research can be messy, but that just makes it more fun, as far as we're concerned.

♦ WHAT'S IN THE BOOK?

There are two parts to this book. Part I is an overview of what we think of as the basics. Chapter 1 is about qualitative data: what they are and how they can be treated for analysis. Chapter 2 lays out the methods for collecting text. Some of this chapter comes from Bernard's earlier books on general social science methods, *Social Research Methods: Qualitative and Quantitative Approaches* (Sage, 2000) and *Research Methods in Anthropology: Qualitative and Quantitative Approaches* (4th edition, AltaMira, 2006). This material, as well as other material from Bernard's earlier books, is used by permission of the publishers. Chapter 3 is on finding themes, and Chapter 4 is on building codebooks. (Chapter 3 is based on our 2003 article in *Field Methods* [volume 15, pp. 85–109].) Chapter 5 is about the basics of data analysis, and Chapter 6 is an intro to conceptual models.

Part II comprises 11 chapters, each treating a different method for analyzing text. Chapter 7 shows how to compare attributes of variables. This chapter will look familiar to those who have analyzed data with Excel or with a statistical package, like SPSS, SAS, Systat, Stata, and the like. That's because the process for comparing attributes of variables in a matrix is the same, whether the data are qualitative or quantitative. Chapter 8, on cultural domain analysis, presents methods for collecting cognitive data—like free listing and pile sorting—and methods for analyzing those data—like multidimensional scaling and cluster analysis.

Chapter 9 is about analyzing words, using simple techniques—like counting and concordances—as well as complex ones—like semantic network analysis. Chapter 10 covers two parts of the enormous field of discourse analysis—conversation analysis and performance analysis and Chapter 11 continues with narrative analysis. Chapter 12 is an introduction to grounded theory—one of the two most widely used methods in the social sciences for analyzing text. The other is content analysis, the subject of Chapter 13. Chapter 14 deals with schema analysis and folk models, methods that derive from psychology and linguistics.

Chapter 15 is on the venerable method of analytic induction (based on logic) and the relatively new method of qualitative comparative analysis that derives from analytic induction. Chapter 16 (based on our 2006 article in *Human Organization* [volume 65, pp. 103–115]) is on ethnographic decision modeling, a method that comes from anthropology. Finally, Chapter 17 deals with issues of sampling in the collection and analysis of qualitative data. There is no hidden message in placing this chapter last. Some colleagues would prefer it right up front, with the basics. Wherever it goes, sampling is very, very important.

Suggestions for further readings are at the end of each chapter. These are meant as pointers to the literature, not as comprehensive reading lists for any topic. Use the Social Science Citation Index and other reference tools to find more literature on all the topics in this book.

The appendix contains information on software for handling various chores in research. We've also put the appendix online so that we can update it. Go to http://www.qualquant.net/AQD.

We don't have a chapter on mixed methods because we start from the idea that mixing methods is the natural order of science and always has been. So, take up any of the methods here and mix them all you want.

Acknowledgments

This book comes out of courses we've taught at the University of Florida (Russ), the University of Missouri (Gery), the Pardee RAND Graduate School in Policy Analysis (Gery), and the National Science Foundation's summer institutes on research design and research methods in cultural anthropology (Russ and Gery). The summer institutes began in 1987, and we have been privileged to work with colleagues whose skills in teaching methods are an enduring source of inspiration: Stephen Borgatti, Jeffrey Johnson, Pertti Pelto, and Susan Weller. We are especially grateful to Clarence Gravlee and Amber Wutich, who continue to teach us about the methods in this book.

Gery thanks his wife, Stephanie for her support and patience as he worked on this project. He thanks the Robert Wood Johnson Clinical Scholars and his colleagues at RAND who presented him with an array of research problems and trusted him to apply and improve new techniques for collecting and analyzing qualitative data, and he thanks David Kennedy, Hank Green, Homero Martínez, and Thomas Weisner for pushing him to new levels of methodological rigor and creativity.

Russ thanks the many students and colleagues—far too many to name—who have helped him learn to talk about research methods. Two of his closest colleagues, Thomas Schweizer and Peter Killworth, are no longer around to hear his thanks, but that neither absolves his debt nor diminishes his gratitude to them.

Finally, our thanks to everyone in editorial and production who worked on this book. C. Deborah Laughton signed the book while she was at Sage and worked with us to refine our ideas and focus our writing. Vicki Knight at Sage ran the editorial end-game. She found the kind of reviewers that authors really, really want—critical and helpful at the same time—and guided us through the revisions. Our production editor, Catherine Chilton, moved us with patience, understanding, and a high commitment to craft, through the hundreds of hidden steps involved in turning raw copy into a book. Carole Bernard (Russ's wife) did yet again what she has done for so many authors. Book authors will all know what we mean. The rest can just look at the bibliography, imagine what it takes to clean that up—and then multiply by ten.

H. Russell Bernard

Gainesville, FL

Gery W. Ryan

Santa Monica, CA

SAGE Publications would like to thank the following reviewers:

Keri L. Heitner
University of Phoenix (Online)

Lawanna Lancaster
Northwest Nazarene University

Aaron Coe
University of Phoenix

Cheryl Winsten-Bartlett
Northcentral University

Dorothy Aguilera
Lewis and Clark College

Judith Preissle
University of Georgia

PART I

The Basics

CHAPTER 1

INTRODUCTION TO TEXT

Qualitative Data Analysis

INTRODUCTION ◆

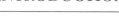

This book is about ways to produce and analyze qualitative data in the behavioral and social sciences.

All sciences rely heavily on—and have well-developed methods for the analysis of—qualitative data. When ecologists pore over satellite images of the Earth's surface, when astronomers listen to recordings of sounds from other galaxies, and when medical researchers listen to heart beats, they are all looking for regularities in qualitative data. "Looking for regularities" is analysis. It's the quintessential qualitative act, and it's common to all traditions of scholarship across the humanities and the sciences.

3

◆ WHAT IS QUALITATIVE DATA ANALYSIS?

Because of a quirk in the English language, the phrase "qualitative data analysis" is mischievously ambiguous. It can mean "the analysis of qualitative data" or it can mean "the qualitative analysis of data." The confusion can be eliminated by distinguishing clearly between data and analysis. Figure 1.1 lays out the possibilities.

The top left cell, A, shows the qualitative analysis of qualitative data. Interpretive studies of texts, like transcriptions of interviews, are of this kind. Investigators focus on and name themes in texts. They tell the story, as they see it, of how the themes are related to one another and how characteristics of the speaker or speakers account for the existence of certain themes and the absence of others. Researchers may deconstruct a text, look for hidden subtexts, and try to let their audience know—using the power of good rhetoric—the deeper meaning or the multiple meanings in it.

The bottom right cell, D, refers to numerical or statistical analysis of numerical data. Lots and lots of data about human behavior come to us as numbers. Closed-ended questions in surveys produce numerical data. So do national censuses. Organizations, from businesses to charities to zoos, produce numerical data, too—data about the socioeconomic characteristics of people who use their products or services, data about how often they have to replace managers, data about how much time secretaries spend on the phone and on e-mail, and on and on.

Figure 1.1   Key Qualitative and Quantitative Distinctions

Analysis	Data	
	Qualitative	Quantitative
Qualitative	A Interpretive text studies. Hermeneutics, Grounded Theory, etc.	B Search for and presentation of meaning in results of quantitative processing
Quantitative	C Turning words into numbers. Classic Content Analysis, Word Counts, Free Lists, Pile Sorts, etc.	D Statistical and mathematical analysis of numeric data

SOURCE: Adapted from: Bernard, H. R., and Ryan, G. W. (1996). Qualitative data, quantitative analysis. *Cultural Anthropology Methods Journal, 8*(1), 9–11. Copyright © 1996 Sage Publications.

The top right cell, B, is the qualitative analysis of quantitative data. It's what quantitative analysts do after they get through doing the work in the quantitative/quantitative cell, D, and it involves the search for, and the presentation of, meaning in the results of quantitative data processing. The qualitative/quantitative cell, B, includes everything from the finding of regularities in a scatter plot to the interpretation of meaning and substantive significance of statistical tests. Without the work in the qualitative/quantitative cell, the kinds of studies shown in the quantitative/quantitative cell are sterile and vacuous.

Which leaves the bottom left cell, C, the quantitative analysis of qualitative data. This involves turning words, images, sounds, or objects into numbers. Scholars in communications, for example, tag a set of television ads from Mexico and the United States to test differences in how older people are portrayed in the two countries. Political scientists code the rhetoric of a presidential debate to look for patterns and predictors of policies. Archeologists code a set of artifacts to produce emergent categories or styles or to test whether some intrusive artifacts can be traced to a source.

In this book, we'll be mostly concerned with cells A (qualitative/qualitative), B (qualitative/quantitative), and C (quantitative/quantitative).

WHAT ARE DATA AND WHAT MAKES THEM QUALITATIVE? ◆

Data—qualitative and quantitative alike—are reductions of our experience (Bernard et al. 1986). Electrons and DNA are things. With a little help from some instruments, we can look at electrons and DNA and we can record what we see. Whatever we choose to record about things like these—their shape, their size, their weight, their speed—are data. If we record numbers, we get quantitative data; if we record sounds, words, or pictures, we get qualitative data.

In the social sciences, we are interested in people's behavior, thoughts, emotions, and artifacts (the physical residue of people's thoughts, emotions, and behavior) and the environmental conditions in which people behave, think, feel, and make things.

When we reduce our experience of those things to numbers, the result is quantitative data. And when we reduce people's thoughts, behaviors, emotions, artifacts, and environments to sounds, words, or pictures, the result is qualitative data.

We create data by chunking experience into recordable units. Consider three researchers observing children at play in a schoolyard or playground. One of them watches the children and writes up field notes on what she or he saw. Another records the frequency of particular behaviors using a checklist. The third uses a video camera to record the children playing. The phenomena of interest—the behavior, the words, the laughter, and the crying of children on a playground—are ephemera, disappearing as they happen. The records of the phenomena—the notes, the checklist, the video recording—remain for us to analyze and understand. Data are the archeological record of experience.

Some qualitative data are produced on purpose—we interview people and transcribe their words; we put children together in a room full of toys and videotape or take notes about what they do—but most of the record about human thought and behavior comes to us as naturally occurring qualitative data. The paintings produced during the first hundred years of the Italian Renaissance, the television ads that aired last week in Mexico that contained images of old people, the articles in the *Wall Street Journal* over the last 20 years that contain the phrase "corporate culture," the diaries of U.S. Civil War soldiers, and the blogs of today's soldiers in Iraq—all are naturally occurring, qualitative data.

Across the sciences, from anthropology to zoology, from sociology to physics, data—all data, qualitative and quantitative—are selections of what's available. Satellites don't record everything going on below them any more than observers of human behavior record everything they see. People—real human beings—decide to measure some things and not others. These decisions are not random. They are sometimes based on unadulterated scientific curiosity, and they are sometimes based on what's fundable. They are sometimes motivated by humanitarian instincts, and sometimes motivated by greed. This does not invalidate the effort to produce data. It does, however, remind us that there is a human component to science, just as there is in art, government, or commerce.

♦ ABOUT NUMBERS AND WORDS

Every reader of this book is aware of the longstanding debate in the social and behavioral sciences about the relative merits of quantitative versus qualitative data. The debate reflects principled stands by colleagues who identify with the positivist tradition and those who identify with the humanist tradition of research. These discussions about epistemology—how we know things at all—have a noble lineage dating to Protagoras' (485–410 BCE) famous maxim that "man is the measure of all things"—meaning that truth is not absolute but is decided by individual human judgment—and to Lucretius' (94–49 BCE) insistence on the material nature of all things, including the mind. (**Further Reading**: the qualitative-quantitative issue.)

The qual-quant conflict plays out in all fields of social and behavioral science. In psychology, most *research* is in the positivist tradition, but much *clinical work* is in the humanist tradition because, as its practitioners sensibly point out, it works. In cultural anthropology, data are collected by fieldworkers—which makes cultural anthropology thoroughly empirical—but much of the data *analysis* is done in the humanist or interpretivist tradition.

Most research in sociology today is positivist, tracing its lineage to August Comte, Adolphe Quételet, and Emile Durkheim. The increasing number of sociologists today who count themselves as interpretivists, however, can trace their epistemological roots to the great tradition of Immanuel Kant, Wilhelm Dilthey, and others in the school of German Idealism. (Idealism here refers not to the pursuit of high purpose, but to the precedence of reason, or ideas, over empiricism in the practice of science.) The same can be said about research in education, nursing, and other fields: Positivists and interpretivists alike have long traditions on their side.

Notice that we don't say anything like "Research in X is mostly quantitative" or that "Research in Y is mostly qualitative." In fact, we never use the distinction between quantitative and qualitative as cover for talking about the difference between science and humanism or between interpretivism and positivism. Lots of scientists do their work without numbers, and many scientists whose work is highly quantitative consider themselves to be humanists as well. Moreover, numbers do not make an inquiry scientific—searching the Bible for statistical evidence to support the subjugation of women doesn't turn the enterprise into science—and the use of qualitative data does not diminish the scientific credibility of any piece of research (see Box 1.1).

Box 1.1

Numbers and Science: What's the Fuss About?

Scholars in the physical and biological sciences wonder what all the fuss is about. They already know how powerful qualitative data are. Satellite images inform geology, meteorology, astronomy, ecology, archeology, and oceanography. Images from electron microscopes inform chemistry, molecular biology, and physiology. Lengthy narratives dictated into a tape recorder by observers inform students of volcanoes, hurricanes, gorillas, and crime scenes.

Researchers in what we usually think of as highly quantitative sciences use a whole family of qualitative methods, called visualization methods, for understanding patterns in numerical data. Multidimensional scaling, for example, is a visualization method that's widely used in the social sciences. In fact, it was developed in the social sciences but, like all useful methods, is used across all sciences now. More on multidimensional scaling in Chapters 5 and 8.

◆ RESEARCH GOALS

There are four main objectives in qualitative research, irrespective of whether it's based on qualitative or quantitative data. The questions associated with each are shown in Table 1.1.

1. Exploration

At this early stage, the goal is to discover themes and patterns and to build initial models of how complex systems work. Whether we're talking about astronomers scanning the night sky in search of new comets and asteroids or grounded theorists studying how people experience illness, exploring means following leads and hunches; taking a step forward and then backtracking; uncovering what's there; experiencing the phenomenon we're studying, if possible; and identifying both its unique features and the features it shares with other phenomena.

Table 1.1 Goals of Qualitative Research

General Aim	Type	Questions
1. Exploration		What kinds of things are present here?
		How are these things related to one another?
		Are there natural groups of things here?
2. Description	Case	What does a case look like?
	Group	What does a set of cases look like?
		Is a particular kind of thing (A) present or not?
		How much of that kind of thing (A) is there?
	Cultural	What does the culture look like?
3. Comparison	Case	How is case X different from case Y?
	Group	How is a group of Xs different from a group of Ys?
4. Testing models	Case	To what degree does a particular case conform to the proposed model?
	Group	To what degree does a group of cases conform to the proposed model?

2. Description

Every field of science depends vitally on good description. Long before the physics of avian flight were worked out, people watched and recorded as faithfully as possible just how birds managed not to fall out of the sky. Every new comet and asteroid that's discovered is described in the scientific literature, as is every new bug and plant and disease.

Descriptions can be qualitative or quantitative, or both, and detailed case studies—with their listings of typical features, idiosyncrasies, and exceptions—are used widely in the teaching of law, medicine, and management. Ethnographic field notes are typically filled with individual case studies.

How much precision should you shoot for in a good description? When you're collecting data, you should get as much as possible. You can always back off on the level of precision later, when you write up your findings. It may be enough in your write-up to say something like "Cambodian refugees comprise the largest ethnic group in this neighborhood." But if you need to know the percentage of each ethnic group in the neighborhood, then you'd better collect that data from the start by asking every refugee what his or her ethnicity (or language or country of origin) is. You can always generalize from specifics, but you can never go the other way.

In describing cultural beliefs and practices, we focus on what people share and what they don't share. Here again, it pays to get as much as possible from the start—and for the same reason: You can only generalize if you have the specifics.

3. Comparison

Qualitative comparison involves identifying features that individuals or groups share and don't share. In the 1930s, Wayne Dennis, a psychologist, collected observational data on 41 Navajo and Hopi babies and on a similar group of White American babies in a study of child-rearing practices. Here's a thoroughly qualitative, comparative statement from his study: "Whereas some American infants are bottle-fed almost from the beginning and many are breast fed but a short time, all Hopi infants are breast fed, none are weaned under one year of age and many are not weaned before two years" (Dennis 1940:307).

Quantitative comparison involves testing whether (and how much) measurements of variables track each other. Does the weight of children between the ages of 10 and 16 vary with their height? If so, how closely do the two variables (height and weight) track each other? Does the tracking vary by ethnic group? By family income?

Just as with description, it pays to collect specific data and not rush to generalize.

4. Testing Models

This is where we test hypotheses against observations. We can do this with only qualitative data, with only quantitative data, or with both. Here is Wayne Dennis again:

> American infants are usually placed on a rigid time schedule of feedings with an interval of several hours between feedings [and are] . . . often expected to cry for a period before being fed. The Hopi infant, on the other hand, is nursed as soon as he cries, and consequently nurses frequently and cries very little. (Dennis 1940:307)

Dennis has drawn a strong conclusion about the relationship between crying and feeding—and has done so without reporting a single number. In fact, he was testing a much, much larger model, or set of hypotheses, about the care of infants. After reporting on Hopi, Navajo, and White American practices for carrying, feeding, and toilet training of infants, Dennis concludes that "beginning roughly at one year of age the patterns of the infant begin to vary in accordance with the culture of the group" as children begin to learn a language and to imitate their parents' distinctly cultural behavior. Dennis concludes that "this corroborates the view that the characteristics of infancy are universal and that culture overlays or modifies a more basic substratum of behavior" (1940:316).

Many projects involve all four of these activities—exploration, description, comparison, and model testing. Some scholars rely on qualitative data for exploration and discovery and rely on quantitative data for testing models. Increasingly, though, research across the social sciences relies on a balanced, commonsensical mix of both kinds of data.

◆ FIVE KINDS OF QUALITATIVE DATA

Qualitative data come to us in five forms: physical objects, still images, sounds, moving images and, of course, written words (see Box 1.2).

Box 1.2

Measuring Smells and Tastes

Interestingly, there are very limited data forms for taste or smell. We know how important these *phenomena* are to people—try to imagine ethnicity in the United States without referring to burritos and lasagna and bagels and moussaka and pirogis. Psychologists and chemists are working on ways to measure taste and smell but, so far, the only easily accessible olfactory and gustatory *data* we have about these things come from our memories or from self-reports. Wine aficionados have developed an elaborate vocabulary about tastes and smells—a vocabulary that turns memory into exchangeable information.

Table 1.2 shows the five kinds of qualitative data, broken down by size and accessibility Material objects range from personal trinkets to vast remains of ancient cities. Videos can be 30-second commercials or 3-hour epic pictures. Graphic data include stick figures drawn by children and murals by Diego Rivera that cover entire museum walls. Texts can be single-word answers to questions or the complete works of Shakespeare or transcribed narratives from ethnographic interviews. Data from public sources are more accessible than are data from private ones.

1. Physical Objects

For archeologists who study preliterate societies—societies that flourished before written communication—physical remains may be the only data available. The study of material culture, however, is not limited to societies of the distant past. Beginning in the late 15th century, the Age of Discovery in Europe produced an enormous market for material objects from societies around the world and by the late 19th century, anthropologists in Germany, Britain, and the United States were avid collectors of artifacts for public museums.

Notes and Queries on Anthropology, the methodological bible for anthropologists up to about 50 years ago, was compiled by the Royal Anthropological Institute of Great Britain. *Notes and Queries*

Table 1.2 Kinds of Qualitative Data Based on Form, Size, and Accessibility

Form	Small		Large	
	Accessibility			
	Public	Private	Public	Private
Physical Objects	Park sculptures, street signs, pottery shards, store merchandise	Personal jewelry, pill bottles, blood samples	Archaeological ruins, buildings, houses, universities, skyscrapers	Household garbage, clothing
Still Images	Magazine ads, cave art, billboards, Web pages, paintings hung in museums	Doodles, line sketches, family portraits, patient X-rays	Large detailed murals, art exhibits	Family albums, art portfolios, CAT scans
Sounds	Jingles, radio ads, intercom announcements, messages you hear while on hold	Memo dictation, answering machine messages, elevator conversations	Political speeches, sports play-by-plays, music albums, focus group tape recordings	Oral histories, demo sound-tracks, in-depth conversations, clinical interviews
Moving Images: Video	TV ads, news footage, sitcoms	Home-movie clips	Full-length movies, documentaries, television programs	Long video recordings of family reunions and special events, like weddings
Texts	Epitaphs, obituaries, personal ads, political buttons, parking tickets	Thank-you letters, shopping lists, short responses to interview questions, e-mails	Books, manuals, religious tomes, court transcripts, Congressional Record, newspapers	Diaries, detailed correspondence, private chat-room discussions

devoted more than a hundred pages to the study of material culture. A sample:

> The study of all aspects of the material side of people's life is of great interest and importance not only from the intrinsic interests of the

artefacts themselves, but for sources of invention, and questions of diffusion. Further, artefacts and techniques have great importance by virtue of their relation to the whole social organization and to religious and other ceremonial practices. (Royal Anthropological Institute 1951:221)

Today, museums around the world provide us with a living record of the diversity of human religious, political, and economic activity, and social scientists from many disciplines continue to study human interaction with material objects.

Researchers in marketing and consumer behavior are vitally interested in material culture (D. Miller 1987; Therkelsen and Gram 2008). Students of the world's religions collect and analyze icons and talismans (Handloff 1982; McColl 1982). Anthropologists have long used material possessions as indicators of status, prestige, and wealth in a community (B. R. DeWalt 1979). Ryan (1995), for example, found that the presence or absence of certain material objects—things like toilets, televisions, cars, corn mills, lamps—in the homes of African villagers predicted the kind of medical treatment that people sought. (**Further Reading**: material culture and museums.)

2. Still Images

For art historians, media and communication specialists, and for those who study popular culture, images, both still and moving, are standard forms of data. As early as 1919, Alfred Kroeber analyzed pictures in American and French fashion magazines and found "an underlying pulsation in the width of civilized women's skirts, which is symmetrical and extends in its up and down beat over a full century; and an analogous rhythm in skirt length, but with a period of only about a third the duration" (Kroeber 1919:257).

Since then, there have been hundreds of social science studies using still images—greeting cards (Bridges 1993), comic strips (LaRossa et al. 2000), pictures in ads (Goffman 1979), photographs (Drazin and Frolich 2007)—as basic data. Malkin et al. (1999) analyzed the covers of 12 popular women's magazines (*Ladies Home Journal, Cosmopolitan,* etc.) and nine popular men's magazines (*Esquire, Sports Illustrated,* etc.). The culturally patterned messages are clear: Men are enjoined to expand their knowledge, hobbies, and activities; women are enjoined to improve their life by losing weight and doing other things to change their appearance.

3. Sounds

Audio data include things like music, narratives, speeches, radio programs, and taped interviews. Alan Lomax (1977), an ethnomusicologist, analyzed speech samples from 114 societies around the world. He found that there are regularities in speech styles in complex, midlevel, and primitive economies. For example, the length of spontaneous utterances is longer, on average, in more complex societies than in less complex ones. Barbara Ayres (1973) discovered a strong preference for systematic, repetitive rhythms in societies where infants are carried in slings and shawls. In societies where infants are rocked in cradles, there is a preference for irregular rhythms.

Sociolinguists and scholars of discourse are dedicated users of audio data. Labov and Waletzky (1997), for example, used tape-recorded narratives to understand differences in class and ethnic markers of Black and White American speech.

Discourse analysis is widely used in the study of human interaction—doctors and patients during examinations, pupils and teachers in classrooms, husbands and wives during counseling sessions, and so on. Part of the content of these interactions—a large part—shows up in basic audio transcriptions. But part of it—the part having to do with tone of voice, pitch, cadence, rhythm—doesn't, and that part may be crucial to understanding what's going on.

For example, Joel Sherzer (1994) compared a tape-recorded, 2-hour traditional chant by Chief Olopinikwa of the San Blas Kuna Indians in Panama, with a phonetic transcription of the event. The transcription left out the chanted utterances of the responding chief (usually something like "so it is"), which was key to understanding the verse structure of the chant. This may seem like an exotic example, but it isn't. It's just an example from an exotic language. In fact, prosodic markers (things like tone of voice, etc.) tell a lot of the story when we want to know the full meaning of an utterance or a piece of dialog. (**Further Reading:** linguistic analysis of discourse.)

4. Moving Images: Video

Moving images, or what we call video in the rest of this book, combines the power of images and sounds through time. Scholars in film studies, sociologists, political scientists, and researchers in gender and media studies have become expert in analyzing video documents such as films, television programs and commercials, political ads, and even home-made movies.

Cowan and O'Brian (1990), for example, studied 474 cases of victims in slasher movies. Most protagonists in those movies are killed (that's the whole point of the genre), but a few survive. Women who survive, it turns out, are less physically attractive than nonsurviving women and are not associated with any sexual behavior. The male nonsurvivors were cynical, egotistical, and dictatorial. Cowan and O'Brien conclude that, in slasher films, sexually pure women survive and "unmitigated masculinity" ends in death (1990:195).

The Third International Mathematics and Science Study, or TIMSS, was a massive study of how math and science were taught in 41 countries around the world in the 1990s. One part of the TIMSS effort was the intensive study of instructional practices and lesson content in three countries: Japan, Germany, and the United States. Researchers studied videotapes of eighth-grade classrooms in the three countries and found very different teaching styles. In the United States and Germany, students spent nearly all their time practicing routine procedures to learn math. In Japan, students spend less than half their time on this kind of learning and a lot of time figuring out new solutions to standard problems—an effort that stimulates conceptual, rather than rote thinking about mathematics (Jacobs et al. 2007; Stigler et al. 1999:vii). (**Further Reading**: images as qualitative data.)

5. Texts

By far the largest trove of qualitative data is the mountain of written texts that have been produced over the centuries. Scholars from the humanist and positivist traditions alike rely on texts as their primary data. Folklorists, sociologists, psychologists, anthropologists, and political scientists have analyzed newspaper articles, novels, congressional reports, brochures published by hate groups, personal want ads, court records, diaries, and, more recently, e-mail messages and web pages.

Most of this book is about analyzing this kind of qualitative data, but almost everything we have to say about finding themes, coding themes, and analyzing text can be applied as easily to objects, images, and sounds as they can to words.

Further Reading

♦ For reviews of the qualitative-quantitative issue in the social sciences, see Guba and Lincoln (1994), Howe (1988), Rossi (1994), and Tashakkori and Teddlie (1998).

♦ For more on the study of modern material culture, see the *Journal of Material Culture*, the *Journal of Social Archaeology*, and the *Journal of Consumer Culture*. See Dant (2005, 2006) for an overview. On clothing and fashion, see Crane and Bovone (2007). See Haldrup and Larsen (2006) on the importance of material objects in the study of tourism. For example, Holly and Cordy (2007) analyze the detritus left by visitors to gravesites as a way to document behavior (like vandalism, magic, legend tripping, and partying) that would be difficult to observe directly without long-term participant observation research.

♦ On material culture as a reflection of gender roles, see Chaterjee (2007). See Cavanaugh (2007) on how the production of a particular kind of food became a symbol for a town in Italy. See Öztürkmen (2003) for how material artifacts are used in the creation of nostalgic narratives about the past.

♦ For more on the role of museums and their artifacts in shaping culture, see Coombes (1994), Hilden and Huhndorf (1999), and P. M. Taylor (1995).

♦ For more on linguistic analysis of discourse, see Drew and Heritage (2006), Schegloff (2007), and Wennerstrom (2001), and see Chapter 10 on conversation analysis. Scholarly journals that focus on this include the *Journal of Pragmatics* and *Text and Talk*.

♦ For more on the use of images as qualitative data, see Chaplin (1994), Collier and Collier (1986), El Guindi (2004), Hockings (2003), Morse and Pooler (2002), Pink 2007, and Van Leeuwen and Jewitt (2001). For more specifically on the use of photographs as data, see Capello (2005), Clark and Zimmer (2001), and S. Gardner (1990). See also the journals *Visual Studies* (from the Visual Sociology Association) and *Visual Anthropology Review* (from the Society for Visual Anthropology).

CHAPTER 2

COLLECTING DATA

◆ INTRODUCTION

Just as with techniques for collecting quantitative data, techniques for collecting words or images have to fit well with the goals of the research project. And just as with techniques for collecting numbers, the techniques we use for collecting words and images play a big part in what we end up with—that is, what we can submit to analysis later on. It's important, then, to know your research goals from the outset so you can choose methods of data collection and analysis well.

We begin with a taxonomy of data collection techniques, both qualitative and quantitative.

◆ DATA COLLECTION METHODS

There are three broad categories of methods for collecting data about human thought and human behavior: (1) indirect observation; (2) direct observation; and (3) elicitation, or talking to people. In addition, many studies involve a mix of the three major kinds of methods. Figure 2.1 lays this out.

The methods in Figure 2.1 have two things in common: (1) they are used equally for collecting qualitative and quantitative data, and (2) they are very, very labor intensive. Anyone who thinks that *qualitative* is a synonym for *easy* has a rude shock coming.

Figure 2.1 Taxonomy of Data Collection Techniques

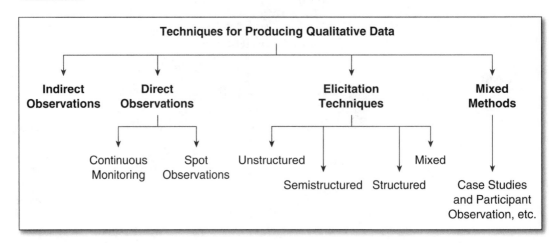

INDIRECT OBSERVATION ♦

Indirect observation involves (1) studying the traces of human behavior and thought; (2) analyzing archival data; and (3) secondary analysis, or reanalyzing data that were collected for other projects.

Behavior Traces

1. The traces of human behavior and thought are everywhere: material objects (pots, statues, buildings, steel mills), texts (diaries, speeches, interviews, lyrics), still images (paintings, graffiti, magazine ads, photographs), moving images (tapes of old radio shows, home videos of family events, newsreels, television ads, commercial movies), and recordings of sound. Some of these remains—like advertisements and political speeches—are created for public consumption; others—like diaries and love letters—are created for private use. But all of these, and much more, have been sources of qualitative data for social research.

There is a long tradition in political science, for example, of analyzing speeches and platforms to understand the policy positions of different candidates and parties (Hill et al. 1997; Laver and Garry 2000). Suedfeld et al. (1990) analyzed all the political speeches from the 10 Canadian elections held between 1945 and 1974. Researchers in media studies and marketing examine printed and television advertisements to track attitudes across time and in different countries about the role of women in the household and on the job (Gilly 1988; McLaughlin and Goulet 1999). Neto and Furnham (2005) analyzed children's ads on Portuguese, English, and American television to look for how gender roles in these three countries were being portrayed.

Personal ads inform us about preferences in mate selection among heterosexuals (Hirschman 1987; Lance 1998; Yancey and Yancey 1997), among gay men (Phua 2002), and among lesbians and bisexuals (C. A. Smith and Stillman 2002a, 2002b). Obituaries of business leaders contain data about men's and women's management practices (Kirchler 1992) and about how people in different cultures memorialize the dead (Alali 1993; de Vries and Rutherford 2004).

The most ubiquitous trace of human behavior is garbage. Archeologists at the University of Arizona have been studying the garbage of people in Tucson for many years. The data—chicken bones, empty beer bottles, empty egg cartons, and all the other detritus of everyday life—arrive at the garbology lab like text, ready for coding and interpretation (Rathje and Murphy 1992).

The Internet, and all its chat rooms, record traces of human thought in ways that were once unimaginable. Among other things, all these data make it possible to study very sensitive topics without invading anyone's privacy. Many people apparently have no compunction about discussing in public chat rooms the most intimate details of their sex lives. Carballo-Diéguez and Bauermeister (2004), for example, studied discussions about intentional, condomless anal sex (a practice known as barebacking) among gay men. Systematic examination of these archived electronic messages provides a window into something that would be difficult, at best, to ask about directly.

Archival Data

2. Research with archival data, like trace data, is inexpensive and nonreactive. Whether you're studying records of court proceedings, migrations, hospital visits, or credit card purchases, people can't change their behavior after the fact. The original data may have been collected reactively, but that's one reason why historians demand such critical examination of sources.

In assessing the value of documents, Guba and Lincoln (1981:238–239), citing G. K. Clark (1967), suggest asking the following questions: What is its history? How did it come into my hands? What guarantee is there that it is what it pretends to be? Is the document complete, as originally constructed? Who is the author? What is the author trying to accomplish? What was the document intended for? What were the maker's sources of information? What was the maker's bias? To what extent was the writer likely to want to tell the truth? Do other documents exist that might shed additional light on the same story, event, project, program, context?

Archives of qualitative data can be examined again and again to answer different research questions. The ads in the *Ladies Home Journal*, for example, have been analyzed for what they say about gender stereotypes in the products advertised to women (Mastin et al. 2004), for what they say about how women's roles have changed over time (Demarest and Garner 1992; Margolis 1984), and for what they say about women's body image (Fangman et al. 2004), among other topics.

The Internet is a rapidly expanding source of data for archival data. The U.S. Library of Congress has an online collection of all known recordings of former slaves (the recordings were mostly made in the 1930s and 1940s) and a collection of 8,000 images documenting Chinese immigration to California between 1850 and 1925. It also has a collection of 2,100 baseball cards from 1887 to 1914, in case you'd like to study what baseball players wore in those days. Libraries across the world are putting collections of primary documents online.

Secondary Analysis

3. Secondary analysis is analysis done on data that were collected for other research projects. All major surveys—the ones that track the buying habits of high school students, the political preferences of people in various ethnic groups, the health of age cohorts, and so on—provide data for secondary analysis, and there are hundreds of published studies based on these analyses.

Less well known, but of enormous value, are the corpora of qualitative data that are available for secondary analysis (Fielding 2004). Hodson observes that there are more than a hundred book-length organizational ethnographies published in English alone. Each of these studies required at least a year in the field, with an additional year analyzing and writing up the results, so this database represents more than 200 years of Ph.D.-level observation and interpretation (Hodson 1999:15).

Historical analysis is largely done on sets of documents about events, communities, organizations, and people, but if you look carefully, you'll find this kind of reanalysis across the social sciences. Khaw and Hardesty (2007) reanalyzed 19 transcripts of long interviews (between 1 and 2 hours) with women who had left relations in which they had experienced physical violence from their partners. The original study, by Hardesty and Ganong (2006), was done to document the parenting histories of the women, but in the reanalysis, Khaw and Hardesty focused on the process by which the women came to the point where they were able to leave the relationship.

The largest archive of ethnographic data in the world is the Human Relations Area Files (HRAF). Started in the 1940s by George Peter Murdock, Clellan Ford, and other behavioral scientists at Yale University, the archive has grown to more than a million pages of text, extracted from nearly 7,000 books and articles, on nearly 400 societies. The archive is growing at about 40,000 pages a year, and about a third of the material is available via the Internet through libraries that subscribe (go to: http://www.yale.edu/hraf/).This archive has been the source of hundreds of published articles. (More about the HRAF in Chapter 13.)

Disadvantages of Archival and Secondary Data

There are at least three problems associated with archival and secondary data: lack of authenticity, lack of representativeness, and measurement error.

The authenticity problem refers to the fact that, in secondary analysis, the data you're examining probably weren't collected with the purpose you have in mind now. If you interview 50 middle-aged women who are caring for frail, elderly parents, *you* decide what issues are important and *you* make sure that you ask each woman about each of those issues. Researchers who code archival data often find that only a few codes that interest them can be consistently applied (Hodson 1999:13). Missing data are a common problem in all research, but at least with data you're collecting yourself, you can go back and fill in the gaps as you find them.

Representativeness is a sampling problem. All data represent something, but in statistics, a representative sample is one in which every unit of analysis (every person, or every church, or every magazine ad) has an equal chance of being selected for the study. Telephone surveys are typically based on random digit dialing because, in theory, everyone in a calling area has the same chance of being contacted. Being contacted, though, doesn't necessarily mean being interviewed. Even in highly industrialized countries, like Holland, Spain, and the United States, response rates of 60% and lower are common (Díaz de Rada 2005:6; McCarty et al. 2006; Poortman and van Tilburg 2005:24).

Thus, the final sample in a well-conducted survey may not represent important segments of the population—like people who avoid surveys. This does not invalidate survey results, but it means that results have to be taken cautiously until they are repeated and that special surveys of nonresponders need to be done to fill in the blanks. We'll have more to say about representative and nonrepresentative sampling in Chapter 17.

Measurement error plagues all data collection, qualitative and quantitative alike. Some states and cities in the United States have implemented gun-control laws. Assessing whether those laws inhibit the use of guns in crime should be simple: Compare the number of crimes in which guns are used before and after each law is implemented. Unfortunately, the basic data—the Uniform Crime Reports, issued by the FBI for each of the 3,142 counties in the United States—are flawed. People in some U.S. counties tend to report when they're robbed at gunpoint. In other counties, the events go unreported and unrecorded.

This doesn't stop research on the effects of gun control laws, either. It creates opportunities to assess error and to make analyses better. All data are reductions of experience. You work with what you have and you try to eliminate bias as best you can. (Further Reading: secondary analysis of qualitative data.)

◆ DIRECT OBSERVATION

In the immortal words of Yogi Berra, "You can observe a lot by watching" (Berra and Garagiola 1998). When you want to know what people do, rather than what they say they do, nothing beats watching them (see Bernard et al. [1984] for a review of the informant accuracy problem). Just sitting and watching the activities of a clinic or hanging out at a truck stop can produce a lot of useful information if you pay attention and take careful notes. The hard part is not taking careful notes—it's paying attention and capturing detail.

Building Explicit Awareness

Paying careful attention to detail is a skill, not a talent. It comes naturally to small children (think of a 3-year-old asking in a loud voice in a supermarket: "Mommy, why doesn't that woman have any hair?"), but it doesn't come naturally to most adults. We learn early to tune out most detail—that's how cultural schemas get imprinted. Those schemas serve us well in everyday life (see Chapter 14), but they are deadly on research. Explicit awareness is a skill that every social researcher needs to develop.

Try this exercise: Holding a notepad, walk by a store window at a normal pace. As soon as the window is out of your vision, write down everything you can remember that was in the window. Go back and check. Do it again with another window. After repeating this exercise a few times, your ability to remember little things will start to improve. You'll find yourself making up mnemonic devices for remembering what you see. After you've done five or six windows, go back to them and try to capture more detail. Keep up this exercise (new windows, old windows) until you are satisfied that you can't get any better at it.

Here's another one. Walk through a city neighborhood, noting the languages or dialects that people speak, the music they play, the foods they eat, the number of singles (people who are alone) and pairs and groups of three or more. Repeat the exercise, going over the exact same route. You'll find yourself listening and watching for more detail and you'll see again how much you can learn from sharpening your skills at on-the-fly observation. Repeat with a new route. Keep this up (new routes, old routes) until you're satisfied that you can't get any better at it.

Here's a more demanding challenge. With two colleagues, attend a religious service that none of you have attended before. Don't take any notes, but after you leave, write up what you saw, in as much detail as you can and compare what you've written. Repeat this exercise—keep attending the service and watching carefully—until the three of you are satisfied that you have reached the limits of your ability to recall complex behavioral scenes and your notes of those scenes are substantially the same. Now repeat the exercise, but at a service with which you are familiar and your colleagues are not. See if your notes are substantially like theirs—that is, if you've been able to develop the ability to see familiar things as if you were seeing them for the first time.

It doesn't have to be a religious service. Any really familiar scene—a bowling alley, a laundromat—will help you improve your reliability as an observer. This doesn't guarantee accuracy, but because reliability is a necessary and insufficient condition for accuracy, you have to become a reliable data-gathering instrument if you want to become an accurate one (see Box 2.1).

Box 2.1

Other Devices for Observation

If you can't take notes during an interview or at an event, then get your thoughts down on paper immediately. Avoid talking to people in the interim. Talking to others before getting your notes down will reinforce some things you heard and saw at the expense of other things (Bogdan 1972:41).

Draw a map—even a rough sketch will do—of the physical space where you spent time observing and talking to people. As you move around the map, details of events and conversations will come to you. In essence, let yourself walk through your experience.

Two formal methods for direct observation of behavior are continuous monitoring and spot observation.

Continuous Monitoring

In continuous monitoring, or CM, you watch a person, or group of people, and record the behavior as accurately as possible. It is hard to do, but it produces uniquely valuable qualitative and quantitative data.

The technique was developed in the 19th century to improve manufacturing. In a classic study, F. B. Gilbreth (1911) measured the behavior of bricklayers—things like where they set up their pile of bricks and how far they had to reach to retrieve each brick—and made recommendations on how to lessen worker fatigue and raise productivity through conservation of motion. Before Gilbreth, the standard in the trade was 120 bricks per hour. After Gilbreth published, the standard reached 350 bricks per hour (Niebel 1982:24).

People who hired bricklayers loved the method. Bricklayers were not as happy, but the method of continuous monitoring of behavior is still used in assessing work situations (Drury 1990; Z. Tang et al. 2007), anxieties and phobias (Carmichael 2001), and the abilities of long-term nursing care patients (Algase et al. 1997; Cohen-Mansfield and Libin 2004). It's used for assessing the quality of interactions among employees and employers (Sproull 1981), pupils and teachers (Meh 1996), police and civilians (Herbst and Walker 2001; R. E. Sykes and Brent 1983), and doctors and patients (M. Silverman et al. 2004; Tabenkin et al. 2004).

Rosalyn Negrón (2007) used CM to find out how much time Spanish-English bilinguals in New York City spent speaking one language or the other and exactly when they code-switched—that is, changed languages (it can happen in the middle of a sentence among bilinguals). There had been dozens of studies on this topic, based on interviews and self-reports of behavior by respondents, but CM helped fill in lots of holes in our knowledge of code switching (see Box 2.2). (Details of Negrón's study are in Chapter 10 on discourse analysis.)

Box 2.2

An Exercise in Continuous Monitoring

To get a feel for the challenge of continuous monitoring, go to an upscale department store on a school day and record the interaction behavior of 60 mother-child pairs for one minute each. (Yes, one minute. It's a long time in the continuous monitoring business.) The children will mostly be under 6 years of age on a school day (ignore mothers with children who are clearly older than that). Select 30 mothers with one child in tow and 30 with more than one child. Record in detail the mother's interaction with each child, including content, tone of voice, and gestures of mothers and children.

Try to guess the ages of the children and the ethnicity and socioeconomic class of the family. It's a real challenge to code for SEC and ethnicity when you can't talk to the people you observe. Try using dress for SEC and language or dialect for ethnicity. Do this with at least one colleague so you can both check the reliability of your observations.

Repeat the exercise at an upscale and at a downscale department store. Then see if you can set up a table of the interactions and find patterns in the behaviors you've recorded.

Spot Observation and Time Allocation Studies

If you are trying to find out *what* people do, the data will be textual, like this:

There are three people home; the grandmother is playing with the toddler, who is about two and is banging a spoon on a the kitchen table; the mother is putting a load of laundry into the washing machine; the grandfather and the father are said to be out playing golf together because it's the father's day off and the grandfather is retired.

Spot observation, or time sampling, is a way to estimate *how much* people engage in a behavior. In this technique, an observer appears at randomly selected places, at randomly selected times, and records what people are doing (Gross 1984). The logic is clear: If you sample a sufficiently large number of representative acts, then the percentage of *times* people are seen doing things (working, playing, resting, eating) is a proxy for the percentage of *time* they spend in those activities. So, if women and men are observed doing some kind of work 38% and 52% of the *times* you observe them, then women work 38% of the *time* and men work 52% of the *time*—plus or minus some amount that's determined by the sample size. Your favorite statistics program will calculate this amount for you and will tell you if 52% is really a bigger number than 38% or might be the result of chance, given the sample size.

Spot observation has been done across the world to track how people actually spend their days and to answer questions like: Do men or women have more leisure time? What fraction of the time are babies left alone or held in someone's arms? (Baksh et al. 1994; A. Johnson 1975; Messer and Bloch 1985; Ricci et al. 1995).

Obviously, spot observation does not capture the *stream* of behavior the way CM does. Nor does it capture whole events in context as ethnography does. But spot observation captures many of the elements that make up the larger context and can be quite revealing when complemented with ethnography and interview data.

Converting Observations Into Data

Like any other phenomenon, the stream of behavior has to be converted to data. This can be done by taking extensive notes or by reducing activities to a set of fixed codes on the fly. Many researchers record their observations on audio or video recorders. It's less tedious than writing; it lets you focus your eyes on what's going on; it lets you record details later that might be left out of an on-the-spot written description; it avoids the limitations of a check list; and it lets you get information about context as well as about the behavior you're studying.

But there are tradeoffs. If you want measurements from qualitative data (like running commentaries on tape or disk), you have to code them. That is, you have to listen to and watch the audio and video recordings over and over again and decide what behaviors to code for each of the people you observe. Coding on the spot (by using a behavioral checklist or by inputting codes into a handheld computer) produces immediate quantitative data, but you lose context.

You can't code and talk into a recorder at the same time, so you need to decide what kind of data you need—exploratory or confirmatory—and why you need them before you choose a method. If you are trying to understand a behavioral process, then focus on qualitative data. If you need measurements of how much or how often people engage in this or that behavior, then focus on quantitative data.

ELICITATION METHODS   ◆

Elicitation, or interviewing, is a social process—you ask people questions and they provide answers—so it's the most reactive of the data collection methods. Interviews can be unstructured, semistructured, or structured. And, of course, you can mix the types in any given study. Figure 2.2 (an expansion of one section of Figure 2.1) lays this out.

Figure 2.2   Taxonomy of Elicitation Methods

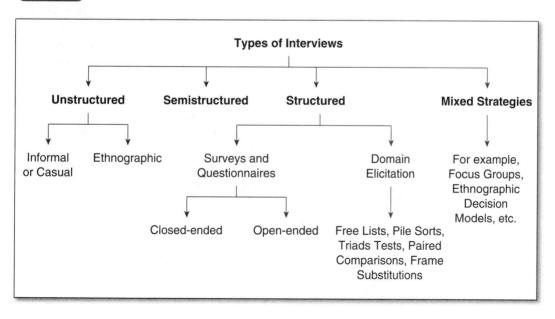

◆ UNSTRUCTURED INTERVIEWS: INFORMAL AND ETHNOGRAPHIC

Informal, unstructured interviews look and sound like casual conversations, but they aren't. They occur everywhere—in homes, in bars, on street corners, in factory lunch rooms—and they're hard to do. Informal interviewing requires self-discipline and a trained memory to recall in detail, from brief notes taken on the fly, what happened to you throughout the day, and what people said to you.

Informal interviewing provides a wealth of information, and in some cases it's the only realistic tool available for gathering information. How else could you talk to commercial sex workers who are out hustling on the street (assuming that you don't have the funds to buy their time for a formal interview)? Or to long-distance truck drivers who are grabbing a quick dinner on the road while their rig is being fueled (assuming that you don't have the time to ride with them all day or all night so you can conduct a formal interview)?

Ethnographic interviews can also look and feel like casual conversations, but they are not. And they are not informal, either. Here are three questions that might turn up in an ethnographic interview: (1) "Can you tell me, from your own experience, how you decided to have an abortion?" (2) "Can you tell me about how your friend decided to have an abortion?" (3) "Can you tell me how women you know decide to have an abortion?" The first question gets directly at lived experience. The second asks for a report on the experiences of others. It's often less threatening and can produce an enormous of amount of data from which cultural norms can be extracted.

The third question goes right for the cultural norms by asking the informant to generalize from experience. The goal in ethnographic interviewing is to understand the cultural norms, but there are many ways to get there. Detailed stories about lived experience are a great way to go, but there are clearly situations in which you have to tread lightly and in which question 2 or even 3 is the best way to start and to build trust.

Typically, ethnographic interviews start with broad, general questions—what Spradley (1979) called *grand tour* questions—and are then followed up with questions about specifics. This is known as a "funnel interview." A study of the dating practices of adolescents might begin with a question like: "What does it mean to date around here?" Later, you would ask for specifics, like: "Who do you and your friends tend to date?" "When people your age are dating, what kinds of things do they do?" And still later, you might probe for information about sexual practices: "When people your age are dating, what kinds of sexual activities do they engage in?" and then "Which of these tends to come first?"

In ethnographic interviews, the idea is to get people on a topic and get out of the way, letting them provide the information that they think is important. This makes ethnographic interviewing a fluid process, and it means that you may not be able to cover all the issues on a topic in a single sitting. Use ethnographic interviews when you have plenty of time—as in participant observation studies—and can return again and again to the same trusted informants.

Informal and ethnographic interviews help you understand the flow of everyday life, the kind of information that people are willing to divulge, and the topics that are sensitive. Informal and ethnographic interviews help build rapport and generate a lot of data—data that can be analyzed on their own or used in designing questionnaires.

SEMISTRUCTURED INTERVIEWS ♦

In semistructured interviews, each informant is asked a set of *similar* questions. In structured interviews, each informant is asked a set of *identical* questions.

If you want to make comparisons across people or groups of people, then you really need to get at least similar information from all of them. Semistructured interviews are based on an interview guide—a list of questions and topics that have to be covered. The interviewer covers each topic by asking one or more questions and using a variety of probes (like "Tell me more about that") and decides when the conversation on a topic has satisfied the research objectives (Cannell and Kahn 1968:527). The interview guide, and its instructions on where and how to probe, are essential when there's more than one interviewer on a project so that people are asked roughly the same questions.

Semistructured interviews occupy an interesting position along the structured-unstructured continuum. Semistructured interviews are flexible in that the interviewer can modify the order and details of how topics are covered. This cedes some control to the respondent over how the interview goes, but, because respondents are asked more or less the same questions, this makes possible comparisons across interviews.

Panchanadeswaran and Koverola (2005) did semistructured interviews of an hour to an hour-and-a-half with 90 Tamil-speaking women in India. All the women were seeking help after having been beaten—many severely— by their husbands. Semistructured interviews let these women speak out, in their own terms, but also ensured that the data could be examined systematically for patterns in the nature of and the consequences of the abuse. For example, almost 80% of the women reported being physically abused every day, and 44% reported the abuse began in the first month of their marriage (Panchanadeswaran and Koverola 2005:741).

Semistructured interviews produce a *lot* of qualitative data quickly. Hardré and Sullivan (2008), for example, studied how rural high school teachers got their students motivated. In addition to applying formal questionnaires, the researchers asked 66 teachers these nine, open-ended questions:

1. What subject areas and classes do you teach?

2. What is your students' general level of achievement in your class?

3. What is your students' general level of motivation for your class?

4. How do you tell when students in your class are unmotivated or disengaged?

5. When you see that students are unmotivated, what do you do or try to do?

6. What do you believe are the features of your classroom environment that facilitate or inhibit students' academic motivation?

7. What do you believe are the features of the larger school environment, outside your classroom, that facilitate or inhibit students' academic motivation?

8. What do you believe are the features of the larger community context, outside the school, that facilitate or inhibit students' academic motivation?

9. Is there anything else that you believe is important for us to know, to understand your students' motivation? (Patricia Hardré, personal communication, December 22, 2008)

The result was 30 hours of transcripts—over 300 pages of single-spaced text in Times 12-point type, or about 135,000 words (Patricia Hardré, personal communication, December 22, 2008).

Semistructured interviews are particularly useful for interviewing people who you really can't interview formally—like children. J. B. Whiting and Lee (2003) interviewed 23 foster children, using a semistructured guide. Each part of the interview—things like "how I came to foster care" or "my family"—was printed on a separate page. The interviewer showed a child each page as a way to stimulate the interview.

Probing

Probing is the key to successful in-depth interviewing; it definitely does not mean prompting. Here's a common question in interviews: "Have you ever lived anywhere except in this city?" If the respondent says, "Yes," then a probe is in order: "Like where?" If the respondent says: "Oh, all over the country," your next response should *not* be "Chicago? New York? Denver?" That's prompting. The correct response is a probe that doesn't put words into your respondent's mouth, like "Could you name some of the places where you've lived before?"

Interview technique, including the use of probes, has been the focus of research since the 1920s. In what follows, we draw on the work by Gorden (1987), Hyman and Cobb et al. (1975), Kahn and Cannell (1957), Merton et al. (1956), Reed and Stimson (1985), Richardson et al. (1965), Warwick and Lininger (1975), Whyte (1960), Whyte and Whyte (1984), and on our own experience. (**Further Reading**: interviewing technique.)

The Silent Probe

The silent probe involves nothing more than waiting for someone to continue their thought. Especially when you start an interview, people will ask for guidance on whether they're "giving you what you want." The silent probe is hard to learn because you have to recognize when people have more to say—and are just thinking—and not take silence as a void that absolutely has to be filled. Doing that can really kill an interview.

The silent probe is also risky. If someone has really completed a response, then silence becomes uncomfortable. In that case, you can lose credibility as an interviewer and wind up with a respondent just going through the motions to complete the task. The silent probe takes practice to use effectively, but it's effective and worth the effort.

The Echo Probe

The echo probe involves simply repeating the last thing someone has said and asking them to continue. It's particularly useful when an informant is describing a process or an event. "I see. So, when you arrest someone, you take them to the station house. Then what happens?" This neutral probe doesn't redirect the interview. It shows that you understand what's been said so far and encourages the informant to continue with the narrative. Don't use the echo probe too often, though, or you'll hear an exasperated informant asking: "Why do you keep repeating what I just said?"

The Uh-Huh Probe

You can encourage an informant to continue with a narrative by just making affirmative comments, like "Uh-huh," or "Yes, I see," or "Right, uh-huh," and so on. Matarazzo (1964) showed how powerful this neutral probe can be. He did a series of identical, semistructured, 45-minute interviews with a group of informants. He broke each interview into three 15-minute chunks. During the second chunk, the interviewer was told to make affirmative noises, like "Uh-huh," whenever the informant was speaking. Informant responses during those chunks were about a third longer than during the first and third periods.

The Tell-Me-More Probe

This probe involves saying: "Could you tell me more about that?" or "Why exactly do you say that?" or "Why exactly do you feel that way?" These stock probes can get tiresome for respondents, though, so use them sparingly. Otherwise, you'll hear someone finishing up a nice long discourse by saying, "Yeah, yeah, and why *exactly* do I feel like that?" (Converse and Schuman 1974:50).

The Long Question Probe

Instead of asking, "Why did you give up drinking?" say: "People have many reasons for giving up alcohol. Can you tell me about why you chose to give up alcohol?" Instead of asking "Why did you join a gang?" say: "Everyone has a story about how they got into this. How did *you* come to join this gang?" Terse questions tend to produce terse answers and longish questions tend to provoke longer answers. Longer is not always better, but when you're conducting an in-depth interview, the key is to keep people talking and let them develop their thoughts. The more people open up, the more you can express your support and develop rapport. This is especially important in the first interview you do with someone whose trust you want to build (see Spradley 1979:80).

Long questions are also recommended for questions about sensitive topics. Instead of asking straight out, "Did you ever steal anything when you were in high school?" you might say: "We're interested in the kinds of things that kids do in high school that can get them in trouble, like shoplifting. Do you know people who shoplifted things?" After the respondent answers, *then* you can ask, "How about you? did you ever steal anything from a store?" (**Further Reading**: improving response to sensitive questions.)

Baiting: The Phased-Assertion Probe

A particularly effective probing technique is called phased assertion (Kirk and Miller 1986:48), or baiting (Agar 1996:142). This is when you act like you already know something to get people to open up. Every journalist (and gossip monger) knows this technique well. As you learn a piece of a puzzle from one person, you use it with the next informant to get more information, and so on. The more you seem to know, the more comfortable people feel about talking to you and the less people feel they are actually divulging anything. They are not the ones who are giving away the "secrets" of the group. Phased assertion also prompts some people to jump in and correct you if they think you know a little, but that you've "got it all wrong."

STRUCTURED INTERVIEWS ♦

In fully structured interviews, each respondent sees or hears the same set of cues. There are two major types of structured interviews. One is systematic ethnography (which we treat in Chapter 8 on cultural domain analysis), and the other is questionnaires.

Questionnaires and Response Effects

The most common instrument for doing structured interviews is the questionnaire. Having a fixed set of questions ensures that everyone we interview responds to the same set of cues. Well, that's the idea. Actually, we know that interviews are social events and that many things can make a difference in how people respond to our questions. Researchers have been studying these *response effects* since surveys began. A lot of what they've learned is as valuable for producing qualitative data as it is for producing quantitative data.

The Deference Effect

Differences in race, gender, ethnicity, and age between an interviewer and an informant can produce lots of deference responses—people telling you what they think you want to know, in order not to offend you. Kane and Macaulay (1993:11) asked a sample of Americans how couples divide child care. Men were more likely than women to say that men and women share this responsibility—if the interviewer was a man. Huddy et al. (1997:205) asked Americans how about various issues affecting women. The answers to those questions were more likely to reflect a feminist perspective—if the interviewer was a woman.

The Third-Party-Present Effect

Interviews are usually conducted one-on-one, but in many cases, the spouse or partner of the person being interviewed may be in the room. Does this affect responses? Zipp and Toth (2002) found that, in Britain, when spouses are interviewed together, they are more likely to agree about many things—like who does what around the house—than when they are interviewed separately. Apparently, people listen to each other's answers and modify their own answers accordingly, which puts on a nice, unified face about their relationship.

Aquilino (1993) found that when their spouse is in the room, people report more marital conflict than when they are interviewed alone. They are also more likely to report that they and their spouse lived together before marriage if their spouse is in the room. Perhaps, as R. Mitchell (1965) suggested long ago, people own up more to things like this when they know it will be obvious to their spouse that they are lying. (Further Reading: third-party present effects.)

Open- and Closed-Ended Questions

Open-ended questions allow people to respond in their own words and capture people's own ideas about how things work. Typically, open-ended questions produce more data and are less boring for people than are their closed-ended equivalents. On the other hand (there's always a trade-off), coding and analyzing open-ended questions are labor-intensive tasks that require lots of inferences and judgment calls. The cost, in time and money, for coding and analyzing the answers to open-ended questions can mount up fast—one reason that research in the qualitative tradition involves a lot fewer respondents than does research in the quantitative tradition.

Open-ended questions also have more missing data than do closed-ended questions about the same topic. Suppose you interview 10 people about the rules of driving. Five people mention driving on the right-hand side of the road; five don't. How to interpret this? You could conclude that half the sample drives on the left (as they do in 50 countries, including England, Japan, Bangladesh, and Cyprus), but instead you go to reinterview the five people who failed to mention the right-hand rule and find that: One is, in fact, from England; another simply forgot to mention the right-hand rule; a third thought that driving on the right was so obvious as not to need mentioning; a fourth is from rural Vermont and drives almost entirely on single-lane roads; and the fifth refuses to be interviewed again.

If you want to know which side of the road people drive on, then a close-ended question—"Do you drive on the right-hand of the road? (Yes or No)"—is the way to go.

In their classic work on interview techniques, Cannell and Kahn (1968) recommended using open-ended questions when the objective is to discover people's attitudes and beliefs and the basis on which someone has formed an opinion. Use open-ended questions, they suggested, when the topic is likely to be outside the experience of many respondents, if you want to assess how much people know about a topic, or if you, yourself, know little about a topic and are in the exploratory phase of research.

But if you already know, from prior research, the range of responses to a question, then, Cannell and Kahn said, use closed-ended questions. This is good advice. Well-formulated, closed-ended questions put a lot less burden on respondents. As they also pointed out 40 years ago—and as thousands of seasoned researchers have learned on the job ever since—"There is no rule against mixing types of questions" (Cannell and Kahn 1968:567).

Short and Long Responses

Answers to open-ended questions can be long, narrative accounts (like an entire life history). They can also be short descriptions of events and experiences (like a one- or two-paragraph account of a recent illness), or even one-liners in response to a specific question. We recently asked people across the United States what they did with the last aluminum can they had in their hands. Most of the answers were one-liners, like "I threw it in the trash," or "I recycled it," or "I was driving and just tossed it out the window."

In general, the longer the texts, the more opportunities there are for discovering new themes and relationships. (More about this in Chapter 3.) Suppose you're studying conflict in married couples. To elicit actual cases of conflict, you might tell each partner separately: "Please describe, in as much detail as you can, the conflicts between you and your partner over the last year." Some responses—the ones from really good informants—will be quite long and will cover many episodes, some serious, others not so serious.

If you want to code the narratives for the presence of anger, frustration, and retaliation, you'll need to break them into episodes of conflict. That's because most people will mention anger, frustration, and retaliation at some point in a narrative about a year's worth of marital conflict. If you leave the narratives whole, you'll wind up with no variation across them, when, in fact, some conflicts are characterized by anger, some by frustration, some retaliation, some by all three of those things, and some by all three possible pairs of those things.

Lists and Relational Responses

Open-ended questions yield two types of answers: lists and relations. When we start to study something, we are typically interested in lists, and lists are generated by the W questions: who, what, why, where, and when. Asking "What did you do last night?" gets you a list of activities. Asking "Why did you do that?" gets you a list of rationales justifying the behavior. Asking a new mother about her birthing experiences, we might ask: "Who was present?" "What medications did they give you?" "Where did the birth take place?" "When did the nurse take your pulse?"

Across many cases, lists tell us about the range, frequency, and distribution of things under study. (See Chapter 8 for techniques to analyze list data.)

Lists from the W questions are very valuable, but, as Becker (1998) argues convincingly, asking *how* questions elicits stories and narratives that tell us about relations among things.

Ask new military recruits, "Why did you decide to join up?" and you'll get answers like: "Well, my father and uncle were in the military and my grades weren't that good, so I figured I would have a hard time getting into college" and "I didn't really want to go to college, but I was getting tired of working at the mall so I figured this would be a good experience and I could use the GI bill to get a college education later." Notice the lists.

Ask them instead, "How did you decide to join the military?" and you'll get stories like this one:

> Well, my grades weren't very good in high school and my folks didn't have much money, so I started working at my uncles' garage. I'd been working for about a year when my best friend came back from boot camp before being transferred to his first station. We talked quite a bit and he said the Army was a great deal. He took me down and we talked to the local recruiter. The recruiter explained what some of the benefits were and told me about all the testing I needed to complete. I started the process the next week. My mother wasn't really sure this was a good idea, but my father and uncle thought it would give me a lot of experience. Eventually my mom said it was my choice. I passed the tests and had good enough scores to get into a mechanic position.

How questions elicit process and relationships. (By the way, this story is from some research we did. The story has been edited to take out all the "umms" and such. Real speech is very messy. Sometimes, as in this case, a full transcription is more than you need. Sometimes, though, as in conversation analysis, you need a true verbatim transcription. We'll cover conversation analysis in Chapter 10.)

Compare-and-contrast questions also elicit how things are related to each other. Try the following experiment the next time you have to make small talk at a party. Instead of asking the standard question, "What do you do?" and waiting for the one- or two-word reply, ask: "So, what is your job like?" If your conversation partner is at all talkative, this should elicit a fairly long descriptive list of his or her day-to-day routine.

Follow up by asking the compare-and-contrast question: "So, how does this job compare to your last job?" This will not only get you a description of a second job, it will give you information about how the two jobs are related or not related.

In our experience, novice interviewers tend to ask more list questions than relational questions.

ACCURACY

When people say that they *prefer* a particular brand of car, or that they *love* their new job, they're talking about internal states. You pretty much have to take their word for such things. But a lot of interviewing involves asking people about their behavior—How often do they go to church? Do they eat out in restaurants? Do they use bleach when they clean their needles?—and about facts in their lives—Where did they spend Thanksgiving last year? How many brothers and sisters do they have? Do they make regular deposits to their 401k? In all these cases, accuracy is a real issue.

People are inaccurate reporters of their own behavior for many reasons. Here are four:

1. Once people agree to be interviewed, they have a personal stake in the process and usually try to answer all your questions—whether or not they know the answers to your questions.

2. Human memory is fragile, although it's clearly easier to remember some things (like recent surgery) than others.

3. Interviews are social encounters, and people manipulate those encounters to whatever they think is their advantage. Expect people to overreport socially desirable behavior (like giving to charity) and to underreport socially undesirable behavior (like cheating on exams).

4. People can't count a lot of behaviors, so they use general rules of inference and report what they think they usually do. If you ask people how many times they ate eggs last month, don't expect the answers to accurately reflect the behavior of your respondents.

Reducing Errors: Jogging People's Memories

Sudman and Bradburn (1974) suggest several things that can increase the accuracy of self-reported behavior:

1. *Cued recall.* In this technique, people might consult their records to jog their memories or you might ask them questions about specific behaviors. With life histories, for example, college transcripts help people remember events and people from their time at school. Credit card statements and long-distance phone bills help people retrace their steps and remember people and events.

2. *Aided recall.* This technique involves giving people a list of possible answers to a question and asking them to choose among them. Aided recall is particularly effective in interviewing the elderly (Jobe et al. 1996). In situations where you do multiple interviews with the same person, you can remind people what they said last time in answer to a question and then ask them about their behavior since their last report.

3. *Landmarks.* The title of Loftus and Marburger's (1983) article on this says it all: "Since the eruption of Mt. St. Helens, has anyone beaten you up? Improving the accuracy of retrospective reports with landmark events." Means et al. (1989) asked people to recall landmark events in their lives going back 18 months from the time of the interview. Once the list of personal landmark events was established, people were better able to recall hospitalizations and other health-related events. (Further Reading: improving accuracy of recall.)

◆ ELICITING CULTURAL DOMAINS

Cultural domains comprise a list of words in a language that somehow "belong together." Some domains, like names for racial and ethnic groups, names of fish, and things to eat for breakfast, are easy to list. Other domains, like things that mothers do or ways to preserve the environment, are harder to list.

Cultural domains are typically hierarchical. For most native speakers of English, lemons are a kind of citrus, which are a kind of fruit, which are a kind of food. But not for everyone. Some people skip the citrus level entirely. And people vary in what they think is the content of any cultural domain. For some native speakers of English, sharks and dolphins are kinds of fish; for others, they are not. For many native speakers of English, chimpanzees are kinds of monkeys; for others, they are kinds of apes and are definitely not kinds of monkeys.

Some cultural domains comprise fixed lists. The list of terms for members of a family (mother, father, etc.) is more or less a fixed list and is agreed on by most members of a culture. But not all. For some native speakers of English, a man's wife's sister's husband is the man's brother-in-law; for others, he's his wife's brother-in-law, and for others, he's no relative at all.

Many cultural domains—like the list of carpenters' tools or the list of muscles, bones, and tendons in the human leg—are the province of specialists. The list of names of major league baseball teams in the United States is agreed on by everyone who knows about this domain, but the list of greatest left-handed baseball pitchers of all time is a matter of heated debate among experts.

The object of cultural domain analysis is to discover the content and the structure of domains—what goes with what, and how they go together.

Data for the content of domains are collected with listing tasks; data on the structure of domains are collected with techniques like pile sorts and triad tests. These tasks generate qualitative data, but because the data are collected systematically, they can be treated quantitatively. We cover the methods for collecting and analyzing data about the content and structure of cultural domains in Chapter 8.

MIXED METHODS ◆

There was a time when combining qualitative and quantitative approaches was a topic of conversation in social research. Today, the practice is so widespread, there are several excellent texts and a scholarly journal devoted to it. (**Further Reading:** mixed methods.)

In fact, many social researchers now routinely begin with ethnography or with unstructured interviews to get a feel for what is going on and then move to semistructured or structured interviews to test hunches or hypotheses—as Laubach (2005) did in his study of informal workplace stratification at a family-owned lending institution. Or they may start with a questionnaire and move on to open-ended interviewing in an effort to better understand the quantitative results—as Weine et al. (2005) did in their study of Bosnian refugees in Chicago.

Focus groups, participant observation, case studies (including life histories), and decision modeling—all of these may (but don't have to) involve a mix of qualitative and quantitative data.

Focus Groups

Focus groups are recruited to discuss how people feel about products (like brands of beer or new electronic gadgets) and for assessing social programs (is the new day care center providing enough support for working mothers?). They are used in getting stakeholder reaction to proposed programs (how do parents, teachers, administrators, and school board members feel about the proposal to move the start of the school year up by a month?). And they are often used in the development of surveys (to explore whether questions seem arrogant or naive to respondents) or to help interpret the results of a survey.

In the hands of a skilled moderator, the group setting stimulates discussions that would not occur in simple two-person interactions and encourages people to explore similarities and differences of opinion (Patton 1987).

Focus groups, however, are not good tools for understanding the distribution of responses in a group. First, the responses that people give to questions are not independent. In fact, the whole idea of a focus group is to get a group dynamic going so that people will feed off one another. This means that some people may dominate while others lurk.

To make sure that we get the whole range of opinions or feelings about a topic, we always ask participants in focus groups to complete a short questionnaire about the topic we plan to discuss *before* we begin the discussion. This gets people thinking about the topic and provides data on the variation in people's beliefs and attitudes about the topic we're studying.

It's tempting to use focus groups in the exploratory phase of research, but, as Agar and MacDonald remind us (1995), you really need to be well along in your research to understand and benefit from the free-flowing rhetoric generated by a group on a roll. When people who talk the same language get together, they abbreviate in almost everything they say.

Listen to ordinary people talking about their computers and you'll hear things like "I really hate it when they put the ports in the back." Think of how much you have to know to fill in around that one: You have to know that ports are either firewire or USB ports, and you have to know that they let you connect to printers, external hard drives, and lots of other things. If you convene a group of teenagers to talk about suicide, you'd better have done plenty of ethnography first or you won't be able to fill in around the cultural abbreviations.

Group interviews are not all focus group interviews. Robert Thornberg (2008) studied what children in Swedish primary schools think about how school rules—don't run in the halls; raise your hand if you want to speak—are made and enforced. During his 2 years of ethnography, Thornberg did 49 interviews with groups of two to four students each. If you're doing field research in a tightly knit community, expect people to just come up and insert themselves into what you think are private interviews. This happened to Rachel Baker (1996a, 1996b) when she interviewed homeless boys in temples and junkyards in Kathmandu. If you insist on privacy in these situations, you might find yourself with no interview at all. Better to take advantage of the situation and just let the information flow. Be sure to take notes, of course—on who's there, who's dominant, who's just listening, and so on—in any group interview. (Further Reading: recruiting and running focus groups.)

Participant Observation

Participant observation is the ultimate mixed method strategy. It has been used for generations by scholars across the social sciences, positivists and interpretivists alike. It puts you where the action is, lets you observe behavior in a natural context (behavior that might be otherwise impossible to witness), and lets you collect any kind of data you want.

A lot of the data collected during participant observation are qualitative: field notes taken about things you see and hear in natural settings; photographs of the content of people's houses; audio recordings of people telling stories; video recordings of people making dinner, getting married, and having an argument; transcriptions of recorded, open-ended interviews; free lists and pile sorts of items in cultural domains. But many participant observers also collect quantitative data about actual behavior—like counting the number of drinks people consume in a bar—and even closed-ended questionnaires.

Participant observation involves going out and staying out, learning a new language (or a new dialect of a language you already know), and experiencing the lives of the people you are studying as much as you can. Unlike passive observation where there is minimum interaction between the researcher and the object of study, participant observation means establishing rapport and learning to act so that people go about their business as usual when you show up (see Box 2.3).

Box 2.3

The Ethical Dilemma of Rapport

Participant observation, for all its virtues, is also the most ethically challenging method for collecting data. Participant observers have taken notes at breast cancer support groups (Markovic et al. 2004), listened while teen-age gangs plotted illegal acts (Fleisher 1998), hidden out with illegal refugees on the run (Bourgois 1990). . . . All of this requires lots of rapport, but the phrase "gaining rapport" is a euphemism for impression management, one of the "darker arts" of fieldwork, in Harry Wolcott's memorable phrase (2005:chap. 6).

Participant observation involves immersing yourself in a culture and learning to remove yourself every day from that immersion so you can intellectualize what you've seen and heard, put it into perspective, and write about it convincingly. When it's done right, participant observation turns fieldworkers into instruments of data collection and data analysis (see Box 2.4). (**Further Reading:** participant observation ethnography.)

Box 2.4

Fieldwork Without Participation

Participant observation implies fieldwork, but not all fieldwork involves participant observation. Gomes do Espirito Santo and Etheredge (2002) interviewed 1,083 male clients of female sex workers and collected saliva specimens (to test for HIV) during 38 nights of fieldwork in Dakar, Senegal. The data collection involved a team of six fieldworkers, and the lead researcher was with the team throughout the three and a half months that it took to collect the data. This was serious fieldwork, but not participant observation.

Case Studies, Life Histories, and Case Histories

Case studies are the "end-product of field-oriented research" (Wolcott 1992:36); a research strategy for developing "a comprehensive understanding" of groups under study (Miles and Huberman 1994:25); and a way to develop "general theoretical statements about regularities in social structure and process" (Becker 1968:233).

In general, the goal of doing a case study is to get in-depth understanding of something—a program, an event, a place, a person, an organization. Often the interest is in process—how things work and why—rather than variations in outcomes, in contexts rather than specific variables, in discovery rather than theory testing (Yin 2008). Like participant observation ethnography, case studies can involve many data collection methods, including direct and indirect observation along with structured and unstructured interviewing.

Case studies are often used in evaluation research (see Patton 2002). They provide lots of descriptive data, are lifelike, and simplify the data that a reader has to assess. Above all, Guba and Lincoln argue, cases studies yield "information to produce judgment. Judging is the final and ultimate act of evaluation" (1981:375).

Merriam (1998) distinguishes among ethnographic case studies (which focus on the culture of a group, like a classroom or a factory), sociological case studies (which focus on social interactions, like those between couples, between student peers, between doctors and patients, etc.), historical case studies (which examine how institutions or organizations change over time), and psychological case studies (which examine the inner workings of people's thoughts and emotions). Freud used case studies in developing his theory of psychosexual development, and Piaget studied his own children to develop his theory of cognitive development.

Life histories are case studies of people—what happened to them and how they felt as they went through various experiences and stages. Life histories produce data from which deductions are made about changes in the culture and social structure of communities. Some life histories are wide-ranging autobiographical accounts, but many life histories are focused on particular topics, like a person's work history, migration history, reproductive history, or sexual history.

When you ask people for their life history, they will try to recount things chronologically but, as in all open-ended interviews, they'll go off on tangents. These tangents provide context and background for the events we're studying, but to keep them from becoming the focus, life histories should be elicited with an interview guide that forces you to cover everything you need to know in a particular project. Life history interviews can take several days, or longer, to complete.

Case histories (also known as event histories or case narratives) are in-depth narratives about specific events. For example, investigators may want to know what happened and how people felt the last time they were sick, the last time they had sex, the last time they fought with their spouse, or the last time they snuck across the border looking for work.

When you analyze a case study, be careful not to overgeneralize. Don't let case studies "masquerade as a whole," warn Guba and Lincoln, "when in fact they are but a part, a slice of life" (1981:377).

Ethnographic Decision Modeling

Ethnographic decision modeling (EDM) is a mixed method that involves ethnographic interviewing, systematic coding, and structured questionnaires. In one of our projects (Ryan and Bernard 2006), we asked 21 people to tell us stories about why they recycled or didn't recycle the last aluminum can they had in their hand. Coding of those stories produced 30 reasons, like "There was a recycling bin handy, so why not?" and "Hey, I was in my car and I didn't want to stain the carpet, so I threw the can out the window" and "I was home and we recycle everything at home, so naturally. . . ."

Then we asked 70 different people what they did with the last aluminum can they had in their hand and, no matter what they said in response, we asked them all 30 of those reasons we had extracted from the story-telling phase: Were you in your car at the time? Do you usually recycle other things at home? Was recycling bin handy? And so on. Finally, using all the responses, we built a model to account for recycling behavior and tested that model on another, independent sample of people. We'll cover this example in depth and EDM in general in Chapter 16.

♦ CHOOSING A DATA COLLECTION STRATEGY

The methods we've outlined here are strategies for collecting data. Each method—participant observation, semistructured interviewing, indirect observation, life histories, and so on—comprises many techniques. And each of these strategic methods has advantages and disadvantages. In deciding which method to use, consider two things: data complexity and data distance.

Data Complexity

Focus groups are more complex than are one-on-one interviews. Open-ended questions produce more complex data than do closed-ended ones. Long interviews produce more complex data than do short ones.

Complex data are likely to be a rich source of information—and quotes that you can use in your write-up—and they are wonderful for:

1. Exploratory questions, like: How do licensed massage therapists feel about having to share their fees with physicians and chiropractors who refer patients?

2. Understanding processes, like: How do people in this community make wine at home?

3. Generating potential explanatory models, like: What causes people to abandon home-based remedies for an illness and consult a nurse or physician?

However, data from broadly focused interviews and from multiple speakers are difficult to compare across individuals. When you want to know the average of anything—whether it's people's age or their weight or how strongly they feel about that new labor contract they're negotiating—you simply have to have data that you can compare across people.

We recommend starting exploratory projects with hypothetical or normative/cultural questions and then moving on to individual/personal questions and finally to episodic questions. For example, if we wanted to talk to cops about violence against them, we might begin by asking a hypothetical question, like: "What would you do if a suspect drew a knife?" Or a normative/cultural question, like: "What's the accepted practice when you happen to come upon an act of domestic violence?"

As the interview progressed, and the respondent felt more comfortable, we might probe about the actual experiences with violence of some colleagues. And if the interview progressed sufficiently, we might ask about their actual experiences with violence and, finally, about the specifics of a real encounter.

Unstructured and semistructured interviews are typically conducted as face-to-face encounters, though it is possible to conduct them over the phone or via chat rooms on the web. Structured interviews can be conducted face-to-face or can be self-administered questionnaires, telephone interviews, or done over the web. Use face-to-face interviews with people who do not usually provide information (like elites), with illiterate people, or with people who have no phone or live in hard-to-reach places.

Face-to-face interviews have several advantages. You can clarify questions as you go, and face-to-face interviews can be much longer than either telephone or self-administered questionnaires. In face-to-face encounters, people can't flip ahead to anticipate questions or change answers they have already given. And in a face-to-face interview, you can be sure that the responses have been provided by the person for whom the questions were intended.

Data Distance

Data distance is about the amount of information lost in the process of recording it. Thinking about data distance is a kind of validity check. It tells us how good a proxy the data are for the phenomenon we're trying to study. A focus group is a complex interaction of individuals discussing a variety of issues. An audio recording of a focus group has no data on hand gestures and facial expressions. Voice tones that indicate emotional, cynical, or enthusiastic responses are lost when the recording is transcribed.

A video camera can record a lot more of the activity, but it can only capture what falls within the range of its lens. You can usually place a video camera so that it captures all movement in a classroom, but the camera can't locate the classroom in its larger school context and cannot assess environmental data like temperature, moisture, or smells.

Human observers can see around moving bodies, can locate a situation in larger contexts, and can record information on environmental conditions. But human observers get overloaded with information very quickly; unless an observer is trained in taking verbatim notes (with shorthand), much of the conversation will go unrecorded, especially when two or more people talk at once.

Field notes are an essential part of all qualitative data collection, even when you have audio or video recordings. But clearly, the notes are a massive reduction of data—which is another way of saying data loss. In writing field notes, we filter what to record, choosing some things and ignoring others, and we lump different observations and events into thematic categories. In this sense, producing field notes is a process of identifying themes, but it can also introduce systematic bias.

The longer you wait to write up your notes, the more errors you're likely to make. There will be errors of omission (we forget events, even whole conversations) and errors of commission (we infer the existence of events and conversations that did not happen). We recommend that all unstructured and semistructured interviews be recorded, unless people explicitly ask not to be recorded. If you must rely entirely on notes, then write them up immediately after each interview. Above all, never sleep on data. They vanish into the night.

As either data complexity or data distance increases, it becomes more difficult to make systematic comparisons. As Figure 2.3 shows, we do not recommend making comparisons using field notes as the only source of data, nor do we recommend making comparisons across complex cases like unstructured focus groups.

Figure 2.3   Data Distance by Data Complexity

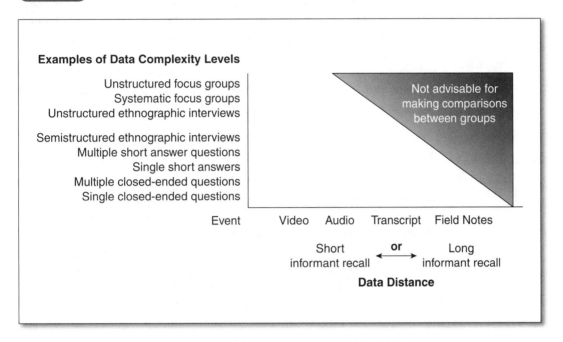

Examples of Data Complexity Levels

Unstructured focus groups
Systematic focus groups
Unstructured ethnographic interviews

Semistructured ethnographic interviews
Multiple short answer questions
Single short answers
Multiple closed-ended questions
Single closed-ended questions

Not advisable for making comparisons between groups

Event   Video   Audio   Transcript   Field Notes

Short   **or**   Long
informant recall ←——→ informant recall

Data Distance

THE MISSING DATA TRAP ♦

All researchers deal with missing data, but the problem is especially acute in the collection of qualitative data. We miss some data because of people's unwillingness to answer a question, but in our experience most missing data come from failure to ask a question in the first place and from failure to probe for detailed answers or to record answers faithfully.

A lot of qualitative research is based on indirect observation and unstructured interviewing, in which the researcher has little or no control. Archival records are often incomplete. Corpora of text, like news articles, may simply not contain information on all events of interest in a study. Focus groups are notorious for producing missing data because not everyone participates fully throughout the discussion. What people think but do not say is missing.

In unstructured and semistructured interviews, everyone may be asked about the same topics but not be asked the exact same questions. Some people are probed on certain questions; others are not. Data are lost when they are not recorded properly. Transcriptions of video and audio eliminate certain kinds of data from the record.

Field notes are the worst offenders when it comes to missing data. Researchers simply cannot write down all they see and hear, and when field notes are written up hours after an event, there is further loss. Human memory is a very poor recorder of events and conversations. In the end, we fill in the gaps with inferences, but missing data make systematic comparisons across cases difficult and make systematic testing of hypotheses questionable. This is one reason we advocate using both systematic and nonsystematic data collection methods in qualitative research.

♦ TURNING AUDIO AND VIDEO INTO OTHER FORMS OF DATA

Before recording was possible, researchers listened hard during interviews and took notes as best they could. This is still a good idea, for two reasons: (1) It shows the respondent that you care a lot of about what she or he is saying; and (2) it lets you record, in writing, your observations about the interview itself.

Beginning in the 1950s, some researchers (mostly anthropologists and linguists) began lugging big, heavy tape recorders to the field. Cassette recorders came on the scene in the mid-1960s and revolutionized the collection of interview data. There will always be cases in which people will absolutely forbid recording of interviews, but these cases are the exception in our experience, especially for research done in industrialized democracies. If you ask people up front, most will let you record interviews.

Today, focus group interviews are typically recorded in video, and some researchers are turning to video to record individual interviews as well.

Audio recordings of interviews comprise raw data. The first step in analyzing those data is to listen to them, several times if need be, to get a feel for the context and nuances they contain. If you have 30–40 hours of interviews, this step is indispensable. You'll be surprised at what you learn by just listening. The next step is to transcribe the interviews and get them into a form that you can analyze more systematically.

If you have 100 hours or more of recorded interviews, the just-listen step will be daunting. And if you have 200 or 300 hours of recorded interviews, the just-listen step will be all but impossible, unless you have assistants who can listen to chunks of interviews.

Transcribing Interviews

The first step in systematic analysis is the conversion of audio into digital text. You'll usually see this step called "transcription," which means listening to a recording and converting it to text by typing the words on a keyboard. From the mid-1960s, when cassette tape recorders became widely available, until the late-1980s, when personal computers became widely available, transcription to hard copy was all there was. Since then, typewriters have become museum pieces and "transcription" means converting an audio recording into digital text (a file on a computer) that can be printed out if you like.

The sheer work of transcribing, though, is intimidating. If you have 40 hours of recorded interviews, plan on working 8 hours a day, every day for 30 days to convert them to text files. The real time may be several months. And if you have 100 hours of recorded interviews. . . . You can see the problem.

If you have the budget for it, the easiest and most pleasant choice is to turn your recordings over to a professional transcriber. If you have to transcribe the interviews yourself, be sure to invest in the right equipment. There are two choices: (1) a combination of transcription hardware and software; and (2) voice recognition (VR) software (see Appendix).

1. With the transcription hardware and software option, you control the recording playback using a foot pedal or a set of hot keys on your keyboard. This lets you listen to a couple of seconds of recording at a time, type everything into the computer, and then move on to the next chunk. Using a foot pedal or a set of keys lets you go back and repeat chunks, all while keeping your hands on the keyboard. (You may also be able to use a mouse, but this takes more time.)

2. With VR software, you listen to an interview through a set of headphones and repeat the words—both your questions and your informant's responses—out loud, in your own voice. The software listens to your voice and types out the words across the screen (see Box 2.5).

Box 2.5

Voice Recognition Software in Other Languages

VR programs are trained to one voice, but you can use them to transcribe focus groups by speaking each participant's part. If you do this, be sure to identify each participant by a pseudonym. VR software is available in several languages (English, Spanish, French, German, Japanese, and Chinese). If you are working in other languages you can listen to a recording and read it back, aloud, in a language that the software understands.

It can take months to train VR software to its maximum accuracy, depending on how much of a workout you put it through. The built-in vocabularies are enormous—something like 250,000 words in English—but the programs still need to learn all the special vocabulary you throw at them. If you say, "Freddie said he didn't want to be friends with me," you would have to spell out "Freddie"—literally, by saying F-R-E-D-D-I-E—and the software would add the word to its vocabulary.

Once the software is up to speed, it can convert digital text from voice with 95%–98% accuracy at about 100–120 word per minute—normal speech, in other words. With a 2%–5% error rate, though, you still have to go over every line of your work to find the errors—you may have to tell it that the word "bloat" should be "float," for instance—and you also have to tell the software where to put punctuation, paragraph breaks, and such. But once a VR program is fully trained, the total time for transcribing interviews can be reduced greatly, compared to regular transcription, especially if you're not a professional at the keyboard. (**Further Reading**: transcription and voice recognition software.)

Once you have data in a computer, the next step is to identify relevant themes (relevant to your particular research project), to tag the data with codes for those themes, and to think about how the themes fit together—the subjects of Chapters 3, 4, and 5.

Further Reading

♦ For more on secondary analysis of qualitative data see Hammersley (1997, 2004), Moore (2007), Silva (2007), and other articles in a special issue of Sociological Research Online (http://www.socresonline.org.uk/12/3/contents.html). See Corti and Backhouse (2005) and other articles in a special issue of Forum: Qualitative Social Research (http://www.qualitative-research.net/index.php/fqs/issue/view/12). There are archives of qualitative data, including http://www.esds.ac.uk/qualidata/about/introduction.asp

♦ For more on interviewing technique, see Converse and Schuman (1974), Gubrium and Holstein (2002), Holstein and Gubrium (1995), Kvale (1996), Levy and Hollan (1998), Mishler (1986), and Rubin and Rubin (2005).

♦ For more on improving response to sensitive and threatening questions, see Bradburn (1983), Bradburn and Sudman et al. (1979), Johnston and Walton (1995), and Tourangeau and Yan (2007). See Catania et al. (1996), Gribble et al. (1999), Hewitt (2002), and Wiederman et al. (1994) for work on how to increase response to questions about sexual behavior. See Johnston and Walton (1995) on the use of computer-assisted self-interviewing for asking sensitive questions. See Joinson et al. (2008) on asking sensitive questions in web-based surveys. See Wutich et al. (2009) on asking sensitive questions in focus groups.

◆ For more on the third-party-present effect, see Aquilino et al. (2000), Blair (1979), Boeije (2004), Bradburn (1979), Hartmann (1994), Pollner and Adams (1997), Seale et al. (2008), and T. W. Smith (1997). For other response effects, see Aquilino (1994), Barnes et al. (1995), Finkel et al. (1991), Javeline (1999), and Lueptow et al. (1990).

◆ For more on improving accuracy of recall in interviews, see Reimer and Mathes (2007), Van Der Vaart and Glasner (2007), and Wansink et al. (2006).

◆ For more on mixed methods research, see Axinn and Pearce (2006), Creswell (2003), Creswell and Plano Clark 2007), Greene and Caracelli (1997), R. B. Johnson (2006), and R. B. Johnson and Onwuegbuzie (2004), Mertens (2005), Saks and Allsop (2007), and Tashakkorie and Teddlie (1998, 2003). For empirical studies using mixed methods, see the *Journal of Mixed Methods Research*.

◆ For details on how to recruit participants and how to conduct a focus group session see Krueger (1994), D. L. Morgan (1997), Stewart and Shamdasani (1990), Vaughn et al. (1996), and particularly Krueger and Casey (2000), D. L. Morgan and Krueger (1998), and Puchta and Potter (2004).

◆ For detailed discussions of participant observation in various disciplines see Agar (1996), Becker (1998), Bernard (2006), Crabtree and Miller (1999), K. M. DeWalt and B. R. DeWalt (2002), Fenno (1990), Gummesson (2000), C. D. Smith and Kornblum (1996), Spradley (1980), and Wolcott (2005).

◆ For more on transcription, see Bailey (2008), Bucholtz (2000), Du Bois (1991), Duranti (2006), Green et al. (1997), Maloney and Paolisso (2001), Matheson (2007), McLellan et al. (2003), and Ochs (1979). For transcription and voice recognition software, see Appendix.

CHAPTER 3

FINDING THEMES

Authors' note: We rely heavily in this chapter on our article Ryan and Bernard, *Field Methods 15*(1): 85–109.
Copyright © 2003 Sage Publications.

◆ INTRODUCTION

Analyzing text involves five complex tasks: (1) discovering themes and subthemes; (2) describing the core and peripheral elements of themes; (3) building hierarchies of themes or codebooks; (4) applying themes—that is, attaching them to chunks of actual text; and (5) linking themes into theoretical models.

In this chapter, we focus on the first task: discovering themes and subthemes. Then, in Chapter 4, we discuss methods for describing themes, building codebooks, and applying themes to text. We move on in Chapters 5 and 6 to building models.

The techniques we discuss here for discovering themes come from across the social sciences and from different methodological perspectives. The techniques range from simple word counts that can be done by a computer to labor-intensive, line-by-line analyses that, so far, only people can do. Each technique has advantages and disadvantages. As you'll see, some methods are better for analyzing long, complex narratives, and others are better for short responses to open-ended questions. Some require more labor and skill, others less. We'll have more to say later about how you choose among these methods. But first. . . .

◆ WHAT'S A THEME?

This question has a long history. Thompson (1932–36) created an index of folktale motifs, or themes, that filled six volumes. In 1945, Morris Opler, an anthropologist, made the identification of themes a key step in analyzing cultures. He said:

> In every culture are found a limited number of dynamic affirmations, called *themes*, which control behavior or stimulate activity. The activities, prohibitions of activities, or references which result from the acceptance of a theme are its *expressions*. . . . The expressions of a theme, of course, aid us in discovering it. (pp. 198–199)

Opler established three principles for analyzing themes. First, he observed that themes are only visible (and thus discoverable) through the manifestation of expressions in data. And conversely, expressions are meaningless without some reference to themes. Second, Opler noted that some expressions of a theme are obvious and culturally agreed on, but others are subtler, symbolic, and even idiosyncratic.

And third, Opler observed that cultural systems comprise sets of interrelated themes. The importance of any theme, he said, is related to: (1) how often it appears; (2) how pervasive it is across different types of cultural ideas and practices; (3) how people react when the theme is violated; and (4) the degree to which the force and variety of a theme's expression is controlled by specific contexts (see Box 3.1).

Box 3.1

Terms for Themes

Today, social scientists still talk about the linkage between themes and their expressions, but use different terms to do so. Grounded theorists talk about "categories" (Glaser and A. Strauss 1967), "codes" (Miles and Huberman 1994), or "labels" (Dey 1993:96). Opler's "expressions" are called "incidents" (Glaser and A. Strauss 1967), "segments" (Tesch 1990), "thematic units" (Krippendorff 1980b), "data-bits" (Dey 1993), and "chunks" (Miles and Huberman 1994). Lincoln and Guba refer to expressions as "units" (1985:345). A. Strauss and Corbin (1990:61) call them "concepts" that are grouped together in a higher order of classification to form categories.

Here, we follow Agar's lead (1979, 1980a) and remain faithful to Opler's terminology. To us, the terms "theme" and "expression" more naturally connote the fundamental concepts we are tying to describe. In everyday language, we talk about themes that appear in texts, paintings, and movies and refer to particular instances as expressions of goodness or anger or evil. In selecting one set of terms over others, we surely ignore subtle differences, but the basic ideas are just as useful under many glosses.

WHERE DO THEMES COME FROM?   ◆

Themes come both from data (an inductive approach) and from our prior theoretical understanding of whatever phenomenon we are studying (an a priori, or deductive approach). A priori themes come from characteristics of the phenomena being studied—what Aristotle identified as essences and what dozens of generations of scholars since have relied on as a first cut at understanding any phenomenon. If you are studying the night sky, for example, it won't take long to decide that there is a unique, large body (the moon), a few small bodies that don't twinkle (planets), and millions of small bodies that do twinkle (stars).

A priori themes also come from already-agreed-on professional definitions found in literature reviews; from local, commonsense constructs; and from researchers' values, theoretical orientations, and personal experiences (Bulmer 1979; Maxwell 2005; A. Strauss 1987). A. Strauss and Corbin (1990:41–47) call the use of a priori themes theoretical sensitivity.

The decisions about what topics to cover and how best to query people about those topics are rich sources of a priori themes (Dey 1993:98). In fact, the first pass at generating themes often comes from the questions in an interview protocol (Coffey and Atkinson 1996:34).

Mostly, though, themes are derived empirically—induced from data. Even with a fixed set of open-ended questions, there's no way to anticipate all the themes that will come up before you analyze a set of texts (Dey 1993:97–98). The act of discovering themes is what grounded theorists call open coding, and what classic content analysts call qualitative analysis (Berelson 1952) or latent coding (Shapiro and Markoff 1997).

There are many variations on these methods and many recipes for arriving at a preliminary set of themes (Tesch 1990:91). We'll describe eight observational techniques—things to look for in texts—and four manipulative techniques—ways of processing texts. These 12 techniques are neither exhaustive nor exclusive. They are often combined in practice. (Further Reading: finding themes.)

♦ EIGHT OBSERVATIONAL TECHNIQUES: THINGS TO LOOK FOR

Looking for themes in written material typically involves pawing through texts and marking them up with different colored pens. For recorded interviews, the process of identifying themes begins with the act of transcription. Whether the data come in the format of video, audio, or written documents, handling them physically is always helpful for finding themes.

Here is what to look for:

1. Repetitions

"Anyone who has listened to long stretches of talk," says D'Andrade, "knows how frequently people circle through the same network of ideas" (1991:287). Repetition is easy to recognize in text. Claudia Strauss (1992) did several in-depth interviews with Tony, a retired blue-collar worker in Connecticut. Tony referred again and again to ideas associated with greed, money, businessmen, siblings, and "being different." Strauss concluded that these ideas were important themes in Tony's life. To get an idea of how these ideas were related, Strauss wrote them on a piece of paper and connected them with lines to snippets of Tony's verbatim expressions—much as researchers today do with text analysis software.

The more the same concept occurs in a text, the more likely it is a theme. How many repetitions make an important theme, however, is a question only you can answer.

2. Indigenous Typologies or Categories

Another way to find themes is to look for unfamiliar, local words, and for familiar words that are used in unfamiliar ways—what Patton calls "indigenous categories" (2002:454; and see Linnekin 1987). Grounded theorists refer to the process of identifying local terms as in vivo coding (A. Strauss 1987:28; A. Strauss and Corbin 1990:61–74). Ethnographers call this the search for typologies or classification schemes (Bogdan and Taylor 1975:83) or cultural domains (Spradley 1979:107–119).

In a classic ethnographic study, Spradley (1972) recorded conversations among tramps at informal gatherings, meals, and card games. As the men talked to each other about their experiences, they kept mentioning the idea of "making a flop," which turned out to be the local term for finding a place to sleep for the night. Spradley searched through his recorded material and his field notes for statements about making a flop and found that he could categorize them into subthemes such as kinds of flops, ways to make flops, ways to make your own flop, kinds of people who bother you when you flop, ways to make a bed, and kinds of beds. Spradley returned to his informants and asked for more information about each of the subthemes.

For other classic examples of coding for indigenous categories see Becker's (1993) description of medical students' use of the word "crock" and Agar's (1973) description of drug addicts' understandings of what it means to "shoot up."

3. Metaphors and Analogies

In pioneering work, Lakoff and Johnson (2003 [1980]) observed that people often represent their thoughts, behaviors, and experiences with metaphors and analogies. Analysis, then, becomes the search for metaphors in rhetoric and deducing the schemas, or broad, underlying themes that might produce those metaphors (D'Andrade 1995; C. Strauss and Quinn 1997).

Naomi Quinn (1996) analyzed over 300 hours of interviews from 11 American couples to discover themes in the way Americans talk about marriage. She found that when people were surprised that some couple had broken up, they said they thought the couple's marriage was "like the Rock of Gibraltar" or that the marriage had been "nailed in cement." People use these metaphors, says Quinn, because they know that their listeners (people from the same culture) understand that cement and the Rock of Gibraltar are things that last forever.

Agar (1983) examined transcripts of arguments presented by independent truckers at public hearings of the Interstate Commerce Commission on whether to discontinue a fuel surcharge. One trucker explained that all costs had risen dramatically in the preceding couple of years and likened the surcharge to putting a bandage on a patient who had internal bleeding. With no other remedy available, he said, the fuel surcharge was "the life raft" that truckers clung to for survival (Agar 1983:603).

Natural human speech is full of metaphors. More on this in Chapter 14, on schema analysis.

4. Transitions

Naturally occurring shifts in content may be markers of themes. In written texts, new paragraphs may indicate shifts in topics. In speech, pauses, changes in tone of voice, or the presence of particular phrases may indicate transitions and themes.

In semistructured interviews, investigators steer the conversation from one topic to another, creating transitions, whereas in two-party and multiparty natural speech, transitions occur continually. Analysts of conversation examine features such as turn taking and speaker interruptions to identify these transitions. More about this in Chapter 10.

5. Similarities and Differences

What Glaser and A. Strauss (1967:101–116) labeled the "constant comparison method" involves searching for similarities and differences by making systematic comparisons across units of data. Typically, grounded theorists begin with a line-by-line analysis, asking: "What is this sentence about?" and "How is it similar or different from the preceding or following statements?" This keeps the researcher focused on the data rather than on theoretical flights of fancy (Charmaz 1990, 2000; Glaser 1978:56–72; A. Strauss and Corbin 1990:84–95). Look at the following exchange:

Interviewer:	So, what can people do to help the environment?
Informant:	(long pause) Ya know the thing that's interesting to me is I don't understand toxic waste roundup, but if there could be more of that . . . it seems that only once a year they round up toxic waste and I know I poured stuff down the sink I shouldn't (laughing) and poured it like on the (pointing to the ground) (pause). Also reporting violations. (pause) I had a friend who reported these damn asbestos tiles (which were on her apartment building roof).

The reference to asbestos is different from the reference to the toxic waste roundup. On the other hand, asbestos is a toxic substance. At this point, we might tentatively record "getting rid of toxic substances" as a theme.

Another comparative method involves taking pairs of expressions—from the same informant or from different informants—and asking: "How is one expression different or similar to the other?" Here's another informant in our study of what Americans think they can do to help the environment:

Interviewer:	Any pressing issues that you can think of right now?
Informant:	Well I don't know what you can do to solve it but the places for hazardous waste are few and far between from what I understand—that some people are dumping where they shouldn't (pause) and I don't know what you can do because nobody wants any of the hazardous wastes near them.

In comparing the two responses, we asked: Is there a common theme here, in hazardous waste and toxic waste? If some theme is present in two expressions, then the next question to ask is: "Is there any difference in degree or kind in which the theme is articulated in both of the expressions?"

Degrees of strength in themes may lead to the naming of subthemes. Suppose you compare two video clips and find that both express the theme of anxiety. Looking carefully, you notice that anxiety is expressed more verbally in one clip and more through subtle hand gestures in the other. Depending on the goals of your research, you might code the clips as expressing the theme of anxiety or as expressing anxiety in two different ways.

You can find some themes by comparing pairs of whole texts. As you read a text, ask: "How is this one different from the last one I read?" and "What kinds of things are mentioned in both?" Ask hypothetical questions like: "What if the informant who produced this text had been a woman instead of a man?" and "How similar is this text to my own experiences?"

These hypothetical questions will force you to make comparisons, which often produce moments of insight about themes.

Bogdan and Biklen (1982:153) recommend reading through passages of text and asking: "What does this remind me of?" Below, we'll introduce more formal techniques for identifying similarities and differences among segments of text, but we always start with the informal methods: underlining, highlighting, and comparing.

6. Linguistic Connectors

Look carefully for words and phrases that indicate attributes and various kinds of causal or conditional relations. The possibilities were first laid out by Casagrande and Hale (1967) in their study of the Papago language, but have since been found in languages across the world (Spradley 1979:111; Werner 1972).

Causal relations: "because" and its variants, 'cause, 'cuz, as a result, since, and the like. For example: "Y'know, we always take 197 [one ninety-seven] there 'cuz it avoids all that traffic at the mall." But notice the use of the word "since" in the following: "Since he got married, it's like he forgot his friends." Text analysis that involves the search for linguistic connectors like these requires very strong skills in the language of the text because you have to be able to pick out very subtle differences in usage.

Conditional relations: "if" or "then" (and if-then pairs), "rather than," and "instead of." "During peak hours at the mall, take 197 instead of 204." "If you wanna get fewer colds, take a lotta vitamin C." "You can drink a lot more [alcohol] if you coat your stomach with milk first."

Taxonomic categories: The phrase "is a" (as in "a moose is a kind of mammal") is often associated with taxonomic categories: "Vitamin C is a great way to avoid colds." Again, watch for variants. Notice how the is-a relation is embedded in the following: "When you come right down to it, lions are just big pussycats."

Time-oriented relations: Look for words like "before," "after," "then," and "next." "There's a trick to that door. Turn the key all the way to the left, twice, and then push hard." The concept of time-ordered events and relations can be very subtle: "By the time I bike home, I'm sweating like a pig." "It's so damn hot, your glasses fog when you go out."

X-is-Y relations: Casagrande and Hale (1967) also suggested looking for attributes of the form X is Y: "Lemons are sour," "The Greek islands are still a bargain," "This is just bullshit," "He's lucky he's alive."

Contingent relations: Look for phrases of the form if X, then Y: "As soon as you feel a cold coming on, you take a boatload of vitamin C" or "You want a strong harvest, you plant with the full moon." Contingent relations can be expressed in the negative, too: "They won't wear a condom, no matter what you do," or "If you want that grant, then don't piss off reviewers."

Spatial relations: Look for phrases of the form X is close to Y: "I found my way around pretty good in the new place [supermarket] because stuff is together. Milk and cheese and eggs and stuff are always together and all that stuff is near the meat" (see Box 3.2).

Box 3.2

More Linguistics Connectors

Operational definitions—X is a tool for doing Y: "You can use Excel to do basic stuff, but if you really wanna work on text you gotta get a real program for that."

Examples—X is an instance of Y: "So now [referring to undergraduates] they're using the Internet to find papers they can use; new technology, same old plagiarism."

Comparisons—X resembles Y: "Iraq is like Vietnam in some ways, but we need to remember the differences."

Class inclusions—X is a member of class Y: "Geeks and nerds are both dorky, but a geek is a nerd who can get hired."

Synonyms—X is equivalent to Y: "Telling me you can't afford to go is just a wimpy way of saying kiss off."

Antonyms—X is the negation of Y: "Not picking up after your dog is the definition of a bad neighbor" [here the implication is that the act is the negation of "good neighbor"].

Provenance—X is the source of Y: "A foolish consistency is the hobgoblin of little minds" [Emerson's famous dictum, 1841].

Circularity—X is defined as X: "Yellow means like when something is lemon colored.

SOURCE: Casagrande and Hale (1967).

7. Missing Data

This method works in reverse from typical theme-identification techniques. Instead of asking "What is here?" we can ask "What is missing?" Women who have strong religious convictions may fail to mention abortion during discussions of birth control. In power-laden interviews, silence may be tied to implicit or explicit domination (Gal 1991). In a study of birth planning in China, Greenhalgh reports that she could not ask direct questions about resistance to government policy. People made "strategic use of silence," she says, "to protest aspects of the policy they did not like" (1994). Obviously, themes discovered like this need to be looked at critically to make sure that we are not finding only what we are looking for.

Gaps in texts may not indicate avoidance at all, but simply what Spradley (1979:57–58) called abbreviating—leaving out information that everyone knows. As you read through a text, look for things that remain unsaid and try to fill in the gaps (L. Price 1987). This can be tough to do. Distinguishing between when people are unwilling to discuss a topic from their simply assuming that you already know about it requires a lot of familiarity with the subject matter. If someone says, "John was broke because it was the end of the month," they're assuming that you already know that many people get paid once a month and that people sometimes spend all their money before getting their next paycheck.

When you first read a text, some themes will simply pop out at you. Mark them with highlighters. Then read the text again. And again. Look for themes in the data that remain unmarked. This tactic—marking obvious themes early and quickly—forces the search for new and less obvious themes in the second pass (Ryan 1999).

8. Theory-Related Material

By definition, rich narratives contain information on themes that characterize the experience of informants, but we also want to understand how qualitative data illuminate questions of theoretical importance. Spradley (1979:199–201) suggested searching interviews for evidence of social conflict, cultural contradictions, informal methods of social control, things that people do in managing impersonal social relationships, methods by which people acquire and maintain achieved and ascribed status, and information about how people solve problems.

Bogdan and Biklen (1982:156–162) suggested examining the setting and context, the perspectives of the informants, and informants' ways of thinking about people, objects, processes, activities, events, and relationships. A. Strauss and Corbin (1990:158–175) urge us to be more sensitive to conditions, actions/interactions, and consequences of a phenomenon and to order these conditions and consequences into theories. "Moving across substantive areas," says Charmaz, "fosters developing conceptual power, depth, and comprehensiveness" (1990:1163).

There is a trade-off, of course, between bringing a lot of prior theorizing to the theme-identification effort and going at it fresh. Prior theorizing, as Charmaz says (1990), can inhibit the forming of fresh ideas and the making of surprising connections. And by examining the data from a more theoretical perspective, researchers must be careful not to find only what they are looking for. Assiduous theory avoidance, however, brings the risk of not making the connection between data and important research questions.

The eight techniques just described require only pencil and paper. Next, we describe four techniques that require more physical or computer-based manipulation of the text itself.

FOUR MANIPULATIVE TECHNIQUES: ♦ WAYS TO PROCESS TEXTS

Some techniques are informal—spreading texts out on the floor, tacking bunches of them to a bulletin board, and sorting them into different file folders—and others require special software to count words or display word-by-word co-occurrences. And, as we'll see, some techniques require a fair amount of skill in computer analysis. But more of that later. . . .

9. Cutting and Sorting

After the initial pawing and marking of text, cutting and sorting involves identifying quotes or expressions that seem somehow important—these are called exemplars—and then arranging the quotes/expressions into piles of things that go together (Lincoln and Guba 1985:347–351).

There are many variations on this technique. We cut out each quote (making sure to maintain some of the context in which it occurred) and paste the material on a small index card. We write down the quote's reference—who said it and where it appeared in the text—on the back of each card. Then we spread the quotes out randomly on a big table and sort them into piles of similar quotes. Then we name each pile. These are the themes.

When it comes to pile sorting, there are two kinds of people: splitters and lumpers. Splitters maximize the differences between items and generate more fine-grained themes; lumpers minimize the differences and identify more overarching themes. At the early stages of data analysis, it's best to identify the widest possible range of themes and leave the lumping for later.

In a project with two or three researchers, each member of the research team should sort the exemplar quotes into named piles independently. This usually generates a longer list of themes than you get in a group discussion.

Barkin et al. (1999) interviewed clinicians, community leaders, and parents about what physicians could say to adolescents, during routine well-child exams, to prevent violence among youth. There were three questions at the center of the project: (1) What could pediatricians potentially do to deal with youth violence? (2) What barriers did they face? (3) What resources were available to help them?

Two coders read through the transcripts and pulled out all segments of text associated with these questions. The two coders identified 84 statements related to potential, 74 related to barriers, and 41 related to resources. All the statements were put onto cards.

Next, four other coders independently sorted all the quotes from each major theme into piles of things that they thought were somehow similar. Talking about what the quotes in each pile had in common and naming those piles helped Barkin et al. (1999) identify subthemes (see Box 3.3).

Box 3.3

Formal Analysis of Pile Sorts

Pile sorts produce similarity data—that is, a matrix of what goes with what—and similarity data can be analyzed with some formidable visualization methods, like multidimensional scaling and cluster analysis. These methods let you see patterns in your data.

Barkin et al. (1999) converted the pile-sort data for each of their three major themes into a quote-by-quote similarity matrix, where the numbers in the cells indicated the number of coders (0, 1, 2, 3, or 4) who had placed the quotes in the same pile. They used multidimensional scaling and cluster analysis to identify groups of quotes that the coders thought were similar.

More about multidimensional scaling in Chapters 5 and 8.

In really large projects, have pairs of researchers sort the quotes and decide on the names for the piles. Record and study the conversations that researchers have while they're sorting quotes and naming themes to understand the underlying criteria they are using. (Further Reading: cutting and sorting.)

10. Word Lists and Key-Words-in-Context (KWIC)

Word lists and the key-word-in-context (KWIC) technique draw on a simple observation: If you want to understand what people are talking about, look closely at the words they use. To generate word lists, you identify all the unique words in a text and then count the number of times each occurs. Computer programs do this effortlessly.

Ryan and Weisner (1996) asked parents of adolescents: "Describe your children. In your own words, just tell us about them." From the transcripts, Ryan and Weisner produced a list of all the unique words. Then they counted the number of times each unique word was used by mothers and by fathers. The idea was to get some clues about themes that could be used for coding the full texts.

Overall, the words that mothers and fathers used to describe their children suggested that they were concerned with their children's independence and with their children's moral, artistic, social, athletic, and academic characteristics, but mothers were more likely to use "friends," "creative," "time," and "honest" to describe their children whereas fathers were more likely to use "school," "good," "lack," "student," "enjoys," and "independent." Ryan and Weisner used this information as clues for themes that they would use later in actually coding the texts. Details about this study in Chapter 9.

Word-counting techniques produce what Tesch (1990:139) called data condensation or data distillation. By telling us which words occur most frequently, these methods can help us identify core ideas in a welter of data. But condensed data like word lists and counts take words out of their original context, so if you do word counts, you'll also want to use a key-word-in-context (KWIC) program (see Appendix).

The KWIC method is essentially a modern version of concordances. A concordance is a list of every substantive word in a text, shown with the words surrounding it. Before computers, concordances were arranged in alphabetical order so you could see how each word was used in various contexts. These days, KWIC lists are generated by asking a computer to find all the places in a text where a particular word or phrase appears and printing it out in the context of some number of words (say, 30) before and after it. You (and others) can sort these instances into piles of similar meaning to assemble a set of themes. More about the KWIC method and word lists in Chapter 9.

11. Word Co-occurrence

This approach comes from linguistics and semantic network analysis. It's based on the observation that many words commonly occur with other words to form a particular idea. The word "shrouded," for example, often occurs near "mystery" or "secrecy" (as in "shrouded in mystery") and sometimes near "mist" or "ambiguity." The word "crime" often occurs with "violent" and "violence" (as in "crime of violence") or with "passion" ("crime of passion") or "thought" ("thought crime") or "century" (crime of the century").

In 1959, Charles Osgood created word co-occurrence matrices—that is, matrices that show how often every pair of words co-occur in a text—and analyzed those matrices to describe the relation of major themes to one another. It was rather heroic work back then, but computers have made the construction and analysis of co-occurrence matrices relatively easy today and have stimulated the development of what's called semantic network analysis (Barnett and Danowski 1992; Danowski 1982, 1993). More about this, too, in Chapter 9.

12. Metacoding

Metacoding examines the relationship among a priori themes to discover potentially new themes and overarching metathemes. The technique requires a fixed set of data units (paragraphs, whole texts, pictures, etc.) and a fixed set of a priori themes, so it's less exploratory than many of the techniques we've described.

For each data unit, you ask which themes are present and, where appropriate, the direction and strength of each theme. The data are recorded in a unit-by-theme matrix. This matrix can then be analyzed statistically. Factor analysis, for example, indicates the degree to which themes coalesce along a limited number of dimensions. Visualization methods—like multidimensional scaling and correspondence analysis—show graphically how units and themes are distributed along dimensions and into groups or clusters. More on multidimensional scaling in Chapters 5 and 8.

Jehn and Doucet (1996, 1997) asked 76 U.S. managers who worked in Sino-American joint ventures to describe recent interpersonal conflicts with their business partners. Each person described two conflicts: one with a same-culture manager and another with a different-culture manager.

Two coders read the 76 intracultural and 76 intercultural conflict scenarios and evaluated them on a 5-point scale for 27 themes that Jehn and Doucet had identified from the literature on conflict. This produced two 76 × 27 scenario-by-theme matrices—one for the intracultural conflicts and one for the intercultural conflicts. Jehn and Doucet analyzed these matrices with factor analysis. This method reduced the 27 themes to just a handful. Jehn and Doucet then pulled out quotes from their original data to illustrate the most important themes.

Quotes that characterized the first factor for intercultural relations were: "There is a lot of hate involved in this situation," and "The dislike is overwhelming," and "I was very angry." Quotes that characterized the second factor were: "I was very frustrated with my co-worker" and "Their inconsistencies really aggravated me." And quotes that characterized the third factor were: "She's a bitch" and "We are constantly shouting and screaming." Jehn and Doucet labeled these factors personal animosity, aggravation, and volatility in intercultural business relations (1997:2).

Numerical methods like these work best when applied to short, descriptive texts of one or two paragraphs. They tend to produce a limited number of large metathemes, but these are just the kinds of themes that may not be apparent, even after a careful and exhaustive reading of a text. Metacoding is a nice addition to our theme-finding tool kit.

SELECTING AMONG TECHNIQUES ◆

Figure 3.1 and Table 3.1 lay out the characteristics of the techniques to help you decide which method is best in any particular project, given your own time and skill constraints. Looking for repetitions and similarities and differences and cutting and sorting can be applied to any kind of qualitative data and don't require special computer skills. It is not surprising that these techniques are the ones used most frequently in qualitative research.

There are five things to consider in selecting one or more of these twelve techniques: (1) the kind of data you have; (2) how much skill is required; (3) how much labor is required; (4) the number and types of themes to be generated; and (5) whether you are going to test the reliability and validity of the themes you produce.

Table 3.1 Practical Characteristics of Theme Discovery Techniques

| Technique | Labor Intensity | Expertise | | | Stage in Analysis | Number of Themes Produced | Type of Theme Produced |
		Language	Substantive	Methodological			
1 Repetitions	Low	Low	Low	Low	Early	High	Theme
2 Indigenous typologies	Low	High	Low	Low	Early	Medium	Theme, subtheme
3 Metaphors	Low	High	Low	Low	Early	Medium	Theme
4 Transitions	Low	Low	Low	Low	Early	High	Theme
5 Similarities and differences	Low-high	Low	Low	Low	Early	High	Theme
6 Linguistic connectors	Low	High	Low	Low	Late	High	Theme
7 Missing data	High	High	High	High	Late	Low	Theme
8 Theory-related material	Low	Low	High	High	Late	Low	Theme
9 Cutting and sorting	Low-high	Low	Low	Low	Early or late	Medium	Theme, subtheme, metatheme
10 Word lists and KWIC	Low	Medium	Low	Low	Early	Medium	Theme, subtheme
11 Word co-occurrence	Medium	Medium	Low	High	Late	Low	Theme, metatheme
12 Metacoding	Medium	Medium	High	High	Late	Low	Theme, metatheme

1. Kind of Data

With the exception of metacoding, all 12 of the techniques we've described here can be applied to lengthy narratives. However, as texts become shorter and less complex, looking for transitions, metaphors, and linguistic connectors is harder to do. Discovering themes by looking for what is missing is inappropriate for very short responses to open-ended questions because it is hard to say whether missing data represent a new theme or is

Figure 3.1 Selecting Among Theme Identification Techniques

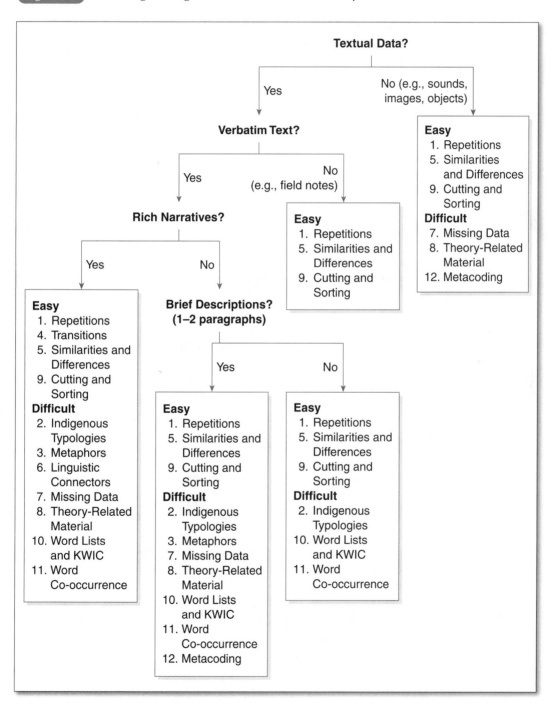

just the result of the way the data were elicited. And short texts are inefficient for finding theory-related material.

For audio and video data, we find that the best methods involve looking and listening for repetitions, similarities and differences, missing data, and theory-related material—and doing sorting or metacoding.

One more reminder about field notes as texts: In writing field notes, we choose what data are important to record and what data are not. Any patterns (themes) that we discover in field notes may come from our informants—but may also come from biases that we brought to the recording process.

2. Skill

Not all techniques are available to everyone. You need to be truly fluent in the language of the text to look for metaphors, linguistic connectors, and indigenous typologies or to spot missing data. If you are working in a language other than your own, it's best to stick to the search for repetitions, transitions, similarities and differences, and etic categories (theory-related material), and to have native speakers do any sorting of exemplars. Word lists and co-occurrences, as well as metacoding, also require less language competence and so are easier to apply.

Using word co-occurrence or metacoding requires know-how about producing and managing matrices as well as skill in using methods for exploring and visualizing data. If you don't have training in the use of multidimensional scaling, cluster analysis, factor analysis, and correspondence analysis, then use techniques that aren't computationally intensive, like cutting and sorting, word lists, and KWIC.

3. Labor

A generation ago, observation-based techniques required less effort than did process techniques. Today, computers and software have made counting words and co-occurrences of words, as well as analysis of matrices very easy, though the cost, in time and effort, to learn these computer methods can be daunting.

Some of the observation-based techniques (searching for repetitions, indigenous typologies, metaphors, transitions, and linguistic connectors) are best done by eyeballing, but this can be really time consuming. In team-based applications research, the premium on getting answers quickly often means a preference for methods that rely more on computers and less on human labor.

In our own work, we find that a careful look at a word frequency list and some quick pile sorts are good ways to start. Studying word co-occurrences and metacoding require more work and produce fewer themes, but they are excellent for discovering big themes that can hide in mountains of texts.

4. Number and Kinds of Themes

In theme discovery, more is better. It's not that all themes are equally important. You still have to decide which themes are most salient and how themes are related to each other. But unless themes are discovered in the first place, none of this additional analysis can take place.

We know of no research comparing the number of themes that each technique generates, but in our experience, looking for repetitions, similarities and differences, transitions, and linguistic connectors that occur frequently in text produces more themes, and looking for metaphors and indigenous categories (which occur less frequently) produces fewer themes. Of all the observation techniques, searching for theory-related material or for missing data produces the smallest number of new themes.

Of the process techniques, the cutting-and-sorting method, along with word lists and KWIC analysis, yield many themes and subthemes; word co-occurrence and metacoding produce a few, larger, more inclusive meta-themes. But at the start of any project, the primary goal is to discover as many themes as possible. And this means applying several techniques until you reach saturation—that is, until you stop finding new themes.

Cutting and sorting expressions into piles is the most versatile technique. You can identify major themes, subthemes, and even metathemes with this method, and, although the analysis of this kind of data is enhanced by computational methods, much of it can be done without a computer. In contrast, techniques that apply to aggregated data such as word co-occurrences and metacoding are particularly good at identifying more abstract themes, but really can't be done without the help of a computer and good software.

5. Reliability and Validity

"There is," says Ian Dey (1993:110–111), "no single set of categories [themes] waiting to be discovered. There are as many ways of 'seeing' the data as one can invent." In their study of Chinese and American managers, Jehn and Doucet (1996) used three different discovery techniques on the same set of data and each produced a different set of themes. All three of their theme sets have some intuitive appeal and all three yield analytic results that are useful. But Jehn and Doucet might have used any of the other techniques we've described here to discover even more themes.

How can we tell if the themes we've identified are valid? The answer is that there is no ultimate demonstration of validity. The validity of a concept depends on the utility of the device that measures it and on the collective judgment of the scientific community that a construct and its measure are valid (Bernard 2006:60; Denzin 1970:106).

Reliability, on the other hand, is about agreement among coders and across methods and across studies. Do coders agree on what theme to assign a segment of text? Strong interrater reliability—about which more in Chapter 13—suggests that a theme is not just a figment of your imagination and adds to the likelihood that the theme is also valid (Sandelowski 1995a).

Lincoln and Guba's (1985) team approach to sorting and naming piles of expressions is so appealing because agreement need not be limited to members of the core research team. Jehn and Doucet (1996, 1997) asked local experts to sort word lists into themes, and Barkin et al. (1999) had both experts and novices sort quotes into piles. The more agreement among team members, the more confidence we have that emerging themes are valid.

Some researchers recommend that respondents be given the opportunity to examine and comment on themes (Lincoln and Guba 1985:351). This is certainly appropriate when one of the goals of research is to identify and apply themes that are recognized or used by the people whom one studies, but it is not always possible. The discovery of new ideas derived from a more theoretical approach may involve the application of etic rather than emic themes—that is, understandings held by outsiders rather than those held by insiders. In these cases, researchers should not expect their findings necessarily to correspond with the ideas and beliefs of study participants. (Further Reading: reliability and validity in qualitative research.)

♦ AND FINALLY. . . .

We have much to learn about the process of finding themes in qualitative data. Since the early 1960s, researchers have been working on fully automated, computer-based methods for identifying themes in text. These computer-based content dictionaries, as they're known, may not sit well with some. After all, if the "qualitative" in qualitative methods means analysis by humans, then how can we give over such an important piece of qualitative analysis—theme identification—to machines?

The answer is that, ultimately, we are responsible for all analysis. We are comfortable using text management software to help us recognize connections in a set of themes, and we are comfortable letting machines count words and create matrices for us from texts. Text analysts of every epistemological persuasion can hardly wait for voice recognition software to become sufficiently effective that it will relieve us of all transcription chores. Computer-based content dictionaries that can parse a text and identify its underlying thematic components will, we believe, be just another tool that will (1) make the analysis of qualitative data easier; and (2) lead to much wider use and appreciation of qualitative data in all the social sciences.

Further Reading

◆ For more on finding themes, see Bradley et al. (2007) and Yeh and Inman (2007). For examples of doing this in group research, see Carey and Gelaude (2008) and MacQueen et al. (2008). On using pictures in the search for themes, see Necheles et al. (2007).

◆ For more on the cutting and sorting technique, see Patterson et al. (1993) and Sayles et al. (2007).

◆ For more on reliability and validity in qualitative research, see E. M. Green (2001), Moret et al. (2007), Sin (2007), and W. Sykes (1990, 1991).

CHAPTER 4

CODEBOOKS AND CODING

INTRODUCTION

In Chapter 3, we discussed how to discover themes. In this chapter, we discuss the actual process of coding—that is, organizing lists of themes into codebooks and applying codes to chunks of text. Finally, we lay out some methods

75

for finding chunks of text that are typical of each theme. This helps us understand the core and peripheral elements of each theme and is an important part of analysis.

◆ THREE KINDS OF CODES

Codebooks contain three kinds of codes: (1) structural codes; (2) theme codes; and (3) memos. Structural codes describe things like features of the environment in which data are collected, features of the respondent, features of the interviewer, and so on (L. Richards and T. Richards 1995; T. Richards 2002). Theme codes show where the themes we've identified actually occur in a text. Memos are field notes about codes and contain our running commentary as we read through texts (A. Strauss and Corbin 1990:18, 73–74, 109–129, 197–219).

Table 4.1 is a piece of a coded focus group transcript showing all three kinds of codes. The transcript is from a study by Mark Schuster and his colleagues (Eastman et al. 2005; Schuster et al. 2000) in Los Angeles about the feasibility of running classes at corporate work sites to help parents better communicate with their adolescent children about relationships and sex.

One structural code (on the far left column in Table 4.1) tells us that the focus group took place in Corporation 1; a second code indicates where different topics in the interview protocol begin and end (in this example, there are two topics represented); a third indicates the gender of the speakers; and a fourth tells us which moderator was running the group at the time of each snippet.

Schuster et al. could have assigned codes for other features of the focus group, like the time of day the group was conducted or whether the focus group met onsite or offsite. And they could have coded for characteristics of the speakers, like age or ethnicity if they'd wanted to.

Thematic codes are the most common kinds of codes. These are the codes we use for marking instances of themes in a set of data. You may see thematic codes called referential codes (L. Richards and T. Richards 1995) because these codes refer to where a theme is located in a text. We might also call them index codes because, like the index in the back of a book, they tell us where to look in a text if we want to find material about a particular theme. There are two thematic codes in Table 4.1. Italicized text marks Theme #1, called "Communication," and underlined text references Theme #2, called "Potential Barriers."

Table 4.1 Examples of Structural Codes, Theme Codes and Memos

Structural Codes				Thematic Codes and Memos
Work Site	Interview Topic	Speaker's Gender	Speaker	Transcript
Corp. #1			Mod.	If we were going to offer a parenting program, what would you like to hear that would catch your interest or make you want to attend this type of program? How could we market it?
	Topic #1	M	1	<u>I don't know. . . . I know my wife would like it a lot. She would lead me into it, but. . . .</u>
		M	2	*Probably stressing the communication, somehow portraying that and the problems communicating because that's a universal. We were talking yesterday, that that's the biggest challenge, or one of the biggest challenges, so somehow portraying that well and grabbing attention that way.* [THIS IS PART II OF A 2-DAY SESSION. PREVIOUS DAY, PARTICIPANTS DISCUSSED HOW THEY COMMUNICATED WITH THEIR ADOLESCENTS ABOUT SEX AND RELATIONSHIPS.]
		F	3	I think you'd have to sell the success. What is it that you plan on accomplishing with this? If you can tell me that at the end of this thing, our relationship will be better, my daughter will be a better achiever, you know, I won't lose my temper as often; that would do it.
		F	4	Money-back guarantee.
	Topic #2		Mod.	If we said, "OK, tonight we want you to have a conversation with your child about sex." What would be hard or easy about that?
		F	4	I've taken a couple of classes through the years, and my kids get a kick out watching me sit and do homework. And so if I let them know, this is my homework, and gosh mom gets homework too, ya, and that could be kinda fun for them to know that you've gotta sit and read a book and do a report or have a discussion. You know, you're my homework tonight.

SOURCE: Adapted from Eastman et al. (2005) and Schuster et al. (2000).

Legend: Italics = Theme #1, communication; underline = Theme #2, potential barriers; small caps = memo. Corp. = corporation; Mod. = moderator.

The segment in small caps between the square brackets is a memo. These features are identified in the legend in the lower right corner of Table 4.1 (see Box 4.1).

Box 4.1

Kinds of Memos

The transcript in Table 4.1 contains some memos embedded right into the running text. A. Strauss and Corbin distinguish three kinds of memos (1990:18, 73–74, 109–129, 197–219): code memos, theory memos, and operational memos.

Code memos describe the researcher's observations and thoughts about the concepts that are being discovered.

Theory memos summarize our ideas about the existence of themes, about how themes are linked, and about what causes themes to exist in the first place. For example, if you are analyzing a set of texts about the experience of giving birth, you may notice that some women mention the pain; others don't, or even play it down. Noticing and memoing how the theme of pain is linked to other themes is an act of theory making, as is noticing and memoing the circumstances in a woman's life that make the mention of pain predictable.

Operational memos are about practical matters. For example, the memo in the middle of the transcript in Table 4.1 indicates that the same participants had met the day before to talk about how they communicated with their adolescent children about sex and relationships. The concept of memoing comes from grounded theory and is an integral part of that method. We'll discuss memos in more detail in Chapter 12, on grounded theory.

Blocking off theme areas makes analysis easier later on: We can search the transcript and find where particular themes occur. This can be done with a word processor, but it's even easier with a text analysis program. And with a text analysis program, you can search for places in the transcript where two or more themes occur.

◆ BUILDING CODEBOOKS

Like themes, codebooks can be built up from data—the inductive approach—or from theory—the deductive or a priori approach—or, as Dey

(1993:104) has long advocated, with a combination of approaches as circumstances dictate.

We're in that camp, too. We find that codebooks are often a work in progress right up until a project is almost over. As coders find more and more examples of themes, their reliability in marking themes—the actual process of coding—goes up (Carey et al. 1996; Krippendorff 1980b:71–84). As coders refine their understanding of the content of a code, the description in the codebook gets more detailed. As Miles and Huberman said so elegantly: "Coding is analysis" (1994:56).

The Evolution of Codebooks I

Karen Kurasaki (2000) studied ethnic identity among *sansei*, third-generation Japanese Americans. She and two research assistants did in-depth interviews, lasting from 1 to 2 hours, with 20 informants, beginning with the question "What sorts of things remind you that you're Japanese-American" (Kurasaki 1997:145–149). The interviews were transcribed and then studied by all three researchers to develop a list of themes.

The first list had 29 themes, but as the researchers studied the texts, they concluded that there were seven major themes, shown in Table 4.2: (1) a sense of history and roots; (2) values and ways of doing things; (3) biculturality; (4) sense of belonging; (5) sense of alienation; (6) self-concept; and (7) worldview. As the analysis progressed, Kurasaki split the major themes into subthemes. For example, she split the first theme into (a) sense of having a Japanese heritage; and (b) sense of having a Japanese American social history.

As the coding progressed further, Kurasaki and her two assistants kept meeting and discussing what they were finding. They decided that one of the major themes, theme 5 (a sense of alienation), was better treated as a subtheme of theme 4 (a sense of belonging). Then they decided that one of the subthemes, 4.4 (searching for a sense of community), was redundant with codes 4.1, 4.2, 4.3, and 4.5, and that code 7.1, social consciousness (shown crossed out in Table 4.2), should instead be labeled an orientation toward promoting racial tolerance (Kurasaki 1997:50–56).

The Evolution of Codebooks II

Here's another example. Across the world, the vast majority of illness episodes are treated at home. Ryan (1995) studied how ordinary people in

Table 4.2   Kurasaki's Inductive Codebook

First-Order Category	Second-Order Category	First Numeric Codes	Second Numeric Codes
Sense of history and roots	Sense of having a Japanese heritage	1.1	1.1
	Sense of having a Japanese American social history	1.2	1.2
Values and ways	Japanese American values and attitudes of doing things	2.1	2.1
	Practice of Japanese customs	2.2	2.2
	Japanese way of doing things	2.3	2.3
	Japanese American interpersonal or communication styles	2.4	2.4
	Japanese language proficiency	2.5	2.5
Biculturality	Integration or bicultural competence	3.1	3.1
	Bicultural conflict or confusion	3.2	3.2
Sense of belonging	Sense of a global ethnic or racial community	4.1	4.1
	Sense of interpersonal connectedness with same ethnicity or race of others	4.2	4.2
	Sense of intellectual connectedness with other ethnic or racial minorities	4.3	4.3
	Searching for a sense of community	4.4	deleted
Sense of alienation	Sense of alienation from ascribed ethnic or racial group	5.1	4.5
Self-concept	Sense of comfort with one's ethnic or racial self	6.1	5.1
	Searching for a sense of comfort with one's ethnic or racial self	6.2	5.2
Worldview	~~Social consciousness~~ Orientation toward promoting racial tolerance	7.1	6.1
	Sense of oppression	7.2	6.2

SOURCE: Kurasaki (1997, 2000:186).

Cameroon react at home when they get sick. Every week for 5 months, Ryan and several assistants visited 88 extended family households in rural Cameroon. They asked if anyone had been sick and, for each of 429 illness episodes, they asked the primary caregiver to describe what happened and what had been done about it.

Ryan knew from earlier work in the village the kinds of treatments that were available to people there, so that part of his codebook was set. He planned to code each illness for the caregiver's ideas about its cause, its severity, and its outcome, as well as for its signs, symptoms, and duration. Because he planned to compare people's responses to illness by age and gender, Ryan included codes for these variables—both for those who were sick and for those who were taking care of them. Ryan's initial codebook is shown on the left of Table 4.3.

Soon after he started collecting data, Ryan realized that people were grouping signs and symptoms by areas of the body: those related to the head, to the chest, to the stomach, and to the skin. He also found that people not in the family of the sick person often offered advice and that people sometimes reported that they avoided the sun and stopped bathing when ill. He added these things to his code list.

Midway though the data collection, Ryan took a break and read over the interview notes and transcripts. He realized that he needed to identify places in his notes where people talked about how the illness had interrupted their daily lives and where they gave specific rationales for their decisions. His reading of the texts suggested that decision criteria were linked to specific characteristics of the illness, to extenuating circumstances and events, or to past illness experiences. He incorporated these new codes into his growing codebook, shown on the right of Table 4.3.

USING EXISTING CODES ◆

Not all codebooks are developed from the ground up. Many researchers rely on, or adapt, standard coding sources. Shelley (1992) studied the social networks of people who had end-stage kidney disease. The traditional therapy is hemodialysis, a blood-cleaning process that requires hooking people up to a machine for several hours every other day. Shelley reasoned that people whose lives depend on those hemodialysis machines will come to have very restricted social networks. Patients who are treated with other therapies, like organ transplants or CAPD (a portable dialysis technology), can work and travel and should not have restricted networks.

Table 4.3 Evolution of Code List for Study of Illness Episodes in Rural Cameroon

Original	Expanded
I. Illness Characteristics	I. Illness Characteristics
A. Diagnosis (Diag)	A. Diagnosis (Diag)
B. Signs/Symptoms (S/S)	B. Signs/Symptoms (S/S)
C. Duration (Dur)	1. Head (S-Head)
D. Severity (Sev)	2. Chest (S-Chest)
E. Perceived causation (Cause)	3. Stomach (S-Stom)
	4. Skin (S-Skin)
II. Treatment Behavior	5. Other (S-Other)
A. Home remedies (HomeR)	C. Duration (Dur)
B. Over-the-counter drugs (OTC)	D. Severity (Sev)
C. Western medical providers	E. Perceived causation (Cause)
1. Nurse (W-Nurse)	
2. Government Clinic (W-Clin)	II. Treatment Behavior
3. Catholic Hospital (W-Hosp)	A. Home remedies (HomeR)
D. Traditional Medical Providers	B. Over-the-counter drugs (OTC)
1. Herbalists (T-Herb)	C. Western medical providers
2. Diviners (T-Div)	1. Nurse (W-Nurse)
E. Other non-professional advisors	2. Government Clinic (W-Clin)
1. Relatives (O-Rel)	3. Catholic Hospital (W-Hosp)
2. Friends/neighbors (O-Friend)	D. Traditional Medical Providers
3. Strangers (O-Strang)	1. Herbalists (T-Herb)
	2. Diviners (T-Div)
III. Patient Characteristics	E. Other non-professional advisors
A. Gender (P-Gend)	1. Relatives (O-Rel)
1. Male	2. Friends/neighbors (O-Friend)
2. Female	3. Strangers (O-Strang)
B. Age (P-Age)	F. Behavioral modifications
	1. Extra sleep (B-Sleep)
IV. Caregiver Characteristics	2. Sun avoidance (B-Sun)
A. Gender (C-Gend)	3. No bathing (B-Bath)
B. Age (C-Age)	4. Other (B-Other)
C. Relation to patient (C-Relate)	
	III. Patient Characteristics
	A. Gender (P-Gend)
	1. Male
	2. Female
	B. Age (P-Age)
	IV. Caregiver Characteristics
	A. Gender (C-Gend)
	B. Age (C-Age)
	C. Relation to patient (C-Relate)
	V. Interruption of Daily Routine
	A. Work/school related (IDR-Work)
	B. Social engagements (IDR-Social)
	VI. Decision Rules
	A. Illness characteristics (Dec-Ill-Char)
	B. Events (Dec-Events)
	C. Past illness (Dec-Past Ill)

Shelley adapted the *Outline of Cultural Materials* (Murdock et al. 2004 [1961]), or OCM, for coding her interviews with patients, hemodialysis technicians, and physicians, as well as her own field notes. The OCM was developed by G. P. Murdock as a way to index and organize ethnographic materials in the Human Relations Area Files. (The full list of the OCM is online. See Appendix.)

Every society in the world has culturally appropriate ways to deal with illness, and the OCM codes 750 to 759 cover this. Few societies have themes relating to hemodialysis or kidney transplants, but Shelley simply added decimal points to the basic OCM code for medical therapy. Table 4.4 shows the original OCM codes and a part of Shelley's codebook—the adaptation of OCM code 757 (medical therapy). More on the HRAF in Chapter 13 on content analysis.

| **Table 4.4** | Shelley's Adaptation of the OCM Code 757 on Medical Therapy |

Original OCM Codes	Shelley's Adaptation
750 SICKNESS	750 SICKNESS
751 Preventative Medicine	751 Preventative Medicine
752 Bodily Injuries	752 Bodily Injuries
753 Theory of Disease	753 Theory of Disease
754 Sorcery	754 Sorcery
755 Magical & Mental Therapy	755 Magical & Mental Therapy
756 Shamans & Psychotherapists	756 Shamans & Psychotherapists
757 Medical Therapy	757 Medical Therapy
758 Medical Care	757.1 Transplantation
759 Medical Personnel	757.2 Hemodialysis
	757.3 CAPD (peritoneal dialysis)
	757.4 Home dialysis
	757.5 Adjustment to dialysis
	757.6 Compliance with medical regime
	757.7 Machinery involved in dialysis
	757.8 Medicines
	757.9 Medical test results
	757.91 HIV test results
	758 Medical Care
	759 Medical Personnel

SOURCE: Shelley (1992).

◆ CODEBOOKS CONTINUE TO DEVELOP

Even for longitudinal projects, codebooks can be permanently works in progress. In 1987, Ronald Gallimore and Thomas Weisner began following 102 families that had young children (3–4 years old at the time) with developmental delays of unknown or uncertain cause. Building on the work of others, Gallimore and Weisner began with a list of 12 environmental and sociocultural factors that might influence the way families organized their everyday routine of family life when they had a child with a developmental disability (Gallimore et al. 1989). The families were interviewed again when the children were 7, 11, and 16 years old (Gallimore et al. 1996; Weisner 2008).

As the research team learned more about how families dealt with developmentally delayed children, and as the children got older, they modified the code list, adding and dropping elements. The final list of 10 major themes for The Ecocultural Family Interview, or EFI, is shown in Table 4.5, and Table 4.6 shows an expansion of one major topic—the overall subsistence base for the family—into four constituent themes that emerged as important over time.

The EFI and its accompanying codebooks have been adapted for studying different communities and family types, including Asian American,

Table 4.5 Major Themes in the Ecocultural Family Interview

Major codebook themes
1. Subsistence domain
2. Services domain
3. Home/neighborhood
4. Domestic workload
5. Connectedness domain
6. Non-disabled support network domain
7. Disability support network domain
8. Diversity domain
9. Service and support domain
10. Information domain

Table 4.6   Expansion of the Codebook for the Subsistence Domain in the EFI

1.   **Overall resilience of subsistence base.**

0, 1, or 2 = Low. Family has low resilience in their subsistence base. They have limited, few back-up resources, live with relatives or rent, have difficulty paying basic expenses between paychecks or live on limited government benefits.

3, 4, or 5 = Moderate. Family has moderate resilience in their subsistence base. They have a moderate income, with some back-up resources, own a home though making payments, have a little something to fall back on as unexpected expenses arise.

6, 7, or 8 = High. Family has high resilience in their subsistence base. They have a high income, own a home, have a fair amount of back-up resources, have income available for "luxuries" and unexpected expenses.

2.   **Overall satisfaction with current subsistence base.**

0, 1, or 2 = Low satisfaction. Family members express dissatisfaction with current status. "0" means family members express virtually total dissatisfaction with current status.

3, 4, or 5 = Moderate satisfaction. Family members express some satisfaction with current status.

6, 7, or 8 = High satisfaction. Family members express great satisfaction with their current status. "8" means family members express virtually total satisfaction with current status.

3.   **Effect of child on father's work arrangements and career decisions.**

0, 1, or 2 = Low. There is little effect of child on father's work. (As examples, father works because he is the family "breadwinner"; father doesn't work because he can't find a job.) "0" means there is virtually no effect of the child on father's work.

3, 4, or 5 = Moderate. (As examples, father leaves work early 2 days a week to drive child to after school activities; father does not pursue better job opportunities in another part of the country because the family is so happy with the child's school services.)

6, 7, or 8 = High. (As examples, father goes into business for himself primarily to have more time available to help child with homework and be involved with child's school and activities; father does not take promotion to new job because it would require a long commute leaving him unavailable to help with the child; father does not take a desired new job because the insurance would not cover the child.) "8" means that father's work is arranged almost completely around the child.

4.   **Effect of child on mother's work arrangements and career decisions.**

0, 1, or 2 = Low. There is little effect of child on mother's work. (As examples, mother works full-time because she feels a career is important; mother works because the family needs the income; mother doesn't work because she believes it's important to be a "full-time Mom.") "0" means there is virtually no effect of the child on mother's work.

3, 4, or 5 = Moderate. (As examples, mother works nights, in part, to be available to deal with child's behavior problems at school during the day; mother started working part time at an early intervention facility at least partly to get information to help the child.)

6, 7, or 8 = High. (As examples, mother works only to obtain health insurance for the child; mother continues to delay employment because she must deal with the child's medical needs and/or behavior problems at school; mother stops working because child needs constant supervision.) "8" means that mother's work is arranged almost completely around the child.

SOURCE: Ecocultural Scale Project (2001:2–3).

Navajo, Japanese, Australian, and Italian families as well as families with children with other health concerns, such as diabetes, asthma, traumatic injury, and cancer. (See Weisner [2002a] for a review of the EFI and its history.) (Further Reading: published codebooks.)

◆ HIERARCHICAL ORGANIZATION OF CODEBOOKS

As codes get refined, they get organized into hierarchies. Here's a five-level hierarchy: plants, trees, evergreens, spruce, blue spruce. Notice that whatever is true about plants is true about trees, and all the defining features of trees are found in evergreens. In other words, items in a well-organized hierarchy are at the same level of contrast.

The number and content of hierarchical levels in a codebook changes as themes become less fuzzy. In the early stages of a project, keep codebooks simple—no more than three levels deep. As the work progresses, you may want to add an additional level or two, but remember, the more levels of contrast, the harder it is for coders to keep things straight in their heads as they work. Kurasaki's codebook (Table 4.2) is just two levels deep. Shelley's (Table 4.4) has three levels (Shelley has 757 for medical therapy, 757.9 for medical test results, and 757.91 for HIV test results).

Remember: Coding is supposed to be data reduction not data proliferation. Matthew Miles (1979:593–594) recounted his experience with a team of three fieldworkers coding data from an ethnographic study of six public schools. The team began with a list of over a hundred codes—which grew to 202 codes as the team got more and more into the research. Of course, each team member felt that his or her codes were essential to the success of the project. The system became so confusing and labor intensive that they stopped coding altogether. Beware of what Lyn Richards calls "coding fetishism"—where "the act of coding becomes an end in itself" (L. Richards 2002:269).

Particularly on projects that you're running yourself, try to get your codebook onto one or two pages of 12-point type so you can refer to it easily as you analyze your texts and, eventually, keep it in short-term memory. For all practical purposes, this means about 50–80 codes (Bogdan and Biklen 1982:166; Miles and Huberman 1994:58). (Further Reading: developing codebooks.)

◆ APPLYING THEME CODES TO TEXT

There are at least three meanings to the word "code" in English.

1. When we code names and places to protect our respondents' anonymity, the word "code" means an encryption device. The object is to hide information, not convey it.

2. Coding texts for themes is different. Here the idea is to tag or index the text or to assign it values of a scale. Suppose you interview a hundred women about their birthing experience and you decide after reading through the narratives that PAIN is a recurrent theme. (It's common to use upper case for themes.) Some women talk about it a lot; others never mention it or minimize its importance.

If you assign the code PAIN to every segment of text in which the theme is mentioned, you're using PAIN as an index code or a tag. These codes, or tags, help you find your way back to the spots in the text where the theme is mentioned, much like the index to a book. If a book's index says that "sampling" is on page 237, then, if you go to page 237, you should be reading about sampling.

3. But suppose you decide that it's important to code for the *amount* of pain, not just the *mention* of pain, by counting words like "torment" and "anguish" as indicating more pain than words like "distress" or by looking at the content and meaning of the text and counting "It was painful, but I got through it" as indicating less pain than "I prayed I would die." In this case, you'd be using PAIN as a value code not as an index code and you'd probably use codes like NO-PAIN, LO-PAIN, MID-PAIN, and HI-PAIN, or something similar.

Examples of the Three Kinds of Codes

Kurasaki's codes for features of Japanese American ethnicity (Table 4.2) and Ryan's codes for features of illness episodes in Cameroon (Table 4.2) are indexing codes, or tags, as are Shelley's codes (Table 4.3) for the narratives of patients with end-stage kidney disease. Table 4.6, by contrast, contains value codes for the Ecocultural Family Index. For each of the four subthemes related to subsistence, the researchers in that project devised an 8-point scale and the coders were asked to apply these scales as they read through the narratives.

There's no rule that says you can't use both kinds of codes—tags and values—in the same project. Table 4.7 shows a portion of Randy Hodson's (1999) coding scheme for workplace ethnographies. Hodson's codebook uses a combination of index and value codes. Codes of2e through of2i, for example, were assigned Yes or No values. Occupation (of2a) used

Table 4.7 Portion of Code Book for Workplace Ethnographies

CASEID: _____

DATE: _____ q1(Mo=) q1a(Da=) q1b(Yr=)

CODER: q2(2 col):

BOOK CODE: q3 (3 col):

T1 BOOK TITLE AND AUTHOR'S LAST NAME:

T2 MODAL OCCUPATION: _____ Page #s: (Include in Text)

T3 INDUSTRY: _____ Page #s: (Include in Text)

T4 COUNTRY/REGION: _____ Page #s: (Include in Text)

T5 OBSERVER'S ROLE: _____ Page #s: (Include in Text)

of1 YEAR STUDY BEGAN: _____ 9999 - No Info Page #s

of1a YEAR STUDY ENDED: _____ 9999 - No Info Page #s:

ORGANIZATIONAL FACTORS

Technology/organization

of2a Occupation: 00 - Professional 01 - Management/Supervisor 02 - Clerical 03 - Sales 04 - Skilled
05 - Assembly 06 - Unskilled 07 - Service 08 - Farm 09 - No Info Page #s:

of2b Craft: 1 - Yes 2 - No 9 - No Info Page #s:

of2c Direct: 1 - Yes 2 - No 9 - No Info Page #s:
Supervision:

of2d Bench: 1 - Straight Piece 2 - Quota/Bonus 3 - Hourly 4 - No Bench Guaranteed 9 - No Info Page #s:

of2e Assembly Line: 1 - Yes 2 - No 9 - No Info Page #s:

of2f Automated: 1 - Yes 2 - No 9 - No Info Page #s:

of2g Microchip: 1 - Yes 2 - No 9 - No Info Page #s:

of2h Bureaucratic: 1 - Yes 2 - No 9 - No Info Page #s:

of2i Corporatist: 1 - Yes 2 - No 9 - No Info Page #s:

of2j Worker Ownership: 1 - Co-op 2 - ESOP 3 - None 9 - No Info Page #s:

of3 Employment Size: (6 col): ___ 999999 - No Info Page #s:

of4 Employment Growth: 1 - Decline 2 - Stable 3 - Growing 9 - No Info Page #s:

of5 Level of Competition: 1 - Low 2 - Medium 3 - High 9 - No Info Page #s:

of6 Product Market Stability: 1 - Stable 2 - Unstable 9 - No Info Page #s:

of7	Productivity:	1 - Declining	2 - Stable	3 - Increasing	9 - No Info	Page #s:
of8	Locally Owned:	1 - Yes	2 - No		9 - No Info	Page #s:
of9	Subcontractor:	1 - Yes	2 - No		9 - No Info	Page #s:
of10	Divisional Status:	1 - Yes	2 - No		9 - No Info	Page #s:
of11	Owned by a Conglomerate:	1 - Yes	2 - No		9 - No Info	Page #s:
of12	Corporate Headquarters:	1 - Yes	2 - No		9 - No Info	Page #s:
of13	Corporate Sector:	1 - Core	2 - Periphery	3 - Industrial 4 - Combined	9 - No Info	Page #s:
of14	Unions (type):	1 - None	2 - Craft	3 - Strong 7 - NA	9 - No Info	Page #s:
of15	Unions (strength):	1 - Weak	2 - Average	3 - High	9 - No Info	Page #s:
of16	Turnover:	1 - Low	2 - Medium	3 - Sometimes 4 - Frequent	9 - No Info	Page #s:
of17	Layoff Frequency:	1 - Never	2 - Seldom	3 - Sometimes 4 - Frequent	9 - No Info	Page #s:

SOURCE: Hodson, R. (1999). *Analyzing documentary accounts* (pp. 74–80). Thousand Oaks, CA: Sage. Copyright © 1999 Sage Publications.

nine nominal values (Professional, Management/Supervisor, Clerical, Sales, Skilled, Assembly, Unskilled, Service, and Farm). Bench (code of2d) used four values (Straight Piece, Quota/Bonus, Hourly Guaranteed, and No Bench).

Hodson's codes of15 through of17 were ordinal variables (that is, they involved ranking) and required the coder to assess the ethnography on a scale of Weak, Average, Strong, or Low, Medium, High, or Never, Seldom, Sometimes, Frequent. Hodson coded Employment Size as an interval variable (that is, a real numerical value) by counting the number of employees. (See Chapter 7 for a discussion of nominal, ordinal, and interval variables.)

With tagging, nothing in the data is lost. You mark and retrieve exactly what people said. The payoff is the ability to retrieve chunks of texts about whatever theme(s) you've marked. Once text is fully coded or tagged, you can ask the computer: "Show me all the text segments that are about X and Y" where X might be "getting help with grocery shopping" and Y might be "reliance on friends."

Value coding reduces text to scales, but, as in Hodson's work, the result is a people-by-themes matrix that can be analyzed statistically. More on building item-by-theme matrices (also called profile matrices) in Chapter 5.

◆ THE MECHANICS OF MARKING TEXT

It's one thing to talk about coding text and quite another actually to do it. There are many computer programs that help with the chore of marking text, but we still recommend starting any text analysis project with pencil-and-paper methods: writing notes in the margins, highlighting chunks of text with different colors, and cutting and sorting multiple copies of notes and transcripts.

As you write down each tag code on a first pass through a text, circle or highlight the exact chunk of text to which it refers. Some chunks will be single words; others may run on for paragraphs.

The physical act of doing this on the first pass will prep you for the really long and tedious process of coding to come. For sound and video, mark segments of tape or disk. For photos and other still images, mark the actual chunks of an image.

Never ever use originals of anything to do this marking.

Coding Data About the Common Cold

Once you get through the first pass, though, and have a draft of a codebook, there is no reason to struggle bravely on without the assistance of a computer. For simple projects, a word processor has everything you need for tagging and retrieving text. Just mark each theme with some attribute, like underlining, italics, boldface, or various colors.

Table 4.8 shows an example of how to do this. These data are from a project in which U.S. undergraduates were asked: "Tell me about the last time you had a cold." Signs and symptoms are tagged with italics; treatments and behavioral modifications are tagged with underlining; and diagnosis is tagged with bold type.

Note that the chunks that are tagged vary in size from a single word (like cold) to several lines. Symptoms and treatment categories take dichotomous values (yes or no). Duration is coded in days, a numerical variable. And gender of informant, a structural variable, is coded as M and F.

Once you have chunks of text marked with underlining or italics or small caps, and so on, you can search for those attributes using your word processor's FIND command. And once you're familiar with the tagging and retrieval process using a word processor, it's easy to automate the procedure so you can find segments very quickly (see Box 4.2).

USING A TEXT MANAGEMENT PROGRAM ♦

For more complex projects—and to make coding easier even for small projects—use a full-featured text management program, like Atlas/ti® or NVivo® or MaxQDA®. Figure 4.1 shows the schema for doing this, using narrative 118 in Table 4.8.

The mechanics vary from program to program, but the idea is pretty much the same in full-featured text management software these days. Basically, the codes are linked to chunks of text or to points in the text, and the codes and memos are all linked. You build a codebook as you go, highlighting a chunk of text ad assigning it a code by opening up a codebook window. If the code exists already (if you've used it before for some other chunk of text), you just click on the code and the highlighted chunk of text

Table 4.8 Example of Tagging and Value Coding

ID	Sex	Narratives	Diagnosis	Signs and Symptoms						Treatments				Duration
				Cough	Sore Throat	Vomiting	Fever	Chills	Fatigue	Home Remedy	OTC	Western Medical	CAM	
108	M	**Sinus/upper respiratory infection/asthma.** *Drainage into lungs, down back of throat, lower breathing capacity, used peak flow meter, shortness of breath, cough, fatigue, wanted to sleep more. Annually occurring. Wheezing, used inhaler three times a day, about every four hours.* Had symptoms for three days before going to health center. Coughing up phlegm, sinus headache, ears popped, runny nose. Amoxicillin for two weeks. *Dizzy, lightheaded.* Lungs felt tight, harder to breathe.	Sinus/ upper respiratory infection/ asthma	Y	N	N	N	N	Y	N	Y	Y	N	3 days or 14 days?
116	F	The last time I had a **cold** my throat was sore. It felt like I had needles in my tonsils. Every time I would swallow it felt like needles were digging in farther and farther. It also felt as though my throat was closing up making it hard to breathe. My nose was stuffed up but it was running like a faucet. There was a lot of pressure in my head like my head was in a vise. I had a horrible headache like someone was smashing my head with a hammer. Every muscle in my body ached. It felt like I couldn't move. I had a 102 degree fever. Sometimes I was so hot I felt like I was on fire. Then the next minute it was like I was in an ice-cube bath! I had difficulty breathing not only because my throat felt like it was closing but also because I felt like someone was sitting on my chest.	Cold	?	Y	N	Y	Y	N	N	N	N	N	?

92

ID	Sex	Narratives	Diagnosis	Signs and Symptoms						Treatments				Duration
				Cough	Sore Throat	Vomiting	Fever	Chills	Fatigue	Home Remedy	OTC	Western Medical	CAM	
118	F	The last time I had a **cold** was back in November, I think. I was tired, crabby, had a sore throat, runny nose, and a *bit of a cough*. I remember going to Wal Mart to look for the new Cold-Eeze throat lozenges that my mother swears by. They have zinc in them and are supposed to reduce the length of your cold. I couldn't find them at Wal Mart because they are a pretty hot item. So I think I just suffered this way throughout the cold with no medication because I'm not a big believer in their benefits (unless, of course, my mother swears by it). I did have some peppermint tea that the midwife at work gave me. (I work as an office assistant at a birth center.) I tried to get more sleep than usual, but I didn't take any time off of work or school. I remember trying not to kiss my boyfriend (that's pretty tough, you know!) so that he wouldn't get sick, too. My cold lasted probably five days. It was about the fourth time I had been sick that semester which is quite unusual for me. I usually only get sick only once or twice a year.	Cold	Y	Y	N	N	N	N	Y	N	N	N	5 days

Legend: Italics, signs and symptoms; underline, treatments and behavioral modifications; bold, diagnosis.

(or the point in the text) is then associated with that code. If you need a new code, you name it and add it to the codebook.

As you code, you think of things to say about the text—memos. Wherever you like, you indicate the presence of a memo. A window opens and you start typing your observations. Memos are hyperlinked to the text so that later, as you read through your marked-up text, you can click on any memo indicator (like the bolded word **memo** in Figure 4.1) and the memo will pop up in a window. You can add, delete, or edit memos as your analysis progresses. Memos are the essence of grounded theory, about which more in Chapter 12. (Further Reading: text analysis software.)

◆ MULTIPLE CODERS

Even on small projects, like those typically associated with MA and Ph.D. theses, you should try to have more than one coder. Constructs typically start out fuzzy

---

Box 4.2

Coding and Inference

Assigning values to a unit of text can be a high- or low-inference act. When someone says they "had a cough, runny nose and headache," it doesn't take much inference to code the variable *coughing* as Yes. But consider narrative 116. The respondent says: "Then the next minute it was like I was in an ice-cube bath!" Coding this as *having chills* requires more interpretation. If you think this is a high-inference problem, think of all the subtle and not so subtle ways in which people can report that they threw up.

And consider Narrative 108. Here, the respondent says that he waited 3 days before going to the health center, but then reports he took Amoxicillin for 2 weeks. So, how long did the episode last? It's common for people to take antibiotics for 2 weeks, but the signs and symptoms probably disappeared long before the pills were gone. If you don't ask "So, how long did that cold last?" you have to decide whether to assign a 5-7–day value to the episode (the time it takes for most colds to come and go) or a 2-week value (the time the informant was on those antibiotics).

Figure 4.1   Linkages Between Texts, Codes, and Memos

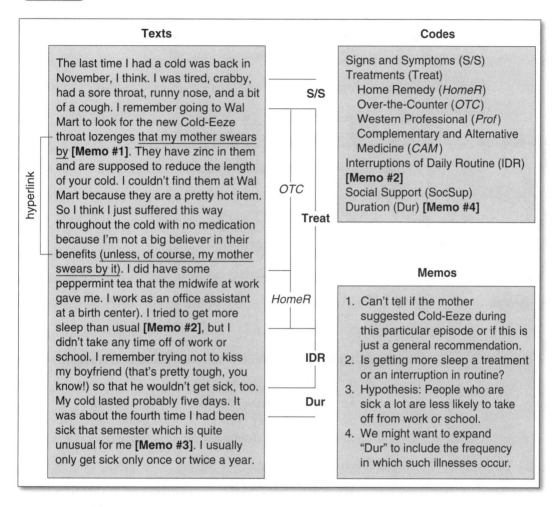

Texts
The last time I had a cold was back in November, I think. I was tired, crabby, had a sore throat, runny nose, and a bit of a cough. I remember going to Wal Mart to look for the new Cold-Eeze throat lozenges that my mother swears by **[Memo #1]**. They have zinc in them and are supposed to reduce the length of your cold. I couldn't find them at Wal Mart because they are a pretty hot item. So I think I just suffered this way throughout the cold with no medication because I'm not a big believer in their benefits (unless, of course, my mother swears by it). I did have some peppermint tea that the midwife at work gave me. I work as an office assistant at a birth center). I tried to get more sleep than usual **[Memo #2]**, but I didn't take any time off of work or school. I remember trying not to kiss my boyfriend (that's pretty tough, you know!) so that he wouldn't get sick, too. My cold lasted probably five days. It was about the fourth time I had been sick that semester which is quite unusual for me **[Memo #3]**. I usually only get sick only once or twice a year.

hyperlink

S/S   OTC   Treat   HomeR   IDR   Dur

Codes

Signs and Symptoms (S/S)
Treatments (Treat)
  Home Remedy (*HomeR*)
  Over-the-Counter (*OTC*)
  Western Professional (*Prof*)
  Complementary and Alternative
  Medicine (*CAM*)
Interruptions of Daily Routine (IDR)
[Memo #2]
Social Support (SocSup)
Duration (Dur) **[Memo #4]**

Memos

1. Can't tell if the mother suggested Cold-Eeze during this particular episode or if this is just a general recommendation.
2. Is getting more sleep a treatment or an interruption in routine?
3. Hypothesis: People who are sick a lot are less likely to take off from work or school.
4. We might want to expand "Dur" to include the frequency in which such illnesses occur.

and become concrete as you become more experienced with a set of texts. And even if you are working on your own, it pays to have at least one other person to talk to about the themes you see in your corpus of text. Also, with more than one coder, you can test for intercoder reliability—the probability that two or more coders see the same thing when they evaluate and code a text.

Intercoder reliability is vital if you're going to do statistical analysis on your data, but it's also important for retrieving examples of text that illustrate themes. If one coder marks themes, you have to rely on that coder—and usually, that means you—not to miss examples of themes. Having multiple coders increases the likelihood of finding all the examples in a text that pertain to a given theme. The best-known measure of interrater reliability is Cohen's kappa. More on kappa in Chapter 13, on content analysis.

Training Coders

We can't stress sufficiently the importance of training coders to recognize themes consistently. There are six principles for this.

1. Give all coders a written codebook to which they can refer during the actual marking of data.

2. After reviewing the codebook as a group, have coders independently code a set of real examples.

3. Review their responses and bring the group together to discuss and resolve discrepancies.

4. Update the codebook as coders come to agreements about the content of themes.

5. Once coders start coding the bulk of the data, do random spot checks to keep coders alert and to find out if they are running into situations that you had not anticipated in designing the codebook.

6. If there are continued problems, repeat steps 3 and 4 and, if you make any changes, go back over previously coded material to make sure it is all coded consistently. (**Further Reading:** training coders.)

How Many Coders Are Enough?

This is a perennial question in text analysis and the answer depends on four things:

1. The experience of coders (some coders are better than others).

2. The core/periphery dispersion of the theme. Themes that have a clear core are easy to pick out in text.

3. The level of inference required to see a theme. The more inference it takes, the harder it is for two or more coders to agree that they see it in a text.

4. The number of times that any given theme appears in the text. The rarer a theme's occurrence and the more important it is to find all occurrences, the more coders you want to look for it.

In large projects, having multiple coders can run into real money. A single 90-minute interview can easily generate 30 to 50 pages of transcribed text. With 150 interviews, that's at least 4,500 pages—about 12 to 16 average size books. Coding all that text, at five pages per hour and $20 per hour, would cost $18,000, not counting the time to get a coder up to speed on recognizing the themes in the text.

Trimming Codes and Coders

We can reduce the workload and the cost by lowering the number of codes, by reducing the amount of text to be coded, and by using fewer coders. Most codebooks are hierarchical, with a small set of superordinate categories and a larger set of subordinate categories. The maximum number of themes that can be dealt with in a journal article is closer to a dozen than it is to a hundred. For some projects, focusing on the major categories is appropriate.

We nearly always wind up with more data than are required in a particular project. We design interviews to capture the broadest range of data and when we build codebooks we tack on every theme that seems useful at the time. As analysis gets underway, however, some of the themes that we thought were so important earlier may not continue to be important. This is a common experience among analysts of text. The three coders on Miles's project to evaluate six public schools developed 202 codes and wound up with just 26 big themes by the time they had done all the trimming (Miles 1979:593ff).

If your analysis interest narrows, focus on the portions of text that are most likely to contain the themes you're really interested in. This is easy to do when you have semistructured interviews because you know where in each text you're likely to find information on each major theme.

For themes that are found throughout a set of texts, it is sometimes enough to analyze a sample of texts, rather than the whole set. Even a smaller sample of texts can be reduced by rapidly scanning for particular themes. Once coders are really familiar with the constructs being studied in a project, they can read very quickly through the material and—especially if they are free to use loose definitions of constructs—identify paragraphs that contain the constructs. More about sampling in Chapter 17.

Whenever a theme of interest is found, the paragraph is cut from the corpus and stored in a separate document of theme hits. To ensure against bias, a second coder should scan the text and look for theme occurrences that the first scanner might have missed. These paragraphs are also pulled and stored in the document of hits.

Finally, the higher the consensus you get among coders, the fewer coders you need for any particular project (Romney et al. 1986:325–327). We can reduce the number of coders by training them very well, though this creates the possibility of another kind of bias—finding themes that we want to find and not others. Giving coders free rein to find lots of new codes or having them look only for codes that we've already determined are of interest in a particular project is a choice. And every choice in research comes with its own problems.

◆ THE CONTENT OF CODEBOOKS

In a good codebook, each theme needs to be described in sufficient detail so that coders can identify and mark the theme when they see it in the data. Table 4.9 shows part of the codebook from Ryan's (1995) study of illness narratives in Cameroon.

Start by giving each theme a mnemonic. Then, as MacQueen et al. (1998) recommend, provide a short description, a detailed description, a list of inclusion and exclusion criteria for each theme, and some typical and atypical examples from the text as well as examples that seem close to but do not represent the theme. This aids in consistency of coding.

Mnemonics

Table 4.9 details three themes: signs and symptoms, over-the-counter drugs, and home remedies. Ryan used S/S, OTC, and HomeR as mnemonics for these themes (see Box 4.3).

No matter how obvious some codes are (like DIV for divorce), you'll never remember the full set of codes for any project a year after you've completed it, so be sure to write up a detailed codebook in case you forget what NAITRAV (has the informant ever traveled to Nairobi?) or whatever-abbreviations-you-dreamed-up-at-the-time-you-did-the-coding mean.

You can use numbers or words as theme codes (whatever you're most comfortable with), but make sure that your codebook is explicit and in plain English (or plain Spanish, or French, or Russian . . .).

Table 4.9   Example of Code Descriptions for Study of Illness Narratives

Mnemonic	S/S
Short Description	Signs and Symptoms
Detailed Description	Signs refer to the observable features that indicate illness such as fainting, sweating, diarrhea, rash, swelling. Symptoms refer to nonobservable features of illness or discomfort such as pain, malaise, and depression.
Inclusion Criteria	Must be felt (either physically or emotionally) by target individual.
Exclusion Criteria	Changes in behaviors.
Typical Exemplars	Pain, fever, vomiting, stomach ache, fatigued, depression.
Atypical Exemplars	For children, changes in behavior (quiet, plays less, crying) count as signs of illness to mother.
Close but no	Dreams, sleeping late, not feeling like going out, bored.
Mnemonic	**OTC**
Short Description	Over-the-Counter Drugs
Detailed Description	The use of pharmaceutical products purchased over-the-counter without a prescription with the expressed intent of alleviating signs or symptoms.
Inclusion Criteria	Nonprescription medications purchased over-the-counter for a current illness.
Exclusion Criteria	Medicines that have been recommended by a doctor or other professional for the current illness episode. Medications purchased for preventive purposes.
Typical Exemplars	Aspirin, decongestants, laxatives, cough medicine.
Atypical Exemplars	Prescription medication that was left over from a previous illness episode.
Close but no	Vitamins
Mnemonic	**HomeR**
Short Description	Home Remedies
Detailed Description	Remedies made at home to alleviate signs and symptoms.
Inclusion Criteria	Remedy must be administered internally or applied externally.
Exclusion Criteria	Products sold in pharmacies for specific purpose of stopping illnesses. Behavioral modifications such as going to bed early, avoiding cold water. Preventive treatments such as regular vitamin intake.
Typical Exemplars	Hot teas, chicken soup, compresses, massages, rice water.
Atypical Exemplars	Large doses of vitamins.
Close but no	Behavioral modifications such as bed rest, not going to school, going to sleep early.

SOURCE: Ryan (1995).

> **Box 4.3**
>
> **Emic and Etic Themes**
>
> Physicians trained in Western medicine distinguish between the signs of illness—the features that they recognize as indicators of an illness—and symptoms—what patients feel and report about an illness. Like most people in the world—and certainly like his informants—Ryan lumps signs and symptoms of illness under one category, labeled S/S.
>
> This means making a decision on whether to search for, and tag, examples of an emic theme (signs and symptoms lumped together) or an etic one (distinguishing signs and symptoms, as physicians do). There is no right or wrong decision here but, as always, each decision in research comes at a price.

Short Descriptions and Detailed Descriptions

Brief descriptions should be a single word or short phrase that communicates the general idea of the theme to co-investigators and readers. These short descriptions can be based on theory or can come directly from the words and phrases of your informants but should be accompanied by a more detailed explanation as well. Start with the most common features of a theme, but don't forget to mention some of the less typical features, too.

List of Inclusion and Exclusion Criteria

This takes the guesswork out of applying the codes to texts. Start by listing the features that must be present for a text segment to be considered a member of the category. Then list any features that would automatically exclude a segment from being considered a member of the category.

For example, in Table 4.8, pharmaceuticals are included as OTC drugs if they are nonprescription medications purchased OTC for a current illness. These medications would not be included, however, if they had been recommended by a doctor or other professional, or if they had been purchased for preventive rather than curative or palliative purposes, even though they could be purchased over the counter.

Typical and Atypical Exemplars

Like MacQueen et al. (1998), we recommend listing typical and atypical examples for every theme. Typical examples are the ones that come easily to mind. Atypical examples are not common, but still count. In Table 4.8, Ryan decided to include the use of prescription drugs that were left over from a previous illness in the OTC theme. In some studies, vitamins might be a fringe member of the OTC drug category, but Ryan decided that for his study, vitamins weren't.

Examples, both typical and atypical, can be whole sentences or even paragraphs, or they can be simply words from the text. These chunks, whatever their size, will help you and other coders develop a sense of the content of the theme—to recognize what you're supposed to be looking for. And they will help you explain the theme to others when you write up your research.

DESCRIBING THEMES: BLOOM'S STUDY OF AIDS ♦

Frederick Bloom (2001) did a series of in-depth interviews with 25 HIV-positive gay men. Bloom wanted to understand how these men, who were living with the knowledge that they were HIV-positive, evaluated their lives and how they worked to preserve or improve their lives.

On average, the men had known their HIV status for 5.8 years and there was great variation in morbidity—some of the men were asymptomatic; others were living with full-blown AIDS. Nine of the men had experienced at least some AIDS-defining illnesses. Each man participated in five to seven interviews over 6 months. A year or two after these interviews, Bloom collected life histories from 13 of the 15 surviving participants.

Bloom identified many themes in the life stories. Some were specific to one or two people in the sample; others appeared in all the informants' narratives. Bloom describes four of the most common themes. They include: (1) SURVIVING (overcoming obstacles and enduring hardships); (2) RECIPROCITY (helping and caring for others in need); (3) APPRECIATION (of one's daily life); and (4) what Bloom calls AVERAGE LIFE (leading an uneventful, simple, or "boring" everyday life.

Figure 4.2 shows Bloom's detailed description of the first theme, SURVIVAL. Like any good codebook (whether for qualitative or quantitative data), Bloom's initial description provides an overview of the theme and its core components. He notes that the theme is quite prevalent (it shows up in 15 of 20 narratives) and distributed across men who were at all stages of the illness.

After the overview, Bloom presents Jerry as a typical example of the theme. In his own words, we hear from Jerry about what it means to survive, to live with HIV, day to day. The description ends with Bloom's own interpretation of the example, tying it back to the theme.

◆ FINDING TYPICAL SEGMENTS OF TEXT

How can you tell what's typical of a theme? One way is to use multiple coders and see which themes all of them, or most of them, agree on (see Ryan [1999], for example). But what do you do when you only have one coder—you—to identify typical chunks of text? The answer is: Use the pile sort method.

Begin by retrieving all instances of a theme from the original text, cutting out the quotes, and writing some identifier on the back (e.g., Interview #22, Female). Then sort them. The six steps for this procedure are laid out in Figure 4.3.

1. First, spread out the quotes on a large table. Make sure you mix up the quotes so that quotes from the same source aren't all together.

2. Next, examine the quotes and identify those that seem to represent the core aspects of the theme. Trust your instincts here. If a quote "feels" like it is a core example of the theme, then move it toward the middle of the table. By the time you are done, the core quotes should be in the center; quotes that are more and more peripheral will be closer and closer to the edge.

3. Refine the core-periphery structure. Start with core quotes and sort them into two groups: those that are most representative of the theme and those that are less so. Call these strong and weak core quotes. Then, try to express in words the characteristics that distinguish between quotes in the strong core and quotes in the weak core. This helps identify primary and secondary components of a theme.

4. Sort the periphery quotes into groups based on their similarity. Make as many groups as you think are necessary. Step 4 in Figure 4.3 identifies three periphery subgroups. These subgroups tell us about the range of features in a theme.

5. Next, select the typical quotes or exemplars that you might want to use in your write-up. Begin by reading over all the quotes in a group. Select a couple that seem (in your intuition) to best represent the group. Typical quotes can be short, direct, and just plain pithy, and they can be detailed, elaborate, and encompassing. Pithy quotes are perfect for hammering a point home as you write. Elaborate quotes are better when you need to provide readers with important details and nuances. If you are doing this alone, you have only your own judgment to trust, but if you can have at least one other person select typical quotes independently, you'll be on much firmer ground.

Figure 4.2   Describing the Theme of Survival

The most common theme is the survival theme, that of overcoming obstacles and enduring hardships. The stylistic orientation associated with this theme is a presentation of the self as a survivor. Stories imbued with this theme focus on past events, difficult situations experienced, and the ability of the narrator to endure or overcome a particular struggle or hardship. These narratives are always instrumental, associating past experiences of survival to present difficulties. Fifteen of the 20 men making up the sample offered at least one narrative expressing this combination of psychocultural theme and stylistic orientation to living with HIV. Survival narratives were presented by men who were quite ill, men who were asymptomatic, and men at various stages of illness in between.

One of the men, Jerry, gives an eloquent example of this theme, style, and narrative-type cluster. He talks about his success in keeping his business going despite numerous difficulties:

> Successes in my life? Surviving as long as I have. I only came back here for a year. It was fun, I guess, to make the business run. Certainly, the odds were against me. I hated coming back to straight, white America, but it was kind of fun for a couple years; making it work, whatever it took. I guess beating the odds on that was good, and when it worked real well it was real good.

Jerry was 37 years old at the time data were collected. He presented himself as having had a difficult life. He related stories of experiencing physical and verbal abuse as a teenager, survival by prostitution while homeless, and intravenous drug use. He learned he was HIV-positive 11 years prior to our meeting. At the time of the study, he still struggled financially, living in a run-down home, surviving only through the generosity of friends.

He had remained relatively healthy until about a year prior to the start of this project. At that time, he developed joint pain, which was particularly severe in his legs, and a decline in his energy level and stamina. During the course of the interviews, Jerry was forced to quit his job because of pain and fatigue.

Though he stated that most of his oldest friends had died from AIDS-related illnesses, he maintained several close long-term friendships. He stated that he had had an ongoing relationship with his lover over the past eight years, though their relationship was characterized by frequent arguments and separations. Jerry also mentioned several friends who stayed with him for months at a time. He talked about his long-term survival with HIV infection:

> I'm a survivor, no matter what, y'know? I can make ends meet. I can get through anything. I guess maybe I get that from the streets, y'know? No matter what happens, you gotta keep going. I can get through anything. I can handle anything. I could live like I feel now and keep going, but certainly not all of the enjoyment in life. There are a lot of people that feel lousy every day for other reasons and you get used to it. You really do get used to it.

Implicit in these statements was Jerry's ability to endure the suffering associated with his illness. The theme was that of overcoming obstacles and enduring suffering. His stylistic orientation placed him clearly as a survivor. However, it is the instrumental nature of his narratives that reveals their meaning. Jerry related that he survived, endured, and overcame obstacles in the past and gave this as reason to expect he would do the same in the future, that he could "handle anything."

SOURCE: Bloom (2001). Reproduced by permission of the American Anthropological Association from *Medical Anthropology* Volume 15(1), 2001: 38-57. doi:10.1525/maq.2001.15.1.38. Not for sale or further reproduction.

Figure 4.3 Finding Typical Quotes Using Pile Sorts

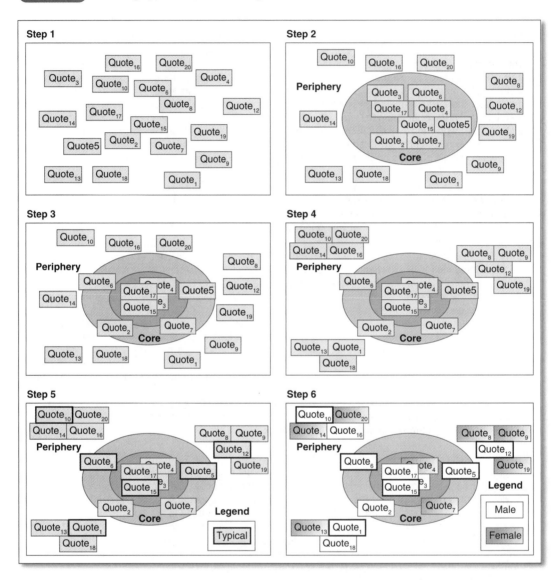

6. With the quotes on the table sorted into core and periphery groups, turn each one over and examine who said it. This serves two purposes. First, it keeps you from using just one or two informants as the sources of quotes. Second, if there is a pattern in the distribution of quotes, you're likely to see it. In step 6 of Figure 4.3, for example, one pattern seems clear: Only two out of eight quotes in the core of the theme are by women ($Quote_4$ and $Quote_7$). The

quotes on the periphery, however, are more or less equally likely to come from men or women.

If we saw this in our own data, we'd want to check the original data to see if the core feature of the theme is one associated mostly with men. The mechanics are easy. Using the Boolean search available in text management programs like NVivo, Atlas/ti, MaxQDA, and many other packages, we'd find all the places where a particular theme appeared AND the speaker was a woman. Then we'd compare these instances with those found from men.

Whatever technique you use to describe themes, the result will be an increasingly detailed codebook, with short descriptions, inclusion criteria, and exemplars that represent the core features of each theme. By the time you're done building the codebook, you've got the basis for your descriptive writing.

Further Reading

♦ Examples of published codes include: B. W. Whiting and J. W. M. Whiting (1975), for observing children in the field; Horizon Research Inc. (2001) for observing classrooms; Miles and Huberman (1994:59–60, 64) for studying school improvement; Patton (2002:516–517) for evaluation research; and Nyamongo (2002) for studying illness reports.

♦ For more on developing codebooks, see Dey (1993:95–151), Miles and Huberman (1994:55–72), and Weston et al. (2001).

♦ For information on text analysis software, see http://caqdas.soc.surrey.ac.uk/ and especially Lewins and Silver (2007), on "Choosing a CAQDAS Package." CAQDAS (pronounced "cactus") stands for computer-assisted qualitative data analysis. Hahn (2008) provides an alternative to using special-purpose, text analysis software and shows instead how to use ordinary database and spreadsheet software for coding text. See Appendix for pointers to text analysis software.

♦ For more on training coders see Hak and Bernts (1996).

CHAPTER 5

INTRODUCTION TO DATA ANALYSIS

INTRODUCTION

Analysis starts even before we begin a research project. No matter how hard we try, there are no purely inductive studies. We choose topics to study because of some prior interest, and we always have ideas about what we'll find and about what's important and unimportant. Systematic analysis, though, is different. That's where we apply methods for finding and laying out patterns in data. This can't begin, however, until we actually have a corpus of data to study.

For practical purposes, this means getting narratives and other forms of qualitative data digitized and into a computer or organized and tagged so that we can apply methods of database management.

◆ DATABASE MANAGEMENT

Qualitative research produces a lot of data. If you do 30 open-ended interviews that average an hour and a half each, you could easily wind up with a thousand double-spaced pages of text to deal with. Long before you try to analyze the data, and long before you try to find patterns in your data, you absolutely must have it packed away in some convenient form. Shoe boxes full of transcripts just won't cut it. That's where database management comes in.

Database management is founded on two basic concepts: records and fields. A record is the unit whose characteristics you want to retrieve. The fields are the characteristics.

If you've got a thousand tunes on your MP3 player and you want to organize them into play lists, then each tune is a record in a database and the fields are things like artist, title, publisher, date of release, and genre. If you have a thousand photographs from a research project, then each one is a record in a database. You can ask the database "Which photos are about children?" or "Which photos are about old men?" or "Which are about children AND about eating?" If you've coded each photo for those themes (children, old men, eating), then the software shows you which records satisfy your query.

If your photos are all on paper, you can number them on the back from 1 to n and use the numbers as the record names in a database. And if your photos are digital (or scanned in from paper or slides), you can code them directly with a database management program. (Microsoft Excel is advertised as a spreadsheet, but you can use it to manage qualitative data.)

When you use your library's online catalogs to find books and articles, you're using database management systems. To find an article on bilingual education and achievement, you would use the Boolean expression "bilingual education AND achiev*." The * is a commonly used "wildcard." In this case, it would mean "find me all the books that are about bilingual education and about anything that starts with achiev, like achieve, achieving, achiever, or achievement."

Text analysis programs are special-purpose database management systems with add-ons. For example, some programs have a tool that lets you map the relation among a set of themes and build a network.

USING A TEXT ANALYSIS PROGRAM ♦

The first thing to say about text analysis programs—like Atlas/ti®, NVivo®, HyperResearch®, Qualrus®, and MaxQDA®—is that they don't do any analysis. They are special purpose database management programs with tools for handling and asking questions of text. The programs do the data management; you do the analysis.

Suppose you have hundreds or thousands of pages of interviews and you ask: "Which pieces of these texts are about migration and about women who are under 30 years of age?" A good text analysis program will: (1) find the segments of text that you've coded for the theme of migration; (2) produce a provisional list of those segments; (3) examine each segment in the provisional list and find the respondent's name or ID code; and (4) look up the respondent in the respondent information file.

If the respondent is a man or is a woman over 30, the program drops the segment of text from the provisional list. Finally, the program reports which, if any, segments of text conform to all the criteria you listed in your question. With the right software, asking questions like this takes a couple of seconds, even with 10,000 pages of text. But deciding which questions to ask—which is analysis, after all—is your job, not the program's.

Many text analysis programs also let you build networks of codes and produce reports and diagrams of how codes are related to one another in a set of texts. (**Further Reading**: text analysis software.)

WHAT IS ANALYSIS? ♦

Analysis is the search for patterns in data and for ideas that help explain why those patterns are there in the first place. Analysis starts before you collect data—you have to have some ideas about what you're going to study—and it continues throughout the research effort. As you develop ideas, you test them against your observations; your observations may then modify your ideas, which then need to be tested again, and so on.

As we pointed out on the first page of this book, analysis is the essential qualitative act. Many methods for quantitative analysis—things like regression analysis, cluster analysis, factor analysis, and so on—are really methods for data processing. They are tools for finding patterns in data. Interpreting those patterns—deciding what they mean and linking your findings to those of other research—that's real analysis.

Where do we get ideas from about patterns? Human beings are really good at this. In fact, they make patterns up all the time. Children look at clouds and make up stories about the shapes. For eons, people have labeled sets of stars and made up stories about them. Psychologists ask people to make up a story about ink blots. Once you have data in your hands, you won't have any trouble seeing patterns. In fact, you'll have to take real care not to read patterns into data. If you work on it, your natural penchant to see patterns everywhere will diminish as you do more and more research, but it's always a struggle. And the problem can get worse if you accept uncritically the folk analyses of articulate or prestigious people.

From a humanistic standpoint, it's important to seek the emic—that is, insider—perspective and to document folk analyses (Lofland et al. 2006). Those analyses may even be correct sometimes. But it is equally important to remain skeptical, to retain an etic—that is, outsider—perspective, and not to "go native" (Miles and Huberman 1994:216).

The Constant Validity Check

As research progresses—as your interviews pile up—work on switching back and forth between the emic and the etic perspectives. Ask yourself whether you are buying into local folk explanations or perhaps rejecting them out of hand without considering their possible validity. It isn't hard to check yourself once in a while during research, but it's very hard to do it systematically.

Here are five guidelines.

1. Watch for disagreements among knowledgeable informants. When knowledgeable informants disagree about anything, find out why.

2. Check informant accuracy whenever possible. For example, check people's reports of behavior or of environmental conditions against more objective evidence. If you were a journalist and submitted a story based on informants' reports without checking the facts, you'd never get it past your editor's desk. We see no reason not to hold social scientists to the standard that good journalists face every day.

3. Welcome negative evidence. If a case turns up that doesn't fit with what you know—a middle-class suburban teenager who doesn't like hanging out at malls, for example—ask yourself if it's the result of: (a) normal intracultural variation; (b) your lack of knowledge about the range of appropriate behavior; or (c) a genuinely unusual case.

4. Continue to look for alternative explanations for phenomena, even as your understanding deepens. American folk culture holds that women left the home for the workforce because of something called women's liberation. An alternative explanation is that the oil shock of the 1970s produced double-digit inflation, cut the purchasing power of men's incomes, and drove women into a workforce where they faced discrimination and unequal pay—and were radicalized (Margolis 1984). Both explanations, one emic and one etic, are interesting for different reasons.

5. Try to fit negative cases into your theory. When you run into a case that doesn't fit your theory, then examine your theory. It's easier to ignore inconvenient data than to reexamine your pet ideas, but the easy way is hardly ever the right way in research.

DATA MATRICES ♦

One of the most important concepts in all data analysis—whether we're working with quantitative or qualitative data—is the data matrix. There are two kinds of data matrices: profile matrices and proximity matrices. Profile matrices are also simply called data matrices. These are the familiar case-by-attribute matrices that are used across the sciences to record data. If you've ever entered data into a spreadsheet, like Excel, you've had experience with profile matrices.

Proximity matrices are a different species altogether. They contain data about how similar or dissimilar a set of things are. Those mileage charts that you see on road maps are proximity matrices. They tell you, for every pair of cities on a map, how far apart they are. We'll have more to say about proximity matrices later. First, profile matrices. . . .

PROFILE MATRICES ♦

The vast majority of analysis in the social sciences, whether it's qualitative or quantitative, is about how properties of things are related to one another. We ask, for example, "Does how much money a family has affect the SAT scores of its children?" "Does having been abused as a child influence whether a woman will remain in a physically abusive marriage?" "Is the per capita gross national product of a nation associated with the average level of education?" "Are remittances from labor migrants related to the achievement in school of children left behind?"

This kind of analysis is done on a profile matrix. You start with a series of things—units of analysis—and you measure a series of variables for each of those things. Each unit of analysis is *profiled* by a particular set of measurements on some variables. Table 5.1 is an example of a typical profile matrix.

In this table, an interviewer has stopped a hundred people who were coming out of a supermarket and recorded seven pieces of information: how much the person spent; the person's gender, age, and education (in years); whether the person lived in a house or an apartment and whether they owned or rented; and how many people lived with them.

These data produce a 100 × 7 (read this as: "100-by-7") profile matrix. Two profiles—two data cases—are shown in Table 5.1.

Person #1 reported spending $67.00, is male, is 34 years old, graduated from high school, and lives in a house, which he rents, with four other people. Person #2 reported spending $19.00, is female, is 60 years old, completed college, and lives in a house, which she owns, by herself.

Profile Matrices With Qualitative Data I—Van Maanen's Study

The profile matrix shown in Table 5.1 was constructed from survey data (asking people the same questions about their grocery shopping experience), but the form of a profile matrix is the same, whether the data are quantitative or qualitative. Van Maanen et al. (1982) compared a traditional commercial fishing operation in Gloucester, Massachusetts, with a modern operation in Bristol Bay, Alaska. Table 5.2 shows what they found in the analysis of their field notes. Simple inspection of Table 5.2 gives you an immediate feel for the results of Van Maanen et al.'s descriptive analysis.

There are two units of analysis in Table 5.2: the two communities where Van Maanen et al. did their ethnographic fieldwork. One community, Gloucester, Massachusetts, represented the traditional American fishing occupation; the other, Bristol Bay, Alaska, represented a more factory-like fishing operation.

Table 5.1   Profile Matrix of Two Cases by Seven Variables

Case	Spent ($)	Gender	Age	Education	Home or Apartment	Own (Y/N)	Number in House
1	67	M	34	12	H	N	5
2	19	F	60	16	H	Y	1

Table 5.2 Van Maanen et al.'s Findings About Kinds of Commercial Fishing

	Traditional fishing (e.g., Gloucester, MA)	Modern fishing (e.g., Bristol Bay, AK)
Social organization		
Backgrounds of fishermen	Homogeneous	Heterogeneous
Ties among fishermen	Multiple	Single
Boundaries to entry	Social	Economic
Number of participants	Stable	Variable
Social uncertainty	Low	High
Relations with competitors	Collegial and individualistic	Antagonistic and categorical
Relations with port	Permanent, with ties to community	Temporary, with no local ties
Mobility	Low	High
Relations to fishing	Expressive (fishing as lifestyle)	Instrumental (fishing as job)
Orientation to work	Long-term, optimizing (survival)	Short-term, maximizing (seasonal)
Tolerance for diversity	Low	High
Nature of disputes	Intra-occupational	Trans-occupational
Economic organization		
Relations of boats to buyers	Personalized (long-term, informal)	Contractual (short-term, formal)
Information exchange	Restrictive and private	Open and public
Economic uncertainty	Low (long-term)	High (long-term)
Capital investment range	Small	Large
Profit margins	Low	High
Rate of innovation	Low	High
Specialization	Low	High
Regulatory mechanisms	Informal and few	Formal and many
Stance toward authority	Combative	Compliant

SOURCE: Van Maanen, J., Miller, M., and Johnson, J. C. (1982). An occupation in transition: Traditional and modern forms of commercial fishing. *Work and Occupations, 9,* 193–216. Copyright ©1982 Sage Publications.

Notice that in Table 5.2, the two units of analysis—the cases—are in the columns and the attributes of the cases are in the rows. This is the opposite of how the data were set up in Table 5.1. It is common in quantitative research to have many units of analysis (like respondents to a questionnaire) and relatively few variables. By contrast, in qualitative research it is common to have a few units of analysis (like informants who provide narratives) and a great many variables (like themes).

Another way of saying this is that in quantitative studies, we typically know a little about many things, and in qualitative studies we typically know a lot about a few things. With just a few units of analysis, it is easier to look for patterns when we have the cases in the columns and the attributes of the cases in the rows.

Table 5.2 tells us that the social organization of the traditional fishing operation in Gloucester is more homogeneous, more expressive, and more collegial than that of the modern operation, but profits are lower. Based on the qualitative analysis, Van Maanen et al. were able to state some general, theoretical hypotheses regarding the weakening of personal relations in technology-based fishing operations. This is the kind of general proposition that can be tested by using fishing operations as units of analysis and their technologies as the explanatory variable.

Profile Matrices With Qualitative Data II—Fjellman and Gladwin's Study

Fjellman and H. Gladwin (1985) studied the family histories of Haitian migrants to the United States. Table 5.3 shows a matrix of information about one family. Table 5.3 is a profile matrix with the cases (the people) in the columns and the variables (the years in which people joined or left the family) in the rows.

The family began in 1968 when Jeanne's father sent her to Brooklyn, New York, to go to high school. The single plus sign for 1968 shows the founding of the family by Jeanne. Jeanne's father died in 1971, and her mother (Anna), sister (Lucie), and brother (Charles) joined her in New York. Thus, there are four plus signs for 1971. Jeanne adopted Marc in 1975. She moved to Miami in 1976, with her mother and Marc, and Lucie and Charles stayed on in New York. The two minus signs in the row for 1976 indicate that Jeanne's sister and brother were no longer part of the household founded by Jeanne.

Lucie married in 1978 (husband not shown), and Charles went to Miami to join Jeanne's household. That same year, Jeanne began applying for visas to bring her cousins Hughes and Valerie to Miami. The asterisks show that these two people were in the process of joining the household in 1982 when the family history data were collected. Aunt Helen (Anna's sister) joined the

Table 5.3 Fjellman and Gladwin's Table for One Haitian Family in the United States

Year	Jeanne	Anna (mother)	Lucie (sister)	Charles (brother)	Marc (adopted son)	Helen (aunt)	Hughes and Valerie (cousins)	Number in Household
1968	+							1
1971	+	+	+	+				4
1975	+	+	+	+	+			5
1976	+	+	−	−	+			3
1978	+	+	−	+	+		*	4
1979	+	+	−	+	+	+	*	5
1982	+	+	−	−	+	+	*	4

SOURCE: S. M. Fjellman and H. Gladwin, Haitian family patterns of migration to South Florida, *Human Organization* 44:307. Copyright © 1985, Society for Applied Anthropology. Reprinted with permission.

family in 1979. Finally, Charles returned to New York in 1982 to live again with his sister, Lucie.

Fjellman and Gladwin present seven of these family history charts in their article, and they provide the historical detail—like why Jeanne went to the United States in the first place and why Charles left Jeanne's household in 1976—in vignettes below each chart. We need the historical detail to understand how the family developed over the years, but reducing everything to a matrix of pluses and minuses lets us see the patterns of family growth, development, and decay. (**Further Reading:** matrices of qualitative data.)

PROXIMITY MATRICES ◆

If profile analysis is about how properties of things are related to one another, then proximity analysis is about how things (not their properties) are related to one another. Profile matrices contain measurements of variables for a set of items. Proximity matrices contain measurements of relations, or proximities, between items.

There are two types of proximity matrices: similarity matrices and dissimilarity matrices. Table 5.4 is a dissimilarity matrix. It shows the

Table 5.4 A Dissimilarity Matrix for Distances Among Nine U.S. Cities

City	Boston	New York	District of Columbia	Miami	Chicago	Seattle	San Francisco	Los Angeles	Denver
Boston	0	206	429	1504	963	2976	3095	2979	1949
New York	206	0	233	1308	802	2815	2934	2786	1771
District of Columbia	429	233	0	1075	671	2684	2799	2631	1616
Miami	1504	1308	1075	0	1329	3273	3053	2687	2037
Chicago	963	802	671	1329	0	2013	2142	2054	996
Seattle	2976	2815	2684	3273	2013	0	808	1131	1307
San Francisco	3095	2934	2799	3053	2142	808	0	379	1235
Los Angeles	2979	2786	2631	2687	2054	1131	379	0	1059
Denver	1949	1771	1616	2037	996	1307	1235	1059	0

SOURCE: Borgatti (1996:28). Reprinted with permission of the author.

driving distances between all pairs of nine cities in the United States. The bigger the number in the cells, the more "dissimilar" two cities are. In other words, the larger the number in any cell, the further apart two cities are on the map.

Seeing Patterns in Proximity Matrices—Visualization Methods

It's much easier to see patterns in graphs of relations than in matrices of them, like Table 5.4. In fact, you could stare at the 9×9 (read: nine-by-nine) matrix of relations in Table 5.4 all day and never see the big picture. Figure 5.1 is a multidimensional scaling (MDS) map of the data in Table 5.4 and it shows the big picture.

MDS is one part of a family of data visualization methods—a way to see all the relations in a matrix of relations. So, in Figure 5.1, we expect New York to be about equally close to Washington, DC, and to Boston. We expect San Francisco to lie between Los Angeles and Seattle and for all three of those

Figure 5.1   Multidimensional Scaling of Distances Among Nine Cities

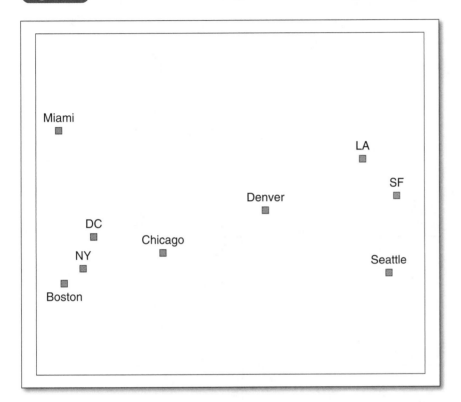

cities to be far from Boston, New York, and DC. And so on. Sure enough, the relations in Figure 5.1 conform to all our expectations.

Well, most of them. Because of our early training in school, we expect Miami to be in the lower right of the map and for Seattle to be in the upper left. The MDS program doesn't care about our culturally derived expectations. It just graphs all the numerical relations in a matrix and all of those relations are, in fact perfectly represented in Figure 5.1. More about MDS in Chapter 8.

If you've had a course in statistics and seen a correlation matrix, then you've had experience with a similarity matrix. The bigger the number in each cell—the higher the correlation—the more alike two things are. Table 5.5 is a similarity matrix of 15 emotions. This matrix comes from a qualitative data collection exercise called a triad test.

In this case, 40 people looked at 70 triads of emotions—Anger/Love/Fear, Sad/Bored/Hate, Anger/Bored/Love, and so on—and told us which emotion was least like the other two. The similarity measurements in Table 5.5 are percentages. Looking across the first row of Table 5.5, we see that love and

Table 5.5 A Similarity Matrix for 15 Emotions

		1	2	3	4	5	6	7	8	9	10	11	12	13	14	15
		LOVE	ANGE	DISG	SHAM	FEAR	ANGU	ENVY	ANXI	TIRE	HAPP	SAD	LONE	BORE	HATE	EXCI
1	LOVE	0.00	0.09	0.08	0.21	0.10	0.08	0.35	0.16	0.10	0.82	0.20	0.14	0.08	0.41	0.74
2	ANGER	0.09	0.00	0.85	0.19	0.59	0.64	0.46	0.32	0.00	0.17	0.40	0.09	0.04	0.95	0.11
3	DISGUST	0.08	0.85	0.00	0.76	0.76	0.66	0.55	0.63	0.08	0.08	0.38	0.08	0.14	0.70	0.13
4	SHAME	0.21	0.19	0.76	0.00	0.22	0.75	0.51	0.38	0.57	0.10	0.57	0.39	0.09	0.47	0.06
5	FEAR	0.10	0.59	0.76	0.22	0.00	0.57	0.40	0.71	0.05	0.11	0.55	0.59	0.08	0.86	0.21
6	ANGUISH	0.08	0.64	0.66	0.75	0.57	0.00	0.85	0.47	0.20	0.10	0.70	0.31	0.08	0.69	0.09
7	ENVY	0.35	0.46	0.55	0.51	0.40	0.85	0.00	0.44	0.06	0.08	0.08	0.30	0.28	0.47	0.11
8	ANXIOUS	0.16	0.32	0.63	0.38	0.71	0.47	0.44	0.00	0.16	0.29	0.30	0.17	0.20	0.39	0.40
9	TIRED	0.10	0.00	0.08	0.57	0.05	0.20	0.06	0.16	0.00	0.14	0.63	0.44	0.73	0.04	0.13
10	HAPPY	0.82	0.17	0.08	0.10	0.11	0.10	0.08	0.29	0.14	0.00	0.34	0.09	0.04	0.08	0.85
11	SAD	0.20	0.40	0.38	0.57	0.55	0.70	0.08	0.30	0.63	0.34	0.00	0.71	0.31	0.24	0.19
12	LONELY	0.14	0.09	0.08	0.39	0.59	0.31	0.30	0.17	0.44	0.09	0.71	0.00	0.59	0.06	0.06
13	BORED	0.08	0.04	0.14	0.09	0.08	0.08	0.28	0.20	0.73	0.04	0.31	0.59	0.00	0.14	0.19
14	HATE	0.41	0.95	0.70	0.47	0.86	0.69	0.47	0.39	0.04	0.08	0.24	0.06	0.14	0.00	0.28
15	EXCITEMENT	0.74	0.11	0.13	0.06	0.21	0.09	0.11	0.40	0.13	0.85	0.19	0.06	0.19	0.28	0.00

Figure 5.2   Multidimensional Scaling of Similarities Among 15 Emotions

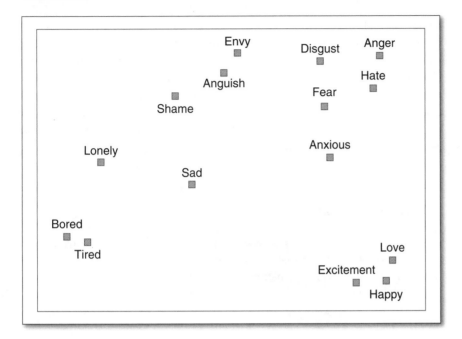

anger are .09 alike, which means that 9% of the time our informants said that love and anger were similar. By contrast, 82% of the time our informants said that love and happy were similar.

If the 9 × 9 matrix of intercity distances in Table 5.4 looked complicated, the 15 × 15 matrix in Table 5.5 is hopeless—far too complex to analyze with the naked eye. Figure 5.2 shows the MDS plot for these data. It's a two-dimensional plot, and it looks like the two dimensions are nice versus not-so-nice emotions (with nice emotions on the bottom of the picture and not-so-nice emotions on the top) and active versus passive emotions (with the most active emotions on the right and the more passive emotions over on the left).

And how is all this qualitative? Well, the triad tests are all qualitative: The informant sees sets of names and chooses one. The data (people's choices) are converted into numbers (Table 5.5), but the numbers are just a way to record the choices that people made in doing the triad task. And the words become numbers only long enough to process them and turn them into a picture—more qualitative data—that we can interpret.

♦ PRESENTING RESULTS AS ANALYSIS

Finally, causal maps represent theories about how things work. They are visual representations of ideas that emerge from studying data, seeing patterns, and coming to conclusions about what causes what. Causal maps do not have to have numbers attached to them, although that is where causal modeling eventually leads, as it's useful to know *how much* one thing causes another as well as the fact that that one thing *does* cause another.

With or without numbers, though, causal models are best expressed as some kind of model, or flow chart, the subject of the next chapter.

Further Reading

- ♦ For more on text analysis software, see http://caqdas.soc.surrey.ac.uk/ and Lewins and Silver (2007) and see Appendix.
- ♦ For more on building matrices with qualitative data, see Miles and Huberman (1994).

CHAPTER 6

CONCEPTUAL MODELS

INTRODUCTION ◆

A major part of data analysis involves building, testing, displaying, and validating models. Models are simplifications of complicated, real things. If you ever played with toy cars or dolls when you were a child, you've had first-hand experience with *physical* models. If you've wasted as much time as we have playing computer games, where you pretend to be a magician or a warrior or a criminal or a crime fighter, you've worked with *virtual* models.

 If you've watched the news during a hurricane and seen predictions of where the hurricane will go and how strong it will be when it gets there, you've seen numerical models that were turned into visual models (to make them easier to understand).

◆ STATISTICAL MODELS AND TEXT ANALYSIS

In fact, understanding numerical models is a very good way to understand modeling in general. If you've ever seen the results of a regression, you've seen a statistical model. Here's a typical statistical model:

STARTING WAGE = .87 +.10EDUC + .08VT + .13PW + .17MARSTAT + .11FO (Graves and Lave 1972:53)

This little model describes the starting wages of 259 Navajo men who migrated during the 1960s from the reservation to Denver. It took Theodore Graves and Charles Lave (1972) about 3 years of tough work to get this model, which says:

1. Start with 87 cents an hour (remember, this was the 1960s).

2. Add 10 cents for every year of education beyond the first 10 years (it turned out that each year of education, up to 10 years, produced the same wage benefit).

3. Then add 8 cents an hour for having strong vocational training (in things like carpentry or plumbing).

4. Add another 13 cents an hour for each dollar the man earned in his best job before migrating to Denver (the PW stands for previous wage).

5. Add 17 cents if the man is married.

6. And finally, because most Navajo men on the Reservation in the 1960s were sheep herders, add 11 cents if the migrant's father had worked for wages (FO is father's occupation) (Graves and Lave 1972:53–54).

It may seem strange for us to present a statistical model in a book on qualitative research methods, but the fact is, although statistical models are built on quantitative data, models are models, no matter what kind of data you have. All researchers, qualitative and quantitative alike, build models of abstract concepts connected by propositions or hypotheses—like this:

$$A \rightarrow B$$

This simple, qualitative model says "Something called A leads to, or causes, something called B." The statistical model by Graves and Lave is a series of abstract concepts (education, marital status, and so on) connected by plus signs, which are propositions to the effect that "all these things added together account for the difference in starting wages when Navajo men get to Denver from the reservation."

If you take the numbers out of the statistical model, you get an entirely qualitative model. Something like Figure 6.1, which says: Five things—education, vocational training, wage on last job on the reservation, father's job on the reservation, and marital status, in no particular order—contribute materially to how much a Navajo man would earn when he migrates to Denver from the reservation.

Adding Weights to Directions

Statistical models can get very complex, with arrows going in both directions and between pairs of concepts. Figure 6.2 shows John Thomas's (1981) model for how men in a small Mayan village in Mexico become leaders.

Figure 6.1   Graves's Initial Conceptual Model of Variation in the Hourly Wage Rate for Navajo Men in Denver

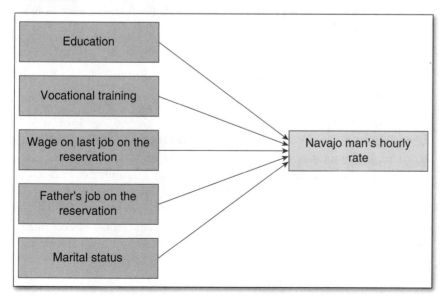

SOURCE: Graves and Lave (1972).

Figure 6.2 Thomas's Model of Leadership in a Mayan Village

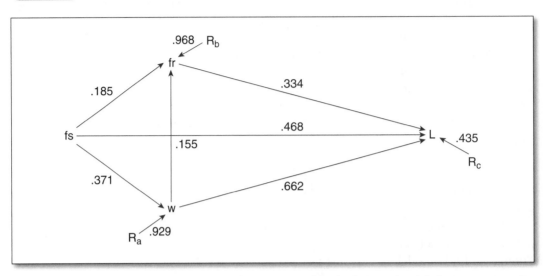

SOURCE: Thomas, J. S. 1981. The economic determinants of leadership in a Tojalabal Maya community. *American Ethnologist* 8:127–138.

Read Figure 6.2 as follows:

1. Men who become leaders (L=leaders) have three key features: lots of material wealth (w=wealth), lots of friends (fr=friends), and big families (fs=family size).

2. Men develop big friendship networks by having wealth and big families.

3. Big families help men develop their wealth *and* their friendship networks (Thomas 1981:133–134).

The model says, then, that to become a leader, you need wealth and friends, but to get wealth and friends, you need a big family. This is because, in agricultural communities, big families imply lots of labor for producing wealth, as long as you have enough land for all of those family members to work.

Thomas developed the model from ethnography and theory. The model is entirely qualitative. The fact that Thomas tested the model quantitatively (he used a statistical method called path analysis) doesn't reduce its essentially qualitative nature one bit: It's a series of concepts connected by hypotheses.

A Different Conceptual Model

Here's one more, from a completely different field. Figure 6.3 is a conceptual model, built from an entirely qualitative study, of the stages of

Figure 6.3 Wysoker's Model of Women's Weight Gain and Weight Loss

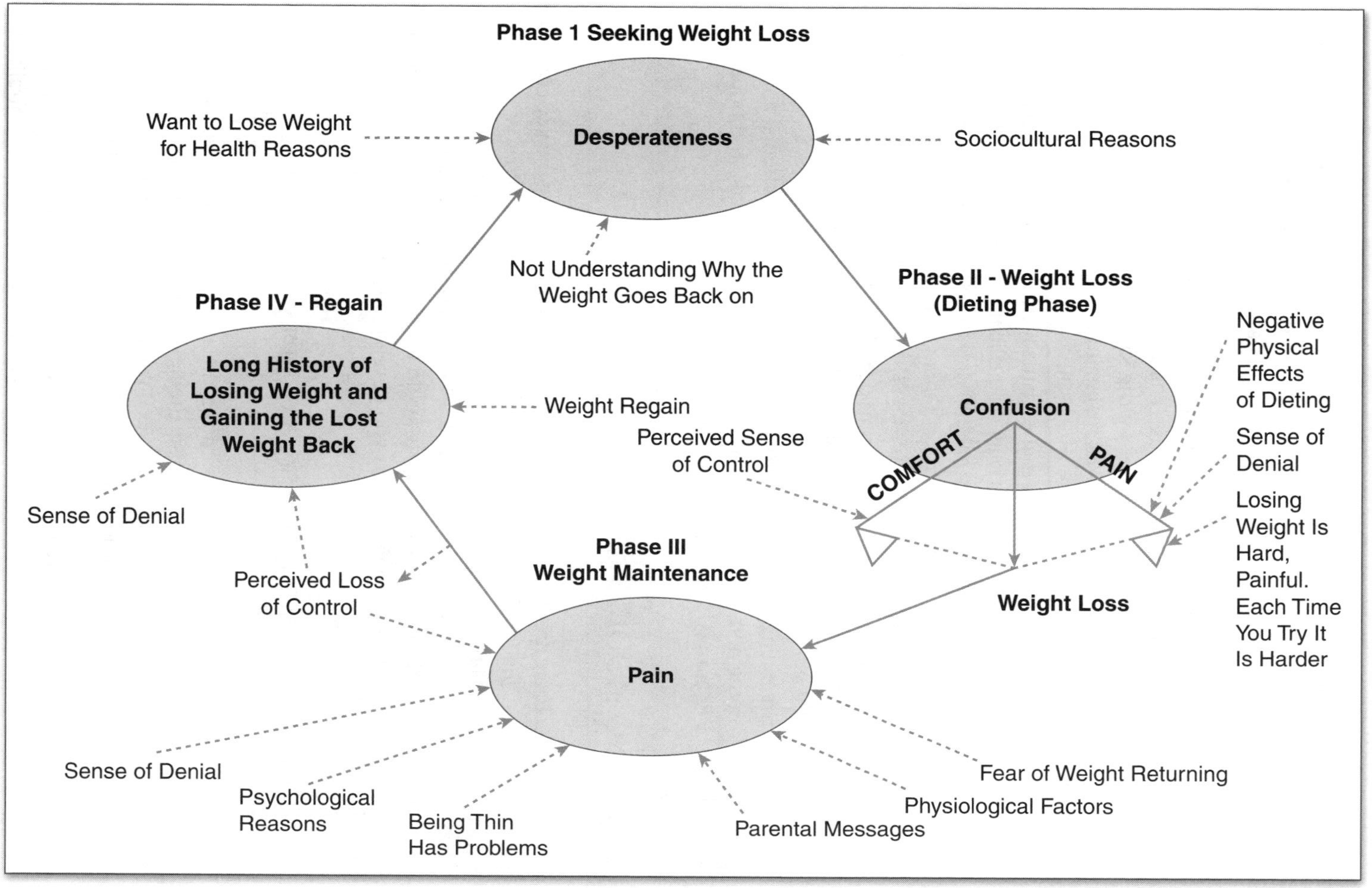

SOURCE: Wysoker, A. 2002. A conceptual model of weight loss and weight regain: An intervention for change. *Journal of the American Psychiatric Nurses Association* 8:168–173. Copyright © 2002, American Psychiatric Nurses Association. Published by SAGE Science Press.

women's weight loss and weight regain. Wysoker (2002:170) wanted to account for the fact that "Women will continue to try to lose weight, despite the long history of losing weight and gaining the lost weight back."

Read Figure 6.3 as follows: In Phase I, women become desperate about losing weight. The desperation comes from two main sources: a concern for health and a desire to conform to social pressures (e.g., about being thin). Desperation leads to dieting (Phase II). Dieting has emotional and physical costs, but those are offset by the satisfaction of weight loss and a sense of control. Phase III involves maintaining the weight loss. This is easier said than done, which leads to weight regain (Phase IV), and this triggers the feelings of desperation that eventually produce Phase I again.

All models, whether built on qualitative or quantitative data, are reductions of complex realities. We build models to better understand these complexities and to help others understand them as well.

The rest of this chapter takes you through the steps in building models and introduces some of the models that researchers use to simplify complex cases or to show how complex processes unfold over time. Variations of these models appear in many different kinds of analyses of qualitative data, including grounded theory, discourse analysis, schema analysis, analytic induction, content analysis, and ethnographic decision modeling. (**Further Reading**: building conceptual models.)

◆ BUILDING MODELS

There are three steps in building models: (1) Identify the key constructs to be included; (2) show linkages among the constructs—that is, identify how the constructs are related and represent the relationships visually; and (3) test that the relationships hold for at least the majority of the cases being modeled.

These steps are not always in sequence. You'll find yourself going back and forth among them as you develop models.

◆ STEP 1: IDENTIFYING KEY CONCEPTS

This is about choosing among the many themes you've identified in your data and prioritizing those themes in terms of their impact on whatever you're studying. In any project, you'll wind up with dozens, even hundreds, of themes in your codebook. Analysis is about whittling the number down and figuring out how the whittled-down set works.

The first step is to separate core from periphery themes, or what grounded theorists call selective coding for salience and centrality. Salience is about how often a concept appears in the data. The more often a concept appears—particularly if it appears across many respondents and in many situations—the more important it is likely to be. Centrality is about the degree to which a concept is linked to other concepts. Concepts that are linked to many others are likely to be at the core of—that is, central to—any model.

Identifying key concepts means making choices about what you can cover in your analysis. No model can cover everything. Some concepts will just have to be excluded, or at least deferred until the next paper. At some point in the process, every researcher has to ask: "Is this something I really need to explain here? Or is it tangential to my main concern right now?"

Getting a Handle on Things

With hundreds of pages of transcripts and notes, how do you actually make those choices?

Richard Addison (1992) followed nine newly minted physicians in their first year of residency in family medicine. He spent hours and hours interviewing them, their spouses, and others involved with their training, and he observed them as they went about practicing medicine. He began to analyze his notes and interviews while he was still collecting data. He started with in vivo coding, highlighting words and phrases that residents used—words like "punting," "pimping," "dumping," and "surviving"—in describing their experiences.

Addison started writing notes about those words and put the notes on index cards. He cut up segments of text from the transcripts and put those on cards, too. He sorted the hundreds of cards into piles that seemed to have some common thread. By the time he was done, he says, "every horizontal surface above floor level was filled with cards and cut-up transcripts." He goes on:

> I began to see progressions and flows. I started making lists of groups of practices, people, reactions, and events and connecting these lists on big sheets of white paper. Since no horizontal surfaces were left, I removed pictures and prints and tacked these lists and categories onto walls. Suddenly, 3 or 4 months after beginning, out of this wealth of seeming chaos, I had a flash of clarity: The central organizing theme for the residents as they began the residency was "surviving." It seemed to both describe and unify their practices in a way that made sense. (1992:117–118)

It is technically possible to use a computer for this pile-sorting task, but when you're really shopping for ideas, nothing beats actually touching and moving your data around.

◆ STEP 2: LINKING KEY CONSTRUCTS

Once key coding categories start to emerge, it's time to link them together in theoretical models. Some grounded theorists call this axial coding. It almost inevitably involves returning to the data for further analysis. For example, after Addison recognized that "surviving" was a central concept in young physicians' experience of their residency, he reanalyzed his transcripts, interviews, notes, and index cards with reference to surviving:

> I began seeing a different, more cohesive organization that seemed to incorporate previously scattered experiences and practices. I constructed a diagram that encompassed most of the lists and categories from my wall charts. This beginning diagram or attempted pictorial whole of what happened to these individuals as they began their residency looked something like a child's drawing of an extraterrestrial's digestive system. It was the first of many attempts to make diagrammatic sense of their existence. (1992:118)

Addison doesn't tell us how he identified (and named) the links between each of his key constructs. We suspect that he did a compare-and-contrast exercise across his transcripts, writing memos and looking for particular types of relationships.

But once he had the links in mind, the next step is to lay them out. And this means choosing a model type. Figures 6.4–6.14 show some common types of models in social research.

Conditional Matrices

Figure 6.4 is an adaptation of what A. Strauss and Corbin (1990:158–175) call a conditional matrix. The small circle at the bottom of the figure represents some action or interaction: a discussion between a doctor and a patient; crossing the U.S.-Mexican border illegally in search of work; moving a dying person to a hospice; buying a $300 pair of running shoes; sharing (or not sharing) a drug needle with a stranger.

In trying to understand the action or interaction we focus on behavior, thoughts, and emotions and on the social and physical circumstances in which thinking, feeling and acting takes place. The circles beyond the behavioral episode represent influences on the action.

The framework can also be presented as a matrix (Table 6.1). The first column represents the episodic action or interaction of interest and can be described in terms of people's behaviors, thoughts, and emotions and the context in which they occurred. Other columns represent larger and larger

Figure 6.4 Conditional Matrix

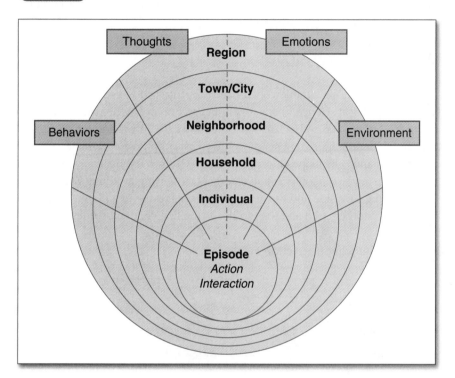

SOURCE: Adapted from Strauss, A., and Corbin, J. (1990). *Basics of qualitative research: Grounded theory procedures and techniques.* Newbury Park, CA: Sage. Copyright © 1990 Sage Publications.

Table 6.1 A General Framework for Key Aspects of Experience and Levels of Influence

	Episode	Individual	Household	Neighborhood	Town/City	Region
Behaviors						
Thoughts						
Emotions						
Environment Social Physical						

SOURCE: Strauss, A., and Corbin, J. (1990). *Basics of qualitative research: Grounded theory procedures and techniques.* Newbury Park, CA: Sage. Copyright © 1990 Sage Publications.

forces that may influence each episode. We often use a table like this one to help us organize questionnaire protocols and to make sense of complex textual data during our analysis phase.

Actor Interaction Models

Figure 6.5 shows a framework for studying interaction events between two actors. In political science, the actors in interaction events are often countries (country A threatens to declare war on country B). In economics, the actors might be organizations (business A buys its supply of raw material from business B and sells its products to business C). In most qualitative research, interactions involve people: A frail elderly person living at home asks for help from a home-care aide and the aide responds; a toddler in a playground grabs a toy from another child and the mother of the first child intervenes.

Figure 6.5 Framework for Studying Interaction Events

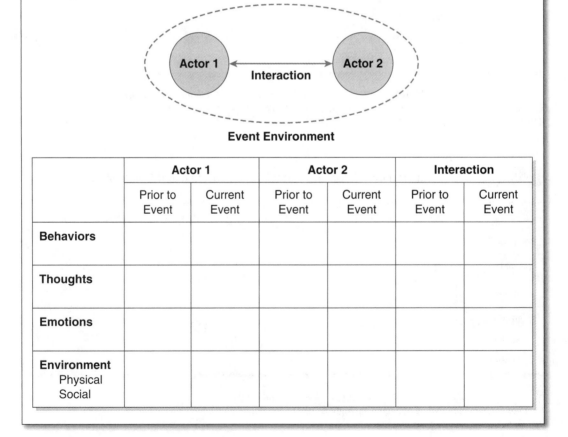

	Actor 1		Actor 2		Interaction	
	Prior to Event	Current Event	Prior to Event	Current Event	Prior to Event	Current Event
Behaviors						
Thoughts						
Emotions						
Environment Physical Social						

In any interaction event, the actors have characteristics that are independent of the interaction itself—things like beliefs and experiences—but which influence the interaction. Each person acts and behaves as an individual before and during an event, but some interactions—ordinary conversations, for example—are the product of joint action. These features of interaction can be represented in a table, also shown in Figure 6.5.

Process Models

Figure 6.6 is a process model that represents how events unfold over time. This framework divides any event into five stages: (1) the event

Figure 6.6 Framework for Studying Processes

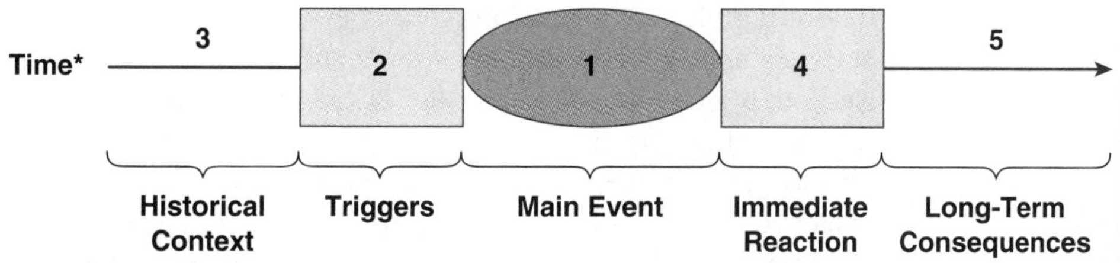

	Historical Context	Triggers	Main Event	Immediate Reaction	Long-Term Consequences
Behaviors Actor 1 Actor 2, etc.					
Thoughts Actor 1 Actor 2, etc.					
Feelings Actor 1 Actor 2, etc.					
Environment Physical Social					

* Order of questions: (1) main event, (2) triggers, (3) historical context, (4) immediate reaction, (5) long-term consequences.

itself; (2) the immediate triggers (environmental, social) that led to the event; (3) the larger historical context in which the event was based; (4) the immediate response or reaction to the event; and (5) the event's long-term consequences.

This model is often combined with the four elements of experience we saw in Figure 6.4 (behavior, thought, emotions, and environment) and can also be represented as a table. Think of using this framework for understanding how people cope with personal problems (like alcoholism or depression or bereavement or being assaulted) over time or to understand people's experiences of positive events (like getting promoted, winning the lottery, or getting engaged).

Decision Models

Figure 6.7 provides a general framework for describing how people make decisions under conditions of uncertainty (Abelson and Levi 1985). Before people can solve a problem, they need to recognize that it exists and they need to label it (even if the label is "I don't know what this is"). Next, they need to generate a list of possible solutions and select one. After the choice is made, it is monitored and evaluated. If it's thought to be the right choice, then the problem is resolved. If not, the decision maker returns to one of the previous stages and begins again.

Decision making often involves whole families, not just individuals. Ryan (1995) studied how lay people in Cameroon decided on treatments for illnesses. The table in Figure 6.7 shows how Ryan laid out the process for all the people involved.

Decision models can be represented in a branching tree diagram—also called a dendrogram—as in Figure 6.8 or in an IF-THEN chart, as in Figure 6.9. The dendrogram in Figure 6.8 shows James Young's model for how people in Pichátaro, Mexico, make their initial decision on how to react to an illness. The IF-THEN chart in Figure 6.9 shows Ryan and Martínez's (1996) model for how mothers in San José, Mexico, decided on how to respond to their infants' and toddlers' diarrhea. More about decision models in Chapter 16.

Transition Models

Figures 6.10 and 6.11 are transition models. When people make decisions about their health care, they move from one treatment to another. Their first reaction may to just wait and see. They may take some pills they

Figure 6.7 A Framework for Decision Making

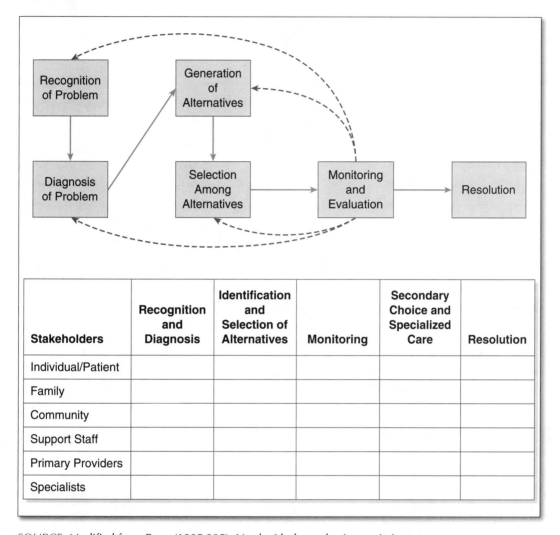

SOURCE: Modified from Ryan (1995:335). Used with the author's permission.

have lying around that they got from a doctor in a previous illness. The models in Figures 6.10 and 6.11 represent these transitions and show how health care decisions unfolded in the village in Cameroon where Ryan worked.

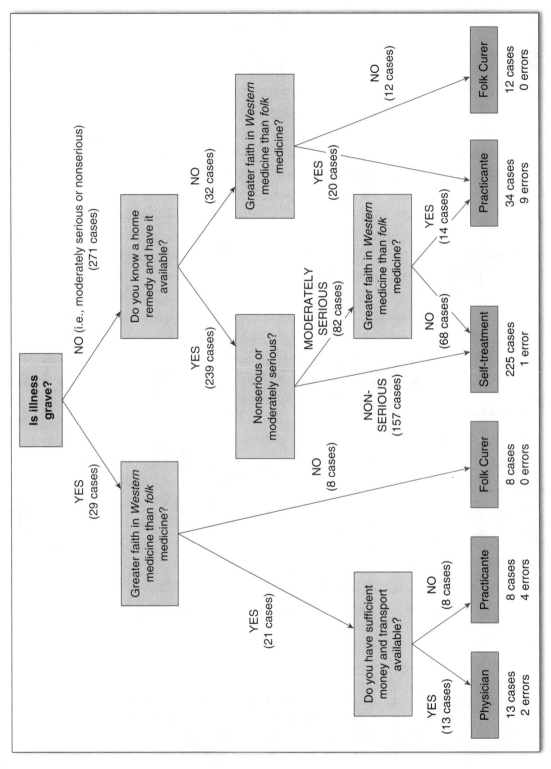

Figure 6.8 Young's Decision Model for the Initial Choice of Treatment

SOURCE: This article was published in *Social Science and Medicine*, 15, Young, J.C. "Non-use of physicians: Methodological approaches, policy implications, and the utility of decision models," pp. 499–507. Copyright Elsevier (1981).

Figure 6.9   Ryan and Martínez's If-Then Model for the Initial Choice of Treatment

Rule 1

IF   child has blood stools OR
        child has swollen glands OR
        child is vomiting

THEN   take child to doctor

Rule 2

IF   diarrhea is caused by
        empacho

THEN   give physical treatment

Rule 3

IF   previous rules do not apply OR
        there is no cure with the
        empacho treatment

THEN   give the highest preferred
        curing treatment that meets
        constraints (see constraint
        chart)

Rule 4

IF   previous treatment did not
        stop diarrhea

THEN   compare the two highest
        treatments of remaining
        options

4.1

IF   one is a curing remedy AND
        meets its constraints

THEN   give this treatment

4.2

IF   both or neither are curing
        remedies AND
        each meet their respective
        constraints

THEN   give the highest ranked
        preference

Rule 5

IF   the previous treatment did not
        stop the diarrhea AND
        the episode is less than 1 week
        long

THEN   repeat Rule 4

Rule 6

IF   the episode has lasted more
        than 1 week

THEN   take the child to a doctor

Constraints on Remedies

IF   you know how to make ORS AND
        your child will drink ORS

THEN   give ORS

Pill or Liquid Medication

IF   you know a medication that
        works for diarrhea AND
        you have it in the house

THEN   give the pill or liquid medication

                        OR

IF   you know a medication that
        works for diarrhea AND
        it is cheap AND
        it is easy to obtain

THEN   give the pill or liquid medication

SOURCE: Ryan and Martínez (1996).

Figure 6.10 Transition Between Types of Treatment

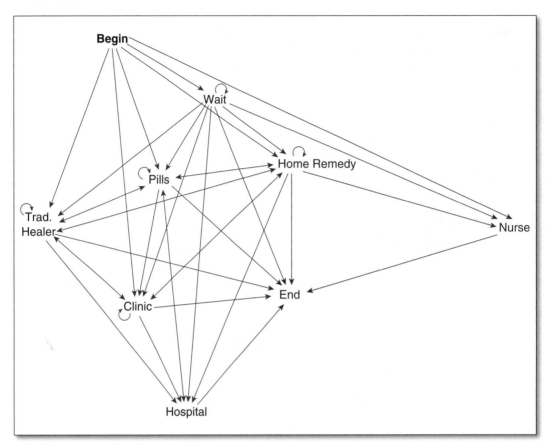

SOURCE: Ryan, G. 1998. Modeling home case management of acute illness in a rural Cameroonian village. *Social Science and Medicine* 4 (2): 209–225.

NOTE: *N* = 429. Arrows indicate that at least one transition occurred.

There are more lines in Figure 6.10 because the cutoff is so low. Ryan had 429 cases of illness in the set of families he studied for a year. If just one transition occurred in a case, it got a connecting line in the model. Figure 6.11 shows what happens when the connecting lines indicate that at least 5% or more had moved from one type of treatment to another. Notice that in both Figure 6.10 and 6.11, there are recursive transitions: People might try one home remedy after another before the illness either stopped or they broke out of the loop and did something else.

Figure 6.11   Transition Between Treatment Modalities

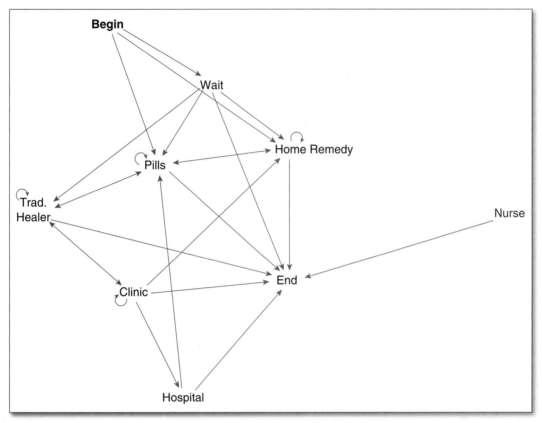

SOURCE: Ryan, G. 1998. Modeling home case management of acute illness in a rural Cameroonian village. *Social Science and Medicine* 4 (2): 209–225.

NOTE: *N* = 429. Arrows indicate transitions that took place more than 5% of the time.

Activity Models

Figure 6.12 is an example of an activity record. This one comes from Werner's (1992) discussion of changing a tire. The model shows that the phrase "change a tire" can have more than one interpretation. At the macro level, the phrase means to get ready, jack up the car, remove the nuts, remove the wheel, put on the wheel, replace nuts, remove the jack, and finish up. At the micro level, it assumes the car is already jacked up and refers only to removing the nuts, removing the wheel, putting on the wheel, and replacing the nuts.

Figure 6.12 An Example of an Activity Record

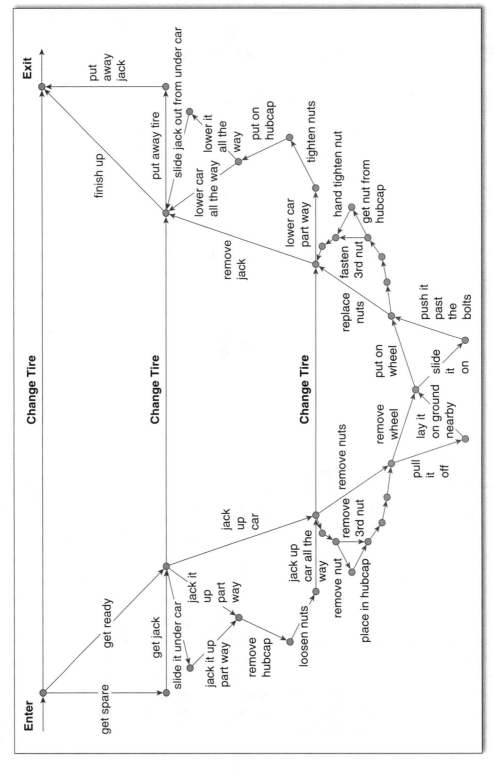

SOURCE: Werner, O. (1992). How to record activities. *Cultural Anthropology Methods Journal, 4*(2), 1–3. Copyright © 1992 Sage Publications.

Taxonomies

Taxonomies are models of how we think a set of things are related. Taxonomies are used in all sciences as models of complex reality (think of the Linnaean tradition of taxonomies of living things in biology, for example). Figure 6.13 is an example of a folk, or cultural, taxonomy. Bernard (2006) elicited this taxonomy of "kinds of cars and trucks" from an informant named Jack in West Virginia in the 1970s. More about building folk taxonomies in Chapter 8 on cultural domain analysis.

Mental Maps

Figure 6.14 comes from a study by James Boster and Jeffrey Johnson (1989) of two groups of fishermen in North Carolina. One group, the experts, were commercial fishermen. The other, the novices, were weekend anglers. Both groups did a pile-sorting task with cards that had pictures of 42 different kinds of fish. The two graphics in Figures 6.14 are models of what the two groups of fishermen thought about how the fish were related. These kinds of models are known as mental maps. They are produced from qualitative data like pile sorts and other systematic data collection methods. More about these methods, too, in Chapter 8.

STEP 3: TESTING THE MODEL ◆

Model building is an iterative process. We start with a case and state a theory. Then we look at another case and see if it fits our theory. If it does, we move on. If it doesn't, then we modify the theory to accommodate the new case. This constant comparison of theory and cases, called negative case analysis, forces us to defend our theories and to look for new explanations.

The danger in negative case analysis is that every new case is seen as unique. In fact, in some sense, every case of anything is unique, but in building and testing models, the idea is to look for the commonalities and to simplify things. If every case is seen as unique, then theories become so complicated and so overspecified that they are useless. (Further Reading: negative case analysis.)

Eventually, we reach some sort of closure—when new cases add little new information. When the incremental improvement in a model becomes minimal with each new case, grounded theorists say they have reached model saturation.

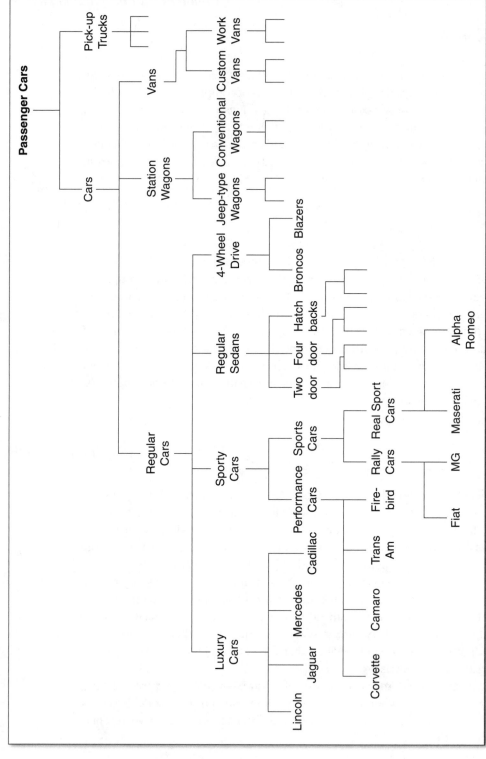

Figure 6.13 Part of Jack's Taxonomy of Cars and Trucks

SOURCE: H. R. Bernard (2006:540). *Research Methods in Anthropology: Qualitative and Quantitative Approaches.* 4th ed. Lanham, MD: Altamira Press.

Figure 6.14 Two Mental Models of Fish

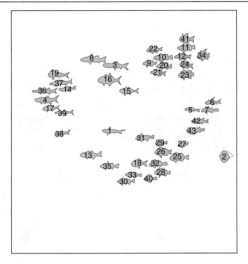
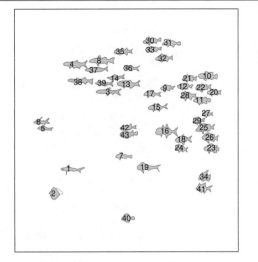

A multidimensional scaling of the similarities among the fish according to the North Carolina experts (Kruskal stress = .18).

A multidimensional scaling of the similarities among the fish according to the North Carolina novices (Kruskal stress = .10).

SOURCE: Boster, J. S. and J. C. Johnson 1989. Form or function: A comparison of expert and novice judgments of similarity among fish. *American Anthropologist* 91:866–889.

The real worth of a model, though, is not in its building, but in its testing—that is, whether it stands up against a new set of cases that weren't used in building the model in the first place.

Go back and look at Figure 6.9, the IF-THEN model that Ryan and Martínez built to account for what mothers in Mexico did in response to episodes of their children's diarrhea. Ryan and Martínez asked 17 mothers in San José, Mexico, who had children under 5 years old, what they did the last time their children had diarrhea. Then they went systematically through the treatments, asking each mother why she had used X instead of A, X instead of B, X instead of C, and so on down through the list.

We'll lay out the process in detail in Chapter 16, on ethnographic decision modeling. For now, the point is that the model in Figure 6.9 accounts for 15 of the original 17 cases (89%). To accommodate the two cases that didn't fit their model, Ryan and Martínez would have had to add more rules—one for each additional case. They tested the model on 20 new cases, and it accounted for 17 (84%). In other words, the model in Figure 6.9, with six rules, does as well on an independent sample as it did on the sample that was used to build it (Ryan and Martínez 1996).

This process of building and testing/validating models is the same for all the analytic methods we describe in the rest of this book. And now, on to the specifics.

Further Reading

♦ For more on building conceptual models, see Miles and Huberman (1994) and Chapter 12 on grounded theory. For some examples of conceptual models based on qualitative data, see Ben-Ari and Lavee (2007), Burton (2007), Dabelko and Zimmerman (2008), Groger (1994), T. F. Morgan and Ammentorp (1993), Polanyi and Tompa (2004), and Radnofsky (1996).

♦ For more on negative case analysis, see Dey 1993, Lincoln and Guba 1985, Miles and Huberman 1994, Becker 1998, and A. Strauss and Corbin 1990, 1998.

PART II

The Specifics

CHAPTER 7

FIRST STEPS IN ANALYSIS

Comparing Attributes of Variables

INTRODUCTION

Many techniques have been developed over the years for systematic analysis of qualitative data. Two of them—semantic network analysis and cultural domain analysis—require the use of computers. Others (comparing attributes of variables, word counts and concordances, content analysis, analytic induction, ethnographic decision modeling, grounded theory, conversation analysis, and schema analysis) don't require the use of computers, but they are greatly facilitated by them.

We begin with the method of comparing attributes of variables. "All knowing is comparative," said Donald Campbell (1988:372), and he was right. Astronomers, historians, and social scientists alike achieve knowledge by making comparisons. This star is brighter than that one; this war was more costly in blood and treasure than that one; women, on average, live longer than men do, in the industrialized societies of the world, but men live longer than women do in the nonindustrialized societies of the world.

Whether we use qualitative or quantitative data, we know things because we compare new experiences with the ones we already have. (Further Reading: analyzing qualitative data.)

♦ FUNDAMENTAL FEATURES OF COMPARISONS

Table 7.1 illustrates how we set up data so we can make systematic comparisons. This table contains a small sample of data (six cases) from a study we did of 60 students at a Midwestern university. We asked the students: "Please recall the last time that you had a cold or the flu and describe it in as much detail as possible." Their answers to this question are in column 3 of Table 7.1.

All the other columns contain information about the student (the ID number in column 1 and gender in column 2) or about the student's answers (in columns 4 to 8) to five questions about the cold or flu episode they described: (1) What kind of illness did you have? (2) Were you ever frightened or overly concerned about your condition? (3) How severe was the illness? (For this one, the students placed a mark on a thermometer-like scale that had marks from 1 to 7.) (4) How bad was the worst point of the episode? (For this one, the students circled a number on a 10-point scale.) And (5) How many days did the illness last?

In making comparisons, we ask three questions:

1. What things are we comparing? What are the units of analysis?

2. What attributes of these units are we using to make the comparison?

3. How will we measure similarities and differences on each of the attributes?

The rows in a data matrix like the one in Table 7.1 represent the units of analysis and define what we're comparing (the answer to question 1). The columns represent the attributes of variables (the answer to question 2). And each cell represents one person's response to each question (the answer to question 3).

Table 7.1 Elicited Illness Descriptions

ID	Gender	Verbatim Illness Description[1]	Nominal/ Categorical — Diagnosis[2]	Measures of Severity			
				Dichotomy — Concern[3]	Ordinal — Overall[4]	Ordinal — At Its Worst[5]	Interval/Ratio — Duration (days)[6]
32	F	Tired, aching, running nose, stuffed nose, sneezing, coughing, difficulty sleeping, uncomfortableness, sore throat—lots of Kleenex.	Cold	Yes	3	7	14
47	F	It was February and I came down with a cold. Just a sore throat, achy body, and a cough. Felt like sleeping all the time and didn't feel like eating anything unless it was salty. It took a week or a week and a half to get over.	Cold	No	1	2	10
17	F	The last time I had the flu I was VERY ill. It began at my head and arms and swept down my body in a big ache. All my muscles were sore, I felt like I was dying. I think I had fever blisters in my mouth, I had a sore throat, but didn't lose my appetite nor was I sick to my stomach. I just remember being laid out on our sofa for 3 days, every muscle in my body aching like I'd been beat up or through severe athletic training. The whole episode lasted around 7 days.	Flu	Yes	7	9	7
18	M	Headache—throbbing in temples—moved around head. Cough—hacking—sometimes—phlegm. Congestion—in sinuses and rib cage. Labored breathing—reduction of 20-10 airflow, tight chest. Fatigue—strong desire to sleep and nap—did not do activities running and going to gym for day to day and a half—felt weak and did not have desire to do much—could not concentrate—bad headache and a little stressed.	Cold	No	4	4	3.5
15	M	The last time I had a cold/flu was in Feb 98. I laid in bed for 2 days with a headache, a stomach ache, fever, body pain. I had spells of dizziness and nausea. I pretty much slept for most of 48 hrs. I was still tired and worn out for a couple of days beyond the initial illness.	Flu	No	5	4	3
24	M	I had the flu 5 months ago. I was always tired and it was hard to think straight. At some points though I actually kind of enjoyed it. No one expected much out of you. I don't know if it was the medicine or the fever, but at times I felt like I had a buzz. Of course I had all the common symptoms. I would wake up at night either sweating my ass off or shaking horribly from being so incredibly cold. I remember one night I was so cold and shaking so bad it woke my roommate up because I was shaking the bunk beds. He was not cold at all.	Flu	No	7	9	14

1. Please recall the last time that you had a cold or the flu and describe it in as much detail as possible. 2. What kind of illness did you have? 3. Were you ever frightened or overly concerned about your condition? 4. Please place a mark on the scale to indicate the severity of your illness (visual scale resembled a thermometer, marked 1–10), with 10 considered to be the worst health state. 5. Please rate the severity of your illness by circling the one number that best describes the severity at its WORST during the episode. 6. How many days did it last?

Units of Analysis

One of the first things to do in any research project is decide on the units of analysis. In Table 7.1, the units are texts and, of course, the people who provided the texts. In fact, in most social research, and especially in qualitative research, the units of analysis are people: female Mexican immigrants, male nurses, bureaucrats in the Department of Justice, women in German trade unions, runaway adolescents who are living on the street, people who go to chiropractors, Hispanic patrol officers in the Los Angeles Police Department.

But other things can be units of analysis, too. Depending on the research you're doing, you can compare newspapers, folk tales, countries, or cities. If it can fit into a row in a matrix—and irrespective of whether the descriptors are words or numbers—then it's a unit of analysis.

The rule about units of analysis is: Always collect data on the lowest level unit of analysis possible. For example, if you want to know a household's income, collect data on the income contribution of each member. Then you can aggregate to the household level. But if you ask people to tell you about their household's income to start with, you can never disaggregate the data to find out how much each person contributed.

If you're studying the relationship between child-rearing practices and religion, collect data on the child-rearing practices of each person in the household—the mother, the grandmother, elder siblings, and so on. You can aggregate those data later and code each household as having, say, strict versus permissive child-rearing practices.

Attributes

We can appreciate qualitative data just by observing them as wholes—looking, listening, feeling—but a different kind of analysis can be done by focusing on features, or variables. A variable is something that can take more than one value, and the values of variables can be words or numbers. Income per year from tips is a variable; number of pregnancies is a variable; gender, religion, political party affiliation—all are variables.

Listen to experts as they discuss different renditions of the same piece of music—say, a piano sonata by Chopin. You'll hear talk about things like harmonic pungency, the force of the attack, the muddiness of the lower registers, and so on. These are all qualitative variables, and, like all variables, they vary from unit of analysis to unit of analysis (in this case, from rendition to rendition of the same piece).

In Table 7.1, the verbatim illness descriptions are in column 3. Then, following that, the descriptions are reduced to a set of variables in columns 4 through 8. Column 4 shows the data for the variable called "Diagnosis." In this project, this variable can take one of two attributes: cold or flu. If we compare informants on this variable, we see that informants 32, 47, and 18 reported having had a cold, and informants 17, 15, and 24 reported that they had the flu.

Univariate Analysis

In column 8, we see that for informants 17, 15, and 18 the illness episodes lasted a week or less, but for informants 32, 47, and 24 the illness episodes lasted more than a week. The previous sentence is an example of univariate analysis, or comparing results within one column at a time. All systematic data analysis should begin with univariate analysis.

Univariate analyses are really, really focused and tell us a lot about a little. Mark Schuster and his colleagues (1998) asked 419 African American mothers who had recently given birth in Los Angeles, "What is your biggest fear for [child's name] growing up?" Mothers were prompted to give more than one answer—"anything else you're afraid of for your child?"

After classifying the responses into 16 categories, Schuster et al. (1998) found that more than half the fears were in the medical and public health categories, but that the number-one concern was fear of gangs, violence, or both (39%). These findings have important policy implications—something the American Academy of Pediatrics has taken up in recommending counseling to families about preventing violence, in general, and firearm injuries, in particular.

Bivariate Analysis

Bivariate analysis involves comparing data across two columns. For example, if we sort Table 7.1 first by diagnosis and then by the variable concern (was the informant ever frightened or overly concerned about the illness), we would find four diagnostic/concern categories: cold/yes, cold/no, flu/yes, and flu/no. In this 4-way categorization, cases 18 and 47 are similar as each belongs to the same cold/no category and cases 15 and 24 are similar as each belongs to the same flu/no category.

Multivariate Analysis

Multivariate analysis involves comparing three or more columns simultaneously. For example, informants 18 and 15 seem quite similar to each other on several variables. Informant 18 rated the overall severity of the illness as a 4, its worst point as a 4, and its duration as about 3.5 days; informant 15 rated the overall severity as a 5, its worst point as a 4, and its duration as about 3 days. Informants 17 and 24 are identical on the first two of these three variables (7 and 9), but informant 24 reported that the illness lasted for 2 weeks—twice as long as the 1 week reported by informant 17.

These two cases seem very different from that of informant 47, who said that she had a very mild cold (rating it just 1 out of a possible 7) that never got very bad (rating its worst point just 2 out of 10)—but it that lasted a long time (10 days).

There are some numbers in these descriptive statements, but the analyses are qualitative. The principle is the same, however, no matter how many cases or how many variables we compare at once: Our knowledge of relations is the result of actively and systematically making comparisons.

But as soon as we get more than a handful of cases, we need more formal techniques than inspection to keep things straight and to calculate similarities and differences. Fortunately, there are many computer programs available today to help you find patterns in both qualitative and quantitative multivariate data (see Box 7.1).

Box 7.1

Multivariate Statistics and Weak Relations

There is a limit to the relations that can be detected in the kind of data we're talking about here—that is, text.

With enough cases, we can use statistical methods to tease out weak relations among multiple variables. Weak relations can be very important in our lives. Some people have an increased risk of certain kinds of cancer because of environmental or genetic factors. Typically, though, it takes population-level studies—studies based on thousands of cases—to detect those increased risks.

African Americans are more likely than Whites in the United States to experience prison, hunger, and violent death. We can tell this because we have population-level studies on which to base the measurement of differences.

◆ LEVELS OF MEASUREMENT

Notice that column entries in Table 7.1 vary in what's known as level of measurement. That is, some columns are filled with qualitative data (words, like cold or flu, or even whole texts, as in column 3), and some contain numbers.

The values of variables come in three major levels of measurement: nominal, ordinal, and interval.

Nominal Variables

The values of a nominal variable comprise a list of names. Religions have names, like Baptist, Hindu, and Shinto, so religion is a nominal variable. Occupations have names, like chauffeur, ornithologist, and zookeeper, so occupation is a nominal variable. Ethnic groups, body parts, rock stars . . . all are nominal variables. The themes in a codebook are nominal variables if they are coded as present or absent.

In statistics, nominal variables are called "qualitative" because they don't involve any quantities. Coding men as "1" and women as "2" does not make gender a quantitative variable. You can't add up all the 1s and 2s and calculate the average gender. Assigning the number 1 to men and the number 2 to women is just substituting one name for another (nominal comes from Latin, *nomen*, or *name*).

Here's an example of a typical nominal, or qualitative, variable from a survey:

Do you identify with any religion? (check one)

☐ Yes or ☐ No.

If you checked "yes," then what is your religion? (check one)

☐ Protestant   ☐ Catholic   ☐ Jewish   ☐ Moslem   ☐ Other religion

---

Notice the use of the "other" category. The defining feature of nominal measurement is that it is exhaustive and mutually exclusive. Inserting the "other" category makes the measurement exhaustive.

Mutually exclusive means that things can't belong to more than one category of a nominal variable at a time. The instruction to "check one" makes the list mutually exclusive. Note, though, that life is complicated. People whose parents are of different races may think of themselves as biracial or multiracial. In 2000, the U.S. Census began offering people the opportunity to check off more than one race—and about seven million Americans did just that. Occupation is a nominal variable, but people can be homeopaths and jewelers at the same time; they can be pediatric oncology nurses and eBay entrepreneurs.

In Table 7.1, whether the informant reported a cold or a flu is a nominal variable. Depending on the analysis, we could add subcategories: simple colds, cold/flu combo, sinus infection, and so on.

Ordinal Variables

Ordinal variables also have the properties of exclusivity and exhaustiveness, but they have an additional property: Their values can be rank ordered. Anything measured as high, medium, or low (like socioeconomic class) is an ordinal variable. Anyone labeled "middle class" is lower in the social class hierarchy than someone labeled "high class" and higher in the same hierarchy than someone labeled "lower class." Ordinal variables, though, do not contain information about how much something is more than or less than something else.

The familiar "on a scale of 1 to 5" preamble to survey questions tells you that an ordinal variable is coming. Consider the variable: "like a lot," "like somewhat," "neutral," "dislike somewhat," "dislike strongly." A person who likes something a lot may like it twice as much as someone who says they like it somewhat, or five times as much, or half again as much. There is no way to tell.

In Table 7.1, Informant 47 said that, overall, her cold was about a 1 on a 7-point scale, and Informant 18 said that his cold was about a 4. We don't know if 4 is four times as bad as a 1 or twice as bad. All we know is that 4 is more serious than 1, at least in the mind of Informant 18.

Thomas Weisner and his colleagues (1991) studied families that had children with developmental delays. Working from interviews and questionnaires, raters assessed each family on: (1) its involvement with and attendance at a church or temple; (2) its shared sense of spirituality; (3) the support it received from a church or temple; and (4) how much religion influenced everyday actions and decisions. Readers of qualitative research reports need context to understand scale values. Weisner and his colleagues provided exemplars in the form of vignettes, shown in Table 7.2, for each of the ordinal categories.

Interval Variables

Interval variables have all the characteristics of nominal and ordinal variables—an exhaustive and mutually exclusive list of attributes that have a rank-order structure—and one additional property: The distances between the attributes are meaningful. Nominal variables are qualitative;

Table 7.2 Qualitative Exemplars of Ordinal Scales

Ordinal Rating	Exemplary Description
Nonreligious family	The Ehrlich family was headed by a grandmother, who was raising her granddaughter who had developmental delays. This family had no religious affiliation and attended no church or temple. They received no support from any religious groups and did not engage in any religious activities in the home. The grandmother was not taking her granddaughter to church at the time. When asked whether religion had provided any kind of support for her, or what else had been helpful, the grandmother replied: "No. Nothing, really. I just, really nothing, (I) just take care of her." As with many other nonreligious families in our sample, the Ehrlich family did have some history of formal religious training or experience in their past, but was not currently involved in religious activity.
Moderately nonreligious family	The Stein family was Jewish and attended temple occasionally, but they were not formal or active members. However, the Steins did indicate that they prayed regularly in their home. When asked whether religion was helpful, this mother replied: "It does play a part, more for me than my husband. But, I am very religious, I guess, in a vague way. My husband is not particularly religious at all."
Moderate to high religious family	The Crandalls had a young son with developmental delays who had several problems at birth and continued to have speech and coordination problems. The family held membership in and regularly attended a nearby Congregational Church. This mother, who taught Vacation Bible School one summer, said of the church, "It's a nice experience for our entire family. Jason loves Sunday School."
Highly religious family	Religion was an integral part of the Robinsons' everyday life. Their daughter Cathy was born prematurely and had major medical problems, necessitating four hospitalizations in her first year; her development was delayed in all areas. The Robinsons were active members of a 7th Day Adventist church, where they were involved in many activities. Prayer was a part of the Robinsons' daily lives. "We started doing things like praying together as a family, and having that faith foundation has strengthened our commitment to one another and our relationship with one another, and I think it's brought us closer together."

SOURCE: Weisner, T.S., L. Beizer, and L. Stolze 1991. Religion and families of children with developmental delays. *American Journal of Mental Retardation* 95:647–662.

ordinal variables are semiquantitative; and interval variables are fully quantitative (see Box 7.2).

Box 7.2

About Interval/Ratio Variables

Technically, most of what we commonly call interval variables are really ratio variables. Ratio variables have all the properties of interval variables, plus one: They have a true zero point. Income for example, is a common ratio variable: $50 is exactly twice $25 and exactly half of $100.

True interval variables—with real intervals and no zero point—are rare. In SAT scores, for example, the difference between a 600 and 700 is 100 points and the difference between 300 and 400 is 100 points. The intervals (SAT points) are the same, but a score of 600 is more than twice as good as a score of 300. Common measurements for temperature are at the interval level. Whether you measure temperature in Fahrenheit or Centigrade, a zero doesn't mean the absence of temperature.

Some examples of interval/ratio variables we've seen recently in the social science literature include: number of times married and number of years married; years in current job and months since last job; distance (in miles or minutes) to the nearest public school; number of pounds of fish caught last week; and number of hours last week spent in preparing food.

"Number of years of education" looks like an interval variable, but a year of grade school is not the same as a year of graduate school, so this variable usually gets chunked into an ordinal one: up to sixth grade, high school, some college, college degree, some postgraduate work; postgraduate degree. Sometimes, you just have to be sensible. And notice that, although a person who is 20 is twice the age of someone who is 10, this says nothing about the difference in social or emotional maturity. Conceptual variables, like social maturity, tend to be measured at the ordinal level.

◆ CONVERTING TEXT TO VARIABLE DATA

There are trade-offs between the complexity and richness of nonvariable data—whole texts, whole pieces of music, whole films, whole television ads—and the simplicity of variable data. On the one hand, nonvariable data, like the verbatim descriptions in Table 7.1 are a rich account of what people thought was most salient to report about their last experience with having a cold or flu. On the other hand, the complexity of nonvariable data makes them difficult to use for making comparisons in their raw form.

Consider cases 32 and 47 in Table 7.1. The two cases are similar in that both report coughing and having a sore throat, but they are quite distinct on many other dimensions. One describes having a runny and stuffed-up nose with sneezing; the other reports having body aches and loss of appetite. One had trouble sleeping; the other felt like sleeping all the time. One reports when the illness started and how long it lasted; the other doesn't cover either of these topics.

How similar are these cases? This question gets even more complex if we want to know whether case 18 (the other case of a cold) is more similar to case 32 than to 47. One way to tackle this problem is to use the value coding processes we covered in Chapter 4. In Table 7.3, we have coded each of the verbatim descriptions in Table 7.1 for eight signs and symptoms: cough, runny/stuffed nose, nausea/vomit, fever, fatigue, sore throat, body ache, and loss of appetite.

Each of the eight themes (variables) in Table 7.3 could take one of three values: 1 if the sign or symptom was mentioned; 0 if it was explicitly mentioned as not being present; and a dot • if it was not mentioned at all. Then (over in the right-hand column of Table 7.3) we summed up all the signs and/or symptoms that were mentioned. Finally, we sorted the table so that examples of cold were at the top and flu at the bottom.

Notice the trade-off here. The eight columns to the right of the diagnosis are now empty except for a number (a 1 or a 0) or a dot. The richness of the original data is gone, but we can systematically compare one illness to another and we can more easily identify patterns. For example, runny nose and cough are only mentioned in cold cases, and fever and nausea/vomiting are only mentioned (either as being present or not) in cases of flu. Fatigue is ubiquitous, and sore throat, body ache, and loss of appetite are associated with both cold and flu.

LEVELS OF AGGREGATION ◆

After you make decisions about the units of analysis (rows), features of comparisons (columns) and level of measurement (cells), the next step is to decide at what level of aggregation you want to make comparisons. There are three levels of aggregation for comparisons: (1) pairwise; (2) within-group; and (3) cross-group.

Table 7.3 Signs and Symptom Codes Derived From Verbatim Illness Descriptions

ID	Sex	Verbatim Illness Description[1]	Diagnosis	Signs and Symptoms								
				Cough	Runny, Stuffed Nose	Nausea, Vomiting	Fever	Fatigue	Sore Throat	Body Ache	Loss Appt.	Sum
32	F	Tired, aching, running nose, stuffed nose, sneezing, coughing, difficulty sleeping, uncomfortableness, sore throat—lots of Kleenex.	Cold	1	1	•	•	1	1	1	•	5
47	F	It was February and I came down with a cold. Just a sore throat, achy body, and a cough. Felt like sleeping all the time and didn't feel like eating anything unless it was salty. It took a week or a week and a half to get over.	Cold	1	•	•	•	1	1	1	1	5
18	M	Headache—throbbing in temples—moved around head. Cough—hacking—sometimes—phlegm. Congestion—in sinuses and rib cage. Labored breathing—reduction of 20-10 airflow, tight chest. Fatigue—strong desire to sleep and nap.—did not do activities running and going to gym for day to day and a half—felt weak and did not have desire to do much—could not concentrate—bad headache and a little stressed.	Cold	1	1	•	•	1	•	•	•	3
17	F	The last time I had the flu I was VERY ill. It began at my head and arms and swept down my body in a big ache. All my muscles were sore, I felt like I was dying. I think I had fever blisters in my mouth, I had a sore throat, but did not lose my appetite nor was I sick to my stomach. I just remember being laid out on our sofa	Flu	•	•	0	•	1	1	1	0	3

ID	Sex	Verbatim Illness Description[1]	Diagnosis	Signs and Symptoms								
				Cough	Runny, Stuffed Nose	Nausea, Vomiting	Fever	Fatigue	Sore Throat	Body Ache	Loss Appt.	Sum
		for 3 days, every muscle in my body aching like I'd been beat up or through severe athletic training. The whole episode lasted around 7 days.										
15	M	The last time I had a cold/flu was in Feb 98. I laid in bed for 2 days with a headache, a stomach ache, fever, body pain. I had spells of dizziness and nausea. I pretty much slept for most of 48 hrs. I was still tired and worn out for a couple of days beyond the initial illness.	Flu	•	•	1	1	1	•	1	•	4
24	M	I had the flu 5 months ago. I was always tired and it was hard to think straight. At some points though I actually kind of enjoyed it. No one expected much out of you. I don't know if it was the medicine or the fever, but at times I felt like I had a buzz. Of course I had all the common symptoms. I would wake up at night either sweating my ass off or shaking horribly from being so incredibly cold. I remember one night I was so cold and shaking so bad it woke my roommate up because I was shaking the bunk beds. He was not cold at all.	Flu	•	•	•	1	1	•	•	•	2

1. Please recall the last time that you had a cold or the flu and describe it in as much detail as possible. 2. What kind of illness did you have? 3. Where you ever frightened or overly concerned about your condition? 4. Please place a mark on the scale to indicate the severity of your illness (visual scale resembled a thermometer marked 1–10), with 10 considered to be the worst health state. 5. Please rate the severity of your illness by circling the one number that best describes the severity at its *worst* during the episode. 6. How many days did it last?

Pairwise Comparison

Pairwise comparisons describe the similarity between any two rows of a table. We can compare informants 32 and 47, 32 and 18, 17 and 15, 17 and 24, and so on. There are six informants in Tables 7.1 and 7.3. The formula for comparing things two at a time from any list is

$$n(n-1)/2$$

so, in this case, with six informants, we can do 6(5)/2=15 comparisons. Going systematically through all possible pairwise comparisons is the central idea in the constant comparative method used by grounded theorists and other qualitative researchers everywhere for finding and themes. (See Chapter 12.)

Within-Group Comparison

If we want to compare more than two things at a time, we use within-group (also called intragroup) comparisons. This involves scanning multiple rows simultaneously to search for things like range, central tendency, and distributions of variables.

For example, the top portion of Table 7.1 contains descriptions of illness by women. We see that two out of three women reported colds and were the same people who reported being somewhat concerned about their condition. Their overall assessment of severity was from 1 to 7 (range) and averaged 3.67 days (1+3+7/3=3.67). These events lasted anywhere from 7 to 14 days (again, range), with an average of 10.33 days.

Cross-Group Comparison

Cross-group (also called intergroup) comparisons takes the process one more step. From Table 7.1, we see that none of the men expressed concern for his health, but two out of three women did. On the other hand, the three men reported colds/flus lasting from 3 to 14 days (average 6.83), with severity ranging from 4 to 7 (average 5.33)—more severe than the colds/flus reported by women but lasting less time than those reported by women.

These are self-report data, so we're dealing here with what people perceive, not with measures of physical reality, as would be the case if we had the results of a physician's examination on all these cases. Also, with so few cases, we can't generalize the results to the whole population. Still, you can see how cross-group comparison can be a very powerful tool for identifying patterns in populations. Even with just a few cases, we can see patterns emerging and can start formulating hypotheses, like "On average, men will report having a harder time with colds and flu than will women but will be reluctant to express concern."

This may not work out when we get more cases, but that's fine. The idea here is to use the data we have in hand and get some ideas about what's going on. These few cases give us something to look for when we collect more cases. In fact, they help us focus interviews as we move through a project. Most qualitative research projects are based on fewer than a hundred interviews. You want to make those interviews count, so start doing the analysis on the first few and keep expanding the analysis as you get more data.

MANY TYPES OF COMPARISONS ♦

Table 7.4 summarizes the comparisons that can be made with combinations of levels of comparisons, levels of measurement, and levels of aggregation. There are two important points here.

First, all the comparisons described in Table 7.4 can be made using qualitative data. In the case of variable-based comparisons, you may need to add an extra step to convert nonvariable data, like text, into nominal-, ordinal-, or interval-level variables.

Table 7.4 Types of Comparisons

Levels of Aggregation	Dimensions of Comparison		
	Univariate	Bivariate	Multivariate
Pairwise	I	IV	VII
	(nv, n, o, ir)	(nv, n, o, ir)	(nv, n, o, ir)
Within-Group	II	V	VIII
	(nv, n, o, ir)	(nv, n, o, ir)	(nv, n, o, ir)
Cross-Group	III	VI	IX
	(nv, n, o, ir)	(nv, n, o, ir)	(nv, n, o, ir)

Levels of Measurement: nv = nonvariable, n = nominal, o = ordinal, ir = interval/ratio.

Second, different methodological traditions emphasize certain types of comparisons over others. For example, classic content analysis of texts (Chapter 13) involves within-group and cross-group comparisons and always requires the conversion of text or images to at least nominal-level variables. Grounded theory and schema analysis (Chapters 12 and 14), by contrast, rely on whole texts—that is, nonvariable data—and rarely involve conversions of texts to variables.

During the discovery phase of both grounded theory and schema analysis, the method of constant pairwise comparison plays an important role in the identification of themes. As the process of building models moves on, within-group and cross-group comparisons become more important.

Analytic induction (Chapter 15), particularly the method known as qualitative comparative analysis (QCA), produces aggregate, within-group models and uses text that has been converted to nominal variables. The analysis of nominal, free list data (Chapter 8) is a type of univariate comparative analysis (usually at the within- and cross-group comparative levels).

If this all seems a bit opaque right now, come back and read this section again after you've gone through the later chapters on all these methods for analyzing texts.

◆ COMPARING THE COLUMNS

Up to this point, we have been making comparisons across pairs of rows or groups of rows (units of analysis). Much of social science research, however, is about identifying general associations between variables and how they are co-distributed in a population. These associations are found by making comparisons across columns.

Table 7.5a shows the bivariate relationship between illness diagnosis (cold, flu) and concern (yes, no) in Table 7.1. The rows in Table 7.5a represent the values associated with one dimension (Diagnosis), and the columns represent the values of the other (Concern). The numbers in each cell represent the number (and percentage) of cases that meet the conditions indicated by the intersection of two variables.

From the data in Table 7.1, we see that informant 32 reported a cold and was concerned, but informants 47 and 18, who also reported colds, were not concerned. From Table 7.5b, we see that only six (14%) of the 43 people who reported a cold also reported being concerned, but nine (about 53%) of the 17 students who reported a case of the flu also reported being concerned. The students in our research see flu as the more serious of the two illnesses.

Table 7.5 Bivariate Comparison of Illness Narratives in Table 7.1

	Table 7.5a[1]					Table 7.5b[2]				
	Concern						Concern				
	Yes		No		Total		Yes		No		Total
Diagnosis	Freq.	%	Freq.	%	Freq.	Diagnosis	Freq.	%	Freq.	%	Freq.
Cold	1	33.3	2	66.6	3	Cold	6	14.0	37	86.0	43
Flu	1	33.3	2	66.6	3	Flu	8	47.1	9	52.9	17
Total	2	33.3	4	66.6	6	Total	14	23.3	46	76.7	60

1. Data taken from Table 7.1 (*n* = 6).

2. Data taken from entire sample on which Table 7.1 was based (*N* = 60).

AND FINALLY. . . . ♦

Many projects that are based on texts involve the kinds of analyses we've outlined in this chapter—that is, comparisons of themes or variables. Some studies may involve only qualitative data and qualitative comparisons. Increasingly, however, we find studies that combine both qualitative and quantitative data and analyses.

It is fashionable to call these mixed-methods studies, but we remind you that a sensible mix of qualitative and quantitative data has always been the natural order of science. Particular studies in any science may be mostly based on qualitative data or mostly based on quantitative data. But all fields of science, from sociology to ornithology, advance as a result of studies based on both kinds of data.

In the next chapter, we take up cultural domain analysis—a truly mixed method that has its roots in several fields, including linguistics, psychology, anthropology, and sociology.

Further Reading

♦ For more on analyzing qualitative data, see Auerbach and Silverstein (2003), Dey (1993), Flick (2002), Miles (1979), Miles and Huberman (1994), and L. Richards (2005).

CHAPTER **8**

CULTURAL DOMAIN ANALYSIS

Free Lists, Judged Similarities, and Taxonomies

◆ INTRODUCTION

Cultural domain analysis (CDA) is the study of how people in a cultural group think about things that somehow go together in their society. These can be physical, observable things—kinds of wine, medicinal plants, ice cream flavors, animals you can keep at home, horror movies, symptoms of illness—or conceptual things like occupations, roles, and emotions. The method comes from work by James Spradley (1972, 1979) and others in cognitive anthropology, but it has since been picked up in other fields as well.

One goal of CDA is to elicit the content of a domain (its elements) and to understand the domain's structure—that is, how its elements are thought by people in a culture to be related to each other. Another goal is to understand how the content and structure of cultural domains vary across cultures or subcultures (Borgatti 1999).

The data for understanding the content of cultural domains are predominantly from free lists. The data for understanding the structure of cultural domains are mostly from tasks of judged similarity, like pile sorts.

The methods for analyzing these data include multidimensional scaling (MDS), cluster analysis, and correspondence analysis. These are all computer-based visualization methods—that is, methods for reducing a welter of data to pictures that we can easily understand and interpret—and they open up many possibilities for researchers who use qualitative data.

◆ WHAT ARE CULTURAL DOMAINS?

A cultural domain is "an organized set of words, concepts or sentences, all of the same level of contrast, that jointly refer to a single conceptual sphere" (Weller and Romney 1988:9). So, for example, most native speakers of English would recognize that apples and oranges are words that stand for "things in the domain of fruits."

Apples and oranges are also at the same level of contrast. The set "apples, oranges, lemons," however, are all elements in the domain of fruits, but at two levels of contrast: One level groups oranges and lemons (as citrus fruits). Apples are a different kind of fruit and, in some culturally appropriate way, "go with" pears and plums. The apple-pear-and-so-on group is culturally at the same level of contrast as the orange-lemon-and-so-on group.

If you ask enough people about this cultural domain, you'll find that—at a higher level of contrast—there are tree fruits and vine fruits and bush fruits and that there are several kinds of each, including citrus fruits and things like apples and pears.

CDA Is About Things

The first principle of CDA is that cultural domains "are about things 'out there' in reality, so that, in principle, questions about the members of a domain have a right answer" (Borgatti 1999:117). What the right answer is, of course, can vary across cultures or subcultures—or gender, for that matter.

The spectrum of visible colors is a physical reality, but around the world, women can name more colors and have a richer vocabulary for describing colors than men do (Rich 1977; Yang 2001). And people in different cultures label chunks of the color spectrum very differently. For example, speakers of Navajo, Korean, Ñähñu, Welsh, and many other languages use one word to identify colors that speakers of English call green and blue. The color is called "grue" in the linguistics literature (Kim 1985).

People who have a word for grue use adjectives to express color differences within the blue-green spectrum. In Navajo, for example, the general term for grue is *dootl'izh*. Turquoise is *yáago dootl'izh*, or sky grue, and green is *tádlidgo dootl'izh*, or water scum grue (Oswald Werner, personal communication).

CDA Is Not About Preferences

Note that none of this is about people's preferences but rather about their perceptions (Borgatti 1999:117). We ask people about which brand of beer they prefer, which political candidate they prefer, and which features they prefer in potential mates because we want to predict their buying, voting, and marrying behavior. We might also ask people about their income, their ethnicity, their age, and so on and then look for packages of variables about the people (single White women under 30, married Black men over 40, etc.) that predict how they will exercise their preferences—what they will buy, for whom they will vote, who they will marry.

In cultural domain analysis, we're interested in the items that comprise the domain—the plants that people use for medicine, the jobs they do—and how people store and retrieve information about those items. We're interested, then, in how people think things in a cultural domain are related to each other (Borgatti 1999; Spradley 1979). (Further Reading: cultural domain analysis.)

FREE LISTS ◆

We begin a cultural domain analysis by getting a list of the items that comprise it. An important method for doing this is the humble free list. Data from short, open-ended questions on surveys can be coded to produce lists, as can transcriptions of ethnographic interviews and focus groups.

In free listing, however, we ask people: "List all the X you can think of," where X might be things they do on weekends, brands of cars, things people do when they get a cold, ways to avoid pregnancy, places in the community frequented by commercial sex workers, and so on.

Prompting

As in any kind of interviewing, people respond with more information if you learn how to probe for it. D. D. Brewer (2002:112) found that semantic cueing increased the recall of items in a free list by over 40%. Ask informants to: "Think of all the kinds of X [the domain] that are like Y," where Y is that first item on their initial list. If the informant responds with more items, you take it another step: "Try to remember other types of X like Y and tell me any new ones that you haven't already said." Do this until the informant says there are no more items like Y. Then you repeat the exercise for the second item on the informant's initial list, and the third, and so on (see Box 8.1).

Box 8.1

Other Prompts

Brewer tested three other kinds of probes for free lists: redundant questioning, nonspecific prompting, and alphabetic cueing. Here's the redundant question that Brewer and his colleagues asked a group of IV-drug users:

> Think of all the different kinds of drugs or substances people use to get high, feel good, or think and feel differently. These drugs are sometimes called recreational drugs or street drugs. Tell me the names of all the kinds of these drugs you can remember. Please keep trying to recall if you think there are more kinds of drugs you might be able to remember. (D. D. Brewer et al. 2002:347)

In nonspecific prompting you ask people "What other kinds of X are there?" after they've responded to your original question. You keep asking this question until people say they can't think of any more Xs. And in alphabetic cueing, you ask informants "What kinds of X are there that begin with the letter A?" . . . "With the letter B?" And so on.

Informants who are very knowledgeable about the contents of a cultural domain usually provide longer lists than others. Some items will be mentioned over and over again, but eventually, if you keep asking people to list things, you get a lot of repeat items and all the new items are unique—that is, mentioned by only one informant. This happens pretty quickly (by the time you've interviewed

15 or 20 informants) with domains like names of ethnic groups, which are pretty well formed. With fuzzy domains, like "things that mothers do," you might still be eliciting new items after interviewing 30 or 40 people.

Long lists don't necessarily mean that people know a lot about the things they name. In fact, in modern societies, people can often name a lot more things than they can recognize in the real world (see Box 8.2).

Box 8.2

Loose Talk

John Gatewood (1983) interviewed 40 adult Pennsylvanians and got free lists of names of trees. He asked each informant to go through his or her list and check the trees that they thought they could actually recognize. Thirty-four out of the 40 informants listed "pine," and 31 of the 34 said that they could recognize a pine.

Orange trees were another matter. Twenty-seven people listed "orange," but only four people said they could recognize an orange tree (without oranges hanging all over it, of course). On average, these 40 Pennsylvanians said they could recognize half of the trees they listed, a phenomenon that Gatewood called "loose talk."

Gatewood and his students (1983b) asked 54 university students, half of them women and half of them men, to (1) list all the musical instruments, fabrics, hand tools, and trees they could think of; and (2) check off the items in each of their lists that they thought they would recognize in a natural setting. Gatewood chose musical instruments with the idea that there would be no gender difference in the number of items listed or recognized; that women might name more kinds of fabrics than would men; and that men would name more kinds of hand tools than would women. He chose the domain of trees to see if his earlier findings would replicate. There were no surprises: All the hypotheses—and stereotypes—were supported (Gatewood 1984).

PLOTTING FREE LISTS ♦

We asked 34 people: "Please write down the names of all the fruits you can think of." Because free list data are texts, they have to be cleaned up before you can analyze them. Only 10 people listed grapes, but another 22 (for a total of 32 out of 34 people) listed grape (in the singular). Before counting up the frequency for each item in the free lists, we had to combine all mentions of grapes and grape. It doesn't matter whether you change grapes into grape or vice versa, so long as you make all the required changes.

Then there are spelling mistakes. In our data, three people listed bananna (wrong spelling), and 27 people listed banana (right spelling); three people listed avacado (wrong), one listed avocato (wrong), and six people listed avocado (right). Cantaloupe was hopeless, as was pomegranate. We got eight cantaloupe (the preferred spelling in the dictionary), six cantelope, two cantelopes, and three canteloupe. We got 17 listings for guava and one for guayaba, which happens to be the Spanish term for guava. We got 10 listings for passion fruit and one for passion-fruit, with a hyphen (when computers list word frequencies, they see those two listings as different).

Once the data were cleaned, we plotted how often each fruit was mentioned. The result is the scree plot in Figure 8.1. ("Scree" refers to the rocks that pile up at the base of a cliff and the telltale L-shape of the pile.)

The shape of the curve in Figure 8.1 is typical for a well-defined domain, like fruits: The 34 informants named a total of 147 different fruits, but 88 of those fruits were named by just one person (prickly pear and quince, for example) and almost everyone named a few items (apple and orange, for example). Compare that to the results for lists of "things that mothers do." For this domain, 34 informants named 554 items, of which 515 were named by just one person and only a handful (love, clean, cook) were named by five or more people.

The difference is that fruits (and animals, and names of racial/ethnic groups, and emotions) are very well defined, but things that mothers do (and things that people can do to help the environment, and things that people might do on a weekend) are much less well-defined cultural domains. Many of the most interesting domains are things that people don't have easy lists for.

Selecting Items From a Free List for Further Study

We use scree plots to choose the set of items that we want to study in more depth. For example, by counting the dots in Figure 8.1, we see that (1) 14 fruits were mentioned by 20 or more of our 34 informants and (2) 58 items were mentioned by at least two of our informants. All the other fruits were mentioned just once.

How many items should we choose from these data as representing the contents of the domain? There is no formal rule here, but a good general rule is to select items that are mentioned by at least 10% of your informants. If you have 40 informants, then choose items that were mentioned by at least four of them. If this still produces too many items, then move up to 15% of informants or more.

There is nothing forcing you to take every item that's mentioned a lot, especially if you already know something about the domain you're studying. If you want to study, say, 40 items in depth, you can choose some that are mentioned frequently and others that are mentioned less frequently—or even by no one at all.

An item mentioned once is usually not a good candidate to include for further work on the structure of the domain. The whole idea of a cultural

Figure 8.1 Scree Plot of Free List of 143 Fruits From 34 Informants

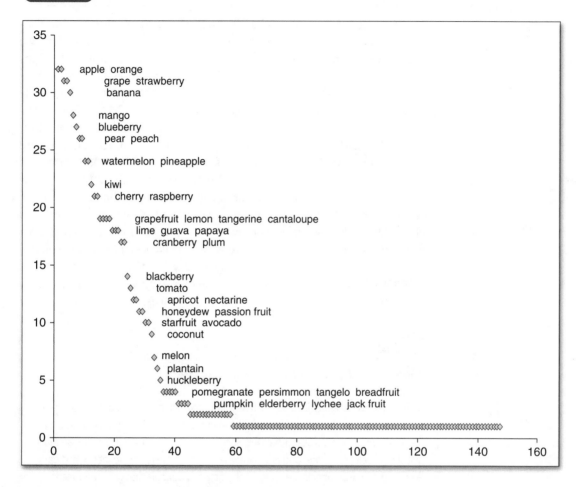

domain, as contrasted with an individual cognitive domain is that the content is shared (Borgatti 1999). On the other hand, we often want to know where a particular item fits within a cultural domain.

In the late 1990s, we studied the domain of green behaviors in the United States—things that people believe they can do to help the environment—under a contract from a motor vehicle manufacturer (Bernard et al. 2009). We collected free list data from 43 people across the United States but nobody, not a single person, mentioned buying an electric or a hybrid car. At the time, there were no electric or hybrid cars on the market, but our client wanted to know where Americans might place the behavior of "buying an electric car" within the domain of green behaviors, so we put that item into the pile-sort task of the study (more on that in a minute).

◆ ANALYZING FREE LIST DATA

Free lists are great for getting a handle on the content of a domain, but they produce very interesting data that can be analyzed in their own right. We asked 42 American adolescents (20 boys and 22 girls) "What health issues are U.S. adolescents worried about?" The results are shown in Table 8.1.

Over three-quarters of the informants (76.2%) mentioned sexually transmitted diseases (STDs), and over a third of them (35.7%) specifically mentioned HIV/AIDS. This is what we expect from adolescents but, surprisingly, nearly half (45.2%) of our informants (all under age 20) were worried about cancer—a worry once associated with older Americans.

When we explored this, we found that just six of the 20 boys in our sample (30%) had mentioned cancer, compared to 13 of the 22 girls (59%). Moreover, when the boys mentioned cancer at all, they ranked it fifth, on average, of the illnesses they were worried about, compared to second for the girls. The girls, it turned out, were very worried about breast cancer, but when the data from both genders were combined, this wasn't noticeable. ANTHROPAC software (Borgatti 1992) makes short work of free lists (see Appendix) (see Box 8.3). (Further Reading: free lists.)

Box 8.3

Measuring the Salience of Free-List Items

The frequency of items in a set of free lists is one indicator of the importance—or salience—of those items to informants. Another indicator is how early, on average, an item gets mentioned. If you ask native speakers of American English to list animals, you'll find that (1) cat and dog are mentioned a lot, and (2) they are mentioned early. In fact, those two animals are typically the first two animals that get mentioned.

Charismatic megafauna—elephants, whales, lions, and so on—also get mentioned a lot, but usually after the common household animals get named. Thus, in addition to frequency, we can measure the average rank that each item appears in a set of lists. Free listing, however, produces lists of varying length. It's one thing to name elephants fifth in a list of 30 animals and quite another to name elephants fifth in a list of 10 animals, and several methods for taking these factors into account are available.

Smith's S (J. J. Smith 1993) takes into account both the frequency of an item and how early in each list it is mentioned and is a popular measure of item cognitive salience. It is also "highly correlated with simple frequency" (Borgatti 1999:149) and so, for most analyses, simple frequency counts of free list data are all that are needed. (Further Reading: salience.)

Table 8.1 Free List Results From 42 Adolescents About Their Health Concerns

Items Mentioned	Total Sample (N = 42)		Girls (n = 22)			Boys (n=20)			Difference Girls% – Boys%
	Freq	%	Rank	Freq	%	Rank	Freq	%	
Cold/Flu	12	28.6	3	10	45.5	9	2	10.0	35.5
Cancer	19	45.2	2	13	59.1	5	6	30.0	29.1
Eating Disorders	10	23.8	4	8	36.4	9	2	10.0	26.4
HIV/AIDS	15	35.7	3	10	45.5	6	5	25.0	20.5
Mono	10	23.8	5	7	31.8	8	3	15.0	16.8
Stress	8	19.0	7	5	22.7	8	3	15.0	7.7
Weight-Obesity	10	23.8	6	6	27.3	7	4	20.0	7.3
Skin-related	13	31.0	5	7	31.8	5	6	30.0	1.8
Hygiene	8	19.0	8	4	18.2	7	4	20.0	−1.8
Disease	8	19.0	8	4	18.2	7	4	20.0	−1.8
Eating Right	7	16.7	9	3	13.6	7	4	20.0	−6.4
STDs	32	76.2	1	16	72.7	1	16	80.0	−7.3
Fitness	12	28.6	7	5	22.7	4	7	35.0	−12.3
Drug Abuse	9	21.4	9	3	13.6	5	6	30.0	−16.4
Alcohol-related	16	38.1	6	6	27.3	2	10	50.0	−22.7
Smoking-related	11	26.2	9	3	13.6	3	8	40.0	−26.4

Once we have identified the items in a cultural domain, the next step is to examine how the items are related to each other. To do this, we ask informants to make similarity judgments. Pile sorts are an effective method for collecting these judgments. (Two other methods, paired comparisons and triad tests, are also used for collecting similarity judgments.) (Further Reading: paired comparisons and triad tests.)

♦ PILE SORTS

Pile sorts are a simple and fun way for informants to identify relationships among items in a domain. Begin by writing the name of each item on a single card (index cards cut in thirds work nicely). Label the back of each card with the number from 1 to n (where n is the total number of items in the domain). Spread the cards out randomly on a large table with the item-side up and the number-side down. Ask each informant to sort the cards into piles according to which items belong together.

Informants often ask three things when we do pile sorts: (1) What do you mean by "belong together"? (2) How many piles should I make? (3) Can I put something in more than one pile? The answer to the first question is that you're really, really interested in what the informant thinks and that there are no right or wrong answers. The answer to the second is that they can make lots of piles, but they can't put every item into its own separate pile and they can't put all the cards in one big pile.

One answer to the third question is that each item can only belong to one pile. This simplifies the analysis, but may not reflect the complexity of people's thinking about items in a domain. For example, in a study of consumer electronics, someone might want to put a DVD player in one pile with TVs and in another pile with camcorders, but might not want to put camcorders and TVs in the same pile. To handle this problem, you can hand people duplicate cards when they want to put an item into more than one pile, though this complicates the data analysis.

When they're done sorting the cards, ask informants to name each pile and describe it in their own words. Record the names and the criteria for each pile in your notes. When you are done, turn the cards over. On a separate line, record all the numbers for each pile.

Recording the Data From Pile Sorts

Table 8.2 shows the pile sort data for one male informant who sorted the names of 18 fruits. The 18 fruits are listed at the top of the table. The bottom of the table shows the five piles that the informant made and which fruits went in each pile. For example, the informant put orange, lemon, and grapefruit in pile #1, and blueberry and strawberry in pile #4.

Table 8.2 Pile Sort Data for One Person for 18 Fruits

1. Apple	10. Strawberry
2. Orange	11. Lemon
3. Papaya	12. Cantaloupe
4. Mango	13. Grapefruit
5. Peach	14. Plum
6. Blueberry	15. Banana
7. Watermelon	16. Avocado
8. Pineapple	17. Fig
9. Pear	18. Cherry

One Person's Sorting of 18 Fruits

Pile #1: 2, 11, 13

Pile #2: 1, 5, 9, 14, 17, 18

Pile #3: 3, 4, 8, 15, 16

Pile #4: 6, 10

Pile #5: 7, 12

Importing the Data From Pile Sorts

We use ANTHROPAC (Borgatti 1992; Appendix) to import these data. The program reads the data and converts them into an item-by-item similarity matrix, shown in Table 8.3 (see Box 8.4).

This similarity matrix is similar to the one we saw in Chapter 5. When the informant put items 2, 11, and 13 (orange, lemon, grapefruit) into a pile, he did so because he thought the items were similar. To indicate this, there is a 1 in the matrix where items 2 and 11 intersect; another 1 in the cell where items 2 and 13 intersect; and another 1 in the cell where 11 and 13 intersect.

And similarly for Pile #2: There is a 1 in the 1-5 cell, the 1-9 cell, the 1-14 cell, and so on. There are 0s in all the cells that represent no similarity of a pair of items (for this informant) and 1s down the diagonal (since items are similar to themselves). Also, notice that if 11 is similar to 13, then 13 is similar

---

Box 8.4

Getting Data Into the Computer

Once you have pile sort data into a computer in the form of a matrix, you can use any full-featured statistics program to analyze them. We used ANTHROPAC (Borgatti 1992) to import the pile sort data and UCINET (Borgatti et al. 2004) to analyze the data and to produce the graphs in this chapter (see Appendix).

A major headache in all computer-based data analysis—whether you're analyzing quantitative or qualitative data—is file compatibility. All major statistics programs can import data from a variety of sources. SPSS for example, can import data from Microsoft Excel. SPSS and Excel do not share file structures, but SPSS will take Excel data and convert them to a file that SPSS can read.

Statistics programs, however, can not easily import the kind of data used in cultural domain analysis. ANTHROPAC is a good utility for doing this. UCINET is used in social network analysis. Network researchers rely heavily on graphics, and UCINET has modules for producing publishable graphics.

We use UCINET in cultural domain analysis because it shares files with ANTHROPAC. Any data you import with ANTHROPAC are available to UCINET for analysis. UCINET also can export data as an Excel file, so you can use the data in your favorite statistics program.

---

to 11, so this particular matrix is also symmetric. In a symmetric matrix, the bottom and top halves (above and below the diagonal of 1s) are identical. (Further Reading: pile sorts.)

◆ ANALYZING PILE SORT DATA: MDS

If you examine it carefully, you'll see that, despite the 1s and 0s, there is not a shred of math in Table 8.3. It contains nothing more than the information in the bottom half of Table 8.2, displayed as 1s and 0s, and there is nothing numerical about those 1s and 0s. They simply stand for whether oranges and papayas and so on were put in the same pile or not. But by substituting 1s and 0s for the relationship between the items, we can use software to look for patterns in the informant's pile sort data.

Table 8.3 Similarity Matrix From One Person's Pile-Sorting of the 18 Fruits

	Ap	Or	Pap	Man	Pea	Blu	Wat	Pin	Per	Str	Lem	Can	Gpf	Plu	Ban	Avc	Fig	Chr
1. Apple	1	0	0	0	1	0	0	0	1	0	0	0	0	1	0	0	1	1
2. Orange	0	1	0	0	0	0	0	0	0	0	0	0	1	0	0	0	0	0
3. Papaya	0	0	1	1	0	0	0	1	0	0	1	0	0	0	1	1	0	0
4. Mango	0	0	1	1	0	0	0	1	0	0	0	0	0	0	1	1	0	0
5. Peach	1	0	0	0	1	0	0	0	1	0	0	0	0	1	0	0	1	1
6. Blueberry	0	0	0	0	0	1	0	0	0	1	0	0	0	0	0	0	0	0
7. Watermelon	0	0	0	0	0	0	1	0	0	0	0	1	0	0	0	0	0	0
8. Pineapple	0	0	1	1	0	0	0	1	0	0	0	0	0	0	1	1	0	0
9. Pear	1	0	0	0	1	0	0	0	1	0	0	0	0	1	0	0	1	1
10. Strawberry	0	0	0	0	0	1	0	0	0	1	0	0	0	0	0	0	0	0
11. Lemon	0	1	0	0	0	0	0	0	0	0	1	0	1	0	0	0	0	0
12. Cantaloupe	0	0	0	0	0	0	1	0	0	0	0	1	0	0	0	0	0	0
13. Grapefruit	0	1	0	0	0	0	0	0	0	0	0	0	1	0	0	0	0	0
14. Plum	1	0	0	0	1	0	0	0	1	0	0	0	0	1	0	0	1	1
15. Banana	0	0	1	1	0	0	0	0	0	0	0	0	0	0	1	1	0	0
16. Avocado	0	0	1	1	0	0	0	1	0	0	0	0	0	0	1	1	0	0
17. Fig	1	0	0	0	1	0	0	0	1	0	0	0	0	1	0	0	1	1
18. Cherry	1	0	0	0	1	0	0	0	1	0	0	0	0	1	0	0	1	1

Figure 8.2 is a multidimensional scaling, or MDS, of these data. MDS is one of several visualization methods—now widely used in all the sciences—that look for patterns in numerical data and display those patterns graphically (see Box 8.5).

The MDS in Figure 8.2 shows the pattern in Table 8.3—that is, it shows how one informant sees the similarities among the 18 fruits.

Box 8.5

Multidimensional Scaling

MDS maps the relations among numbers in a matrix. Look carefully at Table 8.3. There are 1s in the cells 2-11, 2-13, and 11-13. This is because the informant put orange (2), lemon (11), and grapefruit (13) in one pile and nothing else in that pile. This behavior is presented graphically in Figure 8.2 with the orange-lemon-grapefruit cluster shown separated from other clusters.

It's convenient to think of the MDS graph in Figure 8.2 as a sort of mental map—that is, it represents what the informant was thinking when he pile sorted those fruits. We say "sort of mental map" because MDS graphs of pile-sort data are not one-to-one maps of what's going on inside people's heads. We treat them, however, as a rough proxy for what people were thinking when they made piles of cards or words or whatever.

You'll sometimes see MDS called "smallest-space analysis." That's because MDS programs work out the best spatial representation of a set of objects that are represented by a set of similarities. (Further Reading: multidimensional scaling.)

◆ ANALYZING PILE SORT DATA: CLUSTER ANALYSIS

There are two things to look at in an MDS graph: dimensions and clusters. Clusters are usually easier to see. Looking at Figure 8.2, it seems to us like there's a citrus cluster, a berry cluster, and a melon cluster at the top, with a fruit tree cluster and a tropical cluster on the bottom. We can check our intuition about these clusters by running a cluster analysis, shown in Figure 8.3 (see Box 8.6).

Read Figure 8.3 as follows: At the first level of clustering, the informant put 7 (watermelon) and 12 (cantaloupe) together, and he put 6 (blueberry)

Figure 8.2 Multidimensional Scaling of 18 Fruits From One Pile Sort

Grapefruit
Cantaloupe
Lemon
Strawberry
Watermelon
Orange
Blueberry
Plum
Pineapple
Apple
Peach
Mango
Fig
Avocado
Papaya
Pear
Cherry
Banana

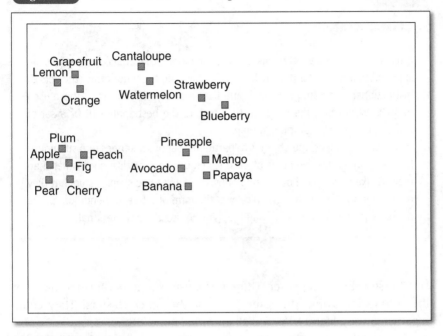

Figure 8.3 Cluster Analysis of 18 Fruits From One Pile Sort

Apple 1
Plum 14
Peach 5
Fig 17
Pear 9
Cherry 18
Lemon 11
Grapefruit 13
Orange 2
Papaya 3
Avocado 16
Banana 15
Mango 4
Pineapple 8
Strawberry 10
Blueberry 6
Cantaloupe 12
Watermelon 7

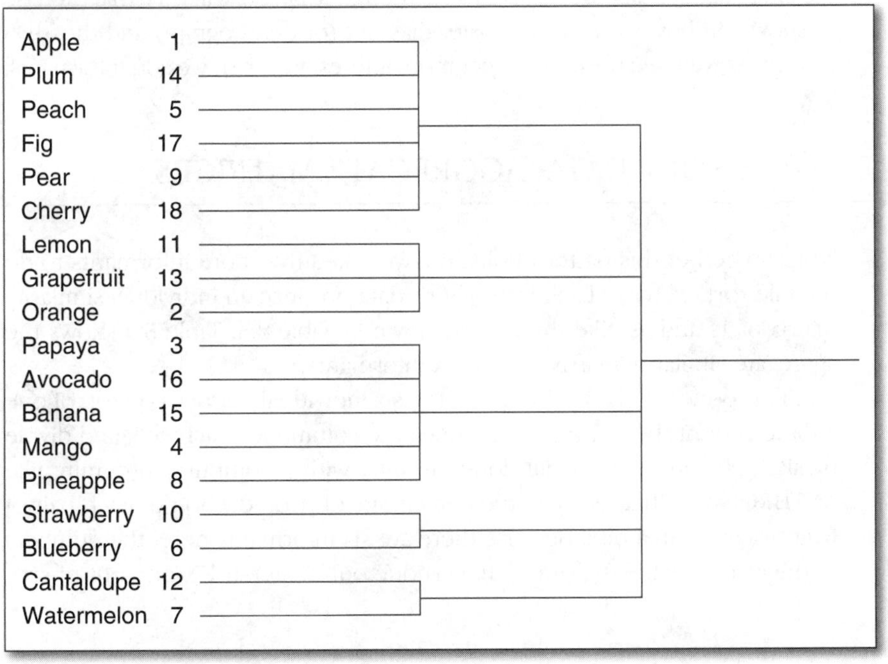

> ### Box 8.6
>
> #### Cluster Analysis
>
> Cluster analysis is another visualization method. Like MDS, it operates on similarity matrices, like that in Table 8.3. However, the algorithms (the sets of instructions) for finding clusters in matrices are very different from those used in MDS. With MDS, the program tries to find the best spatial fit of a set of similarities. An MDS graph is a map.
>
> In cluster analysis, the object is to partition a set of similarities into subgroups (clusters), where the members of each subgroup are more like each other than they are like members of other subgroups. Clusters can be simply listed, but they are commonly represented graphically in the form of a tree, or dendrogram, like the ones shown in Figures 8.3 and 8.5. (Further Reading: cluster analysis.)

and 10 (strawberry) together. These two clusters together form a cluster at the second level. And the same goes for the other clusters: They come together at the second level and all form one big cluster.

Because there is just one informant, there can only be two levels. The first level is the level at which the informant made the separate piles. The second is the entire set of fruits. We've taken you through what looks like a trivial exercise to show you how to read the cluster diagram (or dendrogram) and the MDS picture. As we'll see next, things get more interesting when we add informants.

◆ ANALYZING PILE SORT DATA: AGGREGATE MATRICES

To test whether this pattern holds up, we asked five more informants to do the pile sort exercise. Each informant's data produce an individual similarity matrix of 1s and 0s, like the matrix shown in Table 8.3. Table 8.4 shows the aggregate similarity matrix for the six informants.

To produce Table 8.4, just stack the six individual matrices on top of one another, count the number of 1s down the column for each cell, and divide by six. (Obviously, this is all done instantly with a computer program, like ANTHROPAC.) That tells you the percentage of people who put each pair of fruits together in a pile. Because there are six informants here, the numbers in the cells of Table 8.4 can be 0.00 (none out of six), 0.17 (one out of six),

Table 8.4 Aggregate Similarity Matrix From Six Pile Sorts of the 18 Fruits in Table 8.2

	Ap	Or	Pap	Man	Pea	Blu	Wat	Pin	Per	Str	Lem	Can	Gpf	Plu	Ban	Avc	Fig	Chr
1. Apple	1.00	0.00	0.00	0.00	0.83	0.00	0.17	0.00	0.83	0.00	0.00	0.00	0.00	0.83	0.17	0.00	0.17	0.33
2. Orange	0.00	1.00	0.17	0.17	0.00	0.00	0.17	0.17	0.00	0.00	0.83	0.17	1.00	0.00	0.00	0.17	0.00	0.00
3. Papaya	0.00	0.17	1.00	0.67	0.17	0.00	0.17	0.50	0.17	0.00	0.00	0.17	0.17	0.17	0.33	0.67	0.17	0.00
4. Mango	0.00	0.17	0.67	1.00	0.00	0.00	0.17	0.50	0.00	0.00	0.00	0.33	0.17	0.00	0.33	0.67	0.00	0.00
5. Peach	0.83	0.00	0.17	0.00	1.00	0.00	0.00	0.00	1.00	0.00	0.00	0.00	0.00	1.00	0.17	0.17	0.17	0.33
6. Blueberry	0.00	0.00	0.00	0.00	0.00	1.00	0.00	0.00	0.00	0.83	0.00	0.00	0.00	0.00	0.00	0.00	0.50	0.67
7. Watermelon	0.17	0.17	0.17	0.17	0.00	0.00	1.00	0.17	0.00	0.00	0.00	0.83	0.17	0.00	0.00	0.17	0.00	0.00
8. Pineapple	0.00	0.17	0.50	0.50	0.00	0.00	0.17	1.00	0.00	0.00	0.00	0.17	0.17	0.00	0.50	0.50	0.00	0.00
9. Pear	0.83	0.00	0.17	0.00	1.00	0.00	0.00	0.00	1.00	0.00	0.00	0.00	0.00	1.00	0.17	0.17	0.17	0.33
10. Strawberry	0.00	0.00	0.00	0.00	0.00	0.83	0.00	0.00	0.00	1.00	0.00	0.00	0.00	0.00	0.00	0.00	0.50	0.50
11. Lemon	0.00	0.83	0.00	0.00	0.00	0.00	0.00	0.00	0.00	0.00	1.00	0.00	0.83	0.00	0.00	0.00	0.00	0.00
12. Cantaloupe	0.00	0.17	0.17	0.33	0.00	0.00	0.83	0.17	0.00	0.00	0.00	1.00	0.17	0.00	0.00	0.17	0.00	0.00
13. Grapefruit	0.00	1.00	0.17	0.17	0.00	0.00	0.17	0.17	0.00	0.00	0.83	0.17	1.00	0.00	0.00	0.17	0.00	0.00
14. Plum	0.83	0.00	0.17	0.00	1.00	0.00	0.00	0.00	1.00	0.00	0.00	0.00	0.00	1.00	0.17	0.17	0.17	0.33
15. Banana	0.17	0.00	0.33	0.33	0.17	0.00	0.00	0.50	0.17	0.00	0.00	0.00	0.00	0.17	1.00	0.33	0.00	0.00
16. Avocado	0.00	0.17	0.67	0.67	0.17	0.00	0.17	0.50	0.17	0.00	0.00	0.17	0.17	0.17	0.33	1.00	0.00	0.00
17. Fig	0.17	0.00	0.00	0.00	0.17	0.50	0.00	0.00	0.17	0.50	0.00	0.00	0.00	0.17	0.00	0.00	1.00	0.50
18. Cherry	0.33	0.00	0.00	0.00	0.33	0.67	0.00	0.00	0.33	0.50	0.00	0.00	0.00	0.33	0.00	0.00	0.50	1.00

0.33 (two out of six), 0.50 (three out of six), 0.67 (four out of six), 0.83 (five out of six), and 1.00 (six out of six).

For example, reading across the top row in Table 8.4, we see that five out of six informants (83%) put apple and pear in the same pile. Reading across the third row, we see that four out of six people (67%) put papaya and mango in the same pile. And so on. Just like Table 8.3, Table 8.4 is symmetric (check it and see for yourself).

◆ MDS AND CLUSTER ANALYSIS OF THE AGGREGATE MATRIX

Figure 8.4 shows the MDS plot of the data in Table 8.4. It looks pretty much like Figure 8.2, but there are some differences. Averaging across the six informants, figs and cherries now appear to be in a separate cluster and to be a bridge between the berry group (strawberries and blueberries) and the major tree-fruit group (apples, plums, peaches, and pears). Furthermore, banana, which was in the tropical fruit cluster for our first informant, now appears to be a bridge between the tropical fruit cluster (mangos, papayas, pineapples, and avocados) and the traditional tree fruit cluster (apples, plums, peaches, and pears) (see Box 8.7).

The cluster analysis on the data in Table 8.4 is shown in Figure 8.5. It confirms that our informants saw cherries and figs as related to strawberries and blueberries and saw all four of these fruits as more closely related to apples, plums, peaches, and pears than to all the other fruits. It isn't that our first informant was anomalous or idiosyncratic. In fact,

---

Box 8.7

Clusters and Bridges

What does it mean to say that "figs and cherries appear to be a bridge between the berry group and major tree-fruit group" or that "banana appears to be a bridge between tropical fruits and traditional tree fruits"?

When we interviewed people about why they put various fruits together, some people who put figs and cherries with apples and pears said "These all grow on trees." People who put figs and/or cherries into other piles said things like "Figs are more exotic, but not like mangoes" or "Cherries grow on trees, but they are small and clumpy." Some informants said that banana was a tropical fruit and "went with papaya," but others said it was unique and belonged in a group by itself. One person said it belonged with apples and pears "because you can mix them together to make fruit salad."

We always ask people to explain their pile choices. Later, when we see figs and cherries in an MDS graph lying between a berries cluster and traditional tree-fruit cluster, we have some basis for interpreting the graph.

there is a lot of consensus across the six informants about what goes with what. But the consensus isn't perfect; there is intracultural variation.

This is, of course, well known to all qualitative researchers, but MDS and cluster analysis let us examine the variation and the consensus more systematically (see Box 8.8).

Figure 8.4 Multidimensional Scaling of the Data in Table 8.4

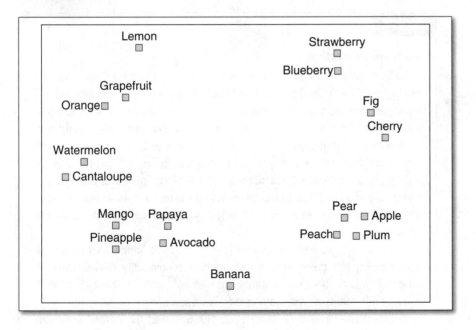

Figure 8.5 Cluster Analysis of the Data in Table 8.4 From Six Pile Sorts

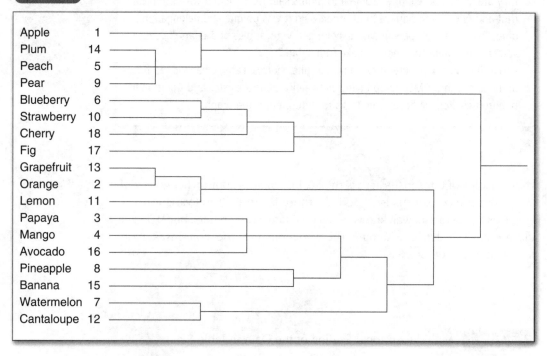

Apple	1
Plum	14
Peach	5
Pear	9
Blueberry	6
Strawberry	10
Cherry	18
Fig	17
Grapefruit	13
Orange	2
Lemon	11
Papaya	3
Mango	4
Avocado	16
Pineapple	8
Banana	15
Watermelon	7
Cantaloupe	12

Box 8.8

Consensus Analysis

There is a formal method for measuring consensus, which we'll describe only briefly here. The method is based on the observation that people who know a lot about something tend to agree with one another (Boster 1986). If you give a test about the rules of baseball to a group of serious fans and a group who never watch the game, you'd find that: (1) The fans will agree on the answers more often than will the nonfans; and (2) the serious fans will get the answers right more often than will the nonfans. This is pretty much like any test you might take in a class. The instructor makes up the test and an answer key with the correct answers. Your job is to match your answers with those on the answer key.

But what if there were no answer key? That's what happens when we ask people to, say, rate the social status of others in a community. We wind up with a lot of opinions about social status, but we don't have an answer key to tell whether informants are accurate in their reporting of this information.

A model developed by Romney et al. (1986)–called the cultural consensus model–shows that, under three conditions, people who agree about the contents of a cultural domain actually know more about that domain. Here are the conditions:

1. People share a common culture and there is a culturally correct answer to any question you ask them. Any variation among people in their knowledge about a cultural domain is the result of individual differences in knowledge, not the result of their being members of subcultures.

2. People answer your test questions independently of one another.

3. All the questions in your test come from the same cultural domain. A test that asks about American kinship and American football would be a poor test.

In practice, the consensus method works as follows:

1. Give a set of at least 30 people a test that asks them to make some judgments about 30 to 40 items in a cultural domain. It is best to use true-false and yes-no questions such as: "You can get AIDS from touching the body of someone who died from it," or "A field goal is worth 7 points." You can use multiple-choice or open-ended, fill-in-the-blank questions, but this makes the analysis tougher.

2. Produce a person-by-person agreement matrix of the answers. If 100 students take a 40-question, true-false test, then each pair of students could agree 40 times, irrespective of whether they got the answer to each question right or wrong. We count the agreement for each pair of students (1 and 2, 1 and 3, 1 and 4, and so on, down to student 39 and 40) and we divide each count by 40. This produces a 100-by-100, student-by-student agreement matrix.

3. Factor the agreement matrix. Factor analysis is based on the simple and compelling idea that if things we observe are correlated with each other, they must have some underlying thing in common. Factor analysis refers to a set of techniques for identifying and interpreting those underlying variables.

If the first factor in the analysis is at least three times the size of the second factor, then: (1) The first factor is knowledge about the domain (because agreement equals knowledge under conditions of the model); and (2) the individual factor scores are a measure of knowledge for each person who takes the test.

Can you really lose the answer key to a test and recover it by analyzing the matrix of agreements among the test takers? We tested this with data from 160 students in a real introduction to anthropology class. The correlation between the percentage of questions they got right, according to the answer key, and their scores on the first factor of the agreement matrix was 0.96—nearly perfect. In other words, as long as the three conditions of the model hold, you can apply consensus analysis to tests of people's responses about who hangs out with whom in an organization, or what people think are proper foods to give infants, or ways to avoid getting AIDS, and so on. (Further Reading: consensus analysis.)

♦ FOLK TAXONOMIES

A taxonomy is a list of things (music, foods, vehicles, electronic gadgets, countries) and a set of rules for organizing those things into related sets. We're all familiar with scientific taxonomies for plants and animals, but listen carefully to ordinary speech and you'll hear people invoking taxonomic rules all the time (see Box 8.9).

Overheard at the supermarket: "Where's the barley?" "It's with the rice, over on aisle 4."

You'll also hear people *negotiating* the rules.

Overheard at the zoo: "What's that monkey doing?" "Actually, it's an ape." "Really? what's the diff?"

Overheard on a college campus: "I can't tell if I like Shania Twain because her music is country or pop, I just know I like her."

Box 8.9

Scientific and Folk Taxonomies

A scientific taxonomy is one that is accepted by a community of scholars. Linnaeus spent years developing the classification system that bears his name, but when he published the first version of it, in 1735, it was one man's ideas about how natural organisms are related. The scheme was quickly recognized as a useful way of classifying living organisms, but new theory and new data changed the system over time. In a sense, then, all taxonomies begin as folk taxonomies and some folk taxonomies develop into scientific ones.

In the social sciences, scholars of ethnobotany and ethnozoology are interested in how people in different cultural groups organize their knowledge of the natural world. Ethnobotanical and ethnozoological taxonomies usually don't mirror scientific taxonomies, but the whole point of folk taxonomic research is to understand cultural knowledge on its own terms.

The conversation that followed that last snippet was about blended gen-res (think New Age–Latin and Reggae-Blues) and about artists who succeed in more than one genre. The people who were having that conversation were relying on the fact that they shared a taxonomy. Every once in a while, they would renegotiate the rules for the taxonomy.

"Glenn Campbell was never really a country singer." "What do you mean? Of course he was."

HOW TO MAKE A TAXONOMY: LISTS AND FRAMES ♦

The most widely used methods for building folk taxonomies are pile sorts, cluster analysis, and frame elicitation (Frake 1964) (Further Reading: frame elicitation.).

Ask a native speaker of American English the following: "List the kinds of foods you know?" A typical list would include things like: "meat, fish, pasta, fruits, vegetables, snacks. . . ."

After the first round, ask the following: "What kinds of meats are there?" and "What kinds of fruits are there?" "What kinds of snacks are there?" . . . and so on. The idea here is to be systematic. That is, take every item the informant named in the first round and ask the follow-up question to expand the list one level down in the informant's taxonomy. A typical answer to the question "What kinds of meats are there?" is "beef, lamb, pork, chicken, turkey, ham, venison, game. . . ." As we get further down into any folk taxonomy, people mix and drop levels of contrast. Here, the informant mentioned chicken and turkey, which are both kinds of poultry, but he didn't mention poultry at all. Poultry is a dropped level of contrast, but it may take several informants to discover the level of contrast called "poultry" in the American English taxonomy of meats. Note, too, that the informant mentioned both venison and game. Here, the informant slipped in two levels of contrast because venison is a type of game.

At this point, you would ask: "What kinds of beef [lamb] [chicken] [etc.] are there?" Do this with several informants and you'll discover that beef is divided into steak, chops, hamburger, and so on and that steak is divided into T-bone and Porterhouse and filet mignon and so on, and you'll find that vegetarians don't make as many distinctions as carnivores do about kinds of meat.

These questions get you the list of items in the domain—in this case, the list of foods—and some idea about the major types. The next step is to find out about overlaps. For example, some foods, like avocados, get classified as fruits by some people and as vegetables by others. Some people think of peanuts as a source of protein; others think of them as a snack. In fact, in real folk taxonomies, you'll find people classifying items differently, depending on the circumstances. You can learn about the possible overlaps in folk categories by using substitution frames:

Is _____ a kind of _____?

Is _____ a part of _____?

Once you have a list of terms in a domain, and a list of categories, you can use this substitution frame for all possible combinations. Are marshmallows a kind of meat? A kind of fish? A kind of snack? This can get really tedious, but discovering levels of contrast—magenta is a kind of red; cashews are a kind of nut; alto is a kind of sax; or ice cream is a kind of dessert—just takes plain hard work. Unless you're a child, in which case all this discovery is just plain fun. In fact, one object of this kind of research is to discover the kind of cultural knowledge that every 10-year-old knows about her or his culture.

A common way to display folk taxonomies is with a branching tree diagram. Figure 8.6 shows a tree diagram for part of a folk taxonomy of passenger cars, elicited in Morgantown, West Virginia, from Jack in 1976 (we saw Jack's taxonomy of cars in Figure 6.13 in the chapter on kinds of models).

Things to Look for in Folk Taxonomies

There are five important points to make about the taxonomy shown in Figure 8.6:

1. Intracultural variation is common in folk taxonomies. That is, different people may use different words to refer to the same category of things. Sometimes, in fact, terms can be almost idiosyncratic. Jack distinguished among what he called "regular cars," "station wagons," and "vans." The term "regular cars" is not one you normally see in automobile ads, or hear from a salesperson on a car lot.

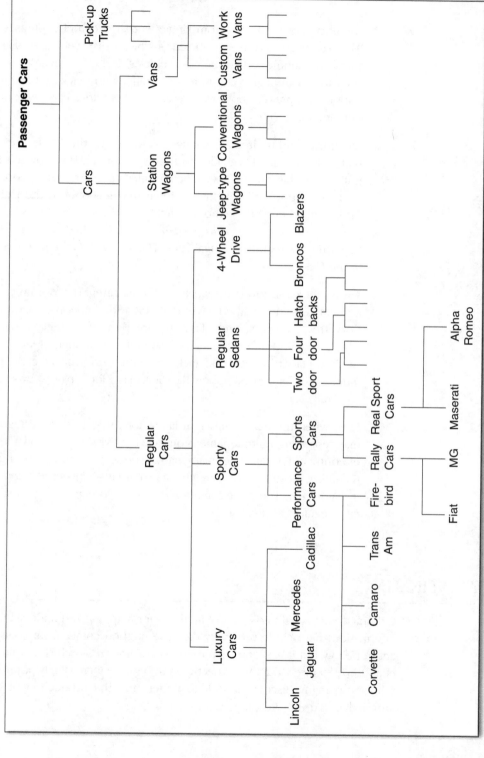

Figure 8.6 Part of Jack's Taxonomy of Cars and Trucks

SOURCE: Bernard, H. R. (2006). *Research methods in anthropology: Qualitative and quantitative approaches* (4th ed., p. 540). Thousand Oaks, CA: Sage. Copyright © 2006 Sage Publications.

2. Category labels can run from single words to complex phrases. In West Virginia, the category labeled "4-wheel drive" vehicles in Figure 8.6 was sometimes called "off-road vehicles" in 1976, or even "vehicles you can go camping in or tow a horse trailer with." Jack said that Jeep station wagons were both wagons and 4-wheel-drive cars you can go camping in.

3. Categories and their labels change over time. By the 1990s, the cars that Jack had called "vehicles you can go camping in or tow a horse trailer with" back in 1976 were being called "utes" by some people— short for "sport utility vehicle." Today, most people in the United States call them SUVs, though small SUVs are sometimes called "cute utes" and *Car and Driver Magazine* had an article in September 2008 titled "Frugal Utes: The 10 Most Fuel-Efficient SUVs in the U.S."

4. Always look for covert categories—that is, categories of things that are real but not named (Whorf 1945). Some people insist that Corvettes, Camaros, and Maseratis are part of a single category, which they find difficult to name (one informant suggested "sporty cars" as a label). Others, like Jack, separate "performance cars" from "sports cars" and even subdivide sports cars into "true sports cars" and "rally cars."

5. Even when there are consistent labels for categories, the categories may represent multiple dimensions, each of which has its own levels of contrast. For example, many native speakers of American English recognize a category of "foreign cars" that cuts across the taxonomy in Figure 8.6. There are foreign sports cars, foreign luxury cars, foreign regular cars, and so on.

◆ AND FINALLY. . . .

Cultural domain analysis is a set of methods for mapping and understanding information that people use every day. The method comes from cognitive anthropology, but it has long been used in consumer research (J. C. Johnson et al. 1987; Stefflre 1972). We expect CDA to become increasingly popular as scholars in many disciplines seek to understand the production of local knowledge. (Further Reading: examples of CDA.)

Further Reading

◆ Key resources for cultural domain analysis include Spradley (1972, 1979) and Borgatti (1999) as well as Borgatti's software (1992; Borgatti et al. 2004). In psychology, see Rosch (1975) and Rosch and Mervis (1975) for important work on the structure of semantic categories.

◆ For more on free lists, see D. D. Brewer (1995), Furlow (2003), Henley (1969), Longfield (2004), Parr and Lashua (2004), Quinlan (2005), Ryan et al. (2000), J. J. Smith and Borgatti (1997), and E. C. Thompson and Juan (2006).

◆ For more on salience measures in free lists, see Quinlan (2005), Robbins and Nolan (1997, 2000), J. J. Smith (1993), and Sutrop (2001).

◆ For more on methods for collecting triad tests and paired comparisons, see Bernard (2006), Borgatti (1999), and Weller and Romney (1988). For examples of triad tests, see D. D. Brewer (1995), Durrenberger and Erem (2005), Furlow (2003), Nyamongo (2002), Reyes-Garcia et al. (2004), and N. Ross et al. (2005). For examples of paired comparisons, see M. L. Burton (2003), Durrenberger (2003), and Durrenberger and Erem (2005).

◆ For examples of the use of pile sorts, see Alvarado (1998), Harman (2001), Nyamongo (1999, 2002), and Trotter and Potter (1993).

◆ For more on multidimensional scaling, see Borgatti (1997), DeJordy et al. (2007), Kruskal and Wish (1978), Mugavin (2008), Pinkley et al. (2005), and Shepard et al. (1972).

◆ For more on cluster analysis, see Aldemnderfer and Blashfield (1984) and Borgatti (1994).

◆ For a review of consensus analysis, see Weller (2007). For examples of consensus analysis, see Caulkins (2001), de Munck et al. (2002), Dressler et al. (2005), Furlow (2003), Harvey and Bird (2004), Horowitz (2007), Jaskyte and Dressler (2004), M. Miller et al. (2004), and Swora (2003).

◆ For more on frame elicitation, see D'Andrade et al. (1972), Garro (1986), and Metzger and Williams (1966).

◆ For some examples of CDA, see Collins and Dressler (2008), Dressler et al. (2007), Eyre and Milstein (1999), and J. L. Ross et al. (2002).

CHAPTER *9*

KWIC ANALYSIS, WORD COUNTS, AND SEMANTIC NETWORK ANALYSIS

INTRODUCTION

Free lists and pile sorts are systematic methods for collecting words and phrases, but most qualitative data come in the form of free-flowing texts.

191

There are four major types of analysis for this latter kind of data. In one, the text is segmented into chunks that conform to a set of themes and the themes are analyzed qualitatively or quantitatively. This is the basis for grounded theory, content analysis, and analytic induction—the subjects of Chapters 12, 13, and 15. In the second type, the entire text is examined closely for patterns. This is the basis for discourse analysis, narrative analysis, and schema analysis—the subjects of Chapters 10, 11, and 14.

Third, there are mixed methods, like ethnographic decision modeling, the subject of Chapter 16.

In the fourth major type of analysis, the text is segmented into its most fundamental components: words. This is the basis for KWIC (key-word-in-context) analysis, word counts, and semantic network analysis—the subjects of this chapter.

◆ KWIC—KEY WORD IN CONTEXT

The key-word-in-context method is summed up in J. R. Firth's famous aphorism: "You shall know a word by the company it keeps" (1957:11). In other words, to understand a concept, look at how it is used. The term KWIC was coined by an IBM engineer (Luhn 1960), but the general method has a very long history. Since at least the 13th century (Busa 1971:595), students of the Old and New Testaments have produced concordances, or lists of every substantive word in those texts, each with its associated sentence, so that people might study the meaning of each word in all its contexts. Concordances have been done on sacred texts from other religions (see Kassis [1983] on the Koran) and on famous works of literature from Euripides (Allen and Italie 1954), to Beowulf (Bessinger 1969), to Dylan Thomas (Farringdon and Farringdon 1980).

Today, any digitized work essentially contains its own concordance. When you search for a word, you see it in context and if you keep searching for the same word, you see it in all its contexts. KWIC programs simply automate this process, searching a text for every use of a particular word or phrase and printing out all the hits, within their contexts. (See Appendix for pointers to KWIC software.) If you run a KWIC program on all the substantive words in a text and then arrange the hits in alphabetical order, by substantive words, you've got a classic concordance.

An Example of KWIC

The concept of "deconstruction" is an abstract term used by social scientists, literary critics, and journalists. Jacques Derrida, who coined the term, did not define it. To Derrida, the meaning of any text is inherently unstable and variable. As an exercise, we wondered if we could understand the term by looking at how one author actually used it. We found an interesting article titled "Deconstructing Development Theory: Feminism, the Public/Private Dichotomy and the Mexican Maquiladoras," by Joanne Wright (1997). Because the article was from a digital database, we were able to download it and search it with KWIC software for each use of the word "deconstruction." There were 19 hits, shown in Table 9.1.

In doing a KWIC analysis, you have to decide on the form of the word that you search for. We searched for the complete word, "deconstruction," but this didn't get us the verb forms "deconstructs" and "deconstructing." Our analysis might be different if we had a larger pool of words and more uses of words that contain the stem "deconstruct." Also, we decided to pull only the sentence in which the word "deconstruction" was found. Here again, our analysis might have been different if we had increased the context and pulled the sentences before and after the sentence in which the word was found—or even the entire paragraph.

To continue our KWIC analysis, we printed each of the sentences that contained the word "deconstruction" on a separate note card and sorted the cards into piles of sentences that we thought somehow "go together." This method taps into the various meanings that we carry around for the word "deconstruction."

The KWIC method gives us a way to deconstruct the meaning of the word "deconstruction," as used by one author. It seems to us that Wright uses it to mean a tool, a process of analysis, the results of an analysis, and a theory. We can see whether our interpretation is idiosyncratic or is shared by others by asking colleagues to sort the 19 statements in Table 9.1 into piles and to explain why they think various statements go together. We can also systematically compare Wright's use of the term "deconstruction" with its use by others by creating tables like 9.1 for other articles.

Finally, we can apply the KWIC method to any word or phrase that we want to analyze. To get an understanding of what the phrase "corporate culture" means, for example, we could examine its use in articles from the *Wall Street Journal* and the *Financial Times of London*. (Further Reading: KWIC.)

WORD COUNTS

Like so many simple things, it's easy to lose sight of how much we can learn from just counting words in a text. Although it's not a perfect relationship, words and phrases that appear more often in a text tend to be more salient

Table 9.1 KWIC Table for the Word *Deconstruction* in Wright (1997)

1	This varied group of postmodern thinkers employs the tool of *deconstruction* to critically evaluate—indeed, to peel back the discursive layers of—development's assumptions: capitalist economics, progress, modernity, and rationality.
2	Their *deconstructions* reveal development's asymmetric dichotomization of the world into modern, Westernized societies on the one hand and traditional, "backward" societies on the other.
3	It will be the purpose of this article to utilize the deconstructive tool from a feminist perspective, to carry the postmodern theorists' *deconstructions* one step further to unravel the elements of development theory that carry Western gender biases regarding proper roles for women and men based on their "true nature."
4	This process of feminist *deconstruction* correlates with a contemporary trend in feminist analysis, that of deconstructing institutions such as the state and law, and discourses of democratic theory and international relations theory, to expose their reliance upon, and infusion with, gender.
5	Feminist *deconstruction*, then, is distinct from the earlier empirical project that enumerates women's experiences with development.
6	Feminist *deconstruction* is "not simply about women," but about the interdependent constructions of masculine and feminine, and about shifting feminist analysis from the margin to the centre.
7	The first step in this exercise is to briefly describe the postmodern approach to Western development theory, following which a theoretical feminist *deconstruction* can be carried out.
8	It will be instructive, as well, to apply this *deconstruction* to an example of development in practice, the maquiladora project of Mexico.
9	*Deconstruction* will be used here to refer to a critical method, a conceptual tool, with which the ideological layers of development are peeled back and examined.
10	The process of *deconstruction* is part of the larger postmodern project, which is to de-naturalize some of the dominant features of our way of life; to point out that those entities that we unthinkingly experience as "natural" (they might even include capitalism, patriarchy, liberal humanism) are in fact "cultural"; made by us, not given to us (Hutcheon 1989:2).
11	Postmodern *deconstructions* of development recognize that world cultures have always been mutually influencing and that there exists no such thing as a "pure" culture to be preserved and cloistered away.
12	A viable *deconstruction* of development can be commenced without relying on the binarism of universal/relative.
13	What *deconstruction* does show is that development has, from its inception, posited a Western model as "the most successful way of life mankind [sic] has ever known" (Ayres 1978: xxxii–xxxiii) and that the implementation of this assumption through development has proved destructive to viable and vital cultures and societies.

14	It is this gap in postmodern theorizing that necessitates a specifically feminist *deconstruction* of the development paradigm.
15	Moreover, a feminist *deconstruction* of development theory takes as axiomatic the idea that women, in practice, transgress the border between public and private.
16	Just as postmodern theory finds the dichotomies of developed/underdeveloped, modern/traditional, and so forth to be central features of development thought, a feminist *deconstruction* reveals that development theory is phallocentric as it organizes social life along the lines of the dichotomies of man/woman, public/private, reason/emotion and knowledge/experience.
17	Rather than trying to reconcile these dichotomies, as women and development theory has tried to do, a feminist *deconstruction* recognizes them as instrumental to the Westernizing project of development.
18	Feminist *deconstruction*, then, must involve changing the parameters of who can know and who can produce theory; it must involve relocating the site of knowledge and theory creation.
19	Derrida, who coined the term, refuses to define *deconstruction*, arguing that any attempt to define it is also subject to the process of deconstruction.

SOURCE: Wright, J. 1997. Deconstructing development theory: feminism, the public/private dichotomy, and the Mexican maquiladoras. *Canadian Journal of Sociology and Anthropology* 34:71–91.

to the writer or speaker who produced the text. Jasienski (2006) found that natural scientists use the word "unexpected" to describe their findings 2.3 times more often than do scholars in the social sciences and humanities. "One might think," says Jasienski, "that academic machismo or realism would cause scientists to downplay their surprise, but, on the other hand, overstating the level of astonishment may occur when striving for media attention" (2006:1112).

Word counts have been used to trace the ebb and flow of support for political figures over time (Danielson and Lasorsa 1997; de Sola Pool 1952) and to help determine the true authorship of disputed texts. Mosteller and Wallace (1964) compared the use of words common to the writings of James Madison and Alexander Hamilton and concluded that Madison and not Hamilton had written 12 of the *Federalist Papers*. You'd be surprised at what we can learn from counting words. (**Further Reading:** authorship studies.)

◆ WORDS AND MATRICES

At the heart of word count analysis is the conversion of text into respondent-by-word matrices. To illustrate, we asked five university students the following:

Please recall the last time that you had a cold or the flu. Take a moment and think about this illness episode. Try to remember as many details as you can. After you have thought about the illness, please describe it in as much detail as possible.

Figure 9.1 displays the results, and Figure 9.2 shows how we converted the data into a word-by-respondent matrix.

◆ STOP LISTS

Before we convert these texts into matrices, we give the software what's called a stop list—a list of common words (like prepositions, conjunctions, and articles) that we don't want counted in the matrix. This is shown in the middle column of Figure 9.2.

Deciding what goes into the stop list is a crucial part of the analysis. Words that are only used once in a corpus of texts can't co-occur, by definition, so they are dropped from analysis. Most researchers ignore common words, like prepositions. Some researchers recode synonyms. We always make sure that there are no misspellings and that orthographic differences are ignored (for example, we combine behavior and behaviour). Many researchers lump singular and plural forms of the same word (product and products, for example) and some lump words with the same root (partial and partially, for example). (See Fox [1989] for a list of words in English that are usually semantically neutral. You can add or subtract from Fox's stop list in any concordance or KWIC program.)

After eliminating the words in the stop list, the software goes through each text and counts each use of each word.

Results of Analyzing the Data in Figure 9.1

The five informants whose texts are shown in Figure 9.1 used a total of 555 words, but they only used 268 different words. Our stop list contained

Figure 9.1   Five Texts From Students About a Recent Experience With a Cold or Flu

#1

I waited till after finals were over to seek care. Had cough, drainage, runny nose, increased wheezing/asthmatic problems. Had symptoms/signs for about three days before going to health center. Receive antibiotics symptoms/signs progressed until almost end of antibiotics. worsened in the middle of illness. Illness lasted for about two and a half to three weeks. Cause fatigue and general run down feeling but did not interfere with life other than mild inconvenience. When symptoms/signs started took home remedy of antihistamine/decongestant and started using inhaler more to help control illness.

#2

I know I'm getting sick by first feeling "puny," you know, weak and tired like you don't want to lift your arms. If I'm really sick it will later be accompanied with "hot flashes." My voice will drop about two octaves (which can be fun since this participant happens to be a girl). Last time I was sick was spring break, I had a terrible congestive cough that would rack my body and wake me up at night, not to mention I would wake up my roommates too. Other than the cough I didn't have too many other symptoms. (Except after coughing a lot I would get dizzy.)

#3

Freshman year, I caught the flu for the first time in three years. I definitely didn't miss not being sick. It started when I began having trouble walking, my body became very weak. Everything on me hurt, and I didn't want to move. After about three hours of laying in bed, I felt like I was going to throw up. Fortunately, I had someone bring up a bucket to my room, however. I threw up repeatedly. When I was finished, I had to brush my teeth, and I figured since I was up, I would take a shower. This was a relieving feeling for me as I sat in the shower for about an hour. This spell of aching body and stomach flu continued for about two days, so I had about twelve hours to study for a test that I hadn't even begun studying for. Everything worked out fine; I guess it was a case of food poisoning or the twenty-four hour flu.

#4

I got the flu last January right before my twenty-first birthday. I took Advil, Tylenol, whatever pain medicine I could find. But it got worse and by two days before my birthday, I went to see a doctor. I wanted to make sure I got well by my birthday so I could party and get my free drinks. Well, it turn out that I had some sort of bad infection of the sinus, and the doctor prescribed for me to take antibiotics for the next ten days, even if I felt better. And because of the antibiotics, I could not drink any alcohol. So I had to wait at least eight days after my birthday before I could drink . . . so after those eight days, I drank up like there was no tomorrow.

#5

The last time I had a cold/flu was in Feb 98. I laid in bed for two days with a headache, a stomach ache, fever, body pain. I had spells of dizziness and nausea. I pretty much slept for most of forty-eight hours. I was still tired and worn out for a couple of days beyond the initial illness.

Figure 9.2 Converting Texts to Matrices

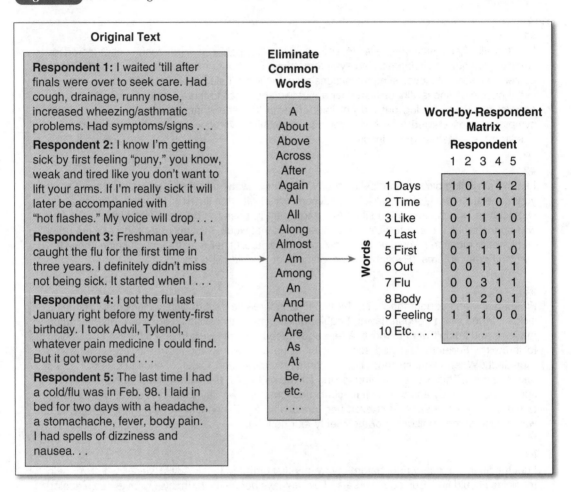

65 words and the five informants used 44 of them. So, not counting those 44 words, the five informants used 224 different words. However, they used 187 of those 224 words just once. Limiting the words in the corpus to those used by two or more informants, we're left with the 37 words in Table 9.2 (see Box 9.1).

Inspecting Table 9.2, we see that the word "days" was mentioned once by persons 1 and 3, twice by person 5, four times by person 4, and never by person 2.

Figure 9.3 is a scree plot (just like the one we used in Chapter 8, on free lists) showing the distribution of the 224 unique words in the five texts and labeling the 37 words used by at least two people.

> **Box 9.1**
>
> ### Words as Variables
>
> Table 9.2 is a profile matrix of five people by the 37 words used at least twice in the corpus of texts. The units of analysis are respondents and the variables are the words they used in their texts. The values for these variables are "used by the informant in a text" (represented by a 1) and "not used by the informant in a text" (represented by a 0).
>
> The usual way to represent profile matrices is with the units of analysis in the rows and the variables in the columns. When we do word counts, however, we may wind up with too many variables to display. That's why, in Table 9.2, the matrix is portrayed with the people in the columns.

PERSONAL ADS ◆

We applied the word-count-matrix method to a set of personal ads. Figure 9.4 shows a couple of typical ads, one from a man and one from a woman, pieced together from ads we found recently online.

These ads have their own vocabulary: SWF means "single White female," DBPM means "divorced Black professional male," ISO means "in search of," LTR means "long-term relationship," and HWP stands for "height and weight proportionate," which is code for "no fat."

We collected 380 of these personal ads—146 placed by women, 234 by men—in 1998 from an Internet website. Table 9.3 shows the 22 words used most frequently by the men and the 21 words most used by the women who placed these ads as they *offered* features about themselves to others. Table 9.4 shows the 21 words used most frequently by men and women who placed these ads as they *sought* features in potential dating partners.

Men and women are about equally likely to mention their hair and eye color when they describe themselves (the differences in percentages are not statistically significant). Some women explicitly seek tall men, but, overall, men are more likely than women to seek a particular kind of body in women (they use adjectives like attractive, slim, fit, slender), and women are more likely to offer a particular kind of body (they use adjectives like full-figured and attractive).

Men and women alike describe themselves in terms of their interests and their physical and personal attributes. But what they seek in others is

Table 9.2   Words Used at Least Twice in Five Texts Shown in Figure 9.1

ID	WORD	INF1	INF2	INF3	INF4	INF5
1	two	1	1	1	1	1
2	not	1	1	1	1	0
3	days	1	0	1	4	2
4	after	1	1	1	2	0
5	first	0	1	1	1	0
6	me	0	1	2	1	0
7	feeling	1	1	1	0	0
8	flu	0	0	3	1	1
9	body	0	1	2	0	1
10	time	0	1	1	0	1
11	my	0	3	3	5	0
12	last	0	1	0	1	1
13	took	1	0	0	1	0
14	since	0	1	1	0	0
15	sick	0	3	1	0	0
16	stomach	0	0	1	0	1
17	weak	0	1	1	0	0
18	pain	0	0	0	1	1
19	cough	1	2	0	0	0
20	bed	0	0	1	0	1
21	going	1	0	1	0	0
22	three	2	0	2	0	0
23	twenty	0	0	1	1	0
24	want	0	1	1	0	0
25	take	0	0	1	1	0
26	illness	3	0	0	0	1
27	symptoms	3	1	0	0	0
28	get	0	1	0	1	0
29	started	2	0	1	0	0
30	hours	0	0	2	0	1

ID	WORD	INF1	INF2	INF3	INF4	INF5
31	didn't	0	1	2	0	0
32	before	1	0	0	3	0
33	felt	0	0	1	1	0
34	eight	0	0	0	2	1
35	antibiotics	2	0	0	2	0
36	tired	0	1	0	0	1
37	even	0	0	1	1	0

Figure 9.3 Scree Plot of the 224 Unique Non-stopped Words in Figure 9.1

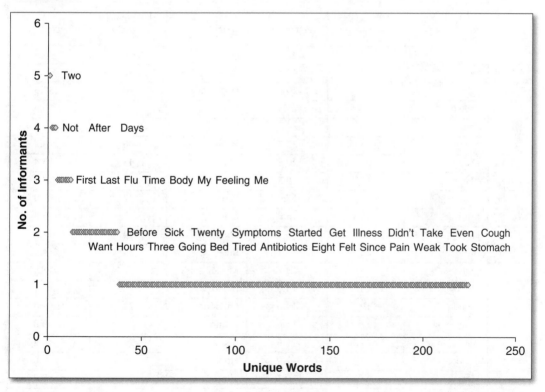

NOTE: The 37 words used by at least two people are spelled out. Words mentioned by only one person are indicated but not labeled.

Figure 9.4 Some Typical Personal Ads

SWF (HWP), 5'6", sandy hair, hazel eyes, fun, adventurous, sensual, passionate, ISO SWM (HWP), 35–40, fun, sexy, and intelligent, for all kinds of outdoor fun and possible LTR.

DBPM, 31, 6'1", 185 lbs, intelligent, employed, ambitious, creative. I like sports, dancing, movies, books, and stimulating conversation. ISO an intelligent SF with similar interests.

Table 9.3 What Men and Women *Offer* in Personal Ads

Rank	Women			Men		
	Term	Frequency (n = 146)	Percentage	Term	Frequency (n = 234)	Percentage
1	Hair	68	46.6	Hair	102	43.6
2	Eyes	64	43.8	Eyes	92	39.3
3	Movies	38	26.0	Employed	76	32.5
4	Brown	37	25.3	Brown	72	30.8
5	Employed	36	24.7	Likes	55	23.5
6	Mom	34	23.3	Fishing	46	19.7
7	Dancing	30	20.5	Movies	43	18.4
8	Outgoing	27	18.5	Camping	43	18.4
9	Reading	26	17.8	Sports	42	17.9
10	Music	23	15.8	Out	37	15.8
11	Likes	22	15.1	Outgoing	34	14.5
12	Blue	22	15.1	Blue	34	14.5
13	Out	20	13.7	Music	27	11.5
14	Full figured	19	13.0	Blond	26	11.1
15	Blonde	19	13.0	Outdoors	23	9.8
16	Gardening	17	11.6	Humorous	23	9.8
17	Attractive	17	11.6	Biking	22	9.4
18	Outdoors	16	11.0	Hobbies	21	9.0
19	Fishing	15	10.3	Fun	20	8.5
20	Fun	15	10.3	Shy	20	8.5
21	Dining	15	10.3	Working	20	8.5
22				Easygoing	20	8.5

Table 9.4 What Men and Women *Seek* in Personal Ads

	Women			Men		
Rank	Term	Frequency (n = 146)	Percentage	Term	Frequency (n = 234)	Percentage
1	Honest	61	41.8	Honest	74	31.6
2	Caring	21	14.4	Sincere	23	9.8
3	Humorous	18	12.3	Relationship	23	9.8
4	Loving	13	8.9	Caring	22	9.4
5	Sincere	13	8.9	Attractive	21	9.0
6	Employed	11	7.5	Fun Loving	18	7.7
7	Secure	11	7.5	Interests	17	7.3
8	Respectful	10	6.8	Possible	15	6.4
9	Interests	9	6.2	Slim	15	6.4
10	Kind	9	6.2	Similar	14	6.0
11	Similar	9	6.2	Compatible	14	6.0
12	Tall	8	5.5	Fit	13	5.6
13	Romantic	7	4.8	Loving	12	5.1
14	Outgoing	6	4.1	Intelligent	12	5.1
15	Good	6	4.1	Slender	12	5.1
16	Life	6	4.1	Humorous	11	4.7
17	Nice	6	4.1	Kind	11	4.7
18	Sensitive	6	4.1	Outgoing	11	4.7
19	Intelligent	6	4.1	Good	11	4.7
20	Meet	6	4.1	Nice	9	3.8
21	Financially	6	4.1	Trustworthy	9	3.8

based primarily on personal attributes, such as honesty, sincerity, caring, and humor—though women are more likely to seek honesty than men are. Men and women both mention their financial status, but women are more likely than men to seek someone who is financially secure.

These findings about what men and women offer each other in personal ads in the United States have been remarkably stable. Hirschman (1987) got similar results in her analysis of personal ads in the 1985 volume of *The Washingtonian* and *New York Magazine*: Men were more likely than women to offer monetary resources; women were more likely than men to seek monetary resources; and women were more likely than men to offer physical attractiveness. (For details of Hirschman's study, see Chapter 13 on content analysis.)

Things may be changing, though. Gil-Burman et al. (2002) found that, although men of all ages in Spain sought physical attractiveness in women and women over 40 sought financial resources (the expected results), women under 40 sought physical attractiveness in men. Gil-Burman et al. interpret this shift in behavior among younger women to economic development in Spain and the participation of women in the workforce. (Further Reading: personal ads.)

♦ DESCRIBING CHILDREN

Here's one more. As part of a longitudinal study of families in Los Angeles, Ryan and Weisner (1996) asked 82 fathers and 82 mothers of teenagers: "What is your teenager like now? Does she or he have any special qualities or abilities?" Parents wrote their answers in short phrases. Figure 9.5 shows three of the responses.

Using a word processor, Ryan and Weisner made sure that each thought (phrase or sentence) was separated by a period. Then they used their word processor and a KWIC program to do some simple counts, shown in Table 9.5 (see Box 9.2).

Dividing the number of characters by the number of words in Table 9.5 shows that mothers and fathers use roughly the same size words (about 5.7 characters each), although, on average, mothers used 26% more words to describe their children than did fathers and 28% more sentences. In all, the 82 mothers produced a total of 1,692 words, of which 666 were unique words; the fathers produced a total of 1,346 words, of which 548 were unique words. Mothers and fathers use the same number of words per phrases (3.20 vs. 3.27), but mothers said more things about their children,

Figure 9.5 Examples of Parents' Descriptions of Their Children

ID-009 (Father's description of son) Loving. Obedient. Maintains own identity. Likes being home. Independent. Anxious to go to California to school.

ID-016. (Father's description of son) Smart. Energetic. Arrogant. Dependent. Slick. Passive. Lack of imagination. Attraction to inner-city lifestyle.

ID124. (Mother's description of daughter) Great kid. Willing to communicate with parents. Listens. Motivated in school. Helpful around the house. Healthy. Active. Lots of friends. She tends to play it safe.

SOURCE: Ryan, G. W., and Weisner, T. (1996, June). Analyzing words in brief descriptions: Fathers and mothers describe their children. *Cultural Anthropology Methods Journal, 8*(2), 13–16. Copyright © 1996 Sage Publications.

Box 9.2

Using Word Processors for Basic Counts

In Table 9.5, to get the average number of characters per word, we just divided the number of characters in the document by the number of words. The number of words and the number of characters are part of a document's basic description in word processors, like MS-Word, OpenOffice Writer, and WordPerfect. WordPerfect also counts sentences, but MS-Word counts paragraphs. To count sentences in MS-Word, just make a copy of your document and make each sentence a paragraph by putting a hard return after each period.

    If you're comfortable with writing macros in MS-Word, use the following macro for counting sentences in MS-Word.

```
Sub MAIN
      StartOfDocument
      Count = 0
      While SentRight(1, 1) <> 0
            If Right$(Selection$(), 1) <>Chr$(13) Then count = count +1
      Wend
      MsgBox "Number of sentences in document:" + Str$(count)
End Sub
```

We used ANTHROPAC to count the unique words, but this function can be found in many KWIC programs, as well as in major text analysis programs (see Appendix).

Table 9.5 Text Statistics for Ryan and Weisner's Data

	Mothers ($n = 82$)	Fathers ($n = 82$)	Total ($N = 164$)
1. Characters	9748	7625	17373
2. Word count	1692	1346	3038
3. Average word length in characters	5.76	5.66	5.72
4. Sentence count	528	411	939
5. Average sentences/phrases per person	6.44	5.01	5.72
6. Average words per sentence/phrase	3.20	3.27	3.24
7. Maximum words per sentence	14	17	
8. Number of unique words	666	548	
9. Type-token ratio	0.39	0.41	

SOURCE: Ryan, G. W., and Weisner, T. (1996, June). Analyzing words in brief descriptions: Fathers and mothers describe their children. *Cultural Anthropology Methods Journal, 8*(2), 13–16. Copyright © 1996 Sage Publications.

and parents all used the same social science questionnaire schema to answer questions—writing a series of terse phrases and words for a minute or so.

Table 9.6 shows an abbreviated list of the mothers' and fathers' words. Mothers mentioned the words "good," "friends," "loving," "out," and "people" at least 11 times and "zest" (the last word on the mothers' list) just once. Fathers mentioned the words "good," "school," "hard," and "intelligent" at least nine times and "zero" (the last word on the fathers' list) just once.

Table 9.6 Mothers' and Fathers' Word Lists in Describing Their Children

Mothers' Descriptions		Fathers' Descriptions	
Rank	Count/Word	Rank	Count/Word
1	22 good	1	23 good
2	12 friends	2	16 school
3	11 loving	3	11 hard
4	11 out	4	9 intelligent
5	11 people	5	8 bright
6	10 doesn't	6	8 independent
7	10 hard	7	8 out
8	10 school	8	8 well
9	9 responsible	9	7 doesn't
10	9 sense	10	7 lack
11	8 caring	11	7 loving
12	8 intelligent	12	7 people
13	8 lacks	13	7 sensitive
14	8 sensitive	14	7 sports
15	7 bright	15	7 student
16	7 honest	16	6 caring
17	7 others	17	6 does
18	7 self	18	6 life
19	7 time	19	6 others
20	7 well	20	6 work
21	7 work	21	5 ability
22	6 creative	22	5 enjoys
23	6 does	23	5 great
24	6 great	24	5 lacks
25	6 mature	25	5 likes

Mothers' Descriptions		Fathers' Descriptions	
Rank	Count/Word	Rank	Count/Word
26	6 sports	26	5 mature
27	5 academically	27	5 own
28	5 artistic	28	5 sense
29	5 cares	29	5 social
30	5 concerned	30	5 wants
31	5 goals	...	
32	5 going	548	1 zero
33	5 humor		
34	5 independent		
35	5 other		
36	5 social		
37	5 times		
...			
666	1 zest		

SOURCE: Ryan, G. W., and Weisner, T. (1996, June). Analyzing words in brief descriptions: Fathers and mothers describe their children. Cultural Anthropology Methods Journal, 8(2), 13–16. Copyright © 1996 Sage Publications.

With 666 unique words in a corpus of 1,692 words, mothers have a type-token ratio of (666/1692) = 0.39, or 39%, almost identical to that for fathers at (548/1346) = 0.41 (41%).

The mothers produced 26% more words than the fathers did (1,692 compared to 1,346). We can't tell from this if fathers have less to say about their children or they just have less to say about all topics, but the type-token ratio shows that men's vocabulary for describing children is as rich as women's vocabulary. The type-token ratio is one of a whole family of measures of lexical richness (see Box 9.3).

Elaborating the Analysis

Looking at Table 9.6, we see that mothers and fathers alike use the word "good" more than any other word in talking about their teenagers. Furthermore, antonyms of good are not prevalent on the word list. This probably reflects a well-known tendency for people to use positive words when responding to questions about their children.

Table 9.6 also suggests that men and women focus on different characteristics of their children. A comparison of the most frequently used

> ### Box 9.3
>
> #### Measures of Lexical Richness
>
> The type-token ratio (TTR) is widely used in linguistics-based text analysis and in bilingual education. Tang and Nesi (2003), for example, used the TTR to assess the difference in lexical richness between two secondary schools in China where the children were learning English.
>
> There is a well-known problem with the TTR: You can get misleading results if the texts on which it is calculated are of very different lengths. Assuming that the mothers and fathers in Ryan and Weisner's sample had similar vocabularies—that is, they were working with more or less the same number of words with which to talk about their children—longer texts could have lower type-token ratios. In this case they don't, and so we conclude that the mothers have a slightly richer vocabulary than the fathers do—at least when they talk about their children. We won't go into them here, but there are many competing measures of text concentration (for a review of these, see Daller et al. 2003).
>
> We lose a lot of information when we examine unique words. Unlike a KWIC analysis, we do not know the context in which the words occurred, nor whether informants used words negatively or positively. Nor do we know how the words were related to each other. But distillations like TTRs introduce very little investigator bias (though we do have to choose what words to leave out of the analysis), and they can help us identify constructs, or themes.

words shows that "friends," "loving," "people," and "responsible" are ranked higher for women than they are for men. In contrast, "school," "hard," "intelligent," "bright," and "independent" are ranked higher for men than for women. This suggests that mothers, on first mention, express concern over interpersonal issues (relationships), and fathers appear to give priority to achievement-oriented and individualistic issues (performance).

We can check this by standardizing the data for men and women—that is, by calculating how many times men would be expected to use each word used by women if the men had used as many words in total as the women did. This is shown in Table 9.7 for the 32 words that were used by both men and women at least four times. Because women used 26% more words than men did (1,692 vs. 1,346), we multiply each of the words used by men by 1.26.

Negative numbers in the column on the far right of Table 9.7 mean that the word was more likely to be used by fathers than by mothers. Positive

Table 9.7 Word Frequencies Sorted by Standardized Frequency to Show Differences in Gender

Word	Mothers	Fathers	Expected Use by Fathers	Standardized Difference
school	10	16	20.16	−10.16
good	22	23	28.98	−6.98
lack	2	7	8.82	−6.82
student	2	7	8.82	−6.82
enjoys	1	5	6.30	−5.30
independent	5	8	10.08	−5.08
extremely	0	4	5.04	−5.04
like	0	4	5.04	−5.04
ability	2	5	6.30	−4.30
own	2	5	6.30	−4.30
wants	2	5	6.30	−4.30
high	1	4	5.04	−4.04
interested	1	4	5.04	−4.04
great	6	5	6.30	−0.30
mature	6	5	6.30	−0.30
humor	5	4	5.04	−0.04
times	5	4	5.04	−0.04
attitude	4	3	3.78	0.22
caring	8	6	7.56	0.44
adult	4	0	0.00	4.00
average	4	0	0.00	4.00
difficulty	4	0	0.00	4.00
goes	4	0	0.00	4.00
kid	4	0	0.00	4.00
lots	4	0	0.00	4.00
respect	4	0	0.00	4.00
talented	4	0	0.00	4.00
uses	4	0	0.00	4.00
honest	7	2	2.52	4.48
time	7	2	2.52	4.48
creative	6	0	0.00	6.00
friends	12	4	5.04	6.96

SOURCE: Adapted from Ryan, G. W., and Weisner, T. (1996, June). Analyzing words in brief descriptions: Fathers and mothers describe their children. *Cultural Anthropology Methods Journal, 8*(2), 13–16. Copyright © 1996 Sage Publications.

NOTE: Data are based on words used at least four times by either mothers or fathers.

numbers mean that the word was more likely to be used by mothers. Numbers close to zero mean that there wasn't that much difference between the men's and women's use of a word.

When we standardize the data, then, we find that men tend to use the word "good" a lot more than women do. Similarly, women use the word "caring" more times in the corpus of texts, but when we standardize, mothers and fathers are equally likely to use the word "caring" in describing their teenagers. Fathers are more likely to use the words "school," "good," "lack," "student," "enjoys," "independent," "extremely," "like," "ability," "own," "wants," "high," and "interested," and mothers are more likely to use the words "friends," "creative," "time," "honest," "uses," "talented," "respect," "lots," "kid," "goes," difficulty," "average," and "adult." These results, by the way, support other research on gender differences in parent-child relations in Western societies (Best et al. 1994).

Word Counts Are Only a Start

These word counting and word examination techniques help us look quickly at very complex data, explore for central themes, and make comparisons across groups. Of course, these are just the first steps in a more detailed analysis of texts. We still want to examine the context in which words occur and how key words are related to each other. We will also want to test hypotheses that emerge from this simple first step. For example, by the time we've done the word counts and are steeped in the contextual data, we may have formed some ideas about how the sex of the teen and that of the parent influence word use. Still, there's a lot to be learned from the simple word-count method. (Further Reading: word counts.)

♦ SEMANTIC NETWORK ANALYSIS

Semantic network analysis goes beyond word counts and examines the relationships among words across a set of texts. The idea is simple and compelling: Texts that share many words—and the people or organizations that produce the words—are more like each other than texts that share few words.

Semantic network analysis begins by producing the kind of similarity matrices we introduced in Chapter 8. To do this for text, we calculate the covariation between all pairs of rows or all pairs of columns in a profile matrix. An example will make this clear.

Table 9.2 (p. 200) is a profile matrix showing how many times each of five informants used each of 37 words in describing their last cold or flu. Table 9.8

shows part of that same data: the 12 words that were used by three or more of the five informants.

Table 9.8 can be converted into a similarity matrix by measuring the covariation of either the rows or the columns. Figure 9.6 shows the process for creating similarity matrices based on simple percentages and provides examples from a variety of studies.

When we have a small number of informants and a matrix with mostly 1s and 0s (as in Table 9.8), the first step is to dichotomize the data. That is, we turn all the numbers in Table 9.8 into 1s or 0s. (You can do this easily with either ANTHROPAC or UCINET. See Appendix.) The number 1 or 0 in Table 9.9 indicates that a word was either used or not used in a text. This makes it possible to compare rows and columns in terms of simple percentages. (As we'll see in a moment, when we have matrices with much denser data, we can use other methods, besides percentages, to calculate similarity between pairs of rows and/or pairs of columns.)

Table 9.8 Data From Table 9.2 Showing the 12 Words Used by Three or More Informants

WORD	INF1	INF2	INF3	INF4	INF5
two	1	1	1	1	1
not	1	1	1	1	0
days	1	0	1	4	2
after	1	1	1	2	0
first	0	1	1	1	0
me	0	1	2	1	0
feeling	1	1	1	0	0
flu	0	0	3	1	1
body	0	1	2	0	1
time	0	1	1	0	1
my	0	3	3	5	0
last	0	1	0	1	1

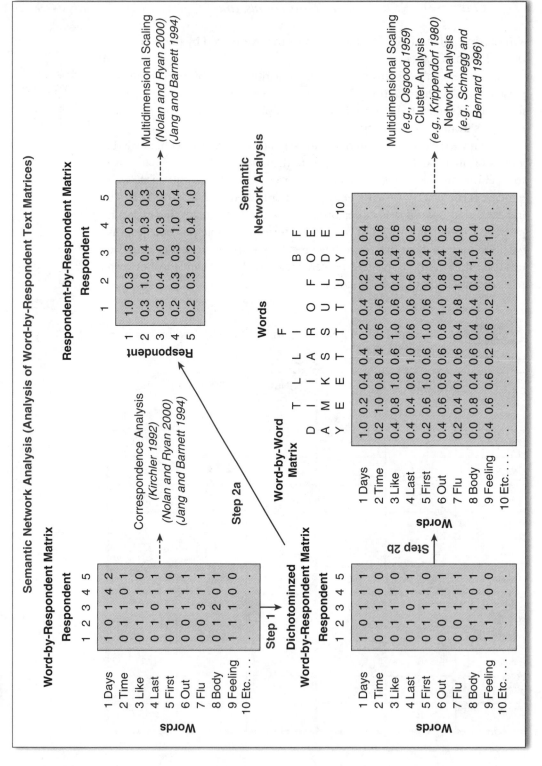

Figure 9.6 Converting a Word-by-Respondent Matrix Into Two Kinds of Similarity Matrices

212

Converting a Profile Matrix to Similarity Matrices

Now we can convert Table 9.9 into two similarity matrices, shown in Tables 9.10 and 9.11, using simple percentages. (Again, you can do this with either ANTHROPAC or UCINET.) The cells in Table 9.10 tell us the similarity among pairs of words—the percentage of times each pair of words co-occurs in the set of five texts.

For example, the words "two" and "days" in Table 9.9 co-occur in four texts (texts 1, 3, 4, and 5), which is 80% of the five texts available. The number 0.80 appears in the first line of Table 9.10, below, where the words "two" and "days" intersect. The word "feeling" is used in texts 1, 2, and 3, and the word "flu" is used in texts 3, 4, and 5, so there's a 0.20 (20%) in the cell where "feeling" and "flu" intersect in Table 9.10. For this set of 12 words in five texts, then, the pair feeling-two is 20% alike and the pair two-days is 80% alike.

In Table 9.10, there is a 1.00 in every cell down the diagonal, signifying that each word universally co-occurs with itself. And Table 9.10 is symmetric. The numbers above and below the diagonal mirror one another: On the first line, there is a 0.60 in the cell for "two" and "me," and there is a 0.60 in the first column where "me" and "two" intersect.

Table 9.9 The Data in Table 9.8, Dichotomized

WORD	INF1	INF2	INF3	INF4	INF5
two	1	1	1	1	1
not	1	1	1	1	0
days	1	0	1	1	1
after	1	1	1	1	0
first	0	1	1	1	0
me	0	1	1	1	0
feeling	1	1	1	0	0
flu	0	0	1	1	1
body	0	1	1	0	1
time	0	1	1	0	1
my	0	1	1	1	0
last	0	1	0	1	1

Table 9.10 The Percentage of Times Each Pair of Words Co-occurs in the Set of Five Texts

WORD	two	not	days	after	first	me	feeling	flu	body	time	my	last
two	1.00	0.80	0.80	0.80	0.60	0.60	0.60	0.60	0.60	0.60	0.60	0.60
not	0.80	1.00	0.60	1.00	0.80	0.80	0.80	0.40	0.40	0.40	0.80	0.40
days	0.80	0.60	1.00	0.60	0.40	0.40	0.40	0.80	0.40	0.40	0.40	0.40
after	0.80	1.00	0.60	1.00	0.80	0.80	0.80	0.40	0.40	0.40	0.80	0.40
first	0.60	0.80	0.40	0.80	1.00	1.00	0.60	0.60	0.60	0.60	1.00	0.60
me	0.60	0.80	0.40	0.80	1.00	1.00	0.60	0.60	0.60	0.60	1.00	0.60
feeling	0.60	0.80	0.40	0.80	0.60	0.60	1.00	0.20	0.60	0.60	0.60	0.20
flu	0.60	0.40	0.80	0.40	0.60	0.60	0.20	1.00	0.60	0.60	0.60	0.60
body	0.60	0.40	0.40	0.40	0.60	0.60	0.60	0.60	1.00	1.00	0.60	0.60
time	0.60	0.40	0.40	0.40	0.60	0.60	0.60	0.60	1.00	1.00	0.60	0.60
my	0.60	0.80	0.40	0.80	1.00	1.00	0.60	0.60	0.60	0.60	1.00	0.60
last	0.60	0.40	0.40	0.40	0.60	0.60	0.20	0.60	0.60	0.60	0.60	1.00

Table 9.11 shows the 5-by-5, informant-by-informant matrix for the data in Table 9.9. The cells in the informant-by-informant matrix show the percentage of words that a pair of people used in common. As a rule, the more words two people use in common, the more similar their texts are. If you look down columns 1 and 2 in Table 9.9, you'll see 1s in the cells for "two," "not," "after," and "feeling," and 0s in the cells for "flu."

So, informants 1 and 2 used four words in common and did not use one word in common. The two informants are 42% similar on this measure (4+1=5/12=.42), called a match coefficient. If we used only the words mentioned by both informants and did not count the words they didn't use in common, then the positive match coefficient would be 33% (4/12=.33) instead of 42%.

Jang and Barnett's Study of CEO Letters

Once you have a similarity matrix, like Table 9.10 or Table 9.11, you can examine it with multidimensional scaling and cluster analysis. Ha-Yong Jang (1995) used this method to examine whether there is a national culture discernible in the annual letters to stockholders from the CEOs of American and Japanese corporations. He selected 35 Fortune 500 companies, including 18 American and 17 Japanese firms, matched by type of business. For example, Ford was matched with Honda, Xerox with Canon, and so on.

All of these firms are traded on the New York Stock Exchange, and each year stockholders receive an annual message from either the CEO or the president of these companies. (Japanese firms that trade on the New York Exchange send the annual letters in English to their U.S. stockholders.) Jang downloaded the 1992 annual letters to shareholders and (applying a stop list of 60 common words) isolated 94 words that occurred at least 26 times across the corpus of 35 letters (Jang 1995:49).

Then Jang created a 94(word)-by-35(company) matrix, where the rows are the 94 words and the columns are the 35 companies and the cells

Table 9.11   A 5-by-5, Informant-by-Informant Matrix for the Data in Table 9.9

INFORMANT	1	2	3	4	5
1	1.00	0.42	0.50	0.50	0.42
2	0.42	1.00	0.75	0.58	0.33
3	0.50	0.75	1.00	0.67	0.42
4	0.50	0.58	0.67	1.00	0.42
5	0.42	0.33	0.42	0.42	1.00

contained a number from 0 to 25, 25 being the largest number of times any word ever occurred in *one* of the letters. (For the curious, the word was "company" and it occurred 25 times in the letter from General Electric.)

Next, Jang created a 35(company)-by-35(company) similarity matrix of companies based on the co-occurrence of words in their letters to stockholders and analyzed that matrix with multidimensional scaling. Figure 9.7 shows the result of running multidimensional scaling on Jang's 35×35 matrix of similarities between companies (from Jang and Barnett 1994).

Figure 9.7 shows that there are two sets of corporate letters to stockholders, one American and one Japanese. Jang and Barnett (1994) found that 13 words were most associated with the American group of companies: board, chief, leadership, president, officer, major, position, financial, improved, good, success, competitive, and customer. From their close reading of all the texts and their knowledge of corporate culture, Jang and Barnett saw these 13 words as representing two themes: financial information and organizational structure.

Figure 9.7 Multidimensional Scaling of Jang and Barnett's Company-by-Company Data

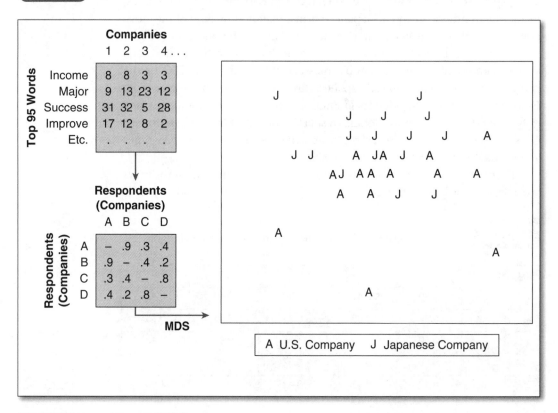

SOURCE: Jang and Barnett (1994).

Six words were more associated with the Japanese companies: income, effort, economy, new, development, and quality. To Jang and Barnett, these words represented organizational operations and reflected Japanese concern for the development of new, quality products in order to compete in the U.S. business environment.

Nolan and Ryan's Study of Horror Films

Here's another example. Nolan and Ryan (2000) asked 59 undergraduates (30 women and 29 men) to describe their "most memorable horror film." Nolan and Ryan identified the 45 most common adjectives, verbs, and nouns used across the descriptions of the films. Next, they produced a 45(word)-by-59(person) dichotomized matrix, the cells of which indicated whether each student had used each key word at least once in his or her description.

Nolan and Ryan correlated the columns of this matrix to produce a 59(person)-by-59(person) similarity matrix of their informants and they analyzed it with multidimensional scaling. Figure 9.8 shows the result.

Though there is some overlap, it's pretty clear that men and women use different sets of words to describe horror films. Nolan and Ryan used correspondence analysis to examine the words that men and women were more likely to use in the texts. Figure 9.9 shows the result.

Like MDS, correspondence analysis produces a map but it scales the rows and columns of a profile matrix simultaneously, so you can see the relation between the objects in a study (the rows of a profile matrix) and the variables that describe those objects (the columns).

The closer things are to one another on a correspondence analysis map, the more alike they are. On the right side of the figure, there is a set of terms (young girl, horror, terrible, evil, devil, father, parents, religious, possessed, and kidnapped) around a group of female informants. Women appear to have focused on themes related to family, terror, and the occult. (Further Reading: correspondence analysis.)

The men in Nolan and Ryan's study were more likely to use the words "disturbing," "violence," "dark," killer," "death," "teenager," "rural," "country," "hillbilly," "massacre," "chainsaw," and "Texas." These last three words are a reference to a famous horror movie, *Texas Chainsaw Massacre*. The prototype film about rural terror for men is *Deliverance*, and, in fact, the men in Nolan and Ryan's sample named that film most often as one of the scariest slasher movies they'd ever seen.

Overall, Nolan and Ryan interpreted these results to mean that the men in their study had a fear of rural people and places, and women were more afraid of betrayed intimacy and spiritual possession. And notice the words in the lower left of Figure 9.9 (words like "rape" and "far") that are shared by

Figure 9.8 MDS of Words Used in Men's and Women's Description of Horror Films

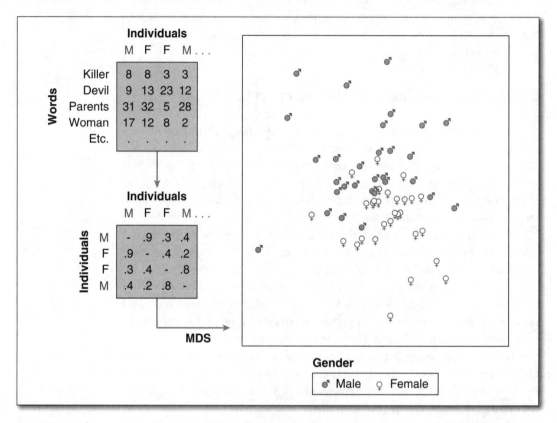

SOURCE: Nolan, J. M. and G. Ryan 2000. Fear and loathing at the cineplex: Gender differences in descriptions and perceptions of slasher films. *Sex Roles* 42(1–2):39–56.

men and women. Nolan and Ryan interpreted this to be a semantic extension of the rural terror theme and reflecting what Clover (1992) called the "rape-revenge" motif in slasher films. (Further Reading: semantic network analysis.)

◆ SOME CAUTIONS ABOUT ALL THIS

One really appealing thing about analyzing word-by-word co-occurrence matrices is that it's done entirely by computer. In fact, the initial analyses can only be done with a computer. This may make it tempting to let the computer do all the work, but in the end it still takes a thoroughly human, interpretive method to make sense of numerical data.

Figure 9.9 Correspondence Analysis of the Words Used by Men and Women in Describing Horror Films

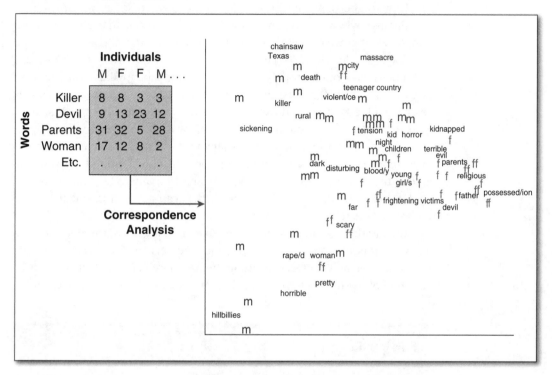

SOURCE: Nolan, J. M. and G. Ryan 2000. Fear and loathing at the cineplex: Gender differences in descriptions and perceptions of slasher films. *Sex Roles* 42(1–2):39–56.

Jang and Barnett, for example, interpreted their results as showing a split between Japanese corporate concern with product innovation and quality versus an American concern with finance and organization. Nolan and Ryan interpreted their results as showing gender differences in what Americans fear. This is the work of cell B in Figure 1.1: the qualitative search for and presentation of meaning in the results of quantitative data processing. No study, no matter how sophisticated the numerical processing, is complete without this step. Don't quit early.

Computer processing of matrices also means that that you have to be especially vigilant about bias going in. One source of bias is the choice of which words to keep in a matrix. This choice begins with the building of a stop list. The bigger the list, the more choices you've made about the analysis—and, as we know, every choice in methods introduces potential bias.

Another choice is the number of words to analyze. Jang chose the top 94 words. We reran his data, using the top 100 words and the top 200 words.

Our findings were substantially the same as his, but they might not have been. Always check this potential source of bias.

How to check? We introduce bias on purpose to see if we can clobber our findings when we use these methods. If we can't, that gives us more confidence that we're seeing something meaningful in the results.

For example, we took Jang's data and removed two really important concept words from his top 94: United States and Japan. What if the dramatic picture in Figure 9.7 was simply the result of the Japanese executives referring a lot to Japan and the U.S. executives referring a lot to the United States? When we removed the words from Jang's data and re-ran the analysis, the plot showing the split between Japanese and U.S. companies became even more dramatic—with one exception. Mitsubishi wound up squarely among the American companies. Was Mitsubishi trying to become more like an American company? Only further analysis can get at this, but that's the nature of research.

We find that, because MDS, cluster analysis, and correspondence analysis show clusters of words, or concepts, they are very useful in the search for themes in free flowing text. Analyzing themes in free-flowing text is the most common of the methods in text analysis, and that's where we go next.

Further Reading

◆ For more on KWIC studies, see E. Johnson (1996) and Weber (1990).

◆ For more on authorship studies, see Martindale and McKenzie (1995) and Yule (1968 [1944]).

◆ A whole literature on personal ads has grown up over the last couple of decades, including studies of Internet ads, studies comparing ads for gay and heterosexual mates, and studies of ads by people of various ethnic groups. See, for example, Badahda and Tiemann (2005), Groom and Pennebaker (2005), Kaufman and Voon Chin (2003), Leighton Dawson and McIntosh (2006), Phua (2002), C. A. Smith and Stillman (2002a, 2002b), and Yancey and Yancey (1997).

◆ For examples of research using word counts, see Arthur et al. (2007), Basturkman (1999), Côté-Arsenault et al. (2001), DeRocher et al. (1973), Doucet and Jehn (1997), Pressman and Cohen (2007), and Ward and Spennemann (2000).

◆ For more on correspondence analysis, see Greenacre (1984), Greenacre and Blasius (1994), Watts (1997), and Weller and Romney (1990).

◆ For more examples of semantic network analysis, see Danowski (1982), Doerfel (1998), Doerfel and Barnett (1999), Kirchler (1992), Rice and Danowski (1993), and Schnegg and Bernard (1996).

CHAPTER 10

DISCOURSE ANALYSIS

Conversation and Performance

INTRODUCTION ◆

Discourse analysis is the study of: (1) grammar beyond the sentence; (2) language in use; and (3) the rhetoric of power (Schiffrin et al. 2001:1). (Further Reading: reviews of discourse analysis.)

1. The first kind of study—grammar beyond the sentence—is about the rules that govern the construction and flow of naturally occurring speech. We're accustomed to thinking about grammar as a set of rules for building sentences, but it's much more than that. Every native speaker of every natural language in the world also learns the grammar—the rules—for building conversations and telling stories. Conversation analysis reveals how people work together, according to a set of rules, to build their interactions, whether those interactions are fun or painful. Performance analysis reveals how people set up stories and how they tell them, whether in speech or in text.

2. The second kind of study—language in use—focuses on how people pursue their goals in naturally occurring speech. Here, the topics range from: how people extract bribes from one another (Mele and Bello 2007); to how teachers get children to behave in classrooms (De Fina 1997; Morine-Dershimer 2006); to how and when bilinguals switch between languages (Negrón 2007; Scotton and Ury 1977).

3. The third kind of study starts from the observation that people in complex societies understand and reenact in speech the power differences that pervade those societies. Studies in this tradition—called critical discourse analysis—focus on how the content of discourse establishes, reflects, or perpetuates power differences between actors in society.

These approaches to analyzing human discourse are not mutually exclusive. The analysis of a single interaction between a doctor and a patient, for example, can contain elements of all three approaches: a discussion of the turn taking (grammar beyond the sentence); a discussion of how the doctor tries to get the patient to comply with orders (language in use); and a discussion of how the rhetoric reinforces the doctor's position of power over the patient (critical analysis). More about this later.

◆ GRAMMAR BEYOND THE SENTENCE

This tradition of discourse analysis is grounded in linguistics. Linguists recognize five levels of grammar: phonology, morphology, syntax, semantics, and discourse.

Phonology is the study of the sounds of a language and the rules governing their use. For example, the guttural ch in the name Bach is used in many languages, but not in English. The vowel sound æ in cat is pretty common, but it doesn't exist in Spanish.

The basic sounds that are available in any particular language are the language's phonemes. There are 42–44 phonemes in English (depending on the dialect). Unfortunately, we only have 26 squiggles in our alphabet to represent all those sounds, but we make do by letting some letters and combinations of letters do double duty. For example, there are three pronunciations of the letter e in the word "represented." (Go ahead, count them. The first is e as in pet. The second is ee as in street. The third is the same sound as the second o in doctor.)

Each level of grammar has its own set of rules. The rules of phonology are learned very early in life, of course. For example, there is a phonological rule in English that forbids the sound combination pt at the beginning of words but allows it in the middle and at the end (think of aptitude and inept). Speakers of Greek, though, don't have this rule, so they have no problem pronouncing the pt in pterodactyl, Ptolemy, and ptomaine poisoning, which speakers of English pronounce as if the p weren't there— as in terodactyl, tolemy, and tomaine.

Morphology comprises the rules for making meaningful units, or lexemes, out of phonemes. Some lexemes are always attached to others (think of ig-, il- and im-, which mean "not" in ignoble, illegal, and immoral), but most lexemes are simply words that stand on their own, like "hairy" and "eggplant."

Syntax is what we usually think of as the grammar of a language. It is the set of rules for stringing lexemes together to make phrases and sentences that native speakers recognize as well formed. Languages with long literary traditions, like English, Arabic, Hindi, Japanese, and such, have developed formal grammars of syntax—all that stuff about parsing sentences you learned in grade school—but the syntax of any language is much, much more complicated than that. It involves all the rules that you follow in decoding new sentences that come your way and in making up new ones every day that others have to decode.

Semantics is one level up from syntax and is the set of rules governing the variable meaning of words and phrases in context. It's the semantic rules of grammar that make word play possible. For example, if someone says to you, "It was so nice to have you here today" (as you're leaving their home), and you reply, "It was so nice being had," you are using your knowledge of the semantic rules of American English grammar to make a joke. And you'd also better know the cultural rules for when you can get away with such things or the joke won't be funny.

Finally, there's discourse, the part of the grammar beyond the sentence. Linguistics-based discourse analysis is the study of the rules governing the construction of whole conversations and narrative performances.

◆ CONVERSATION ANALYSIS

Conversation analysis is the search for the grammar of ordinary discourse, or talk-in-interaction. It is the study of how people take turns in ordinary discourse—who talks first (and next, and next), who interrupts, who waits for a turn.

If you listen carefully to ordinary conversations between equals, you'll hear a lot of sentence fragments, false starts, interruptions, overlaps (simultaneous speech), and repeating of words and phrases. As students of conversation have learned, however, there is order in all that seeming chaos as participants respond to each other (even in strong disagreements and shouting matches) and take turns (Goodwin 1981:55ff).

The grammatical rules of turn taking are, like the rules that govern the formation of sentences, known to native speakers of any language. But unlike the other rules of grammar, the rules for taking turns are flexible and allow turn taking to be negotiated, on the fly, by participants in a conversation. At the molecular level, then, every conversation is unique, but the study of many conversational exchanges can expose the general rules, within and across cultures, that govern how conversations start, evolve, and end (see Box 10.1).

Box 10.1

Turn-Taking Rules in Institutions

In many institutional settings, turn taking in meetings is regulated by someone acting as leader. Even these rules can be subtle. At a convention of Alcoholics Anonymous in Southeast Asia, a meeting described by O'Halloran (2005:541) operated on an unspoken, but apparently well-understood rule: A member would rise and go to the microphone at the speaker's table. This simple act was sufficient to claim a turn.

And pilots all over the world have a special turn-taking rule: They absolutely must learn to let each other finish each sentence before jumping in with the next one (Nevile 2007).

Unique sentences are produced all the time, by speakers of thousands of languages across the world. The sentence you are reading right now might never have been uttered or written before, but every native speaker of

English reading this book knows the rules governing how the sentence was formed. We produced the sentence and you are decoding it on the fly. In natural languages, a finite number of rules, operating on a finite number of words, produce an infinite number of well-formed sentences.

This generative principle for grammar was established in 1957 by Noam Chomsky. The idea—that rule-based systems can produce an infinite number of unique outcomes—is very important. The evolution of life forms is based on rules, but the forms of life (kangaroos here, chimps there) are a set of unique outcomes. Every geological formation—every canyon and bluff—is unique, but we know that their formation and weathering are governed by rules. Every hurricane, every volcano eruption, and every battle is unique and, on the surface, chaotic. But we study hurricanes, volcano eruptions, and battles because we know that there are regularities across many unique events.

Transcriptions

To identify turns and other features of conversations (like adjacency pairs and repair sequences, which we'll take up later), you need detailed records of actual talk-in-interaction. The tactic for signaling the intention to take a turn or to repair a broken turn sequence may be a word or a phrase, or it may be prosodic features of speech (intonation, length of vowels, stress, and so on), or breaths, tokens (like er, ummm, eh), gestures, body language, or gazes (R. Gardner 2001; Goodwin 1994).

Table 10.1 shows one widely used system, developed by Gail Jefferson (1983, 2004), for transcribing speech, including some of the basic prosodic features. (Further Reading: transcribing conversation.)

It takes 6–8 hours to transcribe an hour of ordinary interviews (but less than half that if you use voice-recognition software—see Chapter 2 and Appendix). It can take 20 hours or more to transcribe conversation with the level of detail required for this kind of analysis.

TAKING TURNS

We've known for a long time that there are regularities in conversations (Aristotle observed in *Poetics* IV that "conversational speech runs into iambic lines more frequently than into any other kind of verse"), but Harvey Sacks and his colleagues, Emmanuel Schegloff and Gail Jefferson, are widely credited for developing the systematic study of order in conversations (Jefferson 1973; Sacks et al. 1974; Schegloff 1968; Schegloff and Sacks 1973). Among the

Table 10.1 Conventions for Transcribing Text

Symbol	Definition
ni::::ce	Indicates length of a consonant or vowel. More colons = more length.
>text<	Speech between angle brackets is faster than normal speech.
(text) ( )	Text in parentheses means that the transcriber had doubts about it. Parens with no text means that transcriber could not make it out at all.
(1.6) (.)	Numbers in parens indicate pauses, in seconds and tenths of a second. A period in parens indicates an untimed and quick pause
((text))	Double parens contain comments by the researcher about people's gestures, gazes, and so on. Often in italics.
[ ]	Left square brackets indicate where one person interrupts another or talks simultaneously. Right square brackets mark the end of overlap.
–	An en-dash (longer than a hyphen) indicates an abrupt end in the middle of a word
?	A question mark indicates rising intonation. It does not necessarily mean that a question is being asked.
.	A period indicates falling intonation. It does not necessarily mean the end of a sentence.
=	The equal sign indicates that a person takes a turn immediately as the previous turn ends.
°text°	Text between degree symbols is quieter speech than that surrounding it.
TEXT	Text in caps indicates louder speech than that surrounding it.
<u>Text</u>	Underlining means that the words are emphasized
.hh and hh	These indicate inhaled (with period first) and exhaled (no period) breaths, as often occurs in natural conversation.

SOURCE: After Jefferson (1983).

basic rules they discovered are that the person who is speaking may (but does not have to) identify the next speaker to take a turn (Sacks et al. 1974:700ff). This is done with conversational devices—like "So what do you think, Jack?"—or with gazes or body language (Goodwin 1986, 1994). If the person speaking does not select the next speaker, then any other person in the conversation can self-select to take a turn.

Alternatively, the next speaker may jump in before a speaker has completed a turn, by anticipating the end of a turn—a supportive gesture—or by interrupting and trying to take away the speaker's turn by force—a hostile gesture. Big gaps occur so rarely in real conversations because speakers anticipate the end of turns so well. For example:

1. A: what a cute <u>no::se</u>.
2. B: all [babies ha-
3. A: [no they don't

A takes a turn; B responds and then A says "No they don't" just as the syllable "ba" in "baby" registers. There is no gap at the end of B's turn because the end of B's turn is predictable to A. And even though A contradicts B, the interruption is supportive, in grammatical terms—that is, it doesn't violate any rules—because it keeps the conversation going.

If the turn taking runs out of steam in a conversation, either because it becomes unpredictable or the content gets used up and no one jumps in to take a turn at the appropriate time, then the current speaker may (but does not have to) continue talking. If none of these things happen, there will be a gap in the conversation. Gaps don't usually last very long if the rules of conversation are followed.

The rules are often broken in real conversations. People often do interrupt each other unsupportively and don't wait to take their turns. People who get interrupted don't always push on, trying to finish their turn, but relinquish their turn instead, without finishing. On the other hand, people usually recognize when the preferred order of turn taking has not been adhered to and engage in what are called repair tactics. For example, Sacks et al. (1974) noted that when two people start talking over each other, one of them might just stop and let the other finish. Here's an example from conversation we overheard:

1. A: [It's not like we–
2. B: [Some people are–
3. B: Sorry.
4. A: No, g'head
5. B: .hhhh I wus jus gonna say that some people aren't innerested in sports [at all.
6. A: [right

This is a simple repair tactic that doesn't involve any serious content. Other repair tactics can be more complex. The result of this repair sequence could have come out differently. But in the study of hundreds of natural conversations between equals, we can uncover the rules governing how people open and close conversations, how they repair mistakes (when they break the rules of turn taking, for example), and how they segue from one theme to another.

The turn-taking sequence rules can be suspended in the telling of jokes and stories. If you ask someone "Did you hear the one about . . . ?" and they say "No, tell me," then this suspends turn taking until you're finished with the joke. If they interrupt you in telling the joke, this breaks the rule for this conversation element.

And the same thing goes for story telling. If you say "I was on the flight from Hell coming back from Detroit last week" and the person you're talking to responds by saying "What happened?" then you get to tell the story all the way through. Certain kinds of interruptions are permitted—in fact, you expect people to say "Uh, huh" and other such supportive interruptions when you're on a roll—but sidetracking you completely from the story is not permitted.

It's not expected, but it happens, and when sidetracking happens, one of several repair sequences might kick in. "Sorry, I got you off track. Then what happened?" is a repair sequence. We've all experienced the pain of never getting back to a story from which we were sidetracked in a conversation. When that happens, we might think badly of the person who did it or we might shrug it off—depending on the context and what's at stake. If you're in a job interview and the interviewer sidetracks you, you'd probably think twice about insisting that the interviewer let you finish the story you were telling.

Adjacency Pairs

Among the first things that conversation analysts noticed when they started looking carefully at conversations was ordered pairs of expressions, like questions and greetings (Schegloff and Sacks 1973). Once the first part of a pair occurs, the second part is expected.

For example, as Schegloff pointed out (1968, 1979), if you say "Hello" and you get silence in return, you might take the absence of response as meaningful. If someone asks "How're you doing?" and you respond by saying "Great" but don't follow up with "And how about you?" then the other person might look for meaning in your tone of voice. Did you say "Great" with enthusiasm or with sarcasm? If the former, you might hear "I'm so glad to hear that," in return. But if it was the latter, you might hear "Sorry I asked" or "Excuse me for asking" with equal sarcasm. In other words, other people's interpretation of the content in your turn leads them to adjust the content of their next turn.

Sacks (1992:3ff) noticed that workers at a psychiatric hospital's emergency telephone line greeted callers by saying something like, "Hello. This is Mr. Smith. May I help you?" Most of the time, the response was "Hello, this is Mr. Brown," but on one occasion, the caller responded, "I can't hear you." When the worker repeated his greeting, "This is Mr. *Smith*," with an emphasis on Smith, the caller responded "Smith."

In this case, the rule for an adjacency pair was not really being broken. It was being negotiated by both parties, on the fly, during the conversation. Mr. Smith, the suicide prevention worker, was trying to get the caller to give his name, and the caller was trying not to give his name.

Dynamic Sequences

If conversations are dynamic things, with constant negotiation, then, to understand the rules of conversations, you can't interview people about the rules of, say, greetings. You have to study real conversations in which greetings occur.

Here is an example of an adjacency pair—a question-answer pair—that's broken up between its parts:

1. A: is it good? the Szechuan pork?
2. B: y'like spicy, [uh–
3. A: [yeah
4. B: it's kinda, y'know, hot.
5. A: <u>great</u>
6. B: yeah, me too.

There is a lot going on here. A asks B if a particular dish is good. This is the first part of a question pair, which calls for an answer. B responds with another question, which creates a new expectation for an answer. A anticipates this and answers "yeah" (line 3) before B finishes her thought (which presumably was "y'like spicy, uh, food?").

B doesn't want to give up her turn just yet, so she completes the thought, in line 4. This gives A the opportunity to reaffirm that she does, in fact, like spicy food (that her "yeah" in line 3 was not just an acknowledgment of B's question) before B answers A's first question. A reaffirms her "yeah" response with "great" in line 5. The segment ends with B agreeing that she, too, likes spicy food.

Looking at this segment, it seems like the first adjacency pair, the question about whether the Szechuan pork is good, has never been answered. But it has. The answer is implied in the inserted question in line 2 and the retesting in line 4, all of which is a shorthand for: "Yes, if you like spicy food, then the Szechuan pork is good, otherwise it isn't."

If this seems complicated, it's because it is. It's very, very complicated. Yet, every native speaker of English understands every piece of this analysis because (1) the segment of conversation is rule based; (2) we understand the rules; and (3) we understand that the outcome is the result of cooperation by both speakers, A and B, as they (4) attend to each other's words; (5) draw on cultural knowledge that they share about being out on a date and about Chinese restaurants; and (6) build a conversation dynamically. In this case, two people, in a conversation among equals, have worked together to make everything come out right.

And if you think this is complicated, just add more speakers. With two people in a conversation, A and B, there are two pairs of people—AB (as seen from A's perspective) and BA (as seen from B's perspective)—figuring out each other's motives and behaviors and negotiating their way through the interaction. With three people in a conversation (A, B, and C), there are six pairs (AB, BA, AC, CA, BC, and CB) doing the negotiating. With six people, there are 60 such pairs. Deborah Tannen (1984) analyzed 2 hours and 40 minutes of conversation among six friends at a Thanksgiving dinner. The analysis is a 170-page book, and that doesn't include the hundreds of pages of transcripts on which the analysis is based.

Dinner parties often start out as conversations among six or eight simultaneous participants, but they soon break up into smaller conversations that are easier to manage. Some conversations among large groups of people, however, require special rules so that they don't break up into conversations among shifting subgroups.

◆ TAKING TURNS IN A JURY

Juries in the United States, for example, are composed of six, nine, or 12 members (depending on the rules for trial), and have special kinds of conversation. They have a leader (the jury foreman or forewoman), and people work hard to make sure that the cultural rules for such formal conversations (written down nowhere, but widely understood) are followed. Among other things, the rules require that no one gets completely drowned and sidelined, unless they deserve to be (by breaking the cultural rules themselves).

John Manzo (1996) studied how jurors for a criminal trial managed turn taking in their deliberations. The case was against a man who was charged with possessing a handgun in violation of his parole. The deliberations were videotaped for a PBS documentary. We'll go over Manzo's discovery of one turn-taking rule in this deliberation.

Figure 10.1   Layout of the Jury Table

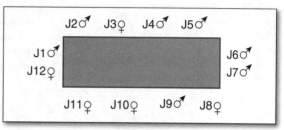

SOURCE: Manzo (1996).

Figure 10.1 shows the layout of the jury table, and Table 10.2 contains the data for one turn-taking sequence. At the start of the deliberations, the foreperson, J1, at the head of the table, on the left, proposed that each juror talk about how she or he felt about the case.

Manzo noticed that, at lines 10 and 12, both juror 2 and juror 12 chime in and support juror 1's suggestion about everyone making an opening statement. It takes 2.5 seconds for juror 2 to respond after juror 12 does, but the foreperson, juror 1, chooses juror 2 (to his left), rather than juror 12. Juror 2 launches right in, down to line 27.

Now, look closely at what happens next. At this juncture, it is still possible for juror 12 to be the next speaker. After all, she had signaled her interest back in line 10. But at the end of his statement, juror 2 turns his gaze toward juror 3, to his left, and then down to the table. Juror 3 cranes her head to see what the foreperson will do next. He nods to juror 3 and she launches into her statement (down to line 39).

The first turn for an opening statement was decided entirely by juror 1, who chose juror 2 over juror 12. The *second* turn, however, is a joint operation, involving three people: the foreperson and jurors 2 and 3. Juror 2's gaze, at the end of his statement, toward juror 3 sets things up; juror 3's craning her neck to see the foreperson is part of the operation; and juror 1's gaze toward juror 3 nails down that it is her turn.

By the time juror 3 completes her turn (at line 39), she only has to shift her weight to her left, for juror 4 to take up the next turn. At this point, the rule is established. No more gazes or instructions from juror 1 are needed.

Table 10.2 Excerpt From a Criminal Jury

Line	Speaker	Text
1 2 3 4 5 6 7 8 9	J1	If I may make a suggestion? rather than- I know that juries uh um >like Mr. ( ) mentioned< like to take a vote right off the bat and. .hh I think if we <u>do::</u> that we'll probably end up discussing it anyhow so let's:: just go around the table discuss the case? and your: .hh views? and uh after:: everybody's said their piece us (.5) we can uh. take a vote on u what we think. if::: that's agreeable to everybody? (1.8)
10 11	J12	uh huh (2.5)
12	J2	sounds good=
13	J1	=so. ((turns to and smiles at J2)) you wanna start?
14 15 16 17 18 19 20 21 22 23 24 25 26 27 28 29 30	J2	mm okay? .hh I found three:: points. that the prosecutor. hadda prove? he proved .hh that the defendant did possess the gun >the defendant <u>knew</u> he possessed a gun< .hh and that uh: the defendant knew he was (.) a convicted felon at the time he uh: possessed a gun. .hh however uh::. because of this case and because of uhm: (1.6) because of the:: record of the defendant uh I 'd have a re- I'd have a real <u>tough</u> time .h uh voting him guiltyu on this a:nduh:- I haven't made up my <u>mind</u> yet .hhh but I see <u>both</u> sides of- both sides of uhm:: <u>both</u> the cases BOTH of the cases as they've been laid out. and uh: rinow? I haven't made up my mind one uh >how I'm goin ta vote. (2.3) ((J2 directs gaze toward J3 and then down to table. J1 then nods in the direction of J3, and J3 cranes her neck in order to meet J1's gaze))
31 32 33 34 35 36 37 38 39 40 41	J3	>Okay I feel the defendant is .< guilty. uh. on all three accusations <u>technically</u>. (.) but I I guess I feel that we should *also* take into consideration the fact that. .h he du::z have a reading disability. as *well* as maybe some <u>other</u> disabilities >I'm not trying to play on your <u>sympathies</u> or anything but. .h it is <u>something</u> that I have to consider tch and right now I haven't (.) determined whether I should name the defendant guilty or innocent. (3.0) ((Juror 3 produces a postural shift toward J4 without eye contact))
42	J4	.hh I fee:l that . . .

SOURCE: Manzo (1996).

A Final Word About Conversation Analysis

Conversation analysis is a highly empirical and highly inductive method, but nothing is a 100% inductive, and in actual practice, it involves both induction and hypothesis testing. You start with a transcript and come at it with as few assumptions as you can and look for regularities in how people manage themselves during conversations. You look for indicator behaviors (gazes, phrases, postures) and, as you pick up clues about these things, you begin to look for repetitions of them.

The process is really hypothesis testing within a transcript. You discover what you think is a regularity, then look for it again to see if you're right. The procedure is the same as that in classical grounded theory, where you let themes emerge from initial narratives and then look for repetitions of those themes. (Further Reading: conversation analysis.)

PERFORMANCE ANALYSIS ♦

In performance analysis, or ethnopoetics, the goal is to discover regularities in how people tell stories, whether in everyday life (Ochs and Capps 2001) or in classrooms (Juzwik 2004). The method is best known in folklore and linguistics and was heavily influenced by the work of Dell Hymes on narratives from the Chinookan languages of Oregon and Washington. We're going to go through Hymes's work in some detail. Because it deals with American Indian languages, it will seem very esoteric at first. But stay with us; its value for all discourse analysis is hard to exaggerate.

The Chinookan Texts

Chinookan is a family of American Indian languages with related but mutually unintelligible branches, like Shoalwater and Kathlemet and Wasco-Wishram. To get an idea of how these languages are related, think of languages, like Spanish, Italian, Rumanian, French, and Portuguese—all branches of (descended from) Latin. Now, between 1890 and 1894, the anthropologist Franz Boas had run into an informant who was fluent in both Shoalwater and Kathlamet Chinook and had collected texts in both languages. Hymes examined those texts as well as texts from Clackamas Chinook (collected in 1930 and 1931 by Melville Jacobs) and in Wasco

(Wishram) Chinook (collected by Edward Sapir in 1905, by Hymes in the 1950s, and by Michael Silverstein in the 1960s and 1970s).

What Hymes found was that features of Chinook that might have seemed idiosyncratic to the speakers of those three Chinook languages—Shoalwater, Kathlamet, and Clackamas Chinook—were actually "part of a common fabric of performance style," so that the three languages "share a common form of poetic organization" in which narratives are "organized in terms of lines, verses, stanzas, scenes, and what many call acts" (D. Hymes 1977:431).

This was a truly important discovery—one with implications for the study of all human discourse. (It also made clear that Native American texts have something to contribute to a general theory of poetics and literature.) Hymes discovered the existence of verses, by recognizing repetition within a block of text. "Covariation between form and meaning," said Hymes, "between units with a recurrent Chinookan pattern of narrative organization, is the key" (1977:438).

Finding Patterns in Performance

In some texts, Hymes found recurrent linguistic elements that made the task easy. Linguists who have worked with precisely recorded texts in Native American languages have noticed the recurrence of elements like "now," "then," "now then," and "now again" at the beginning of sentences. These kinds of things often signal the separation of verses. The trick is to recognize them, and the method is to look for "abstract features that co-occur with the use of initial particle pairs in the narratives" of other speakers who use initial particle pairs. The method, then, is a form of controlled comparison (1977:439).

In a series of articles and books (1976, 1977, 1980a, 1980b, 1981), Hymes showed that most Native American texts of narrative performance (going back to the early texts collected by Franz Boas and his students and continuing in today's narrative performance by American Indians as well) are organized into verses and stanzas that are aggregated into groups of either fives and threes or fours and twos. Boas and his students organized the narratives of American Indians into lines, and this, according to Virginia Hymes, hid from view "a vast world of poetry waiting to be released by those of us with some knowledge of the languages" (V. Hymes 1987:65).

Dell Hymes's method, according to Virginia Hymes, involves "working back and forth between content and form, between organization at the level of the whole narrative and at the level of the details of lines within a single verse or even words within a line" (V. Hymes 1987:67–68). Gradually, an analysis emerges that reflects the analyst's understanding of the larger narrative tradition and of the particular narrator.

This emergent analysis doesn't just happen miraculously. It is, Virginia Hymes reminds us, only through close work with many narratives by many narrators that you develop an understanding of the narrative devices that people use in a particular language and the many ways they use those little devices (V. Hymes 1987).

Sherzer's Study of a Kuna Chant

Joel Sherzer (1994) applied the principles of ethnopoetics to analyze a 2-hour performance that he recorded in 1970 of a traditional San Blas Kuna chant (the Kuna are an indigenous people from Panama). The chant was rendered by Chief Olopinikwa and recorded on tape. After the chant, Sherzer asked his bilingual, Kuna-Spanish-speaking assistant, Alberto Campos, to transcribe and translate the tape. Campos put Kuna and Spanish on left- and right-facing pages (Sherzer 1994:907).

During the performance, another chief, who was in the audience, responded to Olopinikwa, usually with some utterance like "So it is" (rather like hearing "Amen" from worshippers during a sermon at some Christian churches). Sherzer noticed that Campos left those responses out of the translation, but it was just those responses that turned out to be markers for verse endings in the chant.

And Campos left out words like "thus" at the beginning of a verse and phrases like "it is said, so I pronounce," spoken by the narrator at the end of a verse. These phrases also contribute to the line and verse structure of the chant. Campos, in other words, edited the chant to give Sherzer the essentials, but it was the seemingly inessential things—those little framing phrases—that defined cultural competence in performance of the narrative (Sherzer 1994:908). (Further Reading: ethnopoetics and performance analysis.)

LANGUAGE IN USE

This branch of discourse analysis is about how people use language to get things done. Studies in this area involve the detailed analysis of interaction—much like conversation analysis, but paying attention to the content and the motivations of speakers, not just to the structure of their interaction.

People around the world are very adept at using just the right language to find marriage partners (Gal 1978), at using jokes to engage in forbidden political discourse (Van Boeschoten 2006), at using subtle language cues to bribe border officials while giving everyone plausible deniability (Mele and Bello 2007). . . .

One area of interest is situational ethnicity, or ethnic identity switching. This phenomenon—where people adopt different ethnicity markers, depending on the situation—has fascinated social scientists for years (Gluckman 1958 [1940]; Nagata 1974; Okamura 1981). People switch ethnicity by telling jokes, or by choosing particular foods when offered a choice, or by casually dropping cultural-insider phrases that signal ethnicity to others. They may do this to land a job, to get a better price in a bargaining situation, to get a better table in a restaurant. . . .

Negrón's Study of Situational Ethnicity in New York

Rosalyn Negrón (2007) studied situational ethnicity among Puerto Rican American and other Hispanics in New York. Her work focused on how Spanish-English bilinguals use code switching—moving back and forth between two languages—as a marker for ethnic identity switching and for getting things they wanted in various interactions.

One of Negrón's informants was Roberto, a 36-year-old Venezuelan who grew up in New York in a neighborhood of Whites, Blacks, and Latinos. Roberto has blue eyes and white skin. He's married to a Puerto Rican woman and his stepmother is a black Haitian. He is completely fluent in Venezuelan Spanish, two dialects of Puerto Rican Spanish (standard and nonstandard), African American Vernacular English, and New York English.

Roberto sells equipment for street fairs—tables, chairs, canopies, and so on. In the interaction below, Roberto goes into a cellphone store and gives James, the store manager, a flyer about the street-fair business. Like Roberto, James is a Latino who looks European and who speaks English with no Spanish accent at all.

Dropping Hints and Doing Business

As they start to talk, neither one knows that the other is Latino, but both of them have business interests to pursue—Roberto to sell his street-fair merchandise; James to sell his cellphones. Listen:

```
 1   R:    H'you doing.
 2   J:    Alright.=
 3   R:    =You guys ah participating in the street fai(-r)z?
 4   (0.7)
 5   J:    Yeah.
 6   R:    You are? (0.5) 'K. Just in case you need, ah, in
 7         case you need canopies tables and chai(-r)z,
 8   (1.0)
 9         j's gimee a call.
10   J:    Yeah. I don't know when the next one is I
11         haven't got [any-]
12   R:                [May twenty-secon(-d).]
13   J:    Rea:.lly?
14   R:    That's the one with the Chamber and <Clearvie::wz
15         is in deh:: fawl>.
16   (1.0)
17   J:    Mm, well I do the Clearview one over at at my
18         other store.
19   R:    Ah, which store is [that-
20   J:                       [(By the), ah, Junction Boulevard.
21   R:    On Junction?, yeah?
22   J:    Yeah.
23   R:    Well, I got the canopies, tables and chairs. I
24         used to work for Clearview. I worked for Clearview
25         for 8 yea(-r)z.
26   J:    [°Ok.°]
27   R:    [An' ] um I started a canopy company (0.5)
28         that's (0.8) direct contact with dem, so whenever you
29         need one or if you need tables, chai(r)z whatever
30         you need,[ j's give me a cawl ahead of time, let=
31   J:             [°Ok.°
32   R:    =me know what event, give me your spot nuhmbuh and
```

33   it will be there before you get der.
34   (1.0)
35   J: Ok.=
36   R: =And [it'll already be set up.
37   J: [( )=
38   R: =>Yah.<
(Negrón 2007:146)

Roberto is dropping clues all over the place that he's a New Yorker. There's the aw sound (fawl and cawl in lines 15 and 30, instead of fall and call); the use of deh, der and dem instead of the, there and them (lines 15, 28, 33); and the dropped r's in chairs, fairs, years, and numbers (lines 3, 7, 25, 29, 32). So, far, though, there's no hint that either of them is Latino. That soon changes. James looks at the flyer that Roberto gave him:

39   J: Let me give you some information.
40   (5.0)
41   J: *Roberto?!*
42   R: Yeah.
43   J: I had a couple of other customers that that(.) do
44   fairs and stuff.
45   R: O?k.
46   (2.0)
47   J: °Try to give you some info.°
48   (2.0)
49   ((James searches for business card))
50   J: °(Ok)° ((James hands Roberto business card))

In line 41, James reads Roberto's name from the flyer, using perfect Spanish pronunciation of the name. He then hands Roberto his own business card.

51   (3.0)
52   ((Roberto reads business card))
53   R: *Cuchifrito* for Thought.
              ('Puerto Rican soul food')
54   ((Roberto laughs))
55   R: I like that! [That's hot.]
56   ((Roberto looking at business card))
57   J: [(Yeah I),] I own an online magazine
58   called *Cuchifrito* for Thought, it's been around for 8

59   years.
60   R: O?k.
61   J: Ahm, (2.0) I'm working with a company called
62   *Alianza Latina?*
             ('Latino/a Alliance')
63   (.5)
64   J: They did something really big in, ah, Flushing
65   Meadow Park last year.
66   R: *No me diga/h/.=*
             ('You don't say?')
67   J: =Yeah and >it's all *Latino*(-s)< and [and from 21 countries?]
68   R: [*O:h, coño, e(-s)ta (bien)*.]
             ('Oh, damn, that's good.')
69   J: >and they used a bunch [of canopies and stuff like that.]<=
70   R: [°Mm::::h, o?k.°]
(Negrón 2007:148–150)

There's a Lot Going on Here

In line 53, when Roberto reads James's card aloud, he uses perfect Spanish pronunciation for the word *cuchifrito*. *Cuchifritos* are small cubes of fried pork (usually tails, ears, stomach, and tongue) and are a famous Spanish Caribbean dish. Any speaker of Spanish who lives in a Puerto Rican or Dominican neighborhood in New York City would know the word and its ethnic implications. In line 58, when James repeats the word, he, too, uses the Spanish pronunciation. He follows up by telling Roberto that he works for *Alianza Latina*, again code switching from perfect English in line 61 to perfect Spanish in line 62.

A few lines later, in lines 66 and 68, Roberto nails it all down, by responding in Spanish to James's discussion in English about an event in Flushing Meadow Park. And it's not just any old Spanish. In lines 66 and 68, Roberto uses an unmistakably Puerto Rican dialect.

In Negrón's work, we see again how important it is to be steeped in a culture to do this kind of analysis. You have to know, for example, about *cuchifritos*; and you have to know that the aspiration at the end of *diga/h/* in the expression *No me diga/h/* in line 66 is a replacement for an s and that this is characteristic of Caribbean Spanish. (Further Reading: code switching and ethnic identity.)

◆ CRITICAL DISCOURSE ANALYSIS: LANGUAGE AND POWER

The critical perspective in social science is rooted in Antonio Gramsci's discussion (1994; Forgacs 2000) in the 1930s of what he called cultural hegemony. Modern states, Gramsci observed, control the mass media and the schools, the structural mechanisms for shaping and transmitting culture. Marxist theory predicts that the culture (the superstructure) follows the structure, and so the lower and middle classes in modern states come to believe in—even advocate—the entrenched differences in power that keep them subservient to the elite.

In critical discourse analysis, the idea is to show how these power differences—between men and women, for example, or between doctors and patients, employers and employees, and so on—are perpetuated, reinforced, and resisted.

Gender and Discourse

Mattei (1998), for example, counted the number of times male and female witnesses in a U.S. Senate hearing were interrupted. These were panel hearings in the nomination of David H. Souter to the U.S. Supreme Court. There were 30 question periods in these panels, and Mattei counted 76 cases of overlap in the testimony. Thirteen cases of overlap were simply to ask the witness to speak louder or to ask a senator to clarify a question. The other 63 cases were interruptions—that is, cutting off a speaker and trying to take over a turn.

The distribution of these 63 cases is revealing. As we expect, senators (who are in a position of power) interrupted witnesses 41 times; witnesses interrupted senators 22 times. Also as expected, of the 41 interruptions by senators, 34 were against women and 7 were against men. Women, however, were more assertive than men were when it came to interrupting senators: Of the 22 interruptions against senators by witnesses, 17 were by women (see Box 10.2).

Doctor-Patient Interaction

Dozens of studies have established the asymmetry in the doctor-patient relation: Doctors use their knowledge to establish their authority and patients adopt a meek, accepting role.

Box 10.2

Gendered Interruption

Pioneering research by Zimmerman and West (1983 [1975]) showed that, in ordinary conversations, men interrupted women more often than women interrupted men. Later research by these same scholars and by many others has shown how complex the patterns are. Kennedy and Camden (1983), for example, showed that women sometimes interrupt more than men and Kendall and Tannen (2001:552) showed that not all interruptions are equal: some are better characterized as overlapping where the purpose is really "to show support rather than to gain the floor." And West (1995:116) showed that in conversations with men, it is often women's response efforts that enable men to "produce 'something worth listening to' in the first place." (Further Reading: gendered interruption.)

Maynard (1991) analyzed how a doctor delivers bad news to a mother and father of a child who has developmental problems (particularly in language and speech). The parents tell the doctor that their child, J, doesn't seem to be progressing normally in speaking. The doctor says that J is having a problem with language, which, he says, is different from speaking.

The parents don't understand the distinction, and the doctor says:

Language are [*sic*] the actual words. Speech is how the words sound. Okay? J's speech is a very secondary consideration. It's the language which is her problem. When language goes into her brain, it gets garbled up, and doesn't make sense. . . . It has something to do with the parts of her brain that control speech, that control language, and it doesn't work. (Maynard 1991: 454)

What's going on here? The parents are being taught that they don't control certain kinds of information and must therefore accept a subservient role in the interaction. Talcott Parsons had observed this patient-doctor dynamic in his discussion of roles (1951), but Maynard shows that patients don't necessarily come into the doctor's office with that role in mind. Instead, they develop the subservient role, *in cooperation with doctors*, during conversations about the illness.

Coding Doctor-Patient Interactions

Howard Waitzkin and his colleagues (Borges and Waitzkin 1995; Waitzkin et al. 1994) analyzed transcripts of 50 encounters between older patients and primary care internists. Analysis begins by coding the text for elements of interest in the research. In this case, coders were told to "flag instances when either doctors or patients made statements that conveyed ideologic content or expressed messages of social control" and nonverbal elements in the text—like interruptions or shifts in tone of voice or unresponsiveness to questions by patients—"that might clarify a deeper structure lying beneath the surface elements of discourse" (Borges and Waitzkin 1995:35).

When the coders finished their work, they produced a "preliminary structural outline or diagram that depicted how the medical discourse . . . processed contextual issues" (Borges and Waitzkin 1995:35). Then members of the research group met together for several months to review annotated transcripts and preliminary outlines or diagrams. They looked at all the coded instances of ideology and social control—the main topics that they had told the coders to flag—and chose texts to illustrate those and other themes, like gender roles and aging.

There were plenty of instances in which the members of the team disagreed about the meaning of a text. In those cases, they report, "we brainstormed to resolve our disagreements and tried to avoid the discussion's being dominated by one person's views" (Borges and Waitzkin 1995:35).

Recognizing that readers can have different interpretations of the same text, the researchers made all their original data available for reanalysis by filing them at University Microfilms International. Then they present their results, which consist of a series of excerpts from the texts and an analysis of the meaning of each excerpt. (Further Reading: doctor-patient interaction.)

Presenting the Results

This is a common method for presenting results of interpretive analysis: laying out conclusions that are instantiated by prototypical quotes from the transcripts.

For example, a woman visits her doctor complaining of multiple symptoms. The doctor reaches a diagnosis of what's called "suburban syndrome," an illness that affects women who try to do too much outside the home while maintaining all their responsibilities at home as well. The doctor prescribes rest; the patient says that she wants a prescription for tranquilizers. The doctor resists at first, but then relents—and not only gives the patient a prescription, but a renewable one, at that. He tries to reassure the patient that there is nothing wrong with her that withdrawing from a few activities wouldn't fix. Still, the patient returns to her concern about organic disease and the doctor cuts her off:

P: That's what I thought maybe you would give me a blood test today, see if I was anemic

D: [For what? Nah (words)

P: [I sometimes feel light-headed

D: I know.

P: And my mother, and my mother tends to be anemic.

D: Don't choose a diagnosis out of the blue. Buy a medical book and get a real *nice* diagnosis. Well, and you, I'll order them (referring to the tranquilizers). Which drug store do you use?
       (Borges and Waitzkin 1995:40–41)

Borges and Waitzkin comment on this section of text:

From the doctor's viewpoint, a search for an underlying physical disorder is fruitless. Such patients with diverse somatic symptoms can present diagnostic and therapeutic challenges for primary care physicians. The doctor concludes that the patient's physical symptoms reflect troubles in her social context, more than pathophysiology. Yet his attempts to persuade her on this point never quite succeed. . . . A college graduate with young children at home, the patient does not refer at any time to her own work aspirations or to her children, nor does the doctor ask. For the present and the indefinite future, one assumes, her work consists of the housewife's duties. . . . Although the doctor gives a contextual diagnosis, suburban syndrome, potentially important contextual issues arise in the conversation either marginally (brief allusions to the patient's, husband) or not at all (work aspirations, child care arrangements, and social support network). Nevertheless, the doctor manages the patient's contextual difficulties by encouraging rest and prescribing a tranquilizer. Presumably, the patient continues to accept the ideologic assumption that her social role as suburban homemaker is the proper one for her. She thus returns and consents to same social context as before, now with the benefit of medical advice and pharmacologic assistance. (Borges and Waitzkin 1995:41)

Here's another example from the same project—a snippet of interaction between a doctor (D) and his patient (P), an elderly woman who has come in for a follow-up of her heart disease:

> P: Well I should—now I've got birthday cards to buy.
> I've got seven or eight birthdays this week—month. Instead of that I'm just gonna write 'em and wish them a happy birthday. Just a little note, my grandchildren.
> D: Mm hmm.
> P: But I'm not gonna bother. I just can't do it all, Dr. —
> D: Well.
> P: I called my daughters, her birthday was just, today's the third.
> D: Yeah.
> P: My daughter's birthday in Princeton was the uh first, and I called her up and talked with her. I don't know what time it'll cost me, but then, my telephone is my only indiscretion (Waitzkin et al. 1994:330).

Then, the researchers comment:

> At no other time in the encounter does the patient refer to her own family, nor does the doctor ask. The patient does her best to maintain contact, even though she does not mention anything that she receives in the way of day-to-day support. Compounding these problems of social support and incipient isolation, the patient recently has moved from a home that she occupied for 59 years (Waitzkin et al. 1994:330).

And finally, Waitzkin et al. interpret the discourse:

> This encounter shows structural elements that appear beneath the surface details of patient-doctor communication. . . . Contextual issues affecting the patient include social isolation; loss of home, possessions, family, and community; limited resources to preserve independent function; financial insecurity; and physical deterioration associated with the process of dying. . . . After the medical encounter, the patient returns to the same contextual problems that trouble her, consenting to social conditions that confront the elderly in this society.
>   That such structural features should characterize an encounter like this one becomes rather disconcerting, since the communication otherwise seems so admirable. . . . The doctor manifests patience and compassion as he encourages a wide-ranging discussion of socioemotional

concerns that extend far beyond the technical details of the patient's physical disorders. Yet the discourse does nothing to improve the most troubling features of the patient's situation. To expect differently would require redefining much of what medicine aims to do. (1994:335–336)

This interpretive analysis is done from a critical perspective, but the method is hermeneutic: You lay out a chunk of text, add running commentary about what you think is going on, and interpret the result.

Further Reading

♦ For reviews of discourse analysis, see Fairclough (1995), Gumperz (1982), Schiffrin et al. (2001), and Wodak and Reisig (1999).

♦ For more on transcribing conversation, see Atkinson and Heritage (1984), Psathas (1979), and Sacks et al. (1974).

♦ For more on conversation analysis, see Drew and Heritage (2006), Gafaranga (2001), Goodwin and Heritage (1990), Psathas (1995), Silverman (1993, 1998), and Zeitlyn (2004).

♦ For more on ethnopoetics and performance analysis, see D. Hymes (1981, 2003), and for more examples of the method in action, see Bauman (1984, 1986), Blommaert (2006), Juzwik (2004), Poveda (2002), and Sammons and Sherzer (2000).

♦ For more on code-switching as a marker for ethnic identity, see De Fina (2007), Fung and Carter (2007), Gafaranga (2001), and Wei and Milroy (1995). And for other examples (not code-switching) of studies of language in use, see Callahan (2005), Kidwell (2005), and Koven (2004).

♦ For more on gendered interruption, see Anderson and Leaper (1998), Auer (2005), Garrett (2005), James and Clarke (1993), Okamoto et al. (2002), Smith-Lovin and Brody (1989), Tannen (1984, 1994), and ten Have (1991).

♦ For more on doctor-patient interaction, see Heath (1989), Maynard and Heritage (2005), McHoul and Rapley (2005), J. D. Robinson (1998), Robinson and Heritage (2005), ten Have (1991), West (1984), and West and Zimmerman (1983).

CHAPTER **11**

NARRATIVE ANALYSIS

INTRODUCTION

Human beings are natural storytellers, and scholars in every age have been fascinated with the structure of narrative. To tell a story, said Aristotle, is to "speak of events as past and gone . . . nobody can 'narrate' what has not yet happened" (*Rhetoric,* Book III, Chapter 16). A narrative poem, he said, "should have for its subject a single action, whole and complete, with a beginning, a middle, and an end" (*Poetics,* Section 3, Part 23). That was 2,360 years ago, and the study of narrative has never waned.

There are four major traditions of narrative analysis in the social sciences.

1. Sociolinguistics. Analysts in the sociolinguistic tradition focus on the structure of narratives, looking for regularities in how people, within and across cultures, tell stories. Here, the narrative itself is the object of interest.

2. Hermeneutics. Analysts in this tradition look for the larger meaning of narratives by interpreting the content. Here, the narrative is a vehicle for understanding the cultural and historical context in which stories get told.

3. Phenomenology. Analysts in this tradition use personal narratives as windows into the lived experience of the narrators and try to achieve empathic understanding of that experience. Here, the object of study is the experience of the person telling a story, not just the story itself.

4. Grounded theory. For grounded theorists, narratives are data for developing explanations of how things work. We'll treat grounded theory at length in Chapter 12.

◆ SOCIOLINGUISTICS

If you ask a friend to tell you how they met their current partner, you get a narrative. If you're doing interviews and you ask a cop to tell you what happens after they arrest someone, you get a narrative. If you ask someone to tell you what it's like living with chronic back pain, or how they decided to have an abortion, or what it was like to open a McDonald's franchise, you get a narrative.

There is plenty of room for creativity in storytelling, but these decisions are not arbitrary. In every case, the narrator has to think things through and decide what to put in—and in what order—and what to hold back (see Box 11.1).

Box 11.1

Narratives and Discourse

Narrative falls into the part of discourse that operates under the don't-interrupt-this-turn rule (see Chapter 10, on conversation analysis). You are expected to be supportive, inserting an uh-huh here and a you-don't-say there, but the rule is to let the person finish—or at least get to a point where it's appropriate to ask things like: "So, have you met his parents yet?"

Most open-ended interviews in the social sciences are punctuated with lots of little probes like that or with questions that move a respondent from one topic to another. But when people are on a roll, telling a story, the best thing to do is get out of the way. Then, later, you can analyze the narrative for themes and structure—how the plot was laid out, who the characters are, and so on.

Rubinstein's Study of
Women's Reaction to Their Mother's Death

Robert Rubinstein, for example, asked 103 middle-class married women in Philadelphia, ages 40–62, to describe how they reacted to the recent death of their widowed mothers. In the lengthy interviews, Rubinstein asked: "Can you tell me the story of your mother's death? What happened? How did she die?" (1995:259).

The stories of these women ranged from short, chronological sequences (mostly from women who had light or no caregiving duties during their mother's terminal illness, whose mother died suddenly, or who lived at least 2 hours away from their mother by car) to long, complex stories about their mother's illness and death (mostly from women who had heavy caregiving responsibilities and whose mother's terminal illness lasted more than 6 months).

Despite the differences in story length, Rubinstein found strong structural regularities. Most informants began their stories with what Rubinstein calls a "medical preamble" (1995:262) and a "narrative of decline element" (p. 263):

And she even began to notice, you know, something wasn't quite right. All the testing they had done, they said, you know, her mental ability isn't that impaired. And I kinda laughed because in January they had said that she was kinda, like, not too bad for a woman who had seen multiple decline in systems. And I kinda laughed because I wanted to come [back for testing] this year. And they said, "Well, bring her back next year and we'll, you know, assess her. This will be a relative point from which we can determine how gradual her decline is becoming." [So] I call them a year later to say she's dead. (Rubinstein 1995:263)

Most women "medicalized the stories of their mothers' deaths" (Rubinstein 1995:263), with details about visits to emergency rooms and about decisions to have surgery, for example. Most informants also mentioned their mother's personality traits:

So, we didn't push her to move in [with me]. You know, we let her make the decision. And then in May she, uh, we closed up her apartment. She never actually went back and she liked it that way. Yeah, she liked leaving there when she was able to walk [out]. [There's some people for whom] it's almost an insult to their dignity and their independence to be seen that way [starting to physically slide downhill], you know to end up being carted out in a wheel chair. You know, people were noticing that she [mother] wasn't herself, and she was a pretty forceful individual, very dominant, very independent, very outspoken, and her mental abilities had begun to slip a little, but her physical decline was becoming more noticeable. (Rubinstein 1995:268)

Notice the transcription. The author selectively uses "kinda" instead of "kind of" to convey the conversational tone of the story, but he also inserts brackets to indicate things that were implied, but not said, in the narrative. There is only the barest attempt to include the kind of detailed information about false starts and tokens (like umm and uhh) that are required in transcriptions for conversation analysis.

Finally, if women were present at their mother's death, they often described the death scene. Here are two contrasting scenes, which Rubinstein counts as similar parts of these narratives:

1. . . . And she kept on talking. And a lot of it was about things from the past. But whatever it was, even when my brother and sister got there, we couldn't, umm, none of us got through to her. Her eyes were just moving around . . . and she even suffered to the very end, I mean, in her own way. It wasn't a peaceful death, really. (1995:270)

2. Most of the family was there, and my mother was having more difficulty breathing and I had her in my arms trying to talk to her, reassuring her that I loved her and one thing and another. And she died. . . . Yes, right in my arms, which was a beautiful way to die. It was like my mother's gift of peace to me, knowing that I could not have been any closer. (1995:271)

Rubinstein's analysis focuses on the stories themselves, on the themes—like the medicalization of death, the impossible dilemmas that arise in deciding on medical care for the terminally ill, the emotional pain for daughters of not being able to find the "mother-who-was" in mothers who were demented—and on how themes are combined and ordered in predictable ways. (Further Reading: event narratives.)

Comparing Narratives: Bletzer and Koss's Study

Systematic comparison is a hallmark of analysis in the social sciences, whether the data are text or numbers. Keith Bletzer and Mary Koss (2006) analyzed 62 narratives by poor women in the southwestern United States who had survived rape, including 25 Cheyenne women, 24 Anglo women, and 13 Mexican American women. The women in all three groups were, on average, about the same age (mid-30s) and were recruited at health clinics that served their respective communities. In particular, the women recruited had mentioned on a screening survey that they had had an "'unwanted sexual experience' that involved force" (Bletzer and Koss 2006:10).

This is an exemplary sampling design for getting at the research question in the project: How do low-income women of different cultural backgrounds—holding region of the country and socioeconomic status constant—tell the story of being victims of sexual violence? Notice especially that the researchers had participants from the majority culture (Anglo women) so that useful comparisons could be made and that they limited their sample of Mexican American women to those who had been raised at least to adolescence in Mexico.

During the interview, each woman was asked to tell her own story of rape, in her own words. The researchers looked at the stories in terms familiar to students of sexual violence: initial reaction, long-term consequences, mourning, and attempts at recovery. In addition to themes, they looked for narrative structuring devices.

For example, Anglo women used nested stories in their narratives; the Mexican American women made less use of this device; and the Cheyenne women didn't use it at all but typically ordered the phases of their stories more than did the Anglo or Mexican American women (Bletzer and Koss 2006:18). Anglo women also used narrative markers (like "so, then. . . ." "so, anyways. . . ." "and then. . . ." etc.) more than did the women in the other two groups (p. 21).

All the women used the metaphor of feeling soiled and dirty after being raped, and the Anglo women sometimes used triplets in their descriptions (Bletzer and Koss 2006:22):

"Angry, scared, degraded. Felt like I was worthless." (Anglo)

"Then when I got pregnant out of it, it just made me feel dirty." (Anglo)

"I just felt dirty and degraded. I wanted to hide so nobody could see me." (Anglo)

"I felt low, I felt raunchy." (Cheyenne)

"I felt sick, dirty. I wanted to kill myself." (Cheyenne)

"It made me feel like I was dirty, nasty. . . . Made me feel real dirty." (Cheyenne)

"Anguish, very strong. Desperation, and sadness, painful sadness." (*Angustía, muy grande. Una desesperación, y tristeza, dolorosa.*) (Mexicana) (Bletzer and Koss 2006:16)

Bletzer and Koss also note what *isn't* in the narratives: Many of the Anglo and Mexican American women, they say, expressed thoughts of revenge against their assailants, but none of the Cheyenne women did (Bletzer and Koss 2006:17). In fact, the Cheyenne women almost never named men in their accounts of rape; Mexican women named people with whom they had good relations; and the Anglo women named intimates as well as people with whom they had troubled relations (p. 14).

Bridger and Maines's Study of a Heritage Narrative

Across the world, people tell stories about their countries or their communities. These heritage narratives, as Bridger (1996) calls them, can define and sustain people's vision of themselves (see Box 11.2).

Box 11.2

Heritage Narratives

For example, the battle of Masada in Israel "has come to symbolize the heroic affirmation of the Jewish will to resist overwhelming odds and has become a heritage narrative that is compressed into a single phrase—'Never again shall Masada fall'" (Bridger and Maines 1998:324). This narrative, Bridger says, supports the constant need in Israel for military readiness. Similarly, to this day, Serbs talk about the Battle of Kosovo—which they lost to the Ottoman Turks in 1389—as a defining element in the development of Serb nationhood.

It is not just nations that have heritage narratives. Communities have narratives that define them and families have narratives that are only intelligible to people on the inside. Politicians often develop (or encourage others to develop) heritage narratives that make them look good. Narrative, then, is a great way to get at identities, from the personal to the familial to the ethnic to the national.

Bridger and Maines (1998) analyzed the narrative that developed around the planned closing in 1989 of 42 out of 112 Catholic churches in Detroit. In the inner city, the number of Catholic households declined from 104,380 in 1976 to 48,804 in 1988 (p. 327), and some parishes could no longer raise enough money from their declining, and increasingly poor, membership to pay the costs of running a church.

The announcement by then Cardinal Edmund Szoka of Detroit caused a firestorm of protest, with some 400 articles, letters, and editorials in Detroit's two largest newspapers. This corpus formed a heritage narrative around the theme of Detroit's Catholic community and the saving of its churches.

Bridger and Maines analyzed this corpus of text and found three overarching themes, or narrative structures, which they call "White flight," "corporate abandonment," and "Vatican II." These themes emerged sequentially in the data, between September 1988, when Cardinal Szoka announced the closings, and June 1989, when the closings actually began taking place.

In justifying the closings, Szoka emphasized the problem of White flight—the mass post–World War II emigration of Whites from the inner cities of the United States to the suburbs. Indeed, although the population of Catholic households in the inner city dropped, the total number of Catholic households in the diocese grew from 900,000 in 1945 to 1.5 million in 1988 because of growth in the suburbs (Bridger and Maines 1998:328). There were many causes of White flight—running highways through inner city neighborhoods, real-estate blockbusting, school busing—but it was a demographic fact. The narrative was, as Bridger and Maines explain, that no one was to blame for the closing of the churches. It just couldn't be helped.

This narrative played well among some Whites, but for many Blacks in Detroit, White flight was the result of corporate abandonment—the closing of factories and major stores and the subsequent loss of jobs. Corporations that abandoned the inner city justified their move as going where their customers were. For those who remained in the inner city, the church closings were just another expression of the corporate abandonment narrative. For them, the church authorities were treating parishes as "branch plants" and "had abandoned one of the central and historic missions of the church involving ministry to the poor, the weak, and the elderly" (Bridger and Maines 1998:330).

In the final chapter of the story, before the actual closings, people in the inner city, including some local priests, accused the cardinal of abandoning the principles of the Second Vatican Council, held from 1962 to 1965. Vatican II, as it is known, had created a climate of openness in the Catholic church—masses began being held in local languages, rather than in Latin; popular music was introduced in some parishes—and led to more participation by priests and the laity in important local decisions. Cardinal Szoka's critics painted him as an authoritarian who rejected these new principles.

In the end, 31 churches were closed rather than 42, and the final narrative—that Vatican II had mandated more democratic decision making in Catholic parishes and that this principle had been ignored in the decision to close the churches—became the dominant explanation of what had really happened (Bridger and Maines 1998:327).

The big lesson here is that heritage narratives, which define the identity of a community, can have a profound impact on political decisions. This is what happens, for example, when a community mobilizes around a narrative about the importance of small-businesses to stop a Wal-Mart from opening, or around the need to protect the environment to stop a subdivision from being built, or around the need to protect children to stop a park from being sold to developers. (Further Reading: heritage narratives.)

Mathews's Study

Folk tales and myths reflect a society's values, and analysis of these narratives stresses the discovery of those values. Each telling of a folk tale, however, is a whole new narrative. Ask five adults to tell you the story of Little Red Riding Hood and you'll see this variation immediately. In Mexico, people tell a story called "The Weeping Woman." Holly Mathews (1992) collected 60 tellings of *La Llorona* (the weeping woman). Here is one telling:

> La Llorona was a bad woman who married a good man. They had children and all was well. Then one day she went crazy and began to walk the streets. Everyone knew but her husband. When he found out he beat her. She had much shame. The next day she walked into the river and drowned herself. And now she knows no rest and must forever wander the streets wailing in the night. And that is why women must never leave their families to walk the streets looking for men. If they are not careful they will end up like La Llorona. (p. 128)

In another rendition, the husband becomes a drunk, loses all the family money, and La Llorona kills herself. In another, her friends tell her that they've seen her husband with other women. La Llorona, in disbelief, catches him paying off a woman in the streets and kills herself.

Across 60 repetitions, Mathews found differences in the way men and women told the story, but in the end, the woman always kills herself. The morality tale succeeds in shaping people's behavior, says Mathews, because the motives of the characters in the story conform to a schema, shared by men and women alike, about how men and women see each other's fundamental nature (1992:129).

Men, according to Mathews's understanding of the cultural model in rural Mexico, view women as sexually uncontrolled. Unless they are controlled, or control themselves, their true nature will emerge and they will begin (as the story says) to "walk the streets" in search of sexual gratification. Men, for their part, are viewed by women as sexually insatiable. Men are driven, like animals, to satisfy their desires, even at the expense of family obligations. But why should all this lead to women killing themselves if they can't make their marriages work? Most marriages in the rural village where Mathews worked were arranged by parents and involved an exchange of resources between families. Once resources like land are exchanged, Mathews says, parents can't, or won't take back a daughter if she wants out of a marriage. The only way a woman can end her marriage, Mathews explains, is suicide (1992:150). And that, Mathews, says, is why suicide is part of virtually all tellings of the La Llorona tale. The folk tale is a cultural artifact, but its force as a morality play is that it is rooted in a political-economic feature of the speech community that tells and retells it. (Further Reading: folk tales.)

HERMENEUTICS ♦

Hermeneutics, or interpretive analysis of text, has a very long history. It is named for the Greek god, Hermes (known as Mercury in the Roman pantheon), whose job it was to deliver and interpret for humans the messages of the other gods. The ancient Greek word, *hermeneus*, or interpreter, gives us the word "hermeneutics," meaning the continual interpretation and reinterpretation of texts.

Modern hermeneutics in social science is an outgrowth of the Western tradition of biblical exegesis. In that tradition, the Old and New Testaments are assumed to contain eternal truths, put there by an omnipotent creator through some emissaries—prophets, writers of the gospels, and the like. The idea is to continually interpret the words of those texts in order to understand their original meaning and their directives for living in the present (see Box 11.3).

Friedrich Schleiermacher (1738–1834) is credited with first advocating that hermeneutics, as a discipline of interpretation, should apply to all text—oral and written, modern and ancient, sacred and secular—and that it required grounding in historical context (Forster 2008; Schleiermacher 1998). Meaning, after all, is ephemeral, so understanding a text's meaning requires a really solid grasp of local conditions and language. Think, for example, of the stories taught in American schools about Columbus's voyages. The meaning of those stories are quite different for Navajos and for Americans of northern and central European descent.

After Schliermacher, there is an unbroken development of hermeneutics in European and American social science. (Further Reading: modern hermeneutics.)

Box 11.3

Biblical Hermeneutics

Rules for reconciling contradictions in scripture were developed by early Talmudic scholars, about a hundred years after the death of Jesus of Nazareth. For example, one of the rules was that "the meaning of a passage can be derived either from its context or from a statement later on in the same passage" (Jacobs 1995:236). Another was that "when two verses appear to contradict one another, a third verse can be discovered which reconciles them" (Jacobs 1995:236). Today, the 13 Talmudic rules for interpreting scripture remains part of the morning service among Orthodox Jews.

Scholars of the New Testament have used hermeneutic reasoning since the time of Augustine (354–430 A.D.) to determine the order in which the three synoptic gospels (Mathew, Mark, and Luke) were written. They are called synoptic gospels because they are all synopses of the same events and can be lined up and compared for details. There are discrepancies among the writers—about the order of some events, for example—and there are many theories about what caused this—including some that involve one or more of the gospels being derived from an undiscovered source. Research on this problem continues to this day (for a review, see Stein 1987).

Today, in the United States, constitutional law is a form of biblical hermeneutics. It is the task of jurists to interpret that meaning of each phrase in the Constitution in light of current circumstances. It is exegesis on the U.S. Constitution that has produced entirely different interpretations across time about the legality of slavery, abortion, women's right to vote, the government's ability to tax income, and so on.

Although they have not influenced Western social science, there are long exegetical traditions in Islam (Abdul-Rahman 2003; Calder 1993), Hinduism (Timm 1992), and other religions.

Herzfeld's Study of Greek Folk Songs

Michael Herzfeld (1977) studied renditions of the *khelidonisma*, or swallow song, sung in modern Greece as part of the welcoming of spring. Herzfeld collected texts of the song from ancient, medieval, and modern historical sources and recorded texts of current-day renditions in several locations across Greece. His purpose was to show that inconsistencies in the texts come not from "some putative irrationality in the processes of oral tradition" but are, in fact, reflections of structural principles that underlie the rite of passage for welcoming spring in rural Greece.

To make his point, Herzfeld looked for anomalies across renditions—like "March, my good March" in one song compared to "March, terrible March" in another. Herzfeld claims that the word "good" is used ironically in Greek where the referent is a source of anxiety.

Well, is March a subject of symbolic anxiety for Greek villagers? Yes, says, Herzfeld, it is, and we can tell that it is because of widely observed practices like avoidance of certain activities during the *drimata* (the first three days of March). Herzfeld supports his analysis by referring to the *drimes*, a word that denotes the first three days of August, which are associated with malevolent spirits. Because March is the transition from winter to summer and August is the transition from summer to winter, Herzfeld concludes that there is symbolic danger associated with these mediating months. He finds support for this analysis in the fact that February is never referred to with an unequivocally good epithet.

This kind of ever deepening, hermeneutic analysis requires intimate familiarity with the local language and culture, so that the symbolic referents emerge during the study of cultural expressions. You can't see the connections among symbols if you don't know what the symbols are and what they are supposed to mean. (Further Reading: folk songs.)

Fernández's Study of Sermons

James Fernández (1967) recorded and transcribed the sermons of two African cult leaders, Ekang Engono of Koungoulou, Kango, Gabon, and William Richmond of Sydenham, Durban, South Africa. Engono preached in Make (a dialect of Fang) and Richmond preached in Zulu. The sermon by Richmond is 45 pages of text, but the one by Engono is quite short. Here it is in its entirety:

The Ngombi is Fang. The Ngombi is something to take great care of. The Ngombi is the fruit that is full of juice, it is something that can act badly, can feel badly, can cause irritation and trouble. It is better that it should be irritating, that it should burst open. The man who knows well the Fang Ngombi, he has his treasure in the land of the dead. Men must not steal iron because it comes from the forge, it is a man's brother, it is the equivalent of man. The blood of the nursing mother is the food of the afterbirth. We don't know the miracle of the spirit. The Ngombi leaves this on earth with us. We are unfortunate because man does not know the significance of eboka. We are the destroyers of the earth. Our destruction makes noise to God. The miracle is between our thighs. Listen to the words of the wind; listen to the words of the Fang Ngombi, listen to the words of the village. They are of great meaning to you. The widow can not cause trouble through her chatter unless she and another like her marry the same husband. The man without witchcraft is an Angel, he is a dove, hence the ancestors said the poor man is one of two things. He is either worn out or he is without witchcraft. (1967:57)

Fernández interprets each of the esoteric images in the sermon—the Ngombi, the iron, the miracle between the thighs, the blood of the nursing mother, the chatter of the widow—showing how they are components of Engono's general exhortation to his flock to protect marriage and pregnancy. The Ngombi, for example, is a sacred harp, the sound of which (for the members of this cult) is the voice of the goddess of fecundity, and gifts of iron were traditional for bride price.

Fernández's interpretive analysis is a translation of the sermon into the language and worldview of his reader, filling in the gaps and making explicit the implicit linkages that would be understood by a native of the culture. But this is more than just an exercise in interpretation of esoteric images. Fernández points out that in 1960, when he recorded the sermon, the Fang had experienced a dramatic, 40-year decline in fertility, the consequence of an epidemic of venereal disease, and that the existence of the cult was in response to this decline.

Fernández used his intimate knowledge of Fang language and culture to show how the otherwise-esoteric content of a brief sermon addressed societal problems. Perhaps similar sermons are being preached today in Africa in the wake of the staggering die-off from AIDS. We could test that. (Further Reading: sermons, stories, lectures, political speeches, jokes, and life histories.)

♦ PHENOMENOLOGY

Phenomenology is a branch of philosophy that emphasizes the direct experience of phenomena in order to determine their essences, the things that make them what they are. Gold, for example, has been a universal currency for centuries, but variations in its price are accidents of history and do not reflect its essence. This distinction between essential and accidental properties of things was first made by Aristotle in his *Metaphysics* (especially Book VII) and has influenced philosophy ever since.

Phenomenology comes into the social sciences through the work of Edmund Husserl (1964 [1907], 1989 [1913]). Husserl argued that the methods used in studying physical phenomena were inappropriate for the study of human thought and action. Husserl was no antipositivist. What was needed, he said, was an approach that, like positivism, respects the data that we acquire through our senses but that is appropriate for understanding how human beings experience the world (Spiegelberg 1980:210). To do this requires putting aside—or bracketing—our biases so that we don't filter other people's experiences through our own cultural lens and can understand experiences as others experience them (Creswell 1998; Giorgi 1986;McNamara 2005:697; Moustakas 1994).

STEPS IN A PHENOMENOLOGICAL STUDY ◆

A phenomenological study involves six steps: (1) identifying a thing, a phenomenon, whose essence you want to understand; (2) identifying your biases and doing as much as you can to put them aside; (3) collecting narratives about the phenomenon from people who are experiencing it by asking them a really good, open-ended question and then probing to let them run with it; (4) using your now-fresh (after bracketing) intuition to identify the essentials of the phenomenon; (5) laying out those essentials in writing with exemplary quotes from the narratives; and (6) repeating steps 4 and 5 until you are sure that there is no more to learn about the lived experience of the person you're studying.

Steps 2 (bracketing) and 5 (selecting quotes that make clear how the person being studied actually experienced something) are the hardest.

Bracketing

Stepping away from one's biases is easier said than done, but when it comes to bias, less is better, so we do what we can. Zakrzewski and Hector (2004) studied the lived experience of seven men who were recovering from addiction to alcohol. The men were all asked the same, open-ended question "Have you had the experience of alcohol addiction? If so, could you tell me about your experience?" The idea was to get men to talk about whatever they felt were important issues and then to analyze the transcripts to see if there were common themes (p. 65).

Zakrzewski is himself a recovering addict, and he knew that his own experience was a double-edged sword: On the one hand, it gave him plenty of empathy for the men he was interviewing; on the other hand, it meant that he carried a lot of his own biases into the project. To counter this, he went through a bracketing interview in which he was asked the same question that the participants would be asked. By analyzing the transcript of that interview with some fellow doctoral students, Zakrzewski was able to identify themes in his own understanding of addiction. He brought that self-conscious understanding to the process of interviewing his informants and of analyzing the transcripts of those interviews.

Selecting Quotes From Narratives

Selecting quotes that make clear how a person being studied actually experienced something is also easier said than done since it requires that the researcher achieve empathic understanding of the phenomenon being studied. Bramley and Eatough (2005) studied Beth, a 62-year-old woman who was living with Parkinson's disease. They did three in-depth interviews with Beth about her life up to the diagnosis, her medication, and her thoughts about the future. Bramley and Eatough read through the transcripts of the interviews several times to get a feel for the whole picture of Beth's account. They made notes about "anything within the text that appeared interesting or significant" and developed themes "which were felt to capture the essence" of Beth's account (p. 226).

Here is Beth talking about what it's like in the morning before she takes her medicine:

> And I'm in like a fog and it, and it, you can't, you can't think straight, you can't erm, it's a horrible feeling, you feel as if er you you're not connecting, you know, that's all I can explain it, your brain isn't telling your body what to do, it isn't telling you how to speak. (p. 227)

And here is Beth describing what it's like to try and walk:

> And like you have to, when you put your, get up on your feet, you say, "now go on put that foot in front of the other" and you have to physically make yourself do a step and a step at a time, you have to tell your body what to do, it doesn't just doing it by thinking. (p. 228)

Garot's Study of Screeners for Subsidized Housing

Garot (2004) studied government workers whose job it was to screen applicants for subsidized housing. He observed 43 of these screening interviews and took notes on the interactions between the workers and their clients. Right after each screening interview, he interviewed the workers about their reactions to what had happened.

There is a lot at stake in housing eligibility interviews. The resources (the subsidies) available are limited, and the intake workers have to turn people down. The workers can feel terrible guilt, especially when rejected clients get emotional or angry and plead their case—sometimes in tears. Garot describes how the workers deal with this—how they avoid using the word "no," how they develop a kind of "detached concern," and how they ease clients "from hope to rejection" (2004:744). One device is to give the exact same speech to everyone who is being denied—which means memorizing it. Here is what the workers told clients who were ineligible for a housing subsidy:

> You don't have a preference [for a subsidy] at this time. To have a pre-ference, you must either be paying 50% of your income towards your rent, live in substandard housing, or have been evicted for a reason other than the nonpayment of rent. If not, we'll keep you on the waiting list, so that if your situation changes we can call you back in. (Garot 2004:744)

Understandably, people plead in the hope that they can persuade the case worker. Here, Manuel lets the case worker (Anna) know that he and his family could be out on the street.

Anna:	So we'll keep you on the waiting list, and if your income decreases or your rent is higher, review it with us.
Manuel:	Right now, this apartment is not really ours. The owner doesn't wanna rent to us. Where'm I gonna go?
Anna [quietly]:	I don't know.
Manuel:	He prefers Section 8 [a program in which the government subsidizes the rent of private houses to poor people]. I'm gonna be out of a place. That's why I'm applying for this.
Anna:	I suggest you try to find a place here that's not too expensive.
	[Manuel and his family get up and leave the office.] (Garot 2004:744)

This kind of interaction takes its toll. Here's Anna explaining to Garot how she has dealt with this stress:

Anna: I went through a period a few years ago where I was so stressed out, and I was having these horrible migraine headaches. I didn't realize at the time it was because I was having a hard time dealing with saying "no" all the time. [anguished tone] You know, seeing people come in here, and they're like, on the border, where you know, OK they can't qualify by the numbers, but you knew that they were in desperate need. So you couldn't help them. You have to sit there and look at them and say "no." [Anna pauses and looks at me, apparently burdened. Then with a sigh she shrugs off such drama and continues in a more lighthearted spirit.] It took me a while to be able to deal with that, and realize, OK, so I didn't help them, but there's someone else who did qualify who needed it more than they did, but, you know, had the numbers and stuff. It took me a while, but I did. (Garot 2004:758)

As you can see, the method here is to produce a convincing description of what other people have experienced. It may be accompanied by an explanation, but the big goal is to make readers understand the lived experience of the people you've studied. Doing that, like so much of good research, is a craft. You get better and better at it as you do more and more of it. (Further Reading: phenomenology.)

Further Reading

◆ For more on event narratives, see Baker-Ward et al. (2005), Blum-Kulka (1993), Bohenmeyer (2003), Brenneis (1988), Koven (2002), Ledema et al. (2006), and Quinn (2005a). See Reimer and Mathes (2007) on methods for improving accuracy in the collection of event histories.

◆ For more on heritage narratives, see Alkon (2004), Ashworth (2004), Glover (2003), and Hale (2001). Heritage narratives, like the one described in this chapter and the one described by Alkon (2004) are often effective in mobilizing political action. For an analysis of the mobilizing effect of the sit-in narratives of the 1960s, see Polletta (1998).

◆ The classic work in the scientific study of folktales is by Vladimir Propp (1990). The first edition of that work, (which appeared in Russian in 1928) established the study of regularities in folk tale themes around the world. Important modern folklorists include Alan Dundes (1965, 1980, 1989) and Dell Hymes (1981, 2003). For specific examples of research on folktales, see Burke (1998), Doyle (2001), Malimabe-Ramagoshi et al. (2007), and Raby (2007).

♦ Key figures in modern hermeneutics include Wilhelm Dilthey (1989 [1883]) and a collection of Dilthey's essays (1996) and Paul Ricoeur (1981, 1991). For examples of hermeneutic analysis, see King (1996), Mann (2007), and Yakali-Çamoglu (2007).

♦ The systematic study of folk songs was pioneered by Alan Lomax (1968, 2003). For more examples of social science research on folk songs and popular music, see Ascher (2001), Cachia (2006), Harris (2005), Hoffman (2002), Messner et al. (2007), and Stewart and Strathern (2002).

♦ For examples of narrative analysis applied to sermons and stories, see Hamlet (1994), Moss (1994), and White (2006). On analysis of lectures, see Javidi and Long (1989) and Nikitina (2003). And for examples of narrative analysis of political speeches, see Elahi and Cos (2005), Guthrie (2007), Murphy and Stuckey (2002), and Tan (2007).

♦ Jokes are a narrative form in cultures across the world. For examples of narrative analysis of jokes see Davies (2006), Holmes (2006), Lampert and Ervin-Trip (2006), Norrick (2001), and Tsang and Wong (2004).

♦ See Angrosino (1989) and Cole and Knowles (2001) for discussions of life history research and see Hatch and Wisniewski (1995) for a collection of essays on narrative analysis of life histories. For examples of narrative analysis of life histories, see Behar (1990), Hinck (2004), Hoggett et al. (2006), Presser (2004), Rich (2005), and Roy (2006), and see the journal *Narrative Inquiry* (beginning in 1991).

♦ For more on phenomenology, see Giorgi (2006), Moran (2000), Sokolowski (2000), and van Manen (1990). For some additional examples of phenomenological research in the social sciences, see Bondas and Eriksson (2001), Howard (1994), and W. K. Taylor et al. (2001).

CHAPTER 12

GROUNDED THEORY

INTRODUCTION

This chapter and the next are about two very different kinds of text analysis: grounded theory and content analysis. The two methods reflect the two great epistemological approaches for all research: induction and deduction.

Real research is never purely inductive or purely deductive, but for some kinds of research problems, a mostly inductive or a mostly deductive approach is called for. Inductive research is required in the exploratory phase of *any* research project, whether the data are words or numbers. Deductive research is required in the confirmatory stage of any research project— again, irrespective of whether the data are qualitative or quantitative.

In general, the less we know about a research problem, the more important it is to take an inductive approach—to suspend our preconceived ideas as much as we can and let observation be our guide. As we learn more and more about a research problem, the more important it becomes to take a deductive approach.

♦ ON INDUCTION AND DEDUCTION

In its idealized form, inductive research involves the search for pattern from observation and the development of explanations—theories—for those patterns through a series of hypotheses. The hypotheses are tested against new cases, modified, retested against yet more cases, and so on, until something called theoretical saturation happens—new cases stop requiring more testing.

In its idealized form, deductive research starts with theories (which are derived from common sense, from observation, or from the literature), derives hypotheses from them, and moves on to observations—which either confirm or disconfirm the hypotheses.

Suppose we want to understand why preadolescent boys and girls join urban gangs. We would begin by observing some boys and girls who are in gangs and some who aren't. We would look for patterns in their behavior. As we learn about those patterns we would form hypotheses. Here's one: Holding neighborhood constant, kids who have two biological parents are less likely to join gangs than are kids who have one biological parent or are in single parent families or are in foster homes. Eventually, we would want to test our ideas about patterns (our hypotheses, in other words) against new observations.

This paradigm for building knowledge—the continual combination of inductive and deductive research—is used by scholars across the humanities and the sciences alike and has proved itself, over thousands of years. If we know anything about how and why stars explode or about how HIV is transmitted or about why women lower their fertility when they enter the labor market, it's because of this combination of effort.

Human experience—the way real people actually experience real events—is endlessly interesting because it is endlessly unique. In a way, the study of human experience is always exploratory, and is best done inductively. On the other hand, we also know that human experience is patterned. A migrant from Mexico who crosses the U.S. border one step ahead of the authorities lives through a unique experience and has a unique story to tell, but 20 such stories will likely reveal similarities. (Further Reading: induction and deduction in social science.)

OVERVIEW OF GROUNDED THEORY ◆

The same goes for women in Boston who have been through natural child-birth, men in Lagos who have lived through hand-to-hand combat, women in Sydney who are fighting breast cancer, and men in Beijing who are fighting prostate cancer. Each has a unique experience; each has a unique story to tell; and similarities, if there are any, are revealed in the aggregate of those unique stories. Discovering patterns in human experience requires close, inductive examination of unique cases plus the application of deductive reasoning.

And the same goes for social processes. People who are in jail for committing violent crimes, or are living with AIDS, or are studying abroad for a year—all of them have been through a long, long process, with many stages and many choices made along the way. And in each case, the process is unique for each person. But there are patterns, too, with one stage leading to the next and the next. Discovering patterns in social processes also requires close, inductive examination of unique cases plus the application of deductive reasoning.

That's where grounded theory (GT) comes in. The method was developed by two sociologists, Barney Glaser and Anslem Strauss, in a seminal book titled *The Discovery of Grounded Theory: Strategies for Qualitative Research* (1967). As the title implies, the aim is to discover theories—causal explanations—grounded in empirical data, about how things work.

Glaser and Strauss were not the first to recognize the value of qualitative data for developing theory about social processes and human experience. The genius of their book—as important and fresh today, in our view, as it was in 1967—was their systematic, yet flexible methods for doing the job. Glaser and Strauss did more than just claim the usefulness of qualitative data. They showed us how to treat qualitative data as a serious source of scientifically derived knowledge about social and psychological processes.

WHERE DO GROUNDED THEORY DATA COME FROM? ◆

Data for a GT study come from in-depth interviews about people's lived experiences and about the social processes that shape those experiences. All the lessons about interviewing from Chapter 2 apply here. You need to be aware of things like the deference effect—people telling you what they think you want to hear. You need to learn how to probe effectively—to get people talking and then letting them talk. You need to learn to ask questions that may be threatening—about drug use, suicide, sexual behavior—and appear comfortable doing so.

GT interviews can be ethnographic—focused on the culture—but many grounded theorists prefer what Levy and Hollan (1998) call person-centered interviews. In an ethnographic interview, one might ask: "Tell me how people in biochemistry get trained to do science." In a person-centered interview, the question would be: "Tell me how you were trained to do science?"

Kathy Charmaz uses in-depth interviewing "to explore, not to interrogate" (2002:679). Figure 12.1 shows the kinds of questions that Charmaz uses in a GT interview. These are the same kinds of questions that characterize a life story interview (R. Atkinson 1998, 2002), or what Kvale calls a life world interview (1996:5).

Figure 12.1 Examples of Questions in a Grounded Theory Interview

Initial Open-Ended Questions

1. Tell me about what happened [or how you came to _____]?
2. When, if at all, did you first experience _____ [or notice _____]?
3. [If so,] What was it like? What did you think then? How did you happen to _____? Who, if anyone, influenced your actions? Tell me about how he/she influenced you.
4. Could you describe the events that let up to _____ [or preceded _____]?
5. What contributed to _____?
6. What was going on in your life then? How would you describe how you viewed _____ before _____ happened? How, if at all, has your view of _____ changed?
7. How would you describe the person you were then?

Intermediate Questions

1. What, if anything, did you know about _____?
2. Tell me about your thoughts and feelings when you learned about _____?
3. What happened next?
4. Who, if anyone, was involved? When was that? How were they involved?
5. Tell me about how you learned to handle _____.
6. How, if at all, have your thoughts and feelings about _____ changed since _____?
7. What positive changes have occurred in your life [or _____] since _____?
8. What negative changes, if any, have occurred in your life [or _____] since _____?
9. Tell me how you go about _____. What do you do?
10. Could you describe a typical day for you when you are _____? [Probe for different times.] Now tell me about a typical day when you are _____.

11. Tell me how you would describe the person you are now. What most contributed to this change [or continuity]?

12. As you look back on _____, are there any other events that stand out in your mind? Could you describe it [each one]? How did this event affect what happened? How did you respond to _____ [the event; the resulting situations]?

13. Could you describe the most important lessons you learned about _____ through experiencing _____?

14. Where do you see yourself in two years [five years, ten years, as appropriate]? Describe the person you hope to be then. How would you compare the person you hope to be and the person you see yourself as now?

15. What helps you to manage _____? What problems might you encounter? Tell me the sources of these problems.

16. Who has been the most helpful to you during this time? How has he/she been helpful?

Ending Questions

1. What do you think are the most important ways to _____? How did you discover [or create] them? How has your experience before _____ affected how you handled _____?

2. Tell me about how your views [and/or actions depending on topic and preceding responses] may have changed since you have _____?

3. How have you grown as a person since _____? Tell me about your strengths that you discovered or developed through _____. [If appropriate] What do you most value about yourself now? What do others most value in you?

4. After having these experiences, what advice would you give to someone who has just discovered that he or she _____?

5. Is there anything that you might not have thought about before that occurred to you during this interview?

6. Is there anything you would like to ask me?

SOURCE: Charmaz, K. (2002). Qualitative interviewing and grounded theory analysis. In J. F. Gubrium and J. A. Holstein (Eds.), *Handbook of interview research* (pp. 675–694). Thousand Oaks, CA: Sage. Copyright © 2002 Sage Publications.

GT has grown and changed over the years, but in one form or another, it is the most widely used method, across the social sciences, for collecting and analyzing interview data about how people experience the mundane and the exotic, the boring and the enchanting moments of life. Some recent examples: how midwives help mothers make informed choices during pregnancy (Levy 1999); how women in a small town act out class differences while having coffee (Yodanis 2006); how the wives of Japanese students and businessmen in the United States cope during their temporary separation from Japanese culture (Toyokawa 2006) (see Box 12.1). (Further Reading: grounded theory.)

Box 12.1

Changes in Grounded Theory Since 1967

Today, there are several competing schools of grounded theory. Glaser and A. Strauss took different paths, developing competing schools of GT. Glaser has remained more committed to the mostly inductivist approach (1992, 2002); Strauss (first in 1987 on his own and then with Julie Corbin in 1990 and 1998) allowed for more use of deduction. A. Strauss and Corbin (1998:48–52) advocate reading the literature on a topic as part of GT; Glaser (1998) warns against it. Strauss and Corbin are for more use of deduction, Glaser less.

For Glaser (1992), the original two layers of coding in the GT method—fragmenting the text into concepts and then putting it back together in larger theoretical categories—is enough. Strauss and Corbin (1998) have added a third layer they call *axial coding*, in which the researcher looks to discover the relationships among concepts

For Glaser (and for us, by the way), the traditional GT method is applicable to any kind of social research and any kind of data (Glaser 1978, 2001, 2002). For others, the traditional GT method is too objectivist. In an influential series of books and articles, Kathy Charmaz has developed an alternative GT method, called constructivist grounded theory (Charmaz 1995, 2000, 2002). Traditional, objectivist GT, says Charmaz, "accepts the positivistic assumption of an external world that can be described, analyzed, explained, and predicted: truth, but with a small t. That is, objectivist GT is modifiable as conditions change" (2000:524). For constructivists, by contrast, informants and researchers create data together, interactively, during an interview. Charmaz's version of GT is firmly in the tradition of interpretive social science with an emphasis on meaning.

In the original formulation of GT, one of its key elements was *theoretical sampling*—deciding on what cases to study based on the content of the developing theory (Glaser 1978:36; Glaser and Strauss 1967:45–77; Strauss and Corbin 1998:143–161), so that sampling, coding, and theory building all develop together.

Theoretical sampling remains central to the method, even for interpretivists, like Charmaz (2000:519). A review of hundreds of studies, however, in which researchers claim to be doing GT, shows that this key component of the method is not widely followed. Rather, many studies today that fly under the banner of grounded theory are based on the analysis of already collected interview texts. In these studies, scholars may develop a theory on half their data and then check it on the other half. This adds an element of verification to the method as well.

Should all these variations be called grounded theory? Surely, that depends on who you ask, but we think they should. For us, what's important in the end is that useful theories are generated and tested. (For a review of the history of GT and the nuances associated with its various brands, see Dey 1999.)

Whichever epistemological position you favor, objectivist or constructivist, once you have data, all GT analysis involves the same basic steps: (1) coding text and theorizing as you go; (2) memoing and theorizing as you go; and (3) integrating, refining, and writing up theories. Notice that theorizing is in all three steps. GT is a supremely iterative process. You keep building and testing theory all the way through to the end of a project. We treat the three key steps in turn.

1. Coding and Theorizing

In GT research the search for theory begins with the very first line of the very first interview you code. How to get started? Begin with a small chunk of text and code *line by line*. Identify potentially useful concepts. Sandelowski's (1995a:373) advice on this is on the money for us: Mark key phrases, she says, "because they make some as yet inchoate sense."

Name the concepts. Move on to another chunk and do this again. And again. And again. This is what Strauss and Corbin (1998:101–121) call open coding and Charmaz (2002) calls initial coding. Whatever you decide to call it, this is a process of fragmenting data into conceptual components.

The next step involves a lot more theorizing, but now it's in service to *defragmenting* the text. As you code, pull examples of all concepts together and think about how each concept might be related to larger, more inclusive concepts— called categories in the language of GT—that you can look for in texts. This involves the constant comparative method (Glaser and A. Strauss 1967:101–115; A. Strauss and Corbin 1998:78–85, 93–99), and it goes on throughout the GT process, right up through the development of complete theories. Coding for categories is variously called focused coding (Charmaz 2002:686) or theoretical coding or axial coding (Strauss and Corbin 1998:123–142).

Milica Markovic (2006) used this method in her study of 30 Australian women—17 immigrants and 13 native born—who had been diagnosed with some form of gynecological cancer (ovarian, cervical, endometrial, uterine). Markovic's goal was to understand why many women in Australia delay getting medical help for obvious symptoms of these cancers. Table 12.1 shows part of her first interview, with Tipani, a 59-year-old immigrant.

Notice the italics in Markovic's transcript (the right-hand column of Table 12.1). Markovic read the text a line at a time, tagging pieces with italics and creating

Table 12.1 Markovic's Open Coding of an Interview

Open coding	Interview With Tipani
Physical symptoms	I've been *bleeding for about 3 months* actually, when I finally had to go in. I am now nearly 59 and my period had already stopped, I think when I was about 54–55. *It did sort of come*
Lay understanding of symptoms	*as a surprise,* when I started to bleed again, and *I thought,* oh, no, this is just one of those
Using a familiar metaphor to explain unfamiliar event	things, *it's all bad blood coming out,* anyway so, really, didn't really worry me to the extent
Lack of understanding as reason for postponing medical attention	that I even wanted to go to the doctor, and tell the doctor about it, no, I just thought it was one of those things. *The other women I had*
Informal health-advice seeking	*spoken about it,* a couple of *other women 60 years old, and one of them said,* oh, yes, *I've had blood now and again,* and *the other one* said, no, *mine had stopped completely.* And I thought, I am in that group that do have some s ort of period, you know, it really didn't really bother me, I mean, not really, but *when I went*
Reasons for initially seeking advice from a health provider	*to my doctor* because I am on *high blood pressure tablets,* and I said to her, oh, I've been bleeding for about, at that stage for about 2 months, and she was stunned, she said, "What?" so I repeated, and she said, *"Well,*
Health professional's advice	*you shouldn't be bleeding at your age, it must be something wrong,* I want you to *come back and get your smear test done.* Five days, let your period stop, and then 5 days after that you come back, and have your smear." Well, *that didn't happen,* because it never got
Duration and severity of symptoms	stopped. . . . Two months, *I bled really*
Reasons for subsequent presentation to a health professional	*heavily* . . . one night, I was *standing like in a pool of blood.* . . . I had to go to the emergency [in the study hospital] . . . they said to me that there is *definitely something wrong,*
Medical test to find underlying cause of her health problem	so they examined me and the doctor said I had to have a *curette* the next day . . . a week later, it was explained to me that they found some traces of cancer. (Markovic 2006:417)

SOURCE: Adapted from Markovic, M. 2006. Analyzing qualitative data: health care experiences of women with gynecological cancer. *Field Methods* 18:413–429.

codes—that is, names—for the italicized pieces whenever she could. You can do this with a word processor (italics, underlining, highlighting, various type fonts), or even by hand, using different colored highlighter pens, though most researchers today would use a text management program.

The important thing is to get your impressions about concepts down and to give the concepts descriptive names. This gives you a map of what to look for in subsequent interviews. For example, Tipani had at first seen her symptoms as something positive—as "bad blood coming out." Markovic interpreted this as Tipani's applying familiar ideas (menstruation and menopause) to an unfamiliar situation and, more generally, as an example of "women's lay understanding of health problems" (see Box 12.2).

Markovic engaged in constant comparison as she coded each text, thinking about each theme as it appeared and asking whether it was like any other theme that had come before. Markovic's next informant, Betty, in talking about her urine burning, said "It's *just women's things*, there is always something." Markovic labeled it "lay understanding of a health problem." As concepts like these emerge, the grounded theorist looks for them in subsequent interviews. (Further Reading: the constant comparative method.)

Markovic used the constant comparative method to isolate and refine themes, but you can use the method to stimulate the production of themes by applying it to sentences ("How is Sentence 1 similar to or different from Sentence 2?"), paragraphs, interviews, respondents, and whole cases. Constant comparison forces you to think about each theme you develop. How did I use it earlier in the text? Is it the same thing here? If not, should I make a new theme? If so, should I go back and re-code earlier segments to reflect my new understanding (see Box 12.3)?

2. Memoing and Theorizing

Keep running notes about each of the concepts you identify, including hypotheses about how the concepts may be related. This is memoing (Charmaz 2002:687–689; Glaser 1978:283–292, 116–127; Strauss and Corbin 1998:217–223). Memos are more than annotations. They are field notes (which can run on for pages) about concepts in which you, as the theorist, lay out your observations, hunches, and insights on the fly. Memoing begins with the first concept you identify and continues right through the process of defragmenting the text and of building theories.

"Memo writing," says Kathy Charmaz, "is the intermediate step between coding and the first draft of the completed analysis" (2000:517). In a series of powerful works, Charmaz (1987, 1991, 1995) has studied how people learn to live with chronic illness. Table 12.2 shows Charmaz's line-by-line coding of

---

Box 12.2

Naming Concepts and Categories

Notice the names that Markovic gave to the concepts she identified in Table 12.1: "physical symptom," "duration and severity of symptoms," "informal health-advice seeking," and "lay understanding of a health problem." These are constructs that Markovic came up with. She might have used the vocabulary that informants use themselves, like "women's things." This is called *in vivo* coding in GT (Glaser 1978).

Richard Addison (1992) followed nine medical graduates through their three years of residency as they trained to become family physicians. As he read through his interviews with the residents, Addison tagged words like punting (pretending you have the answer to a problem while you're desperately looking for it), pimping (grilling of young physicians by older ones on fine points of medicine), dumping (transferring by private hospitals of unprofitable patients to public hospitals), and surviving (getting through the hell of residency).

These were, said Addison, words that the residents had used and that stood out to him as being significant for understanding what the residents were going through.

Using the vocabulary of your informants to name concepts is a great idea if you run into words, like the ones Addison co-opted in his work, that are clearly important concepts for your informants.

Most codes, however, are not of the in vivo kind, but are rather investigator derived and are the first cuts at analysis. Suppose you see this in an interview: "We didn't have car seats when I was a kid and we had a great time playing in the back seat on trips. To hear people talk today, you gotta wonder how anyone my age survived childhood." Suppose you code this as "nostalgia for simpler times."

Not as catchy as pimping and dumping, but it shows that you're well into data analysis. It also shows that, as Lincoln and Guba point out, concepts don't somehow miraculously emerge from text. Detecting and naming concepts text takes a lot of "effort, ingenuity, and creativity" (1985:340).

---

a snippet from one interview with Christine, a 43-year-old woman who was suffering from lupus. The woman had been hospitalized eight times and was just getting back to work.

Box 12.3

Intercoder Reliability

Most GT projects are small—the kind of thing that can be run by one investigator. In team research, with lots of coders, the design will always call for multiple checks of intercoder reliability all along the way—to make sure that all the coders are seeing the same thing when they read a chunk of text.

Formal checks for intercoder reliability are a hallmark of content analysis, so we'll discuss this in the next chapter, but having at least two people code any set of texts is always better than having just one person do it. If (because of lack of time or money) you must do all your own coding, have at least one other person code some sample chunks of texts to make sure that your coding is not idiosyncratic.

The highlighted items in Table 12.2 are Charmaz's focused codes. These are the codes that appear again and again in the texts and become labels for categories, or sets of lower-level codes. (In the end, a GT analysis is a story that integrates these focused codes—the main categories of events and ideas in a set of texts. But you can't get to focused codes without doing the fine-grained coding first.) One of Charmaz's focused codes in Table 12.2 is suffering as a moral status. Figure 12.2 shows part of Charmaz's memo about this concept.

Read the material in Figure 12.2 carefully. Notice how Charmaz plays with words ("worth less" and "worthless") and how she puts in extra words ("seen known") to make sure that all her thoughts get down in the memo. And notice how she copies the chunk of the interview on which she is commenting directly into the memo. She says she finds it helpful to do that (2002:689), but you might be more comfortable hyperlinking your memos to the original text. These are matters of style. Whatever other disagreements they had about GT, Glaser and Strauss agreed that getting memos and hypotheses down early and often is indispensable (Glaser 1978:58; Strauss 1987:127).

3. Building and Refining Theories

As coding categories emerge, the next step is to link them together in theoretical models around a central category that holds everything together (Glaser and Strauss 1967:40; Strauss and Corbin 1998:146–148).

Here again, the constant comparative method comes into play, along with negative case analysis—looking for cases that do not confirm your

Table 12.2 Charmaz's Open Coding of an Interview

Open Coding	Interview With Christine
Recounting the events Going against medical advice Being informed of changed rules Suffering as moral status Accounting for legitimate rest time Distinguishing between "free" and work time Receiving an arbitrary order Making a moral claim Finding resistance; tacit view of worth Having a devalued moral status because of physical suffering Taking action Learning the facts Making a case for legitimate rights Trying to establish entitlement Meeting resistance Comparing prerogatives of self and other Seeing injustice Making claims for moral rights of personhood	And so I went back to work on March 1st, even though I wasn't supposed to. And then when I got there, they had a long meeting and they said I could no longer rest during the day. The only time I rested was at lunchtime, which was my time, we were closed. And she said, my supervisor, said I couldn't do that anymore and I said, "It's my time, you can't tell me I can't lay down." And they said, "Well you're not laying down on the couch that's in there, it bothers the rest of the staff." So I went around and I talked to the rest of the staff, and they all said, "No, we didn't say that, it was never brought up." So I went back and I said, "You know, I was just was talking to the rest of the staff, and it seems that nobody has a problem with it but you," and I said, "You aren't even here at lunchtime." And they still put it down that I couldn't do that any longer. And then a couple of the other staff started laying down at lunchtime, and I said, you know, "This isn't fair. She doesn't even have a disability and she's laying down," so I just started doing it.

SOURCE: Charmaz 2002:677-678. Qualitative interviewing and grounded theory analysis. *Handbook of Interview Research: Context and Methods.* J. F. Gubrium and J. A. Holstein, eds. Thousand Oaks, CA: Copyright 2002 © Sage Publications.

model (Lincoln and Guba 1985:309–313). The procedure is simple and clear: You generate a model about how whatever you're studying works, right from the first interview, and you see if the model holds up as you analyze more interviews.

This is how Markovic proceeded, as she analyzed those 30 interviews with women in Australia who had been diagnosed with some form of gynecological cancer. Here is her model, based entirely on the interview with Tipani (shown in Table 12.1):

Figure 12.2 Charmaz's Memo About the Concept of Suffering as a Moral Status

Suffering is a profoundly moral status as well as a physical experience. Stories of suffering reflect and redefine that moral status. With suffering comes moral rights and entitlements as well as moral definitions—when suffering is deemed legitimate. Thus the person can make certain moral claims *and* have certain moral judgments conferred upon him or her.

Deserving

Dependent

In Need

Suffering can bring a person an elevated moral status. Here, suffering takes on a sacred status. This is a person who has been in sacred places, who has seen known what ordinary people have not. Their stories are greeted with awe and wonder. The self also has elevated status. . . .

Although suffering may first confer an elevated moral status, views change. The moral claims from suffering typically narrow in scope and power. The circles of significance shrink. Stories of self within these moral claims may entrance and entertain for a time—unless someone has considerable influence and power. The circles narrow to most significant others.

The moral claims of suffering may only supersede those of the healthy and whole in crisis and its immediate aftermath. Otherwise, the person is less. WORTH LESS. Two words—now separate may change as illness and aging take their toll. They may end up as "worthless." Christine's statement reflects her struggles at work to maintain her value and voice.

And so I went back to work on March 1st, even though I wasn't supposed to. And then when I got there, they had a long meeting and they said could no longer rest during the day. The only time I rested was at lunchtime, which was my time, we were closed. And she said, my supervisor, said I couldn't do that any more and I said, "It's my time, you can't tell me I can't lay down." And they said, "Well you're not laying down on the couch that's in there, it bothers the rest of the staff." So I went around and I talked to the rest of the staff, and they all said, "No, we didn't say that, it was never brought up." So I went back and I said, "You know, I was just was talking to the rest of the staff, and it seems that nobody has a problem with it but you," and I said, "You aren't even here at lunchtime." And they still put it down that I couldn't do that any longer. And then a couple of the other staff started laying down at lunchtime, and I said, you know, "This isn't fair. She doesn't even have a disability and she's laying down," so I just started doing it.

Christine makes moral claims, not only befitting those of suffering, but of PERSONHOOD. She is a person who has a right to be heard, a right to just and fair treatment in both the medical arena and the workplace.

SOURCE: Charmaz, K. (2002). Qualitative interviewing and grounded theory analysis. In J. F. Gubrium and J. A. Holstein (Eds.), *Handbook of interview research* (pp. 675–694). Thousand Oaks, CA: Sage. Copyright © 2002 Sage Publications.

In the presence of an unusual symptom, women (more specifically, immigrant women) seek advice from their peers. If they (or those whom they ask for advice) interpret their symptoms in light of their previous life experiences and normalize the severity of the symptoms, women wait until their next regular appointment for an ongoing health problem before reporting their cancer symptoms to a health professional. On the other hand, if women experience disruptions to their everyday life (that is, symptoms that cannot be normalized easily), this influences their decision to report the symptoms to a health professional earlier. (Markovic 2006:418)

Markovic's second informant, Betty, produced some new themes, but overall, Betty's story confirmed the preliminary hypothesis. Betty's symptoms were not the same as Tipani's, but like Tipani, Betty found reasons to normalize her symptoms and the result was the same: a delay in diagnosis despite the fact that the symptoms were disruptive of daily life.

Markovic's third informant, Tulip, reported that she went to see a physician at the first signs that something was wrong. According to Tulip, her first physician referred her to another, the second one referred her to a third, and the third referred her to a hospital for tests. The tests confirmed that Tulip had ovarian cancer. Markovic modified her hypothesis to accommodate this otherwise negative case.

Unusual symptoms that cannot be interpreted as normal, given the woman's individual life circumstances, influence her prompt seeking of advice from a health professional. A health professional, however, may provide referral for diagnostic tests and to a specialist other than a gynecologist, which can lead to diagnostic delays. (Markovic 2006:420)

Markovic's next informant, Barbara, reported being sent for several ultrasounds that came back negative. The doctor told her she had an enlarged liver from "all that alcohol you drink." Barbara shot back:

Listen here, if the pubs had to depend on me buying alcohol, they'd go broke. . . . I said to him, "*Aren't you getting sick and tired of sending me for all these ultrasounds* and everything?" So he said, "Look, I'll refer you to [a woman's hospital] to see what they say." (2006:420)

With each new interview she coded, Markovic compared all reported events to one another—the constant comparative method again—and found that many women had experienced incorrect diagnoses and having their concerns dismissed by clinicians. She modified her hypothesis again, "to accommodate the reported lack of responsiveness of health providers to women's distress and women's perception that the onus was being placed on them to be persistent in seeking professional health advice" (Markovic 2006:421).

In the end, 19 of the 30 women whom Markovic interviewed said they had experienced delays in diagnosis. This became the core category for analysis. Among the 19 who experienced delays, 14 *had not* normalized their symptoms and *had* told their doctors that the symptoms were disruptive. Seven of those 14 reported having had their symptoms initially dismissed by physicians and six of the seven were immigrants.

Figure 12.3 shows Markovic's final grounded theory, or model, to account for all 30 of her cases.

Figure 12.3 Markovic's Grounded Theory of Delays in Diagnosing Women's Cancer in Australia

1. If women can normalize their symptoms by placing the symptoms in the context of their life cycle or as normal signs of female physiology, they are likely to delay seeking advice from a professional, causing a delay in proper diagnosis. The likelihood of this happening in these cases is low: 5 out of 30 women (17%) fall in this category.

2. These women eventually visit a health professional when the symptoms become more severe. This suggests that public education about the signs of gynecological cancer is an appropriate intervention for this part of the problem.

3. Among the 25 women who visited doctors soon after symptoms appeared, fourteen reported that their physicians either dismissed their concerns (i.e., normalized the symptoms) or referred them to inappropriate diagnostic tests and specialists. These tests, which did not suggest any underlying pathology, caused further delays in proper diagnosis by the clinicians, according to these women.

4. Most women reported that they experienced some delay in accessing the public health care system (they were put on waiting lists), but most women would not have been on the list for longer than a couple of weeks or so.

5. The report of a prompt diagnosis (11 of 30 cases) was accompanied by any or some combination of the following: reports of regular screening and a Pap test (which detected cervical cancer), symptoms incongruent with women's life cycle (lump on the vulva, vaginal bleeding among younger women), accidental finding of gynecological cancer during regular health exams, and diagnostic acumen on the part of clinicians.

SOURCE: Markovic, M. (2006). Analyzing qualitative data: Health care experiences of women with gynecological cancer. *Field Methods, 18,* 413–429.

A GT PROJECT: SCHLAU'S STUDY OF ♦ ADJUSTMENT TO BECOMING DEAF AS AN ADULT

Let's go through one more GT project to illustrate the pieces. Jane Schlau (2004) used GT in her doctoral research on the adjustment to acquired deafness—that is, adjustment to deafness among people who, like her, lost their hearing after learning to communicate with full hearing. She interviewed 24 people by e-mail (the perfect medium for interviewing the deaf) about their experiences and generated 216 pages of material. Schlau did not use theoretical sampling. This was her complete corpus. She coded line by line and, as is typical at the initial stage of GT, she generated a lot of codes—128 of them—shown in Table 12.3.

Next, Schlau compared and contrasted all these initial codes across all her respondents, looking for similarities and differences and reducing the number of codes. She combined codes like ambivalence, denial, and depression into a category she called emotional reactions. She combined bluffing, lip reading, and several other open codes into one she called

Table 12.3   Listing of 128 Open Codes From Schlau's Study of the Deaf

Acceptance	Death	Groups	Meeting others	Self
Accommodations	Denial	Guilt	Mental health	Self acceptance
ADA	Dependence	"Hearies"	Mental illness	Self-concept
Adaptation/change	Depression	Hearing again	Money	Sign
Adjustment	Disability	Hearing aids	Music	Sleep
Advocacy	Disclosure	Hearing dogs	Notice	Social
Ambivalence	Discovery	Helping others	Other disabilities	Speechreading
Asking for help	Doing for others	Holidays	Others	Stigma
Attitude	Dreams	Humor	Phone	Stress
Avoidance	Driving	Identity	Pity	Substitutes
Awareness	Drugs	Impact on life	Positives	Suicide
Before hearing loss	Educating others	Inclusion	Preconceived attitudes	Support
Bias/choice	Education	Interventions	Pretending	Surrender
Bluffing	Effects on others	Intimacy	Process	Talk to others
Can't do's	Emotions	Isolation	Psychology	Talking about it

Career	Employment	Knowing others	Reading/ research	Technology
Changes	Escape	Knowledge	Reality	Time
Choice	Exclusion	Kübler-Ross	Realization	Tolerance
CI	Existentialism	Learning	Reflection	Travel
Communication	Expectations	Life	Regrets	Treatment
Communication needs/assertiveness	Family	Limits	Religion	Trust
Confirmation	Fatigue	Lip-reading	Replacements	Vocational Rehabilitation
Control	Final comments	Loss	Resentment	Voice
Conversations	Friends	Lost words	Responsibility	Wanting to hear again
Courage	Gave-up	Marriage	Risk	
Deaf	Grief	Medical	Safety	

SOURCE: Schlau (2004:71).

communication. She reduced the 128 codes to 44, shown in Table 12.4 and then reduced all of those codes to just seven major codes: In the Beginning, Reactions/Stigma, Symptoms, Talking about it, Defining Moments, Coming to terms/New reality, and Learning (Schlau 2004:73–74).

Schlau saw these seven codes as parts of a core theme, adjusting to acquired deafness. When she reached this point in her analysis, Schlau went back over the texts and did *selective coding* to learn in-depth as much as her data could tell her about how each of the 24 participants in her research had adjusted to acquired deafness. Everyone adjusted, but not everyone adjusted in the same way. All 24 of Schlau's informants reported similar experiences at the onset of hearing loss. That's the in-the-beginning code, and all of them reported defining moments (like the first time they realized that they couldn't talk on the phone).

Shlau's grounded theory of adjustment to acquired deafness is shown in Figure 12.4.

Table 12.4   Forty-Four Open Codes in the Second Stage of Schalu's Coding

Acceptance	Driving	Intimacy	Self/identity
Adjustment	Education	Isolation	Sign Language
Advocacy	Effect on/from others stigma	K-R/death	Social
Avoidance/escape	Emotions	Medical	Stress
Can't do/limits	Family	Music	Substitutes
Career/employment	Fatigue	Phone	Psychiatric
Changes/adjustment/ dealing	Final Comments	Positives	Talks about deafness to family/others/disclosure
CI	Finances	Reading/research	Technology
Communication	Hearing aids	Reality	Travel
Control vs. uncontrollable	Impact on life/loss	Reflection	Vocational Rehab
Dependence	Interventions/support/LDAs	Religion	Voice

SOURCE: Schlau (2004: 73).

◆ VISUALIZING GROUNDED THEORIES

Many grounded theorists find that visualizing the emerging theory with one or more of the modeling formats described in Chapter 6 helps them integrate their models of how things work.

Margaret Kearney and her colleagues (1995) interviewed 60 women who reported using crack cocaine an average of at least once weekly during pregnancy. The semistructured interviews lasted from 1 to 3 hours and covered childhood, relationships, life context, previous pregnancies, and actions taken in the current pregnancy related to drug use, prenatal care, and self-care.

Kearney et al. coded and analyzed the transcripts as they went. As new topics emerged, investigators asked about the topics in subsequent interviews. In this way, they linked data collection and data analysis in one continuous effort. As they identified categories, they looked to see how

Figure 12.4   Schlau's Grounded Theory of Adjustment to Acquired Deafness

The discovered grounded theory illustrates how the process of becoming deafened begins the same way for everyone. All participants, once aware of hearing loss, sought medical attention. When hearing loss was confirmed, they had strong emotional reactions. These emotional reactions were also noted in my pilot study. As participants went through medical procedures and experienced countless emotions, they also obtained hearing aids, in an effort to mitigate the effects of hearing loss.

Following these reactions, the process participants went through varied based upon the individual. Factors such as personality, the influences of parents and upbringing, are just a couple of the variables that effected individual adjustment. However, all participants experienced the physicality of deafness—the symptoms of being deaf. All participants discussed changes in their lives, based upon the effects of deafness on communication. The reciprocity of communication, as stated by Goffman (1959, 1967) structures our everyday interactions. When this basic tenet of communication breaks down, due to deafness and the resultant inability to receive communication, reality is changed. As reality changed for the participants, as they experienced the effects and symptoms of deafness, they all had some defining moment, where the realization of the need for change "hit." The loss of the ability to use or participate in an activity that once took no thought—such as watching television or using the phone—was a reality check for all participants. This brought the participants to the point of coming to terms with being deafened and forming a new reality.

Here is where differences among participants were clearly noticeable. Those who were "Accepted" all had deaf friends. They all had some family support; all signed to some degree; all found positives in deafness; all were willing to disclose their deafness and all reflected and learned to be deaf. Those who were "Struggling" all collected SSDI. They all had little or no family support; they did not sign; they did not have deaf friends; they either told selected people they were deaf or they tried to hide their deafness. Ultimately, they did not experience double loop learning and avoided internalizing a change in their reality.

Those who were "Resigned" to deafness also generally had little family support. They were not interested in sign language; generally found nothing positive about their deafness; told only select people they were deaf; and had only hearing friends or were isolated. They also did not experience double-loop learning through reflection, but most did experience some reflection and were often aware of changes they could make but had not internalized these changes.

SOURCE: Schlau (2004:161–162).

categories were related to other things and to one another. They recorded their ideas and impressions about these interactions in the forms of memos and they used the relationships they discovered to form a preliminary model.

With each subsequent transcript, they looked for negative cases and pieces of data that challenged their emerging model and adjusted it to include the full range of variation that they found in the transcripts.

By the end of their analysis, Kearney et al. (1995) identified five major categories that they called "value," "hope," "risk," "harm reduction," and "stigma management." Women valued their pregnancy and their baby-to-be in relation to their own life priorities (value); women expressed varying degrees of hope that their pregnancies would end well and that they could be good mothers (hope); and they were aware that cocaine use posed risks to their fetus but they perceived that risk differently (risk). Women tried in various ways to minimize the risk to the fetus (harm reduction) and they used various stratagems to reduce social rejection and derision (stigma management).

By the time they had coded 20 interviews, Kearney et al. realized that the categories harm reduction and stigma management were components of a more fundamental category that they labeled "evading harm" and that the categories value, hope, and risk were components of a more fundamental category that they labeled "facing the situation."

After about 30 interviews had been coded, they identified and labeled an overarching psychological process they called "salvaging self" that incorporated all five of the major categories. This was the core category in their theory. By the time they'd done 40 interviews, Kearney et al. (1995) felt they had reached theoretical saturation—they were not discovering new categories or relations among categories. Just to make sure, they conducted another 20 interviews and confirmed the theoretical saturation.

Figure 12.5 shows the graphic model that Kearney et al. produced to represent their understanding of how the process worked. Notice how each of the substantive themes in their model is succinctly defined by a quote from a respondent. (Further Reading: visualizing models.)

Verifying the Model

Once the theory was built, Kearney et al. took the next step by doing what Lincoln and Guba (1985:314–316) call member checks. They took their model back to stakeholders in their study—members of the project staff, health and social service professionals who were familiar with the population, and a group of 10 pregnant drug users who were not among those interviewed for the study—and asked if the model rang true.

It did. Kearney later studied women who were trying to recover from drug and alcohol addiction but weren't pregnant. Those women reported that they, too, were trying everything they could to salvage some sense of self (Kearney, personal communication; see also Kearney 1996, 1998).

Figure 12.5 The Development of Kearney's Core Category in a Grounded Theory of Cocaine Use Among Pregnant Women

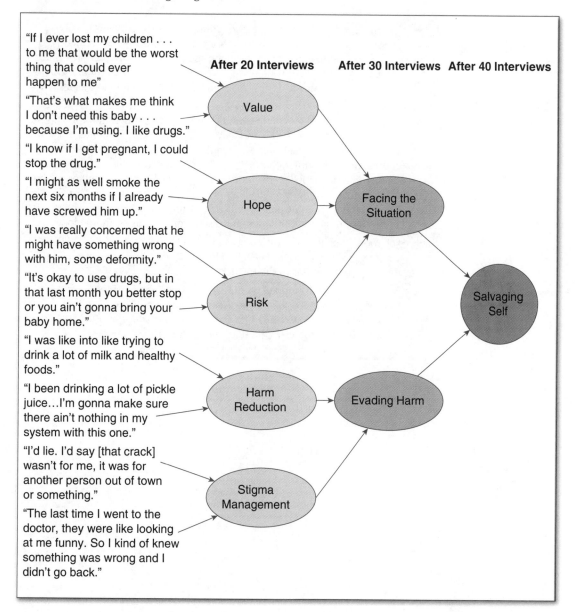

SOURCE: Adapted from Kearney, M. et al. 1995:210. Salvaging self: A grounded theory of pregnancy on crack cocaine. *Nursing Research* 44(4) July/August:208–213.

Further Reading

♦ For more on induction and deduction, see Kaplan (1964). This is a classic on research methods for the social sciences. See Scott (1991) for a review of philosophical issues in the social sciences. Two philosophers associated with the problem of induction and deduction are David Hume and John Steward Mill. See P. Jones (1996) on Hume and Harrison (1996) on Mill.

♦ In addition to the key volumes on GT already mentioned in the text, see Bryant and Charmaz (2007) and Dey (1999). For more examples of GT in action, see Brudenell (1996), Churchill et al. (2007), Ekins (1997), Hebert and Papadiuk (2008), Schraw et al. (2007), and Van Vliet (2008). Many studies that are labeled as grounded theory lack one or another of the elements of GT as developed either by Glaser and Strauss (1967) or Glaser (1992) or Strauss and Corbin (1997). See Cutliffe (2005) and Greckhamer and Koro-Ljungberg (2005) and for discussions of this phenomenon.

♦ For more on the constant comparative method, see Boeije (2002) and Glaser (1965). See Conrad (1978), Hedley (2002), and Scott et al. (2007) for some applications of the method.

♦ For more on visualization of models and theories, see Chapter 6. For recent examples of grounded theories represented graphically, see Churchill et al. (2007), Weaver and Coleman (2005), and Witavaara et al. (2007). A key work on using graphics in the sciences is Tufte (1997).

CHAPTER 13

CONTENT ANALYSIS

INTRODUCTION

Content analysis is a set of methods for systematically coding and analyzing qualitative data. These methods are used across the social sciences and the humanities to explore explicit and covert meanings in text—also called manifest and latent content—and for testing hypotheses about texts. Whether the research task is exploratory or confirmatory, content analysis is usually quantitative analysis. This is one thing that distinguishes content analysis from grounded theory.

But the big difference between grounded theory and content analysis is their epistemological pedigree: In grounded theory, the idea is to let understanding emerge from the close study of texts. This comes from the great tradition of inductive science. Content analysis involves the tagging of a set of texts or other artifacts with codes that are derived from theory or from prior knowledge and then analyzing the distribution of the codes, usually statistically. This comes from the great tradition of deductive science.

There is no point in talking about which of these traditions is better. They're both terrific if you use them to answer appropriate questions. (For more on induction and deduction, see the beginning of Chapter 12 and Further Reading in Chapter 12.)

◆ HISTORY OF CONTENT ANALYSIS

Content analysis has very deep roots. Wilcox (1900) studied the content for June and September 1898, and September 1899, of 147 newspapers in the 21 most populous cities of the United States. He came up with 18 categories of content—including war news (the Spanish American was big news that year), foreign news, business news, sporting news, society news, news of crime and vice, editorials, want ads, retail ads, and so on—and estimated the number of column inches devoted to each category in each paper.

At the time, newspapers were being criticized for focusing too much on sensational stories, particularly about crime and vice (the cliché "If it bleeds, it leads" was as true then as it is now). Wilcox found that the worst offender devoted 19% of its space to crime and vice, and, on average, just 3% of the total space in American newspapers in 1898 was devoted to crime and vice (1900:67, 70). Still, as Krippendorff notes (2004a:5), Wilcox criticized the greed that drove some publishers to focus on sensational news.

Wilcox's methods were crude. He doesn't tell us how he came up with the 18 categories and he made all the decisions about coding the papers himself. But for the time, Wilcox's study was front-edge work. Since then, of course, there have been great advances in sampling and measurement and content analysis has become an important method of investigation across the social sciences.

The systematic application of scientific methods for analyzing text got a real boost with the study of political propaganda, particularly in the period before and during World War II. (See Krippendorff [2004a:6–12] and Neuendorf [2002:23–45] for excellent reviews.) (See Box 13.1.)

Box 13.1

How Evidence From Content Analysis Became Admissible in Court

When the Nazis came to power in the 1930s, the U.S. Federal Communications Commission began monitoring short-wave radio broadcasts from Germany. Analysts established 14 major propaganda themes in the Nazi media. In 1942, the U.S. Department of Justice sued William Dudley Pelley for sedition, claiming that Pelley was publishing pro-Nazi propaganda in the United States while the United States was at war with Germany.

In court, the Department of Justice relied on work by independent coders who had been asked to classify 1,240 items in Pelley's publications as belonging or not belonging to one of those 14 Nazi propaganda themes. Harold Lasswell, a political scientist and expert on propaganda analysis, testified that 1,195 of the items (96.4%) "were consistent with and suggested copying from the German propaganda theme" (*United States v. Pelley* 1942). Pelley was convicted, the conviction was upheld by the U.S. Circuit Court of Appeals, and the admissibility in court of evidence based on this simple method of content analysis was established (Goldsen 1947; Lasswell 1949:49).

In 1955, the Social Science Research Council's Committee on Linguistics and Psychology sponsored a conference on content analysis, bringing together experts from across the social sciences. Their contributions appear in a landmark volume edited by de Sola Pool (1959). Since then, extensive reviews have appeared every decade or so. (Further Reading: reviews of content analysis.)

DOING CONTENT ANALYSIS ♦

There are seven big steps in content analysis—and a lot of little ones:

1. Formulate a research question or a hypothesis, based on existing theory or on prior research.

2. Select a set of texts to test the question or hypothesis.

3. Create a set of codes (variables, themes) in the research question or hypothesis.

4. Pretest the variables on a few of the selected texts. Fix any problems that turn up with regard to the codes and the coding so that the coders become consistent in their coding.

5. Apply the codes to the rest of the texts.

6. Create a case-by-variable matrix from the texts and codes.

7. Analyze the matrix using whatever level of analysis is appropriate.

We'll go over these, in turn, using two studies—one by George Cunningham and colleagues (2004) and one by Elizabeth Hirschman (1987). The one by Cunningham et al. tests research questions; the one by Hirschman tests formal hypotheses.

Cunningham's Study of Media Bias

Interest in media bias has never waned since Wilcox's day. Cunningham et al. (2004) studied whether the coverage of women athletes in the *NCAA News* reflected women's place in college athletics in general. Following the seven steps outlined above, here's how they did the research:

1. *Formulate a research question or a hypothesis, based on existing theory or on prior research.* In 1972, a law was passed in the United States to ensure that colleges and universities made all academic and sports programs available equally to men and women. Since then, more and more women have been participating in college sports, but coverage of women's sports in the media has not kept pace. Many studies have documented the fact that proportionately more coverage is given to men's sports in newspapers, magazines, radio, and television.

Those media are for-profit businesses and may be responding to what they think their customers want. But Schifflett and Revelle (1994) found that from 1988 to 1991, even the *NCAA News*—which is distributed to members of the National Collegiate Athletic Association—was biased against coverage of women's athletics.

Cunningham et al. (2004) set out to test whether things had changed in the *NCAA News* in the decade after Shifflett and Revell did their study. Cunningham et al. didn't have any hypotheses, but they did have two solid research questions:

Research question 1. Did the *NCAA News* provide equitable coverage for men's and women's athletics in 1999–2001?

Research question 2. Did the coverage of women's athletics in the *NCAA News* improve since Shifflett and Revelle's (1994) study?

2. Select a set of texts to test the questions or hypotheses. After setting up a research question, the first thing to do is decide on the units of analysis—that is, what segments of text or other qualitative data will be coded and analyzed. Among content analysts, this is known as unitizing (Krippendorff 2004a:98; Neuendorf 2002:71–74).

The NCAA News was published twice a month in 1999 and 2001, so the sampling universe was 48 issues. Rather than just selecting a random grab of issues, Cunningham et al. (2004) randomly selected one of the two issues of the *News* published each month during 1999 and 2001. The sampling universe here was 48 issues, of which 24 issues (one for each month of 1999 and one for each month of 2001) were selected.

This sampling procedure ensured that whatever patterns Cunningham et al. found in their sample could be generalized with confidence to the rest of the issues for 1999 and 2001. Later, during analysis, they would test whether the patterns they found in 1999 and 2001—like the proportion of space devoted to pictures of male athletes and the proportion devoted to female athletes—were statistically different from one another. If the findings were statistically indistinguishable, then they could generalize their findings with confidence to the 3-year period 1999–2001, not just to 1999 *and* 2001.

Next, Cunningham et al. (2004) went through the 24 issues they had selected and marked all the articles that were about athletes, coaches, and teams, rather than about schools, facilities, administrators, and so on. This is what Schifflett and Revelle (1994) had done in their earlier study of the *NCAA News*. To make their analysis comparable to that of Schifflett and Revelle, that's what Cunningham et al. did, too. The articles marked for study comprised 5,745 paragraphs and 1,086 photographs to read and code. In the Cunningham et al. study, then, the paragraph and the photo were the units of analysis.

3. Create a set of codes (variables, themes) in the research question or hypothesis. Exactly as Shifflett and Revell had done, Cunningham et al. coded the articles for gender (that is, whether an article was primarily focused on men, primarily focused on women, focused on both sexes or on neither sex); location (where the article appeared in the issue); length (in square inches); and content. Paragraph content was coded as: (1) factual information related to athletics; (2) factual information not related to athletics; (3) personal information related to athletics; and (4) personal information not related to athletics (Cunningham et al. 2004:863).

The photos were coded for six themes: (1) competing athlete; (2) athlete in competitive context but not competing; (3) head shot of the athlete(s) or coach(es); (4) head shot of a person other than an athlete or coach (i.e., administrator); (5) a group photograph of persons other than players or coaches (e.g., committee members); and (6) other (Cunningham et al. 2004:863).

For location, Cunningham et al. coded articles and photos as appearing on: (1) the front page; (2) the back page; or—for pieces inside the issue—(3) at the top of the page; or (4) somewhere else on the page.

Of the 5,745 paragraphs, 2,342 were about men and 1,723 paragraphs were about women, for a total of 4,065 codeable paragraphs. The other paragraphs were about neither sex or about both sexes and were not coded.

4. Pretest the variables on a few of the selected texts. Fix any problems that turn up with regard to the codes and the coding so that the coders become consistent in their coding. For the paragraphs, Cunningham et al. (2004) did pretests on three issues of the *NCAA News* that were not part of the main sample. For the photos, they found nearly perfect agreement on the content codes and the length for 50 photos selected from one issue of the *News*.

5. Apply the codes to the rest of the texts. Keep checking for coder reliability. Cunningham et al. used latent coding in marking the paragraphs. In manifest coding, only words and phrases in the text count as indicators of themes. In other words, the meaning is *manifest* in the language itself. Latent coding, in contrast, involves interpretation—reading for meaning, taking context into account, and identifying the presence of constructs or themes. In the early days of content analysis, some researchers insisted on sticking to manifest coding to ensure reliability (see Berelson 1952:18, for example), but over the years, with the development of statistical tests for reliability, latent coding has become the norm.

Manifest coding is highly reliable. You only have to train coders, or a computer, to see a list of words and phrases to ensure high reliability. Latent coding, however, gives you the freedom to find themes in texts, even if certain words are not there. This is very important. It is, in fact, why we tell ethnographers to code their field notes every day. You can attend a wedding ceremony, for example, and write five single-spaced pages of notes that night about your observations—and never use the word "marriage." When you go back to your notes 6 months later and do a computer search for everything about marriage, your five pages of notes about that wedding won't even pop up.

Cunningham et al. (2004) kept checking their coders' work by reading randomly selected paragraphs out of context. All of this attention paid off:

Cohen's kappa, a popular measure of coder reliability (more about how to calculate kappa later), was very high for all their themes. When the coding phase was over, the investigators talked about and resolved any inconsistencies in the coding.

Cunningham et al. found 100% agreement on the coding for 100 photos from two randomly selected issues. At that level of agreement on a large sample of items in a study, it is unnecessary to run a complete interrater reliability check.

6. *Create a case-by-variable matrix from the texts and codes.* There were two data matrices in the Cunningham et al. study—one for paragraphs and one for photos. The matrix for paragraphs would have had 4,065 rows and six columns and would have looked something like Table 13.1.

Column 1 is a unique identifier—just a number—between 1 and 4,065. These refer to the 2,342 paragraphs about men and the 1,723 paragraphs about women. Column 2 would have the year 1999 or 2001, but might just as well have a 1 or a 2 to identify which year each paragraph came from. With just two genders to mark, column 3 will have a 1 or 2, but can just as well be

Table 13.1 Schematic for the Data Matrix of the Study by Cunningham et al. (2004)

Paragraph	Year	Gender	Location	Length	Content
1					
2					
3					
4					
5					
•					
•					
•					
•					
•					
4065					

coded with a 1 or a 0. There are four possible locations (front page, back page, etc.), so column 4 will have a number from 1 to 4. Length, in column 5, will contain a real number, like 3.4 or 4.1, indicating the number of square inches taken up by paragraph. Finally, because the researchers were coding for four possible content themes, column 6 will contain a number from 1 to 4.

Cunningham et al. (2004) first tested whether the amount of news coverage for women's teams, as measured by the percentage of paragraphs devoted to those teams, was different for the two years. In 1999, women's teams received 41% of all coverage compared to 44% in 2001. This meant that Cunningham et al. could combine the data from the 2 years for the rest of their analyses.

7. *Analyze the matrix using whatever level of analysis is appropriate.* Recall the first research question: Did the *NCAA News* provide equitable coverage for men's and women's athletics in 1999–2001? Well, it depends on what you count and how you count it. Women comprised 42% of all college athletes in those years and received 42.4% of the coverage in the *NCAA News* (and 39.7% of the photo coverage). Also, the average length of paragraphs was identical for men and women (2.25 square inches) and paragraphs about women and women's teams were equally likely to contain information about athletics (rather than personal information) as were paragraphs about men and men's teams. On these measures, women received coverage equal to that for men.

Paragraphs about women and women's teams, though, were more likely to appear in prominent spots (front or back page or top of a middle page) than were paragraphs about men and men's teams. On that measure, women did better than the men. On the other hand, 51% of all intercollegiate athletic teams in those years were women, so getting 42.4% of the coverage was somewhat less than that for men.

What about the second research question: Did the coverage of women's athletics in the *NCAA News* improve since the Shifflett and Revelle (1994) study? In 1990–91, women were 33% of all student athletes, and women's teams were 46% of intercollegiate competition. Shifflett and Revelle found that women got 26.5% of the coverage in the *NCAA News*. The data from the Cunningham et al. (2004) study show the *NCAA News* had erased all of the deficit in coverage of individual women athletes by 1999–2001 and had cut the deficit of women's team coverage from 19.5% (the difference between 46% and 26.5%) to 8.6% (the difference between 51% and 42.4%). (Further Reading: content analysis of media.)

Hirschman's Study of People as Products

1. *Formulate a research question or hypothesis, based on existing theory or on prior research.* Drawing on social exchange theory and on studies of human mate selection, Elizabeth Hirschman (1987) analyzed the content of personal advertisements. In social exchange theory, human interaction is seen as a series of exchanges of goods and services. The goods can be material, but they can also be nonmaterial—things like beauty, prestige, recognition, love, respect, and so on (see Blau 1964, Donnenworth and Foa 1974, and Homans 1961). Researchers of human mate selection have shown that women tend to prefer men of higher social and economic status and that men tend to prefer women of greater physical beauty (see Buss 1985, Dunbar and Barrett 2007, Pawlowski and Jasienska 2008, and Sefcek et al. 2007).

From the literature on exchange theory, Hirschman reasoned that men and women would offer and seek 10 kinds of resources from one another in personal ads: physical characteristics, money status, educational status, occupational status, intellectual status, love, entertainment, and information about demographic characteristics (age, marital status, residence), ethnicity, and personality. From the literature on mate selection, Hirschman expected to find a pattern, shown in Table 13.2, of resources offered and sought.

Table 13.2 The Expected Pattern of Resource Exchange in Personal Ads

Women Are Expected to Offer and Men to Seek	Men Are Expected to Offer and Women to Seek
Physical attractiveness	Money
Love	Educational status
Entertainment	Intellectual status
Information about their demographic characteristics (age, marital status, residence)	Occupational status
Ethnicity	
Personality	

SOURCE: Hirschman (1987:103).

Table 13.2 is a schematic for a series of hypotheses. Two hypotheses, for example, are: (1) Men seek physical beauty and love more than women do in personal ads; and, conversely, (2) women offer physical attractiveness and love more than men do. To test her hypotheses, Hirschman needed a corpus of personal ads . . . which brings us to step 2.

2. *Select a set of texts to test the question or hypothesis.* Hirschman randomly sampled 100 female-placed ads and 100 male-placed ads in *New York Magazine* and *The Washingtonian* from May 1983 to April 1984.

By sampling the ads at random, Hirschman was assured that whatever she found in the corpus she analyzed could be generalized to the content of all the ads in the two magazines. It could not, of course, be generalized to all magazines in the New York or Washington area, much less to magazines in any other city.

For example, in another New York–area magazine, *The Village Voice*, explicitly sexual traits and services were already common in personal ads in the 1980s. In *New York Magazine* and *The Washingtonian*, sexual traits and services were less than 1% of all resources sought and offered in 1983–84, so Hirschman excluded those from her analysis. If you wanted to replicate Hirschman's study today—for any magazine or Internet personal-ads site anywhere—you would sample ads that do not contain explicitly sexual services or characteristics.

3. *Create a set of codes (variables, themes) in the research question or hypothesis.* In this case, the variables, or themes, are the 10 resources that Hirschman had posited would be in the ads. The real work here is building a coding scheme—deciding on how to code the text in the ads. For example, "NYU grad" or "MA in modern French lit" would count as "educational status." "Tall," "thin," "shapely," "good looking," "handsome," and so on, would count as "physical features." Information about personality might be words and phrases like "shy," "fun loving," "young at heart," "active," and so on. Information about ethnicity would be things like "Black," "White," "Hispanic," "Asian," and so on, and "small town girl" would be coded as demographic information (residence).

4. *Pretest the variables on a few of the selected texts. Fix any problems that turn up with regard to the codes and the coding so that the coders become consistent in their coding.* Hirschman gave 10 men and 11 women the list of ten resource categories and a list of 100 resource items taken from 20 additional ads. She asked the 21 respondents to match the 100 resource items with the resource category that seemed most appropriate. In this case,

Hirschman did not do a pretest with her actual coders. The 21 pretest respondents, however, provided strong support for the variables that Hirschman had developed. The respondents were able to categorize all 100 test items.

5. *Apply the codes to the rest of the texts.* Hirschman gave a male and female coder the entire set of 405 ads. (She wound up with 405 ads instead of 400 because she miscounted in the sampling and decided to keep the five extra ads. This kind of human error is easy to make in any study like this.) There were a total of 3,782 resources offered or sought in the 405 ads. The two coders worked apart and did not know the hypotheses that Hirschman was testing. They coded each of the 3,782 resources into the 10 resource categories. The coding took 3 weeks. This is not easy work to do.

Hirschman then checked for problems. Of 3,782 resource items coded, the coders differed on their categorization of 636 (16.8%) and in another 480 cases (12.7%) one coder neglected to categorize an item that the other coder had tagged. Hirschman resolved the 636 coding discrepancies—that is, she decided which coder was right. For the 480 coding omissions, Hirschman checked the ad and made sure that the resource item was correctly coded by the one coder who saw it. If this was the case (as it always was, apparently), then the resource was assigned to the ad by both coders.

6. *Create a case-by-variable matrix from the texts and codes.* In this case, the data matrix would have looked something like Table 13.3.

The first column of Table 13.3 is the number of the ad, from 1 to 405. These are the cases, or units of analysis for this data set. Column 2 is for the name of the magazine. With just two magazines, the entries in column 2 would be 1 or 0, where 1 might mean *New York Magazine* and 0 would mean *The Washingtonian*. The cells in column 4 would have a 1 or a 0 to indicate whether the ad had been placed by a man or a woman. Next would come 20 columns, two for each of the 10 resource categories. For each of the 405 ads, these columns would indicate how many of each of the 10 resource categories had been sought or offered.

7. *Analyze the matrix using whatever level of analysis is appropriate.* Hirschman analyzed her data statistically. Her main concern was to test for differences in gender. Is the content of female-placed ads different from that of male-placed ads? Before doing this, she tested whether there were differences in the content by city. If the content of the ads placed in Washington were really different from those placed in New York, then she would have had to analyze the two data sets (one for Washington and one

Table 13.3 The Data Matrix for Hirschman's Study of Personal Ads

Ad #	Mag	Female placed	Physical features offered	Physical features sought	Money offered	Money sought	Educ status offered	Educ status sought	Occup status offered	Occup status offered	Etc.
1											
2											
3											
4											
•											
•											
•											
•											
•											
405											

for New York) separately for the effects of gender. Hirschman ran an analysis of variance, or ANOVA, and found that, whatever differences there were by gender in the content of the ads, those differences weren't affected by the city of origin. For the rest of the analyses, Hirschman could combine all her data, from both cities.

To set up the tests for gender effects, Hirschman counted the number of times each of the ten resources were offered and sought in each ad. Because the ads were of different length (some people included three or four of the 10 resources in their ad; some included six or seven . . . or even 10; and some repeated resources two or more times), Hirschman converted the counts of resources in each ad to percentages. If an ad listed six resources and two of them were about physical characteristics (tall, wavy hair), then physical characteristics were counted in that ad as 2/6, or 33%. Now Hirschman had a set of percentages, like those in Table 13.4.

Table 13.4 The Data From Hirschman's Study of Personal Ads

Resource	Mean Offered by Women	Mean Sought by Women	Mean Offered by Men	Mean Sought by Men
Physical status	.221	.090	.151	.223
Money	.018	.080	.059	.010
Educational status	.013	.008	.013	.009
Occupational status	.067	.032	.086	.011
Intellectual status	.048	.050	.030	.059
Love	.061	.168	.063	.158
Entertainment services	.107	.071	.080	.103
Demographic info	.217	.219	.283	.195
Ethnicity info	.091	.007	.090	.053
Personality info	.144	.200	.131	.150

SOURCE: Hirschman (1987:104–105).

We can tell a lot just by looking at the data in Table 13.4. For example, men mentioned money (think words and phrases like "solid income" and "well-paying job") in 5.9% of their offers, and women mentioned something to do with money in 1.8% of theirs. Women sought monetary resources more than men did (8% vs. 1%). Women offered something to do with physical status (think of words and phrases like "tall," "trim," "fit," "full figured") more than men did (22.1% vs. 15.1%), and men sought physical traits more than women did (22.3% vs. 9%). These statistics are pretty much what is expected from prior research on this topic. Men and women seek and offer the rest of the resources—including love—in more or less the same proportions.

We say "more or less" because that's the way the numbers look to us when we read the table. Fortunately, there is a simple test to tell if pairs of proportions, like those in Table 13.4, are statistically different—that is, if the differences are big enough to indicate that they probably didn't occur by chance. The results are in Table 13.5. (We do not cover how to calculate the statistics in this book. The appropriate tests are covered in all standard statistics texts.)

Four of Hirschman's hypotheses were confirmed: (1) Men seek physical attractiveness more than women do. (2) Women offer physical attractiveness more than men do. (3) Women seek money more than men do. (4) Men offer money more than women do. All the other comparisons were statistically nonsignificant.

Washington, DC, and New York City are supposed to be hip places, yet the way men and women wrote their own personal ads in 1983–1984 conformed to traditional gender role expectations. Have things changed since then? Are the stereotypes of how men and women market themselves to one another very different today?

Table 13.5 Summary of Hirschman's Findings

Resource	Hypotheses		Confirmation	
	Men	Women	Men	Women
Physical status	Seek	Offer	Seek	Offer
Money status	Offer	Seek	Offer	Seek
Education status	Offer	Seek	ns	ns
Occupation status	Offer	Seek	ns	ns
Intellectual status	Offer	Seek	ns	ns
Love	Seek	Offer	ns	ns
Entertainment	Seek	Offer	ns	ns
Demographic info	Seek	Offer	ns	ns
Ethnicity info	Seek	Offer	ns	ns
Personality info	Seek	Offer	ns	ns

SOURCE: Hirschman (1987:104).

Note: ns = not significant statistically.

This is a developing area of research. (Further Reading: content analysis of personal ads.)

INTERCODER RELIABILITY ♦

The reliability of coding has long been a concern for content analysts (Woodward and Franzen 1948), and the measurement of reliability has been a major theme in all reviews of the field (Berelson 1952:171–195, Holsti 1969:127–149, Krippendorff 1980:129–168, 2004a:144–166; Neuendorf 2002:211–256; Weber 1990:17–24). With two or more coders, we can test whether people think that the same constructs apply to the same chunks of text. The benefit of this is that we can be more certain of the counts we make when we add up the number of times any particular theme is mentioned in a text. In turn, reliable counts mean increased confidence in measures of association between themes.

Consider the following two sentences:

Among the 12 men in our study, 10 (83%) said that they were abused by police who arrested them, and 9 of those 10 (90%, or 75% of all men in our sample) described arguing with police during the event. Among the 16 women arrested during the demonstration, 5 (31%) said that they were abused and 1 of those 5 (20%, or 6% of all women in our sample), described arguing with police during the event.

The counts and associations in these two sentences are more credible if two or more coders marked the texts on which the analysis is based *and* agreed with one another about the presence of each theme (report of being abused, report of arguing with police).

There is an obvious and simple way to measure agreement between a pair of coders: line up their codes and calculate the percentage of agreement. This is shown in Table 13.6 for two coders who have coded 10 texts for a single theme, using a binary code, 1 or 0—that is, they are coding the text for whether the theme is present or absent, not whether the theme is there a little bit or a lot or not at all.

Both coders have a 0 for texts 1, 4, 5, 7, and 10, and both coders have a 1 for text 2. These two coders agree a total of six times out of 10—five times that the theme, whatever it is, does not appear in the texts, and one time that the theme does appear. On four out of 10 texts, the coders disagree. On text 9, for example, coder 1 saw the theme in the text, but coder 2 didn't. Overall, these two coders agree 60% of the time.

Adjusting for Chance

The total observed agreement is a popular method for assessing reliability, but it has long been recognized that coders can agree on the presence or absence of a theme just by chance. Many statistics have been developed to adjust for this, and there is a substantial literature about which measure is best under various conditions. (See Lombard et al. [2005] for a review.)

For example, themes may be binary—present or absent—or they may be nominal variables with more than two attributes (male, female, gay, lesbian, transgender; or Protestant, Catholic, Jew, Muslim, other; etc.). They may be ordinal variables, like attitudes (happy, neither happy nor sad, sad) or interval-level variables, like age or income. In general, the more attributes a variable has, the harder it is for coders to agree. Different measurements of agreement can take this into account.

For nominal variables, many researchers use a statistic called Cohen's kappa (Cohen 1960), or k, or a variant, developed by Fleiss (1971), which allows for more than two coders. (The more coders, the more difficult it is to achieve perfect agreement.) Kappa measures how much better than chance is the agreement between a pair of coders with regard to the presence or absence of binary (yes/no) themes in texts. Here is the formula:

$$k = \frac{\text{observed} - \text{chance}}{1 - \text{chance}}$$

Table 13.6   Measuring Simple Agreement Between Two Coders on a Single Theme

Coders	Units of Analysis (Documents/Observations)									
	1	2	3	4	5	6	7	8	9	10
1	0	1	0	0	0	0	0	0	1	0
2	0	1	1	0	0	1	0	1	0	0

When k is 1.0, there is perfect agreement between coders. When k is zero, agreement is what might be expected by chance. When k is negative, the observed level of agreement is less than what you'd expect by chance. And when k is positive, the observed level of agreement is greater than what you'd expect by chance.

Table 13.7 shows the data in Table 13.6 rearranged so that we can calculate kappa.

The observed agreement between Coder 1 and Coder 2 is:

$$\frac{(a + d)}{n}$$

Here, Coder 1 and Coder 2 agreed that the theme was present in the text once (cell a) and they agreed that the theme was absent five times (cell d), for a total of 6, or 60% of the 10 texts.

The probability that Coder 1 and Coder 2 agree by chance is:

$$\frac{(a + b)}{n} \bullet \frac{(a + c)}{n} + \frac{(c + d)}{n} \bullet \frac{(b + d)}{n}$$

Here, the probability that Coder 1 and Coder 2 agreed by chance is .08 + .48 = .56. Using the formula, we calculate kappa:

$$k = \frac{6 - .56}{1 - .56} = 0.909$$

Table 13.7 The Coder-by-Coder Agreement Matrix for the Data in Table 13.6

		Coder 2		
		Yes	No	Coder 1 Totals
Coder 1	Yes	1 (a)	1 (b)	2
	No	3 (c)	5 (d)	8
Coder 2 Totals		4	6	10 (n)

In other words, the 60% observed agreement between the two coders for the data in Table 13.6 is only about 9% better than we'd expect by chance. When overall agreement is 70% for two coders marking 10 texts, kappa increases to 0.348, or 35% better than chance. At 80% raw agreement, kappa is 0.60 for two coders marking 10 texts. However, for two coders marking 20 texts, rather than just 10, a raw agreement of 80% produces a kappa of 0.58. The more units of analysis being coded, the harder it is to get a high kappa score (see Box 13.2).

Box 13.2

Problems With Measuring Reliability

These and other statistical issues with kappa are the source of discussion in the literature about what constitutes acceptable reliability (see Krippendorf 2004b).

   The most versatile of the measures of reliability is Krippendorff's alpha (2004a:221ff). It can be used with nominal, ordinal, and interval variables; it can be used with any number of coders; and it corrects for missing data (which occurs when coders mark up overlapping, but exactly the same, sets of texts).

   Krippendorff recommends that analysts rely only on variables that attain an alpha coefficient of 0.80 or better, but would allow variables with coefficients between 0.667 and 0.800 to be used for "drawing tentative conclusions" (2004a:241). Krippendorff's alpha is not as widely used as, say, Cohen's kappa, perhaps because the most popular statistical packages do not yet include it. However, macros for calculating Krippendorff's alpha are being published in articles (for example, Kang et al. 1993) and on the Internet.

How Much Intercoder Agreement Is Enough?

This is a fair question, but the answer depends partly on what's at stake. X-rays are texts, after all. We'd like a pretty high level of intercoder agreement if a group of physicians were deciding on whether a particular feature meant our being sent for surgery or not. In text analysis, the standards are still evolving and there is not yet any real agreement on what constitutes sufficient intercoder reliability.

Landis and Koch (1977:165) developed a set of benchmarks for agreement, based on empirical tests with kappa. Their recommendations for kappa were:

<0.00 Poor
0.00–0.20 Slight
0.21–0.40 Fair
0.41–0.60 Moderate
0.61–0.80 Substantial
0.81–1.00 Almost perfect

Most researchers today would accept $k = 0.80$ or better as strong agreement or high reliability and $k = 0.70$–0.79 as adequate, but these standards are ad hoc and are still evolving.

A REAL EXAMPLE OF USING KAPPA: CAREY ET AL.'S STUDY ◆

Carey et al. (1996) asked 51 Vietnamese refugees in New York State 32 open-ended questions about tuberculosis. Topics included knowledge and beliefs about TB symptoms and causes as well as beliefs about susceptibility to the disease, prognosis for those who contract the disease, skin-testing procedures, and prevention and treatment methods. The researchers read the responses and built a code list based simply on their own judgment. The initial codebook contained 171 codes.

Then Carey et al. broke the text into 1,632 segments. Each segment was the response by one of the 51 respondents to one of the 32 questions. Two coders independently coded 320 of the segments, marking as many of the themes as they thought appeared in each segment. Segments were counted as reliably coded if both coders used the same codes on it. If one coder left off a code or assigned an additional code, it was considered a coding disagreement.

On their first try, only 144 (45%) out of 320 responses were coded the same by both coders. The coders discussed their disagreements and found that some of the 171 codes were redundant, some were vaguely defined, and some were not mutually exclusive. In some cases, coders simply had different understandings of what a code meant. When these problems were resolved, a new, streamlined codebook was issued, with only 152 themes, and the coders marked up the data again. This time they were in agreement 88.1% of the time.

To see if this apparently strong agreement was a fluke, Carey et al. tested intercoder reliability with kappa. The coders agreed perfectly ($k = 1.0$) on 126 out of the 152 codes that they'd applied to the 320 sample segments. Only 17 (11.2%) of the codes had final k values ≥ 0.89. As senior investigator, Carey resolved any remaining intercoder discrepancies himself (Carey et al. 1996).

How Many Coders Are Enough?

The answer to this question depends on: (1) the level of inference required to identify themes, and (2) the prevalence of themes.

1. If you have texts from single mothers about their efforts to juggle home and work, it's easier to code for the theme "works full time" than it is to code for the theme "enjoys her job." For themes that require high inference, one should expect more coder disagreement a priori than for themes that require low inference. This means more training to bring coders into agreement and this means more time and money.

2. Highly prevalent themes are easier to identify than are rare ones, simply because coders see prevalent ones more often. For rare themes, then, we expect higher disagreement than for common themes, and this, too, means more coder training.

If a theme occurs a lot, any given coder is likely to find at least one example of it, even if the coder is not very good at inferential coding. If a theme occurs rarely, the likelihood of finding a single example decreases, and it decreases even more if a coder is not very good. Researchers are usually willing to miss a few examples of a theme that occurs a lot, but they can't afford to miss any examples of a theme that occurs rarely. It makes sense, therefore, that the rarer a theme's occurrence and the more important it is to find all occurrences, the more coders you want to look for it. (Further Reading: intercoder reliability.)

◆ AUTOMATED CONTENT ANALYSIS: CONTENT DICTIONARIES

Computer-based dictionaries are used in automated content analysis. To build these dictionaries, words are assigned, one at a time, by human coders, to one or more categories, or themes, according to a set of rules. The rules are part of a computer program that parses new texts and assigns words to categories. Over time, researchers can assign new words to one of the categories or add new categories. As the dictionary grows, it becomes more sophisticated, making automated content analysis increasingly powerful. When you hear "This call may be monitored for quality assurance purposes," it's likely that the conversation will be turned into text that will be submitted to a computer for content analysis.

Work began in the 1960s on a system called the *General Inquirer* (Kelly and Stone 1975; Stone et al. 1966) and continues to this day (http://www .wjh.harvard.edu/~inquirer/). An early version was tested on 66 suicide notes—33 written by men who had actually taken their own lives and 33 written by men who were asked to produce simulated suicide notes. The control group men were matched with the men who had written actual suicide notes on age, occupation, religion, and ethnicity. The *General Inquirer* program parsed the texts and picked the actual suicide notes 91% of the time (Ogilvie et al. 1966).

The latest version of the dictionary for this system is the *Harvard Psychosocial Dictionary*, version IV-4, or simply *Harvard IV-4* (Kelly and Stone 1975). It incorporates the *Lasswell Value Dictionary* (Namenwith and Weber 1987) and can tell whether the word "broke" means "fractured," or "destitute," or "stopped functioning," or—when paired with "out"—"escaped" (Rosenberg et al. 1990:303).

Rosenberg et al. (1990) used this system to analyze 71 speech samples from people who had been diagnosed with one of three psychological disorders (somatization disorder, $n = 17$; paranoia, $n = 25$; depression, $n = 12$) or with lung or breast cancer ($n = 17$). Here's what interviewers said to patients:

> We're interested in how people seeing doctors feel about things and how they express themselves. We'd like you to talk for 5 minutes about anything you like. So talk about anything—it could be about things at home with your family, or work, or school, or books, the past, present, future, or anything. We don't care so much what you say but will be interested in the words you use to say it. (Rosenberg et al. 1990:302)

The transcripts were scored by a human researcher on 12 scales that had been developed by Gottschalk and Gleser (1969), including scales to measure death anxiety, separation anxiety, inward hostility, overt hostility, and the like.

Then the transcripts were analyzed with the *General Inquirer*. The expert coder identified the three previously diagnosed psychiatric disorders correctly in 62% of the 71 cases. The computer correctly classified 85% of the cases, using the *Harvard IV* dictionary. The difference was statistically significant. Meanwhile, using the Gottschalk-Gleser coding, the human researcher identified 94% of the cancer patients, versus 77% for the *General Inquirer* and *Harvard IV.* This difference was not statistically significant (Rosenberg et al. 1990:307).

Content Dictionaries Don't Have to Be Big to Be Useful

In his study of Navajo and Zuni responses to thematic apperception tests, Colby's (1966:379) initial impression was that the Navajo regarded their homes as havens and places of relaxation and that the Zuni depicted their homes as places of discord and tension. To test this idea, Colby created a special-purpose dictionary that contained two-word groups that he and his colleagues had developed before looking at the data.

One word group, the "relaxation" group, comprised the words assist, comfort, easy, affection, happy, and play. The other, the "tension" group, comprised the words destruction, discomfort, difficult, dislike, sad, battle, and anger. Colby examined the 35 sentences that contained the word home *and* one of the words in either of the two-word groups. Navajos were more than twice as likely to use words from the relaxation group when talking about home as they were to use words from the tension group. Zuni were almost twice as likely to use tension words as they were to use relaxation words.

Colby (1966:378) also found that the Navajo were more likely to use words associated with exposure such as storm, cold, freezing, hot, heat, windy. Colby was not surprised at the results, noting that the Navajo were sheepherders and were concerned about protecting their sheep from the elements and the Zuni were crop growers and were concerned about the water they need to grow their corn. What *was* surprising was that the texts were generated from pictures that had nothing to do with sheep or crops.

Content dictionaries are attractive because they are so reliable. The rules built into a computer program are applied to a text in the same way every time. There are still plenty of cases where only humans can parse the subtleties of meaning reflected in context (Shapiro 1997; Viney 1983). And, of course, we are nowhere near having computers take over all text analysis. Still, dictionary-based markup of text is producing better and better results as time goes on. As with all technology, we won't be surprised to see computers doing text analysis in ways we don't currently imagine. (Further Reading: automated content dictionaries.)

CROSS-CULTURAL CONTENT ANALYSIS: HRAF ◆

Finally, we want to point to a particular use of content analysis: the content coding of ethnographies and the testing of cross-cultural hypotheses. The Human Relations Area Files (HRAF) at Yale University is the world's largest archive of ethnography. Since the 1940s, professional coders have been theme-coding ethnographies of cultures from around the world. Today, the archive is about a million pages of text, taken from almost 8,000 books and articles, on over 400 cultural groups. The archive is growing at about 40,000 pages a year, and about 40% of the material is available on the Internet through libraries that subscribe (http://www.yale.edu/hraf/).

The coders at HRAF follow a codebook developed by Murdock and others (2004 [1961]). For example, there are codes for demography, family, entertainment, social stratification, war, health and welfare, sickness, sex, religious practices, and so on. Within each major theme, there are subthemes, just like any other codebook for analyzing text. For example, under demography, there is a subcode for mortality, another for external migration, and so on. Under the code for family, there are subcodes for marriages, nuptials, termination of marriages, and so on.

Doing Cross-Cultural Text-Based Research

There are five steps in doing an HRAF study (Otterbein 1969):

1. State a hypothesis that requires cross-cultural data.

2. Draw a representative sample of the world's cultures.

3. Find the appropriate OCM (Outline of Cultural Materials) codes in the sample.

4. Code the variables according to whatever conceptual scheme you've developed in forming your hypothesis.

5. Run the appropriate statistical tests and see if your hypothesis is confirmed.

For example, Barber (1998) found that the frequency of male homosexual activity was low in hunting and gathering societies and increased with the complexity of agricultural production. Ethnographic reports of male homosexuality were also more likely for societies in which women did not control their own sexuality—a well-known correlate of increased reliance on complex agriculture.

Landauer and Whiting (1964) coded 65 societies for the practice of physical stress on male infants—things like piercing (lips, nose, scarification, circumcision) or molding of arms or legs or head. Adult men in societies with these practices are significantly taller than their counterparts in which these practices are absent (about 2 or 3 inches taller). The researchers controlled for, and ruled out, variations in sunlight (and hence in the body's production of vitamin D) and variations in population genetics—two factors that are well known to cause variations in height.

But they could not rule out the possibility that parents who put their infants through this kind of stress give those children more food or better medical care, which supports growth, or that boys who are stressed during infancy become more aggressive and only the tallest survive. As the researchers themselves acknowledged, correlation doesn't mean cause (Landauer and Whiting 1964:1018). (Further Reading: cross-cultural studies of ethnographic text.)

Further Reading

◆ For reviews of content analysis, see Gerbner et al. (1969), Holsti (1969), Krippendorf (1980, 2004a), Neuendorf (2002), Roberts (1997), and Weber (1990).

◆ For more on content analysis of media, see Christopherson et al. (2002), Dardis (2006), de Vreese and Boomgaarden (2006), Murray and Murray (1996), Riffe et al. (2005), and Shanahan et al. (2008). See Parmelee et al. (2007) on analysis of political ads.

◆ For more on content analysis of personal ads in the United States, see Butler-Smith et al. (1998), Cameron and Collins (1998), Goode (1996), Wiederman (1993), and Willis and Carlson (1993). See de Sousa Campos et al. (2002) for a content analysis of personal ads in Brazil; Parekh and Berisin (2001) for an analysis of ads in the United States, India, and China; Badahdah and Tiemann (2005) for personal ads placed by Muslims in the United States; and Yancey and Yancey (1997) for analysis of personal ads of people seeking interracial relationships in the United States. See Groom and Pennebaker (2005), Gudelunas (2005), A. Smith (2000), and C. A. Smith and Stillman (2002a, 2002b) for analyses of gay and lesbian personal ads. Stalp and Grant (2001) show how to use personal ads in teaching undergraduates about coding.

◆ For more on intercoder reliability, see Krippendorff (2004b), Kurasaki (2000), Lombard et al. (2004), and Muñoz Leiva et al. (2006). The problem of assessing intercoder reliability is important in all observational studies. See, for example, and Hruschka et al. (2004) and Thompson et al. (2004).

◆ For more on automated content dictionaries, see Carley (1988), Fan and Shaffer (1990), Ford et al. (2000), Gottschalk and Bechtel (2005), Hart and Childers (2005), and Schonhardt-Bailey (2008).

◆ For more on cross-cultural studies of ethnographic text, see Dickson et al. (2005), Ember et al. (2005), and Otterbein (1986).

CHAPTER 14

SCHEMA ANALYSIS

INTRODUCTION ◆

This chapter is about cultural schemas, also known as cultural models. The methods for identifying cultural schemas come from psychology, linguistics, anthropology, and sociology, and schema analysis, in one form or another, is practiced in all these fields today.

Schema analysis is based on the idea that people must use cognitive simplifications to help make sense of the complex information to which they are constantly exposed (Casson 1983:430). Schemas are what let culturally skilled people fill in details of an event (Schank and Abelson 1977). And schemas are, as Wodak says (1992:525), what lead us to interpret Mona Lisa's smile as evidence of her perplexity or her desperation.

◆ HISTORY OF SCHEMA ANALYSIS

Schema analysis comes from Frederick Bartlett's (1964 [1932]) pioneering experiments on memory and meaning. In the early days of modern psychology, the most influential researcher on memory was Hermann Ebbinghaus. Prose, said Ebbinghaus, contained phrases that could, by turns, be funny or sad, soft or harsh. All of this variation was uncontrollable, so Ebbinghaus developed 2,300 nonsense syllables by systematically putting vowels between pairs of consonants . . . bok, gub, tiv, and so on (1913:22–23). The idea was to test people's memory without introducing the clutter of meaning.

Bartlett argued that meaning was integral to memory and sought a different experimental technique. It would be messier, but it would let him study memory and meaning together. He hit on the idea of asking subjects—Cambridge University students—to memorize and repeat back folk tales (prose with meaning) that were culturally bizarre to them. Around 1916, Bartlett began asking people to read and recall a Kathlamet Indian folktale called "The War of the Ghosts." The tale had been collected in Bay Center, Washington, by Franz Boas, who translated it into English (Boas 1901:5; D. Hymes 1985:392). Here it is:

One night two young men from Egulac went down to the river to hunt seals and while they were there it became foggy and calm. Then they heard war-cries, and they thought: "Maybe this is a war-party." They escaped to the shore, and hid behind a log. Now canoes came up, and they heard the noise of paddles, and saw one canoe coming up to them. There were five men in the canoe, and they said: "What do you think? We wish to take you along. We are going up the river to make war on the people." One of the young men said," I have no arrows." "Arrows are in the canoe," they said. "I will not go along. I might be killed. My relatives do not know where I have gone. But you," he said, turning to the other, "may go with them."

So one of the young men went, but the other returned home. And the warriors went on up the river to a town on the other side of Kalama. The people came down to the water and they began to fight, and many were killed. But presently the young man heard one of the warriors say, "Quick, let us go home: that Indian has been hit." Now he thought: "Oh, they are ghosts." He did not feel sick, but they said he had been shot. So the canoes went back to Egulac and the young man went ashore to his house and made a fire. And he told everybody and said: "Behold I accompanied the ghosts, and we went to fight. Many of our fellows were killed, and many of those who attacked us were killed. They said I was hit, and I did not feel sick." He told it all, and then he became quiet. When the sun rose he fell down. Something black came out of his mouth. His face became contorted. The people jumped up and cried. He was dead. (Bartlett, F. 1964 [1932]. *Remembering: A Study in Experimental and Social Psychology.* Cambridge: Cambridge University Press. Reprinted with the permission of Cambridge University Press.)

In some of Bartlett's experiments, people read the story twice and were asked to recall it after a few minutes or, in some cases, after several years. This was long before tape recorders, so Bartlett took detailed notes about what people recalled and didn't recall. Over time, Bartlett saw some pattern emerge in the way people recalled this story.

One key finding was what W. F. Brewer (2000:72) calls transformations to the familiar—recasting unfamiliar things into more familiar terms. So, for example, instead of repeating "Something black came out of his mouth," someone in pre–World War I England might have said "He foamed at the mouth" or "His soul passed from his mouth" (p. 73). People also left out things that seemed irrelevant to them—like the fact that the young man made a fire when he went to his house. This event, said Brewer (p. 72), was not crucial to the plot and so was forgotten when subjects repeated the story. But this detail would have made perfect sense to any Kathlamet man in 1899: The first thing you do when you come home, he would have said, is make a fire. (Further Reading: schema analysis.)

MENTAL MODELS ◆

Bartlett sought a theory to explain the systematic distortions and transformations over time in the retelling of stories. Even before his work, it was well known that human beings process thousands of bits of information every day about real objects and events. Bartlett reasoned that our experience of this reality is far too complex to deal with on an image-by-image basis. There must be some underlying structures—some simplifications—that help us make sense of the information to which we are exposed (Casson 1983).

These underlying simplifications, or schemas, are what Rumelhart (1980) famously called "the building blocks of cognition." They are generalizations from our prior experience and comprise "rules . . . for imposing order on experience" (Rice 1980:153). Schema analysis, then, is the search for those rules and how they are linked together into mental models.

Like physical models—of airplanes or DNA molecules—mental models are reduced, simpler versions of complex realities, but they exist in our minds, like grammars for actions rather than for words. When we run into a new situation—an object, a person, an interaction—we compare it to the schemas we have already stored in memory—not to each individual object, person or interaction we've experienced over the years (D'Andrade 1991).

For example, when we buy a car, we expect to haggle over the price, but when we order food in a restaurant, we expect to pay the price on the menu. We know instinctively not to leave a tip at a fast-food counter, though this rule can be relaxed (as at Starbucks) if we see a big jar, labeled "Tips," on the counter where we pay for the food. And when someone we hardly know says "Hi, how's it going?" we know that they don't expect us to stop and give them a full rundown on how our life is going these days. If we did stop and launch into a peroration about our life, we'd be acting outside the prevailing schema—breaking frame, as Goffman (1974) put it—and making people very uncomfortable. (Further Reading: mental and cultural models.)

Abbreviating

In an influential book, Schank and Abelson (1977) postulated that schemas—or scripts, as they called them—make it possible for culturally skilled people to fill in the details of a story.

Consider this seemingly uncomplicated utterance: "Alice had to go out to Los Angeles last week and deal with this client's ego." Think about all the information you need to understand that sentence, including its implications. For example, if you are in New York when you hear this sentence, you know that Alice traveled by plane. You know that "last week" is less than 7 days ago. Even if you don't know that Los Angeles is 2,753 miles from New York, you know that it's much too far for Alice to have driven to LA and back or to have taken a train in the time available. You also know that, although Alice would rather she didn't have to, she thinks it's worth spending a lot of time and money on keeping this client happy.

Here's another one: "Fred lost his term paper because he forgot to save his work." This is a causal statement (A happened *because of* B). We know that Fred's forgetting to save did not actually *cause* him to lose his term paper. Several links in the causal chain are left out. These links are easily filled in by listeners who have the background to do so: Fred was going along, happily typing his term paper into a computer. He neglected to save his work periodically, as he had surely been advised to do many times over the years. Without warning, some unforeseen event occurred—like a total crash of Fred's hard disk—and Fred wound up having to type his term paper in all over again. Again, think of all the information—about computer crashes and data-loss disasters, not to mention term-paper typing—you need to fill in and understand this sentence.

As with many kinds of text analysis, the most important methodological skill you can have for schema analysis is to be really, really steeped in the language and culture of the people you are studying.

KINDS OF SCHEMAS ◆

Some schemas—the what-goes-with-what schemas—are about objects: What kinds of foods go together in a Chinese meal? What kinds of clothing and accessories are appropriate for a bride? What kinds of animals will you find in a zoo? One important schema for Americans is about how the components of a good marriage fit together (Quinn 1997). More on this later.

Some schemas—what-happens-when schemas—are culturally shared scripts about how regularly occurring sets of behaviors play out.

One famous script, for going out to a restaurant, was described by Schank and Abelson (1977). The script has four main components: ENTERING, ORDERING, EATING, and EXITING. (Upper case is conventionally used to represent those underlying—that is, unspoken, perhaps even unconscious— "building blocks of cognition" that Rumelhart [1980] talks about.)

Each of the main components contains one or more additional scripts. The ORDERING script, for example, comprises scripts for: EXAMINING the menu, CHOOSING food, SUMMONING the waiter or waitress (Casson 1983:448; Schank and Abelson 1977:42–43). The EXITING schema has scripts for PAYING THE BILL, TIPPING, and LEAVING.

These ordered schemas together tell you when to order (after entering and sitting down); when to pay (after you've eaten); and when to tip (after paying the check). Schank asked his daughter, Hanna, to tell him what it's like to go to a restaurant. Beginning at less than 3 years and 4 months of age, she was already developing a complex script for this activity. By 4 years and 2 months of age, Hanna had integrated paying at the end of the meal into the script.

There are culturally shared scripts for appropriate behaviors while waiting in a doctor's office for an appointment and scripts for how to enter and leave a classroom after the lecture has begun.

And some schemas—the how-things-work schemas—are folk theories. There is a cultural schema in Mexico for how people get diabetes (Daniulaityte 2004) and another in Haiti for how people contract AIDS (Farmer 1994). There are culturally shared schemas about why you see your breath outdoors during the winter (Collins and Gentner 1987) and about how thermostats work to keep your house warm (Kempton 1987). We'll take you through the THERMOSTAT AS VALVE versus THERMOSTAT AS FEEDBACK metaphor at the end of this chapter.

Universal, Individual, and Cultural Schemas

Some schemas may be universal, reflecting the fact that there are some experiences that are common to all humanity. Lévi-Strauss (1963), for example, observed that all human beings experience the world as a set of binary categories—like male-female, sacred-profane, and raw-cooked. Kinship systems across the world are organized around very clear distinctions, many of them binary—like lineal and collateral kin, male and female kin, consanguineal and affinal kin, and so on (D. Jones 2003, 2004:215).

Every human being is born into a system in which parents are powerful and infants are helpless. This common experience by every person in the world, argues Govrin (2006:629), produces a universal "underdog schema"— the tendency to feel sympathy with the oppressed.

On the other hand, because every human being grows up with a unique set of experiences, some schemas are idiosyncratic—the unique angle that each of us has on some things. The sales tax in New York City is 8.38%. A local cultural rule in New York says "Double the tax on restaurant bills to figure out the tip." But some people have a rule that says tip exactly 20% of the bill in a restaurant, no matter what. So, if the bill is $34.28, the tip (with a separate, rounding-up-to-the-nearest-penny rule applied) would be $6.86. Others may apply a 15% rule and others may have a complicated algorithm, taking into account the kind of restaurant, the perceived markup rate on the wine (yes, really; we know people who do this), and the judged quality of service.

Somewhere between universal and idiosyncratic schemas are cultural schemas: They are developed through experience but are held by a population (Rice 1980:154). For example, Blair-Loy (2003) describes the conflict that some women in executive positions feel about two widely held and competing schemas in current U.S. culture: DEVOTION TO FAMILY and DEVOTION TO WORK.

♦ METHODS FOR STUDYING SCHEMAS

There are three widely used methods for studying schemas: (1) experiments; (2) interviewing; and (3) analyzing metaphors.

1. Experiments

Building on Bartlett's pioneering work, Rice (1980) conducted some experiments using Eskimo folk tales. First, following Rumelhart (1975), Rice developed what she called the American cultural schema for telling a story: There is a PROTAGONIST who has a PROBLEM or series of problems; the protagonist EVALUATES THE SITUATION in each problem and TAKES ACTION; and the action has some RESOLUTION, which can be positive or negative in terms of solving the protagonist's problem.

In one experiment, Rice made two versions of some Eskimo stories. One version was the complete Eskimo version, in English. The other version was adapted to make it fit the idealized American story schema, with a protagonist, a problem, an action, and a resolution. The participants in this experiment read the story and then wrote it out from recall. They also came back a week later and recalled the story again.

Rice's results provide strong support for Bartlett's earlier findings: People add the American schema structure to the stories that lack it (1980:163). For example, in one story, the protagonist is a boy who is reproached for not hunting even though he is old enough to do so. The boy doesn't respond and nothing happens to him as a result. This is a violation of the American story schema in which outcomes of one kind or another—good, bad, or indifferent—are expected for a problem in a story. "By the one-week recall," says Rice,

> 8 of the 12 subjects had modified this sequence so as to mend this hole. There are two strategies for this. Five subjects provided some sort of response on the boy's part: "but he didn't want to" or "he preferred to beg." Another three dropped the admonition altogether, an efficient solution. (1980:166)

When the passages fit the American story schema (as the passages did in the Americanized versions of the stories), people agreed about which events they remembered. And people recalled more exactly worded phrases from the Americanized versions of the stories than from the Eskimo versions. Thus, as Bartlett had found in his early work, people distort stories in recall to fit their cultural expectations (their schemas) about what stories ought to be like.

2. Interviewing: Schemas From Text

Naomi Quinn and her students collected and transcribed interviews about marriage from 11 North American couples. Some of the couples were recently married; others had been married a long time. The couples came from different parts of the country and represented various occupations, educational levels, and ethnic and religious groups. Each of the 22 people was interviewed separately for 15–16 hours, and the interviews were transcribed.

In a series of articles, Quinn (1982, 1987, 1992, 1996, 1997, 2005b) has analyzed this body of text to discover and document the concepts underlying American marriage and to show how these concepts are tied together—how they form a cultural model, a schema, shared by people from different backgrounds about what constitutes success and failure in marriage.

Quinn's method is to "exploit clues in ordinary discourse for what they tell us about shared cognition—to glean what people must have in mind in order to say the things they do" (1997:140). She begins by looking at patterns of speech and the repetition of key words and phrases, paying particular attention to informants' use of metaphors and the commonalities in their reasoning about marriage (see Box 14.1).

Box 14.1

Linkages and Language Competence

Schema analysis requires a deep understanding of the metaphors that informants use in talking about marriage or dinner parties or energy costs or Little League. . . . This means either native or near-native competence for this kind of analysis. Language competence is nine-tenths of method, when it comes to schema analysis.

D'Andrade notes that "perhaps the simplest and most direct indication of schematic organization in naturalistic discourse is the repetition of associative linkages" (1991:294). "Indeed," he says, "anyone who has listened to long stretches of talk—whether generated by a friend, spouse, workmate, informant, or patient—knows how frequently people circle through the same network of ideas" (p. 287).

In a study of blue-collar workers in Rhode Island, Claudia Strauss (1992) refers to these ideas as "personal semantic networks." On reading and rereading her intensive interviews with one of the workers, Strauss found that he repeatedly referred to ideas associated with greed, money, businessmen, siblings, and "being different." Strauss displays the relationships among these ideas by writing the concepts on a sheet of paper and connecting the ideas with lines and explanations.

This is the same method used by grounded theorists. In fact, one of the key features of many late-model text management programs is the ability to build on a computer screen the networks of themes that represent underlying schemas.

For example, Nan, one of Quinn's informants, uses a popular metaphor: "Marriage is a manufactured product"—something that has properties, like strength and staying power, and that requires work to produce. Some marriages are "put together well," and others "fall apart" like so many cars or toys or washing machines (Quinn 1987:174).

Sometimes Quinn's informants would talk about their surprise at the breakup of a marriage by saying that they thought the couple's marriage was "like the Rock of Gibraltar" or that they thought the marriage had been "nailed in cement." People use these metaphors because they assume that their listeners know that cement and the Rock of Gibraltar are things that last forever (1997:145–146).

Quinn concluded that just eight themes were needed to classify the hundreds of metaphors about marriage in her corpus of text:

> (1) metaphors of *lastingness,* such as, "It was stuck together pretty good" or "It's that feeling of confidence about each other that's going to keep us going"; (2) metaphors of *sharedness,* such as, "I felt like a marriage was just a partnership" or "We're together in this"; (3) metaphors of *mutual benefit,* such as, "That was really something that we got out of marriage" or "Our marriage is a very good thing for both of us"; (4) metaphors of *compatibility,* such as, "The best thing about Bill is that he fits me so well" or "Both of our weaknesses were such that the other person could fill in"; (5) metaphors of *difficulty,* such as, "That was one of the hard barriers to get over" or "The first year we were married was really a trial"; (6) metaphors of *effort,* such as, "She works harder at our marriage than I do" or "We had to fight our way back almost to the beginning"; (7) metaphors of *success or failure,* such as, "We knew that it was working" or, conversely, "The marriage was doomed"; and (8) metaphors of *risk,* such as, "that so many odds against marriage" or "The marriage was in trouble." (1997:142)

These eight classes of metaphors, Quinn argues, represent underlying concepts that are linked together in a schema that guides the discourse of ordinary Americans about marriage:

> Marriages are ideally lasting, shared and mutually beneficial. Marriages that are not shared will not be mutually beneficial and those not mutually beneficial will not last. Benefit is a matter of fulfillment. Spouses must be compatible in order to be able to fill each other's [emotional] needs so that their marriages will be fulfilling and hence beneficial. Fulfillment and, more specifically, the compatibility it requires, are difficult to realize but this difficulty can be overcome, and compatibility and

fulfillment achieved, with effort. Lasting marriages in which difficulty has been overcome by effort are regarded as successful ones. Incompatibility, lack of benefit, and the resulting marital difficulty, if not overcome, put a marriage at risk of failure. (Quinn 1997:164)

The use by informants of similar metaphors and the repetition of similar words and phrases indicates commonalities in how people share their reasoning. In other words, just as in the search for themes in any set of texts, the search for cultural models involves being alert to patterns of speech and to the repetition of key words.

3. Analyzing Metaphors

Quinn's work owes a lot to Lakoff and Johnson's (2003 [1980]) pioneering study of metaphors. Scholars of literature have always recognized the importance of metaphors in rhetoric. Lakoff and Johnson studied metaphors in everyday discourse and distinguished between conceptual metaphors—deeply embedded similes, like LOVE IS WAR—about how the world works—and metaphors that are simply surface representations of conceptual metaphors in language. "The way we think," argued Lakoff and Johnson, "what we experience, and what we do every day is very much a matter of metaphor" (p. 3).

Listen carefully to everyday speech and the power of Lakoff and Johnson's insight becomes clear. If someone says, "He's drowning in debt," the image of a person drowning is not meant literally, but the metaphor works as a "figure of speech" (literally, an image made with words) because native speakers of English share some basic concepts. We understand, for example, when someone says "Debt can sink you," or "Debt can bury you" or "He got into a really big hole when he took on that mortgage." The underlying concept—the conceptual metaphor—is that DEBT IS STRUGGLE, but it is reflected in many linguistic metaphors.

One way to get a list of metaphors is to collect a large amount of text, as Quinn did, on a particular topic, and comb through it. For many languages today, however, there are compilations of metaphors and proverbs—short phrases or sayings that encapsulate the cultural wisdom of a people. Those archival resources offer the opportunity for schema analysis.

Lakoff and Kövecses (1987), for example, studied idiomatic expressions in American English that focus on the concept of anger. They found about 300 entries in Roget's *University Thesaurus* under "anger," including things like:

He lost his cool.
He channeled his anger into something constructive.
He's wrestling with his anger.
You're beginning to get to me.
Watch out! He's on a short fuse.
When I told my mother, she had a cow.

Lakoff and Kövecses argue that, not only do all these surface expressions have something to do with anger, they have something to do with each other. For example, one underlying idea is that anger is the HEAT OF A FLUID IN A CONTAINER. Lakoff and Kövecses find this in such metaphors as:

Simmer down!
You make my blood boil.
Let him stew.

This proposed schema is corroborated by the extension that when anger becomes too intense, the person explodes (1987:199), as in:

She blew up at me.
We won't tolerate any more of your outbursts.
When I told him, he just exploded.
He blew a gasket.
She erupted.
She's on a short fuse.
That really set me off.

Lakoff and Kövecses argue that the underlying metaphor for anger is that ANGER IS HEAT (1987:197), but that this is further subordinated to a more general metaphor of the BODY AS A CONTAINER FOR THE EMOTIONS ("she couldn't contain her joy; he was filled with anger; she was brimming with rage"). Thus, anger is the HEAT OF A FLUID IN A CONTAINER ("you make my blood boil; let him stew; simmer down!") (p. 198). (Further Reading: metaphor analysis.)

FOLK THEORIES: KEMPTON'S ♦ STUDY OF HOME THERMOSTATS

Folk theories, or folk models, are everyday theories about how things work or why things exist: Why do so few women go into physics? Why have

American automobile manufacturers lost ground to Japanese and European manufacturers? How is obesity related to overall health? To understand these theories, we need to study "cognition in the wild" (Hutchins 1995).

Kempton (1987) interviewed 12 people in Michigan about how they controlled the heat in their homes during the winter. He inferred from the interviews that people were applying one of two possible theories—the THERMOSTAT AS FEEDBACK THEORY or the THERMOSTAT AS VALVE THEORY—about heat control. People who have the feedback theory—we can call it the feedback schema—about how their heating system works believe that the furnace gets turned on when the thermostat senses that the temperature has fallen below some level. If the thermostat is set at, say, 72 degrees, then, when the temperature falls below 72, the furnace comes on and pours out heat until the house is at 72 again. Then the furnace shuts off.

There is, in other words, a "feedback" between the thermostat and the furnace. In this theory, the thermostat regulates the amount of *time* that the furnace runs, but while it's running the furnace is thought to run at a constant speed and intensity. As Kempton points out, this emic understanding of how furnaces work is thought by heating engineers to be simplified, but essentially correct (1987:228).

People who hold the THERMOSTAT AS VALVE THEORY see the thermostat as analogous to the gas pedal on a car. Just as a car goes faster the more you push on the gas pedal, so the furnace works harder, and puts out more heat, the higher the thermostat is set. As Kempton shows, this widely held schema translates into energy-inefficient behavior. If they walk into their house on a cold day and the house is at 50 degrees, they may turn their thermostat up to 90 degrees, figuring that the house will heat faster than it would if they set the thermostat to 70. They figure they can turn the thermostat down to 70 when the temperature in the house reaches that mark. Much of the time, however, they miss the mark and are reminded to turn the thermostat down when the temperature in the house reaches 80 degrees and they notice that it feels too hot.

Kempton came up with the hypothesis that people have either a feedback or a valve theory about how the thermostat works early in his study of home heating control. He went back later and looked through the corpus of text for all 12 of his informants to see if his hypothesis was correct. He looked through each interview for statements or metaphors that indicated which, if either, theory people held. One informant said: "You just turn the thermostat up and once she gets up there [to the desired temperature] she'll kick off automatically" (Kempton 1987:228). That informant was using a feedback theory. Another informant said that the furnace was like ". . . electric mixers. The higher you turn them, the faster they go" (p. 230). That informant was clearly using a valve theory.

If you've ever tried to make an elevator come more quickly by repeatedly hitting the call button, you might have a valve theory of elevators. (**Further Reading:** folk theories.)

Further Reading

♦ For more on schema theory, see Mandler (1984) and Saito (2000). For gender schema theory, see Bem (1981, 1983, 1985) and Hudak (1993). On schema theory in the study of literacy, see McVee et al. (2005).

♦ For more on mental and cultural models, see D'Andrade and C. Strauss (1992), Gentner and Stevens (1983), Halford (1993), Johnson-Laird (1983), Morgan et al. (2002), and Wierzbicka (2004). Other examples of searching for cultural schemas in texts include Holland's (1985) study of the reasoning that Americans apply to interpersonal problems, and C. Strauss's (1997) study of what chemical plant workers and their neighbors think about the free-enterprise system.

♦ For more on metaphor analysis, see Allan (2007), Bialostok (2002), Ignatow (2004), Rees et al. (2007), Saban et al. (2007), Schmitt (2005), Steger (2007), and L. H. Turner and Shuter (2004).

♦ For more on folk theories, see Cho et al. (2005), Cornell (1984), Li (2004), Martin and Parker (1995), Reid and Valsiner (1986), Slaughter (2005), and Watts and Gutierres (1997).

CHAPTER 15

ANALYTIC INDUCTION AND QUALITATIVE COMPARATIVE ANALYSIS

INTRODUCTION ◆

Analytic induction is a qualitative method for building up causal explanations of phenomena from a close examination of a small number of cases (see Manning [1982] for a review). It flourished in the 1940s and 1950s with a series of books by scholars from the Chicago School of Sociology—which emphasized participant observation fieldwork and the study of real human problems—but fell out of favor for several decades for reasons we'll lay out below.

The method of analytic induction was revived in 1987 with the publication of Charles Ragin's *The Comparative Method. Moving Beyond Qualitative and Quantitative Strategies.* Ragin's method, called qualitative comparative analysis, or QCA, is a Boolean generalization of analytic induction (more about this later). Analytic induction has always been attractive for studies that rely on a small number of cases—which means most studies based on text—but it is more accessible to scholars today than ever because of new computer programs that aid with data management and analysis. (Further Reading: computer programs for analytic induction.)

◆ INDUCTION AND DEDUCTION—AGAIN

As we saw in Chapter 14, induction is reasoning from observation to formulate rules. It is contrasted with deduction, which involves reasoning from general rules to infer what should be out there and available for observation. For example, once we know that abject poverty causes despair, and that despair causes people to engage in destructive and self-destructive behavior, we can use those rules to infer that there is more child abuse and alcoholism among people who are poor than among people who are not. Then we can collect data to test this deductively derived hypothesis.

By contrast, we would use inductive reasoning if we were at an earlier stage in research and were shopping for ideas about what causes some phenomenon in which we're interested. We might examine many cases of child abuse and look for what those cases have in common. If we notice that many cases involve despair, we'd formulate a hypothesis about the relationship between child abuse and despair and figure out a way to test it.

In practice, induction and deduction are used by all empiricists, whether they rely on qualitative or quantitative data. There is no way to decide if deduction or induction is better, but some branches of the social sciences rely more on one kind of inference than the other. For example, as we saw in Chapters 13 and 14, grounded theorists tend to be inductivists, and content analysts tend to be deductivists.

The Induction Tradition

Credit for the distinction between inductive and deductive reasoning (the "two ways of searching into and discovering truth") goes to Francis Bacon (1864 [1620]:71). Bacon's method of induction involved making and comparing lists of observations. One list would comprise examples of something we want to explain. Another would comprise things that are *like* those in the first list, but in which the thing we want to explain is absent.

For example, Bacon was interested in the phenomenon of heat and what caused it. In collecting many examples, he noticed that some animals are hotter than others and that the insides of animals were hotter than the outsides. He also noticed that animals were hotter after exercise. From these and many other observations, he concluded that motion was a cause of heat. Not a bad conclusion, considering he was writing in 1620 (see Box 15.1).

Box 15.1

Bacon's Death

To Bacon goes the honor of being the first "martyr of empiricism." In March 1626, at the age of 65, Bacon was driving through a rural area north of London. He had an idea that cold might delay the biological process of putrefaction, so he stopped his carriage, bought a hen from a local resident, killed the hen, and stuffed it with snow. Bacon was right—the cold snow did keep the bird from rotting—but he himself caught bronchitis and died a month later (Lea 1980).

Bacon did not tell us how we actually get from lists to conclusions about cause and effect. The rules for inductive logic—"the means which mankind possess for exploring the laws of nature by specific observation and experience"—were formalized by John Stuart Mill (1898:259). Two of Mill's rules—what he called "the method of agreement" and the "method of difference"—are the foundation of analytic induction.

The method of agreement states that if two or more cases of a phenomenon (like getting sick) are different in every way but have one thing (like eating a particular food) in common, then that thing is the cause or the effect of the phenomenon. The method of difference states that if two cases of something (like getting sick) are alike in every respect, except for one thing (like not eating a particular food), then that thing is at least part of the cause or effect of the phenomenon (Mill 1898:255, 256).

ANALYTIC INDUCTION ♦

Florian Znaniecki introduced the term "analytic induction" in 1934, in his book on sociological method (pp. 235ff), observing that the method had a long history, especially in the physical sciences. He contrasted the method with what he called enumerative, or statistical induction (pp. 221ff) and analytic induction has been part of the social science tool kit ever since (see Box 15.2).

Box 15.2

Statistical Induction

By the 1920s, with the development of things like the correlation coefficient and the t-test, statistical induction had become very popular in the social sciences. In statistical induction, you see if the distribution of two things (like age and weight) are related and you try to infer cause and effect.

Many social scientists quickly noticed the flaw in statistical induction: Just because the number of hours of daylight and the number of drownings per day are associated doesn't mean that one of those things causes the other. They're both caused by summer, nice weather, and lots of people at the beach. In other words, the correlation between the number of daylight hours and the number of drownings is spurious.

Still, with proper precaution, statistical induction is an excellent start in the search for rules governing social phenomena.

The idea of analytic induction is to formulate ironclad rules about the causes and effects of social phenomena—with none of the wishy-washy tendencies and associations that are the product of statistical analysis. (Think of the difference between saying: "Whenever you see X you will see Y" and "Whenever you see X, there is a 62% chance that you'll see Y".) Several qualitative methods—including grounded theory, schema analysis, and decision modeling—are based on the logic of analytic induction.

W. S. Robinson (1951) laid out the rules for the method. Here's the algorithm:

Start with a single case and develop a theory to account for that one case.

Then, look at a second case and see if the theory fits.

If it does, go on to a third case.

Keep doing this until you run into a case that doesn't fit your theory. (If you see something called "negative case analysis," or "deviant case analysis," this is what it means; see Emigh 1997.)

At this point, you have two choices: modify the theory or redefine the phenomenon you're trying to explain.

Repeat the process until your theory is stable—that is, until it explains every new case you try (W. S. Robinson 1951:813). No fair explaining cases by declaring them all unique. That's an easy way out, but not an option of the method.

How many cases in a row do you need to explain before declaring victory? As in any science, the answer is that you're never home free. No matter how many cases your theory explains, there's always the possibility that the next one will fail the test. Still, if a theory is built on 10–20 cases, and it goes on to explain another, independent sample of 10–20 cases, that's strong evidence in any science that the theory should be accepted (see Box 15.3).

An Example: Cressey's Study of Embezzlers

Among the best-known studies to use analytic induction is Donald Cressey's classic on embezzlers. Cressey (1950, 1953) interviewed 133 prisoners at the Illinois State Penitentiary at Joliet—men who had been convicted of stealing money from their employers. This is the part of analytic induction where you define and redefine the phenomenon you want to study. Cressey could have defined the phenomenon as simply "stealing from employers," but he decided to focus only on men who had taken their jobs with no intention of becoming embezzlers. During a screening interview to find prisoners who were eligible for his study, Cressey listened carefully and chose men who said they had never intended to steal—that it just sort of happened (1950:740).

Cressey began with the hypothesis that men who were in positions of financial trust—like accountants—would become embezzlers if they came to believe, on the job, that taking money from their employers was just a "technical violation" and not really illegal (1950:741). Unfortunately, as soon as he started doing his interviews, real-life embezzlers told Cressey that they knew all along that what they were doing was illegal. So, Cressey formulated a second hypothesis: Men will embezzle when they have some need—like a family emergency or a gambling debt—that they can interpret as an emergency and that they can't see being met legally.

This hypothesis was abandoned when Cressey ran into two kinds of negative cases: men who reported having emergencies that did not drive them to steal and men who stole when they had no financial emergency. One

---

Box 15.3

Large and Small *N*s

Some research problems demand a really big number of cases. Clinical studies around the world long ago confirmed that mothers who breastfeed their children are less likely to develop breast cancer than are mothers who don't. Clinical studies, though, are often on a small number of cases. Even with a few hundred cases, it's impossible to test for small but potentially important effects. For example, if women who breastfeed are more likely to avoid breast cancer, then do mother who breastfeed longer have an even better chance?

It turns out that they do. For every year a mother breastfeeds her children, she cuts her risk of cancer by 4.3%, and for every baby she has, she cuts her risk by 7%. In countries where women have six or seven babies and breastfeed each of them for up to 2 years, the combined effect (more babies and longer breastfeeding of each one) lowers the lifetime risk of breast cancer from 6.3 per 100 women (the rate for the industrialized nations) to 2.7 per 100. But researchers couldn't detect this until they brought together studies from around the world with data on a total of about 150,000 women (Collaborative Group 2002).

On the other hand, many research problems in the social and behavioral sciences involve a really small number of cases. Freud, Piaget, and Skinner all produced their big theories—the theories of psychosexual development, cognitive development, and operant conditioning, respectively—from careful study of a few cases. Comparing the transcripts of clinical interviews from three or four schizophrenics can produce a lot of insight about the illness. Comparing the historical details of how four or five countries (like Chile, Taiwan, Uganda, and South Korea) changed from autocratic to democratic regimes yields a lot of insight about political processes.

Intensive case studies like these are important because they yield insight and understanding about how things work—information about process, not just about presence. They also typically produce hypotheses that can be tested on large samples of people or countries, or whatever.

---

of the prisoners told Cressey that no man would steal if he always confided in his wife about financial problems, but Cressey had to reject this hypothesis, too (1950:741).

Cressey was getting closer, though. His next hypothesis was that men who have the technical skill to embezzle would do so if they had any kind of problem (financial or otherwise) that they felt (1) could *not* be shared with anyone; and (2) *could* be solved with an infusion of money.

Some men told Cressey that they had been in this situation and had not embezzled because the circumstances were not sufficiently clear to make stealing something they could reconcile with their values. That's when Cressey added the final piece of the theory: Men had to be able to square "their conceptions of themselves as trusted persons with conceptions of themselves as users of the entrusted funds or property" (195:742).

This theory explained all 133 cases that Cressey collected. In fact, it also explained about 200 cases that had been collected by others in the 1930s (1950:740).

Another Example: Manning's Study of Abortions

Peter Manning used analytic induction in his study of 15 college women who sought and obtained abortions (Manning 1971). In 1969, when Manning did his study, abortion was illegal in the United States. Getting an abortion required getting information, finding an abortionist, and then making the decision to actually have the procedure.

Manning thought at first that the decision would be facilitated in cases in which women had a close relationship with the biological father who could encourage the woman to have the abortion. Women did not always have a close relationship with the biological father, so Manning reformulated the theory to "a network of supporting people who encourage the abortion, rather than the single potential father" (Manning 1982:292).

Just as Cressey had found two decades earlier in his study of embezzlers, the women in Manning's study had to "develop a self-conception as law-abiding people while making an exception" for their own illegal act. Here's the final theory in Manning's study, derived inductively, by trial and error:

> An abortion takes place when an unmarried woman defines herself as pregnant, is neither willing to marry at that time nor to rear a child, is advised by friends to solve the problem by abortion, neutralizes her self-concept as deviant, and finally is able to locate an abortionist. (Manning 1982:286)

This theory accounted for all the cases of abortion. If any of the conditions were false—if the woman married, for example, or did not come to terms with the problem of self-image—the result was no abortion. (Further Reading: analytic induction.)

Critique of Analytic Induction

Analytic induction is a powerful, qualitative method, but sociologists in the 1950s were quick to point out its flaws (W. S. Robinson 1951; R. Turner 1953). The most obvious is that the method accounts for data you've already collected but does not allow prediction about individual cases. Cressey could not predict, a priori—that is, without data about actual embezzlers who had been arrested and jailed for their crime—which bank workers would violate the trust of their employers. Manning could not predict, a priori, which pregnant women would ultimately seek an abortion. Cressey's theory, however, was superb, a posteriori, as was Manning's.

The critique, then, is that, much as in grounded theory, theories derived from analytic induction explain what's already known. This is not as strong a critique as it may appear. Retrospective understanding of a small set of cases, especially if achieved with systematic methods of data collection and analysis, allows us to make strong predictions about the set of uncollected cases yet to come. In other words, analytic induction does not produce perfect knowledge for the prediction of individual cases, but it can do as well as statistical induction—the standard in social science—in predicting the outcome in aggregates of cases, and it does so with a relatively small number of cases.

It's true that collecting and analyzing case histories of phenomena is much more labor intensive than, say, collecting questionnaire data by telephone. But if you want and need context to derive a theory in the first place or to understand the complexity of a phenomenon, then case histories, analytic induction, and patience produce powerful results.

Finally, one of the critiques of analytic induction has long been that it is based on simple, binary input and output variables. In Manning's theory, women were either persuaded to seek an abortion or they weren't. In Cressey's case, the men either rationalized having violated their employer's trust or they didn't. Like all methods, analytic induction is useful for some problems and not useful for others. It's not very good at handling shades of grey. But for many phenomena, simple black-and-white explanations are enough. (Further Reading: critiques of analytic induction.)

◆ QUALITATIVE COMPARATIVE ANALYSIS—QCA

In any event, with all the critiques, analytic induction fell out of favor for several decades. It has enjoyed a revival, though, since Charles Ragin

(1987, 1994) formalized the logic of the method using a Boolean approach. Boolean algebra involves two states: true or false, present or absent, one or zero. With two dichotomous conditions, A and B, there are four possible combinations: (A and B), (A and not-B), (not-A and B), and (not-A and not-B). With three dichotomous variables, A, B, and C, there are eight combinations; with four, there are sixteen combinations; and so on. Ragin called the method he developed qualitative comparative analysis, or QCA.

An example will make this clear.

Haworth-Hoeppner's Study of Eating Disorders

Susan Haworth-Hoeppner (2000) used QCA in her study of why White, middle-class women develop eating disorders. She interviewed 30 of those women, 21 of whom were either anorexics or bulimics, for 2 hours each about their body image and eating problems. She used open coding to find major themes in these interviews; four themes emerged as factors in the development of eating disorders:

1. A family in which the woman was constantly criticized, by one or both parents as she was growing up about almost everything—her weight, her looks, her personality, her appearance, her performance. In the analysis that follows, this is called C, for "critical family environment."

2. Parents who tried to control everything the woman did by yelling and hitting and by laying down rules, particularly rules about food. This is called R, for "coercive parental control."

3. Parents who made the woman feel unaccepted and unloved. This is called U, for "unloved."

4. A family in which all the conversations seemed to revolve around weight or appearance. This is called D, for "main discourse on weight." (Haworth-Hoeppner 2000:216)

Next, Haworth-Hoeppner coded each of the 30 transcripts for these four concepts. Did the woman live in a family where she was always being criticized for her appearance? Were her parents controlling? Unloving? Always going on about weight and appearance? Finally, she coded for the dependent variable: Was the woman herself bulimic or anorexic? The resulting data are shown in Table 15.1

Table 15.1 Data Matrix for Haworth-Hoeppner's Study

Case	Critical family environment	Coercive parental control	Unloving parent-child relationship	Main discourse on weight	Suffers from eating disorder
1	1	0	0	0	0
2	0	1	0	0	0
3	1	0	1	0	0
4	0	0	0	0	0
5	0	0	0	0	0
6	0	0	0	0	0
7	0	0	0	0	0
8	0	0	0	0	0
9	0	0	0	0	0
10	1	1	1	0	1
11	1	1	0	0	1
12	0	0	0	1	1
13	0	0	0	1	1
14	1	0	0	1	1
15	1	0	0	1	1
16	1	1	0	1	1
17	1	1	0	1	1
18	1	1	0	1	1
19	1	1	0	1	1
20	1	0	1	1	1
21	1	0	1	1	1

Case	Critical family environment	Coercive parental control	Unloving parent-child relationship	Main discourse on weight	Suffers from eating disorder
22	1	1	1	1	1
23	1	1	1	1	1
24	1	1	1	1	1
25	1	1	1	1	1
26	1	1	1	1	1
27	1	1	1	1	1
28	1	1	1	1	1
29	1	1	1	1	1
30	1	1	1	1	1

SOURCE: Susan Haworth-Hoeppner (from Haworth-Hoeppner 2000:218 and personal communication).

Look at Table 15.1 carefully. It has 30 lines, one for each person in the study, and five columns. The four independent variables (the hypothesized causes) are coded (1 or 0) in the first four columns (after the case number) and the one dependent variable, the outcome, is coded (also 1 or 0) in the last column. Consider case number 3. This woman's narrative was coded as having the themes of C and U present (she reported growing up in a critical family environment and having unloving parents) but was not coded for R and D (coercive parental control and a main discourse on weight). From the narrative, there was no evidence that woman #3 was a bulimic or an anorexic, so there is a 0 in the column on the far right.

In fact, 9 of the 30 women showed no evidence of an eating disorder. Six of the nine had *none* of the four factors identified by Haworth-Hoeppner. You can see that in Table 15.1 by looking for the 6 cases that are in the 0000 condition. Nine women (cases 22–30) reported growing up in families where *all four* hypothesized causes were present. In every one of those nine cases—shown as the 1111 condition in Table 15.1—there was evidence of either bulimia or anorexia.

Arranging Data in a Truth Table

Next, Haworth-Hoeppner arranged her data in the form of what's called a Boolean truth table in logic. This is shown in Table 15.2. This table has only 16 rows, not 30 because here, the rows are the combinations of conditions, not the profiles of individual people. As there are four hypothesized causal variables, and each one can be present or absent, there are 2^4, or 16 possible combinations, and so there are 16 rows in the table (see Box 15.4).

Table 15.2 Truth Table for Haworth-Hoeppner's Data

Critical family environment	Coercive parental control	Unloving parent-child relationship	Main discourse on weight	Outcomes: Presence of eating disorders (# of cases)
1	0	0	0	1 (0)
0	1	0	0	1 (0)
0	1	0	1	X
0	0	1	0	X
1	0	1	0	1 (0)
0	0	1	1	X
0	1	1	1	X
0	1	1	0	X
0	0	0	0	6 (0)
1	1	1	0	1 (1)
1	1	0	0	1 (1)
0	0	0	1	1 (2)
1	0	0	1	1 (2)
1	1	0	1	1 (4)
1	0	1	1	1 (2)
1	1	1	1	1 (9)

SOURCE: Haworth-Hoeppner (2000:218).

NOTE: X = condition not observed; 1= condition observed; ( ) = # of cases.

Box 15.4

The Logical-But-Absent and the Null Cases

Five of the 16 conditions—0101, 0010, 0011, 0111, and 0110—though logically possible, did not occur in Haworth-Hoeppner's 30 informants.

For example, the 0101 condition involves (1) the absence of a critical family environment, (2) the presence of coercive parental control, (3) the absence of unloving parents, and (4) a main family discourse on weight. In other words, it involves a loving, supportive family in which the parents exert coercive control and are always going on about weight. It's an unlikely combination and, indeed, it did not occur in Haworth-Hoeppner's data.

These logical conditions that did not occur in the data are shown as Xs in Table 15.2. A truth table forces us to consider all logical possibilities, even though some combinations of features are unlikely to occur in real data.

Four conditions—1000, 0100, 1010, and 0000—were present in Haworth-Hoeppner's informants but did not produce an eating disorder. The first three of these conditions produced a single case each (of absence of an eating disorder) and the 0000 condition produced six cases in which eating disorders were absent. We show these nine cases in parentheses in Table 15.2. These nine cases do not get explained in the analysis. QCA (and analytic induction in general) is best used for explaining the cases where factors lead to a phenomenon (Haworth-Hoeppner 2000:218).

Still, if we can explain the existence of a phenomenon like eating disorders among a set of White, middle-class women, that would be quite a lot.

Simplification

The next step in QCA is to simplify the truth table—to cut it down to its prime implicants. The last seven lines of Table 15.2 show the configurations that produce eating disorders:

1110
1100
0001
1001
1101
1011
1111

Letters are easier to comprehend than 1s and 0s. Haworth-Hoeppner used upper-case C, R, U, and D to represent the presence of the four factors that produce eating disorders and lower-case c, r, u, and d to represent the absence of those factors. The configurations that produced eating disorders (the bottom seven lines in Table 15.2) are shown in the top panel of Table 15.3.

Table 15.3 Simplifying Haworth-Heoppner's Data

The seven configurations that produce eating disorders				
Configurations in Table 15.1 that produced eating disorders	C Critical family environment	R Coercive parental control	U Unloving relationship with parents	D Main discourse on weight in family
1	C	R	U	d
2	C	R	u	d
3	c	r	u	D
4	C	r	u	D
5	C	R	u	D
6	C	r	U	D
7	C	R	U	D
Simplifying to eight pairs of the seven configurations above				
		Call these	Simplifying again	
1+2	CRd	1	1+7	CR
1+7	CRU	2	2+3	CR
2+5	CRu	3	5+8	CD
3+4	ruD	4	6+7	CD
4+5	CuD	5	4	ruD
4+6	CrD	6		
5+7	CRD	7		
6+7	CUD	8		

SOURCE: Haworth-Hoeppner (2000:219).

SUMMARY: Eating disorders = CR + CD + ruD

Using Ragin's method, Haworth-Hoeppner simplified the configurations in Table 15.1 by examining pairs of configurations and looking for terms that are unnecessary. On the first pass, she found that she could reduce the 21 configurations to just eight combinations of the four variables, in sets of three. These are shown on the left-hand side of the bottom panel in Table 15.3 (see Box 15.5).

Box 15.5

Finding the Simplest Set, or Prime Implicants

To find the simplest set of features—the prime implicants—that account for the dependent variable (eating disorders) requires a systematic comparison of all pairs of configurations that produce eating disorders.

There are $n(n-1)/2$ pairs of anything. With three elements in a set, A, B, and C, there are $3(2) = 6/2 = 3$ pairs. Here they are: AB, AC, BC. With four elements (cars, people, countries, whatever), there are $4(3) = 12/2 = 6$ pairs. There are, then, $7(6)/2 = 21$ pairs of the seven configurations in the top panel of Table 15.3.

    Pair 1 and 2, for example, is: CRUd and CRud

    Pair 1 and 3 is: CRUd and cruD

    And so on, down to pair 6 and 7: CrUD and CRUD

    Notice that both C R U D and C r U D produce the same outcome (an eating disorder). This makes R superfluous. On the other hand, R is needed for the pair C R U d and C R u D, but in that case, U is superfluous (Haworth-Hoeppner 2000:219–220).

    The method here is to examine all pairs of conditions and see if we can reduce the number of combinations that account for the outcomes in the truth table. Then we see if we can reduce the number of combinations again until we find the minimum number of variables and their combinations that account for a set of cases in a truth table. These are called the prime implicants in Boolean logic.

Haworth-Hoeppner gave these eight configurations new numbers and repeated the process. There are $8(7)/2 = 28$ pairs of eight configurations, but in the end, Haworth-Hoeppner found that only three combinations of variables (CD, CR, and ruD) were needed to account for the 21 cases of eating disorders in her data. Those configurations are shown in the right-hand column of the bottom panel of Table 15.3. The final result—the prime implicants for eating disorders—is expressed in the Boolean formula:

$$\text{Eating disorders} = CR + CD + ruD$$

We read this as: "Eating disorders are caused by the simultaneous presence of C AND R, AND by the simultaneous presence of C AND D, AND by the presence of D in the absence of R and U" (Haworth-Hoeppner 2000:219–220).

Note how U dropped out of the picture entirely. From the literature about eating disorders, Haworth-Hoeppner expected to find that unloving parents were a prime factor in creating the problem for women. But from the QCA, she learned that this feature was simply not needed to explain the cases in her sample. This sets up an entire agenda for future research.

Like classic content analysis and cognitive mapping, analytic induction and its Boolean incarnation QCA require that human coders read and code text and produce a matrix. The object of the analysis, however, is not to show the relationships between all codes but to find the minimal set of logical relationships among the concepts that account for a single dependent variable.

With four binary independent variables, as in Haworth-Hoppner's data, there are 16 configurations to simplify. With each additional variable, the analysis becomes much more difficult. Fortunately, computer programs are available for this kind of analysis (**Further Reading**: QCA.)

Further Reading

♦ For more on computer programs and other resources for QCA, see the COMPASS resource site for small-*n* research: www. compasss.org. Computer programs for analyzing truth tables include FS/QCA (Ragin et al. 2006), Tosmana (Cronqvist 2007), fuzzy (Longest and Vaisey 2008), and ANTHROPAC (Borgatti 1992).

♦ For more on analytic induction, see Crouch and McKenzie (2006), B. A. Jacobs (2004), S. I. Miller (1982), and Tacq (2007).

♦ For critiques of QCA, see Hicks (1994), Lieberson (1991), and Romme (1995).

♦ For more on QCA, see Cress and Snow (2000), Hicks et al. (1995), Hodson (2004), Kilburn (2004), Rantala and Hellström (2001), Rihoux (2003, 2006), Rihoux and Ragin (2008), Schweizer (1996), Smilde (2005), Stokke (2007), Wickham-Crowley (1991), and Williams and Farrell (1990).

CHAPTER **16**

ETHNOGRAPHIC DECISION MODELS

INTRODUCTION

Ethnographic decision models (EDMs) are qualitative analyses that predict episodic behaviors. Any recurring decision—to buy or not buy a computer; to use (or demand the use of) a condom during sex; to attend or not attend an eight-o'clock class—can be modeled using the EDM method.

    Like analytic induction and qualitative comparative analysis (Chapter 15), EDMs are based on logic. Unlike analytic induction and qualitative

Authors' note: This chapter is adapted from Ryan and Bernard (2006). Used by permission, Society for Applied Anthropology.

comparative analysis, EDMs produce probabilities for behavioral outcomes: Given X, and Y, and Z, people are predicted to make a particular decision with a particular probability. So, EDMs take negative cases into account by incorporating them into a prediction.

EDMs are typically built from interviews with 20–60 people and are tested on a similarly small sample—just the sort of samples used by researchers who rely on qualitative data. Even with such small samples, EDMs typically predict 80%–90% of all outcomes (see Box 16.1).

Box 16.1

EDMs and Binary Outcomes

EDMs are easiest to build for questions about behaviors that can be answered yes or no. Breslin et al. (2000), for example, applied the EDM method to referrals for outpatient treatment by clinicians of drug-abuse patients; Beck (2000) used the method to model the decision by psychologists in British Columbia to report suspected cases of child abuse to the authorities. Both of these are yes-no decisions: to refer a patient for treatment or not; to report suspected abuse to the authorities or not.

EDMs are not limited, however, to binary decisions. Ryan and Martínez (1996) modeled the decision by mothers in a Mexican village of when to take their children to the doctor. In that case, there were four options: Do nothing; use various home remedies; engage the services of a *curandera* (local curer); or take the child to the doctor. The Ryan-Martínez model accounted for 15 out of 17 cases (89%) in their original model and 17 out of 20 cases (84%) in their test of the original model.

◆ HOW TO BUILD EDMS

Christina Gladwin (1989) made the method of ethnographic decision tree modeling widely accessible. Here are the steps: (1) Select a specific behavioral choice to model and elicit decision criteria from a convenience sample of respondents. (2) Further elaborate and verify the decision criteria on a purposive, heterogeneous sample of informants. (3) Use the ethnographic data from step 1 and the survey data from step 2 to build a hierarchical decision model. (4) Test the model on an independent and, if possible, representative sample from the same population.

We will add a fifth step: (5) Validate the model with responses from people about why they acted as they did.

Step 1. Selecting a Behavioral Choice to Model and Eliciting the Decision Criteria for Recycling

In one of our projects (Ryan and Bernard 2006), we modeled people's decision to recycle (or not) the last aluminum beverage can they had in their hand. We chose this decision because: (1) It is very common; (2) the consequences are economically and ecologically great; and (3) a lot is already known about it. We wanted to know whether an EDM, based on a small, ethnographic sample, would reflect what has long been known, in general, about recycling, from large surveys: When it's convenient, people will do it. When it's not convenient, they won't.

To start, we did exploratory, free-ranging interviews with a convenience sample—some men, some women, some older, some younger—of 21 informants in Florida and North Dakota.

We asked each informant three questions: (1) Think about the last time you had a can of something to drink in your hand—soda, juice, water, beer, whatever. When was that? (2) What did you do with the can when you were done? (3) Why did you [didn't you] recycle?

The goal was to elicit as many possible reasons for why people recycled or not. By the time we got through 21 informants, there were few new rationales being mentioned, so we stopped. The results are shown in Table 16.1 Most people claimed to have recycled the last can they had in their hand, so there are more reasons for recycling than for not recycling. Of course, there is a social-desirability effect, and we expect some people to claim to have recycled when they hadn't. This may affect the final results, but it doesn't affect the building of the model.

Step 2. Collecting Data for a Preliminary Model

In Step 2, we collected survey data from a new group of ethnographic informants and used these data to build a preliminary model of the behavior. Ethnographic informants are people who know about the behavior of interest and about the culture surrounding the behavior. That is, they can knowledgeably respond to questions about their own behavior (in this case, getting rid of an empty beverage can) and about their reasons for their behavior. The data collected from these informants are survey data because every informant is asked the same set of questions.

Table 16.1   Reasons for Recycling or Not Recycling From 21 Informants

Reasons for Recycling	Reasons for Not Recycling
1. It's wasteful to just throw it away.	1. I was traveling and I had no place to recycle it.
2. The city has a recycling program. The garbage man picks it up.	2. Bins aren't around. I didn't have a recycling bin. There aren't enough recycling bins available.
3. To help save the environment.	
4. Recycling bins are conveniently located.	3. There's no recycling program where I live. No city recycling program.
5. That's what big blue is for.	4. Because I don't have Big Blue.
6. My kid made a pact with a TV club so she now recycles.	5. I didn't think about it.
7. I'm concerned about the environment.	6. I gave it to kids who turn it in for money.
8. It's environmentally sound.	7. Forgot.
9. Land is not a renewable resource.	8. Recycling is not available to me.
10. I save cans to get money for them.	9. Laziness.
11. The people I'm staying with recycle, so I do, too.	10. The recycling bin was not conveniently located.
12. The bins were around.	11. Because I have to separate out cans from my garbage and that's a problem.
13. It's useful and can be used again.	12. Lack of education.
14. To keep the environment clean.	13. I don't have enough time.
15. Because of habit; we usually put it in big blue.	
16. Because I'm environmentally conscious.	
17. To preserve the environment for my kids.	
18. It's not biodegradable.	
19. It's no good in the landfill.	
20. Because it's just good to recycle.	
21. It's easy to do.	
22. Because it's the right thing to do.	
23. Because it's the big thing to do these days.	
24. Because someone told me to.	
25. We shouldn't cover the land up with garbage.	
26. To buy more beer.	
27. Because if you don't you have to pay a fee.	

SOURCE: Ryan and Bernard (2006). Material used with permission of the Society for Applied Anthropology.

We interviewed 70 informants, 37 in Florida and 33 in North Dakota. Here again, we purposefully selected a diverse group of informants (age range 18–71 years, education 1–23 years, 48% male) in hopes that we could build a robust model that would account for can-recycling behavior across a wide range of people (see Box 16.2).

Box 16.2

Sample Size for EDMs

Our sample size was based on some crude calculations. We wanted enough cases to be able to build a tree (see Figures 16.1 and 16.3 below) that was at least three levels deep and where each endpoint would contain at least five people. Having at least five cases at each endpoint gives us confidence that the decision criteria are nontrivial. We calculate the minimum sample size for such a tree as follows:

Minimum Sample Size = Minimum cases in each endpoint $\times\ 2^{(\#\ of\ Levels)}$

In our case, the minimum sample size would have been $(5 \times 2^3) = 40$. The reason this is a minimum is that our assumptions are met only if the cases bifurcate perfectly at each decision point in the tree. Our experience with decision trees, however, suggests that this rarely happens, so we try to more-or-less double the minimum sample size to insure that we wind up some cases at each endpoint... hence, our 70 survey cases for building the model.

We began our interviews with the same initial questions we had asked in Step 1: "Think about the last time you had a can of something to drink in your hand—soda, juice, water, beer, whatever. Did you recycle the can? Why [Why not?]" Then we asked each of those 70 people 31 questions derived from Table 16.1. The 31 questions are shown in Table 16.2.

Note that some of the questions are about general behavior ("Do you normally recycle cans at home?"); some are about structural conditions ("Was a recycling bin handy?"); and some are about attitudes ("Do you consider yourself environmentally conscious?"). Also note that questions 7–11 are expansions of the question "Where were you when you had that used beverage can in your hand?" into five binary questions. This ensures that all informants are given the same set of cues as the data are collected to build the preliminary model.

Table 16.2 Questions Asked in the Recycling Study

After asking about the last can and the reasons for recycling, ask each of the following:

1. Does your city have a recycling program?
2. Can you return aluminum cans for redemption in your town or city?
3. Did you live in a house or apartment?
4. If you live in a house, is there a special pickup for recycled materials (e.g., Big Blue)?
5. Are there special bins for recycled materials in your apartment building, etc.?
6. Are there recycling bins for cans where you work?

The last time you drank from an aluminum can were you:

7. at home?
8. at work?
9. driving in your car?
10. inside or outside?
11. at someone else's house?
12. The last time you drank from an aluminum can did you get the can from a vending machine?
13. The last time you drank from an aluminum can was there a recycling bin conveniently located nearby?
14. The last time you drank from an aluminum can were you busy?
15. The last time you drank from an aluminum can were there other people around when you finished your drink?
16. If so, do these people usually recycle cans?
17. If so, did anyone suggest that you recycle the can?
18. Do you have children?
19. Do you habitually recycle material such as cans, newspapers, and plastics at home?
20. Do you habitually recycle material such as cans, newspapers, and plastics at work?
21. Do you consider yourself environmentally conscious (not at all, a little, some, a lot)?
22. How much do you think that recycling helps to save the environment (not at all, a little, some, a lot)?
23. How much are you concerned about the environment (not at all, a little, some, a lot)?
24. How much do you think recycling helps to keep the environment clean (not at all, a little, some, a lot)?
25. How important is it for you to preserve the environment for children (not at all, a little, some, a lot)?
26. Do you think it's wasteful to throw away an aluminum can?
27. Do you think that there is a lot of social pressure nowadays to recycle?
28. Do you think that cans are bad for landfills?
29. Do you think that recycling aluminum cans is useful?
30. Do you recycle any materials besides cans?
31. If so, what other materials do you recycle?

Step 3. Building the Preliminary Model

In Step 3, we looked for patterns among the decision criteria in Step 1 and the reported behaviors in Step 2 and built an explicit logical model to account for the behaviors.

This is the most difficult of the steps and the hardest to describe because it involves a lot of trial-and-error. There are formal approaches, but we use the method of analytic induction recommended by C. Gladwin (1989): closely examine cases that do not fit the model, and modify the model accordingly until it achieves some desired level of accuracy, say, at least 80% (see Box 16.3).

Box 16.3

Formal Approaches for Decision Modeling

One formal method is to produce vignettes that lay out all possible combinations of factors identified as important in a decision.

> For example: You're [standing at a bus stop] [at home] [at work]. You're [alone] [not alone] and your children [are there] [not there]. You have a can of [soda][juice][beer] in your hand. When you finish the can, you [throw it in the garbage] [put it in a recycle bin] [leave it anywhere that's handy, like a desk or on the ground].

The modal responses from vignettes like these can be used to generate the decision rules in the model. The vignette method is attractive but, like all methods, it has its limitations. Even with just eight binary factors, there are $2^8 = 256$ combinations. In a small-n study—the kind usually done by qualitative researchers—each informant would have to see 256 vignettes. There is an alternative to this full-scale approach, in which informants see a random sample of vignettes, but this requires a large number of informants. (See Rossi and Noch [1982] for more on this method.)

Another formal approach involves the use of artificial intelligence (or data mining) algorithms to build and prune decision trees (Mingers 1989a, 1989b). These algorithms semi-automate the model-building procedure by identifying the possible combinations of factors (and the order of those factors) that produce the various outcomes (here, recycled or didn't). Some tree-pruning procedures are available in statistical packages such as SYSTAT's "Classification and Regression Tree Analysis" (SYSTAT 2008).

From the responses to our EDM survey of 70 informants in Florida and North Dakota, we drafted models of the decision process, trying different combinations of variables. The result was a preliminary model, shown in Figure 16.1.

We got to this first model by going through the questions in Table 16.2 one at a time and asking: How many errors (that is, outcomes that are not predicted by the model) would this question produce? The idea is to find the one question that produces the fewest errors. That question then becomes the first branch of a proposed model.

In examining the data, the question "Were you at home when you had that can in your hand?" produced the fewest errors. Thus, guessing that everyone at home recycled and that everyone not at home did not recycle produces 6 errors (22% of the 27 cases) on the left-hand branch and 11 errors (26% of the 43 cases) on the right-hand branch, for a total of 17 errors and an accuracy rate of 53 out of 70 cases, or 76%.

The six errors on the left-hand branch of Figure 16.1 are the $4 + 2 = 6$ people who did not recycle when the single-criterion model (at home, not at home) predicted they did. Similarly, the 11 errors on the right-hand side of Figure 16.1 comprise those who said they recycled ($7 + 2 + 1 + 1$, including 2 of the 3 singleton errors on the right-hand branch of Figure 16.1) when the single-criterion model predicted they did not.

Balancing the Advantages of Complexity and Simplicity

A slightly more complex model improves the results from 76% to 90%. First, the left-hand branch of the model: Of the 27 informants who were at home, the best predictor of who did or who did not recycle was to ask whether they recycled any other products. Of the 23 who said they recycled other products, 21 (91.3%) recalled recycling the last can they had in their hand. All four of those who said they didn't recycle other products also recalled not recycling the can. The rule here is: For those at home who recycle other products, guess "recycled the can"; otherwise, guess "didn't recycle the can." This results in just 2 errors out of 27 cases, or 92.6% correct.

On the right-hand branch of the model, just guessing that nobody recycled produced 32 out of 43 correct answers, or 74.4% correct. This improves to 88.4% correct by distinguishing whether those not at home were at work or elsewhere, and then asking: "Was a recycling bin conveniently located nearby?"

First, as shown in Figure 16.1, when bins were nearby, seven of the eight (87.5%) respondents who were at work recycled. When bins were not

Figure 16.1   Decision to Recycle Cans (Ethnographic Sample, N = 70)

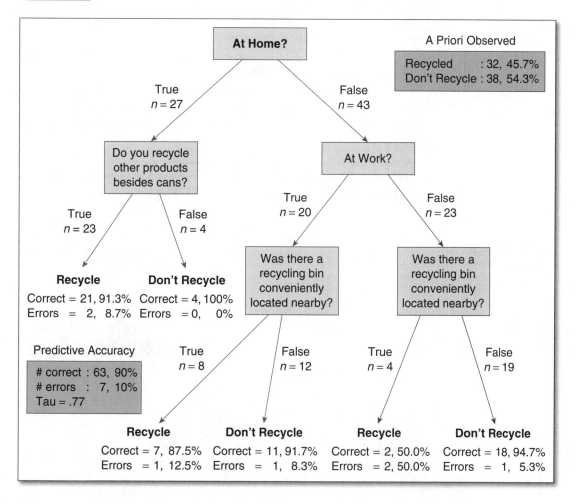

nearby, 11 of the 12 respondents (91.7%) who were at work said that they didn't recycle. This branch of the model gets 18 out of 20, or 90% correct. Second, among the 23 respondents who were neither at home nor at work, asking if a recycling bin was nearby produces a model with just three errors, or 87% correct.

Overall, on the right-hand branch, the model produces five errors (88.4% correct), and the accuracy of the complete model (both left- and right-hand branches) is 63 right out of 70, or 90%. This is 77% better than expected by chance (and is indicated by Klecka's *tau* = .77 in Figure 16.1; see Klecka 1980:50–51).

Now, the model in Figure 16.1 can be made simpler by collapsing the two paths "At Work?" and "Not at Work?" as shown in Figure 16.2.

This change has no affect on the error rate, since most of the predictive power on the right side of the model is based on a bin being nearby. The extra criterion in the model, however (at work–not at work in Figure 16.1), with its two extra paths, shows that people at work recycle more than do those who are neither at home nor at work—40% (7 + 1 = 8 of 20), compared to 13% (2 + 1 = 3 of 23).

The extra criterion thus provides information on the size and location of the problem—information that suggests where to put recycling bins if we don't have an unlimited supply of them. More about this in Step 4.

Figure 16.2 Decision to Recycle Cans—Simplified Model (Ethnographic Sample, *N* = 70)

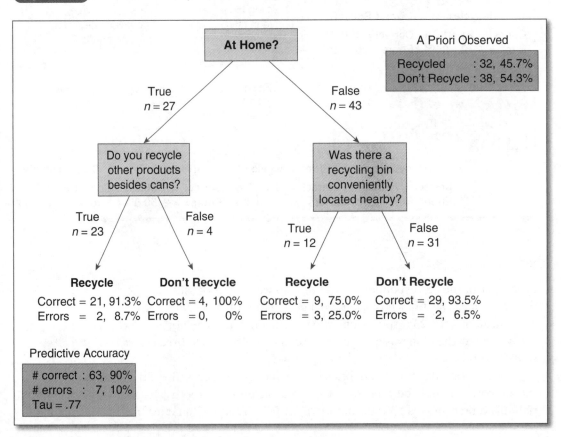

Step 4. Testing the Model
on an Independent Sample

An accuracy rate of 90% may seem high, but it's hardly a surprise when a model accounts for the data on which it is built. All we are doing in Figure 16.1 is representing graphically what people told us they did. Models, however, are hypotheses. Their validity doesn't depend on how they are derived but on how well they stand up to tests on an independent sample of people who were not involved in building the model in the first place.

To see how our model EDM did on a larger population, we tested it on a representative, national sample of 386 respondents in the United States. The results are in Figure 16.3 (see Box 16.4).

If you compare Figures 16.1 and 16.3, you'll see a lot of differences in the distribution of answers. For the ethnographic model, we interviewed people wherever we could find them, while for the national survey, we called people at home. Sure enough, 58% of the national respondents said they were at home when they had that last beverage can in their hand, compared to only 39% of our ethnographic informants.

Box 16.4

Samples for Testing EDMs

Samples for testing EDMs are typically drawn from the same local populations that are used to build the models. Strong agreement between two, independently derived EDMs is the equivalent of repeating a laboratory experiment in terms of reliability and internal validity. There are two cautions here:

1. EDMs usually predict 80%–90% of episodic behaviors, but these are almost always reported, not observed behaviors. Thus, EDMs are subject to the same problem as are all studies of self-reported behavior.

2. Strong reliability and internal validity are not a proxy for external validity. However, the credibility—and hence, generalizability—of results from small experiments increases with each repetition of the experiment. If you repeat a small experiment on cultural content in Florida, North Dakota, and California and you get consistent—that is, reliable—results, the credibility of those results—that is, the confidence in their external validity—increases.

Figure 16.3 Decision to Recycle Cans (National Sample, $N = 386$)

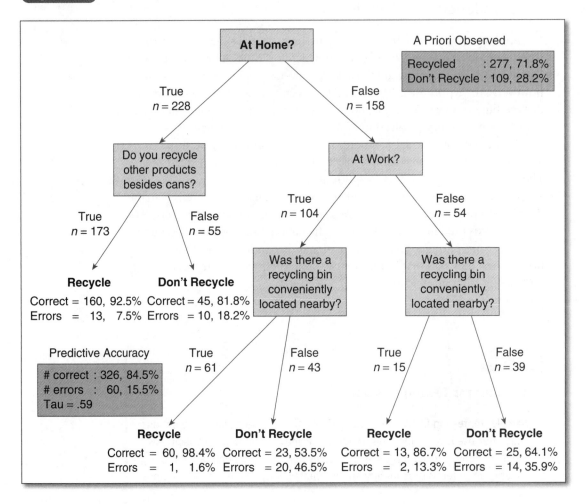

Complexity Versus Simplicity Again

And still, the ethnographic model held up well in a national test. Of the 173 people who were at home and who also said they recycled other products besides cans, 160 (93%) recalled recycling the can, compared to 91% in the ethnographic sample. Of the 55 people at home who reported not recycling other products besides cans, 45 (82%) recalled not recycling the can, compared to 100% for the ethnographic sample. And the overall accuracy of the national model is 85%, compared to 90% for the ethnographic model.

Just as with the ethnographic model, adding the question about where the behavior took place (at work vs. at home) has no effect on prediction power. It does, however, corroborate the policy-relevant information produced in the ethnographic model regarding where to put scarce resources if we want to increase recycling behavior. Of the 158 people in the national sample who said they were not at home when they had that last beverage can in their hands, 20% (20 + 1 = 21 out of 104 in Figure 16.3) said they didn't recycle if they also said they were at work. By contrast, 50% (25 + 2 = 27 out of 54 in Figure 16.3) of the not-home people said they didn't recycle if they also said they were not at work.

It may be tempting to go after the 50% error rate, but the not-home/not-at-work condition covers people who are at football games, or driving on the freeway, or visiting other people's houses, or window shopping. With so many conditions, and limited resources with which to put out recycling bins, it is going to be tough to have an impact on that 50% error rate. In the short term, it's easier to imagine incentives for getting employers to put out those bins.

Step 5. Assessing the Validity of Ethnographic Decision Models

We can take the process one step further and bring qualitative information into assessing the model's validity. We asked 33 of our ethnographic informants to tell us, in their own words, why they recycled, *before* we asked systematically about the decision criteria. For these informants, we can examine the fit between their justifications of their choice to recycle or not and the model's predictions.

We do this by flowing individual recycling cases down the decision tree and examining the degree to which each end point in the tree (each final decision) corresponds to our informants' own accounts. The results are shown in Table 16.3.

The top right-most cell of Table 16.3 contains the rationales from people who reported that they were at home and recycled other things besides cans. At home, only one person said it was *easy* to do. Three people, however, said it was a *good thing* to do or that it was *mandatory*. Nowhere else in the rationales do these latter two themes arise.

The next cell down shows the rationales from people who reported that they were at home but did *not* recycle other things. The model correctly predicted that the first three of the respondents would not recycle. Unlike those who had recycled, none of the three mentioned that it was important or good to recycle—or that it was mandatory. The three cases that were misclassified more closely resemble the rationales in the cell above.

The rationales for those at work are clearly divided between those respondents who reported having a recycling bin conveniently located nearby and those who did not. Those who had a bin nearby reported its

Table 16.3 Verbatim Justifications for 33 Recycling Choices From an Ethnographic Sample

Decision Rules					Choice	Verbatim Justification
At home?	Yes	Recycle other things?				
		Yes			Yes	• I know you can recycle it and the bin was easy to get to. • I believe in it, and it's good for the environment. • I feel that it's some form of token effort in trying to protect the environment and keep stuff out of landfills. • I recycle as much as I can. • For recycling—because garbage just doesn't disappear— if you recycle there is less garbage then. • They pick it up on Wednesday—because it's a good thing to do. • It is required to recycle cans. • It is mandatory, and I believe in recycling. • It is mandatory.
		No			No	*Correct* • I don't recycle. I didn't think about it and I don't like storing it around home because it brings pests. • I was too lazy. • Sometimes I keep 'em for my brother but. . . . I give them to him. . . . I just didn't this time. *Incorrect* • I take them to a place where they take aluminum cans and gets money for 'em. • I did it to recycle . . . no reason just to recycle. • It's easy to do and they pick 'em up.
	No	At work?	Yes	Bin nearby?		
				Yes	Yes	• I always recycle aluminum cans. . . . I don't know . . . because I can, because it's available. • It's an automatic thing at work; we all recycle there. • I wasn't gonna mess with it—it was easy. • One of the operators collects them at work, and she takes the bag weekly to put it . . . to take in for recycling.
				No	No	• We're not allowed to keep cans on the job. • There was no recycling center nearby. • A lady at work collects them—so I put them in the bag to give to this one lady.

Decision Rules						Choice	Verbatim Justification
At Home?	No	At Work?	No	Bin nearby?	Yes	Yes	*No examples available.*
						No	*Correct* ♦ It wasn't convenient I guess. ♦ There was no obvious place to put it for recycling. ♦ I don't know—I didn't have a container to put it in. ♦ I was not home—I was someplace in town. ♦ I was at someone's house. ♦ I was driving—I threw it out the window—it was a beer can—the environment—I'm down with it but there are too many rules—I threw it out so I wouldn't get caught with it in my car. ♦ I wasn't at home—at home I would've put it in the recycling bucket—If it weren't illegal to put it in my car. . . . I'd've taken it home with me—more people would recycle if it weren't for those open container laws. *Incorrect* ♦ Well I didn't know what to do with it. ♦ That's better on the environment. ♦ I take 'em in and turns 'em in for money. ♦ I think it's a good thing—why use new things when you can reuse old things.

availability and the ease with which one could recycle. Those who didn't have a bin spontaneously mentioned not being able to keep cans on the job or not having a recycling center.

The last cell shows the rationales for those who were not at home or at work and who did not have a recycling bin nearby. Of the eight cases that the model predicted correctly, half spontaneously mentioned either the lack of convenience or the lack of a recycling bin. The other half mentioned explicitly where they were and clearly implied that place had something to do with their behavior. The two people who said that they threw the can out of the car identified a factor we hadn't thought of before—laws against drinking and driving might have an impact on environmentally friendly behaviors.

Resolving Errors With Ethnography

Why do people recycle when the model predicts that they shouldn't and don't recycle when the model predicts that they should? Again, we turn to the verbatim comments of our informants. Those who recalled recycling a can despite not being at home or at work and not having a bin conveniently located were likely to justify their behavior by citing their beliefs in environmentalism or citing financial benefits for doing it. This may be the result of positive attitudes about recycling—attitudes that give people the extra impetus they need for recycling when bins aren't handy.

This is worth testing, but note that attitudes (or whatever else is at work) can account for no more than 10% of responses in the local sample (because the model predicts 90% of responses there) and no more than 15% of responses in the national sample (because the model predicts 85% of responses there).

We don't have ethnographic data to account for those not at home who reported not recycling a can despite having a recycling bin handy—because none of our 33 informants were in that category. In fact, only three out of 76 people in our national sample reported not recycling despite having a bin handy. Clearly, just putting a lot of recycling bins around will increase recycling behavior. This has been known for some time, of course, but the fact that we can validate a well-understood piece of information like this gives us confidence in the EDM method for answering questions that are not this obvious. (Further Reading: ethnographic decision modeling.)

Further Reading

◆ For more on EDMs, see C. E. Hill (1998). Much of the research based on EDMs focuses on the choices that people make in response to illness—like Ryan and Martínez's study (1996) of when mothers in rural Mexico decide to take their children to a doctor (see Box 16.1 above). For more studies of illness decisions, see Dy et al. (2005), Mathews and Hill (1990), Montbriand (1994), Weller et al. (1997), and Young and Garro (1994 [1981]).

◆ In other areas, Bauer and Wright (1996) used EDMs to study the decision of Navajo mothers to breastfeed or use formula; Heemskerk (2000) studied the decision of men and women in Suriname to go into gold mining; Fairweather (1999) modeled the decision by farmers in New Zealand to use organic or conventional methods; and Morera and Gladwin (2006) modeled the decision by farmers in Honduras to practice soil conservation.

SAMPLING

INTRODUCTION ◆

All good research starts with a solid research design and this means solving two kinds of problems—problems of sampling and problems of measurement. Deciding what to study is a measurement problem. Deciding what themes to code in a set of texts is a measurement problem. Deciding when to ask sensitive questions during the course of an interview is a measurement problem, as is deciding whether it's ethical to ask certain questions at all.

Sampling problems are different. In most projects, it's impossible to collect data about every unit of analysis in a population, so we sample those units. In content analysis, the units of analysis might be issues of a monthly magazine over a period of years. In grounded theory, the units of analysis are usually people who have personal experience we want to understand—like coping with widowhood, or crossing the U.S.-Mexican border in search of work, or living with AIDS.

The art and science of measurement addresses this question: Do the data you collect from a set of people (or magazines, or whatever) represent well the phenomenon you're studying? The answer to this question—known as the internal validity problem—depends ultimately on whether your colleagues believe the data and findings you report.

The art and science of sampling, on the other hand, addresses this question: Can you generalize from your findings about the people (or other units of analysis) you've actually studied to the population at large of those units? The answer to this question—known as the external validity problem—depends on whether the things being studied are part of a probability sample or not.

◆ TWO KINDS OF SAMPLES

There are two kinds of samples in research: those based on probability theory—random sampling—and those that are not. Which kind of sample you use depends on your research objective. When it comes to sampling, though, the same three rules apply to all researchers, including those who deal with qualitative data as well as those who deal with quantitative data. Here's the first rule:

1. If your objective is to estimate a parameter from a sample of data to a larger population, then only probability sampling will do. Collect data from a sufficiently large, randomly selected, unbiased sample of the larger population.

Here's the second rule:

2. If your research objective demands a statistically representative sample but there is no way to get one (because of logistical or ethical problems), then don't agonize. Use a nonprobability sampling method—more about this below—apply it systematically, and let everyone know in your write-up exactly what you did.

And, finally, here's the third rule:

3. If your research objective requires a nonprobability sample, then choose an appropriate sampling method and apply it systematically.

Sample Size in Probability Sampling

In classical sampling terminology, a parameter is a real number that you want to estimate. In any group of, say, 1,000 people, for example, the true average height—the height parameter—is the sum of all the measured heights of the people, divided by 1,000. This parameter can be estimated from an unbiased sample of the heights of those 1,000 people. An unbiased sample implies random selection, which means that every unit of analysis—in this case, people—has the same chance of winding up in the sample (see Box 17.1).

Box 17.1

Why Sampling Theory Is Important in Qualitative Research

Although ethnography, grounded theory, and other research strategies in the qualitative tradition rely heavily on nonprobability sampling, it is important for all social scientists to understand the basics of statistical sampling theory as well as the value of nonprobability samples. As we've stressed throughout this book, we see the great divide between qualitative and quantitative in social research as dysfunctional. It keeps good social scientists in both traditions blinded to the value of work in both traditions.

We can't cover sampling theory here, but coverage is widely available in other methods books. (Further Reading: sampling theory in social science.)

By eliminating bias—by taking the decision out of your hands—random selection ensures that whatever you find out about the sample can be generalized to the population from which it was taken, give or take a known amount of potential error.

For example, when you read that a political leader has an "approval rating of 41%, plus-or-minus 3 points," and assuming the poll was done on an unbiased sample of, say 400 people, you know that if the poll were taken 10,000 times, then 95% of the time the parameter would be estimated to lie between 38% and 44%—that is 41%, plus-or-minus 3 points.

The amount of error, given random selection, depends on sample size, not on the proportion of the population taken as a sample. A random sample of 400 out of a population of 10,000 has the same error bounds as a sample of 400 out of a population of 10,000,000. Determining the sample size in survey research may be complicated, but it's a science that has known error bounds. (Further Reading: sampling theory in social science.)

Sample Size in Nonprobability Sampling

The problem of sample size is not quite as well understood when it comes to ethnography, grounded theory, schema analysis, narrative analysis, and the like, but a lot of progress has been made. There is growing evidence that 20–60 knowledgeable people are enough to uncover and understand the core categories in any well-defined cultural domain or study of lived experience.

We know from Chapter 8, on cultural domain analysis, that 20–30 informants are needed for a free-listing exercise to identify the contents of a cultural domain—even such loosely defined domains as "things mothers do."

Once you've identified knowledgeable people, even fewer informants are needed. Weller and Romney (1988:77) showed that just 10 knowledgeable informants are needed to understand the contents of a cultural domain. And that's when the average knowledge of the informants is only .70—that is, informants who would get a C on a test of knowledge about the domain. The number of informants needed rises to a lofty 13 if the average knowledge slips from .7 to .5. This is very good news for all researchers of experience and cultural knowledge—the kind retrieved with in-depth interviews (and see Handwerker 2001:93–96).

M. G. Morgan et al. (2002:76) did in-depth interviews with four different samples of people about various risks in the environment. The researchers did the usual coding for concepts, but they also plotted the number of new concepts in each interview across the four different studies. Their results are in Figure 17.1. In every case, the shape of the line is the same: The first few interviews produce a lot of new data, but by 20 interviews, the curves flatten out and hardly any new information is retrieved.

This finding has been corroborated by Guest et al. (2006). These researchers interviewed 30 sex workers in Ghana and another 30 in Nigeria. They coded the transcripts in batches of 6, completing all the interviews from Ghana and then moving on to the interviews from Nigeria. Figure 17.2 shows the plot of the number of new themes uncovered in the coding. Of the 114 themes identified in the entire corpus, 80 turn up in the first six interviews. Another 20 themes turn up in the second batch of six interviews. Only five new themes were added to the codebook to accommodate the 30 interviews from Nigeria. Clearly, most of the information extracted from the interviews was obtained early on.

Morse (1994) recommended a minimum of six interviews for phenomenological studies and 30–50 interviews for ethnographic studies and grounded

Figure 17.1

The Number of New Concepts Retrieved in Interviews Tapers Off After Just 20 Interviews

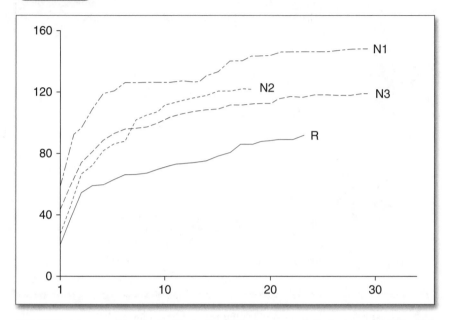

SOURCE: Morgan, M. G., B. Fischoff, A. Bostrom, and C. J. Atman 2002. *Risk Communication: A Mental Models Approach.* New York: Cambridge University Press. Reprinted with the permission of Cambridge University Press.

NOTE: N = three separate sets of interviews on nuclear power in space vehicles; R = interviews on radon in homes.

theory studies. Now, the data from two studies—shown in Figures 17.1 and 17.2—tend to support Morse's experience-based guess. (Further Reading: problems of sampling qualitative research.)

Remember: Every sample represents something. An unbiased sample represents a population with a known probability of error. A nonprobability sample lacks this one feature. For a very, very large number of research questions, this is simply not a problem.

KINDS OF NONPROBABILITY SAMPLES ♦

The most widely used nonprobability sampling methods are: quota sampling, purposive sampling (also called judgment sampling), convenience sampling, network sampling, theoretical sampling, and key informants.

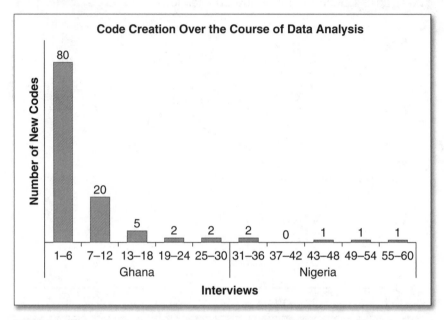

Figure 17.2 Number of New Themes Tagged in 60 Interviews

SOURCE: Guest, G., Bunce, A., and Johnson, L. (2006). How many interviews are enough? An experiment with data saturation and variability. *Field Methods, 18,* 59–82. Copyright © 2006 Sage Publications.

Table 17.1 Quota Sampling Grid With Three Binary Independent Variables

Variables							
Salaried				Self-Employed			
≤39		≥40		≤39		≥40	
Men	Women	Men	Women	Men	Women	Men	Women
5	5	5	5	5	5	5	5

Quota Sampling

Quota sampling involves the production of a sampling grid of mutually exclusive subpopulations. Table 17.1 shows a typical sampling grid for a study of 40 people, all of whom are employed full time. Given the time and money to study 40 people, the researcher has decided to sample five men and five women in each of two categories: the salaried versus the self-employed people, and younger (under 40) versus older (40 and over).

Silverman et al.'s Study of Breast Cancer

E. Silverman et al. (2001) did in-depth, hour-long interviews to learn "how women view breast cancer, their personal risk of breast cancer, and how screening mammography affects that risk" (p. 231). The researchers began by calling women across the United States at random. The first question they asked was whether the women had ever had breast cancer. If the answer was no, the woman was eligible for the study. Silverman et al. used a quota system to select women for in-depth interviewing. Here is how they described their sample:

> To fill our quota sampling, we approached 191 women randomly selected within strata defined by census tract income and age provided by NDS. Ninety-eight women were disqualified because they did not meet racial, age, or socioeconomic criteria; 52 refused; and 41 agreed to participate. Of note, 35 of these women requested the personalized breast cancer risk report, and all 41 accepted the $20 payment. (E. Silverman et al. 2001:233)

Table 17.2 shows the key sampling criteria used in the Silverman et al. study. Table 17.3 shows the diverse demographics of Silverman et al.'s final sample of 41 informants.

Table 17.2 Sampling Grid for the Quota Sample in Silverman et al.'s Study

Income							
Up to $25,000 per year				Above $25,000 per year			
Race							
White	Black	Other		White	Black		Other
Age							
≤39	40–49	50–69	≥70	≤39	40–49	50–69	≥70

SOURCE: Assembled from data in Silverman (2001:232). Silverman, E., S. Woolshin, L. M. Schwartz, S. J. Byram, H. G. Welch, and B. Fischoff 2001. Women's views on breast cancer risk and screening mammography: A qualitative interview study. *Medical Decision Making* 21:231–240. Copyright © Society for Medical Decision Making c/o George Washington University.

| Table 17.3 | Participant Characteristics for 41 Women in the Silverman et al. Study |

Demographics	Percentage
Age	
Younger than 40	15
40–49	37
50–69	34
70 or older	15
Race	
White	51
Black	24
Asian	12
Hispanic	7
Native American	5
Annual Income	
Less than $25,000	51
Education	
Did not finish high school	20
High school graduate	41
College degree	39
Ever had a mammogram	80
Breast cancer risk factors	
Family history of breast cancer	12
Personal history of breast biopsy	23

SOURCE: Silverman, E., S. Woolshin, L. M. Schwartz, S. J. Byram, H. G. Welch, and B. Fischoff 2001. Women's views on breast cancer risk and screening mammography: A qualitative interview study. *Medical Decision Making* 21:231–240.

Quota samples are much less expensive and are easier to implement than are random samples. Quota samples are not unbiased but they often approximate the results of probability sampling.

But not always. In 1948, in a famous polling debacle, many pollsters predicted, on the basis of quota sampling, that Thomas Dewey would beat Harry Truman in the U.S. presidential election. The *Chicago Tribune* was so confident in those predictions that they printed an edition announcing Dewey's victory—while the votes were being counted that would make Truman president.

The lesson was that quota sampling cannot be used for estimating proportions that are close to 50-50. Quota samples are excellent, however, for understanding variation in people's experience. If you want to know how children's sports— Little League Baseball, Pop Warner football, Youth Soccer, high school football— function in small communities across the United States, you'd ask people who have children playing those sports. To get at the intracultural variation, open-ended interviews with five or six really knowledgeable people in each subgroup (like Blacks, Whites, and Hispanics, for example, or young parents and grandparents) will produce the relevant data about the range of ideas that people have about these institutions. (Further Reading: quota sampling.)

Purposive or Judgment Sampling

Purposive sampling is quota sampling without a grid. You simply decide the purpose you want informants to serve and you take what you can get (see Box 17.2).

Box 17.2

Other Units of Analysis

Remember, units of analysis can be people (organic tomato farmers, female fire fighters, recovering alcoholics), groups (classrooms, countries, Fortune 500 companies), and objects (nonresidential buildings in a city).

Or even time. Experience sampling, for example, involves calling people up at random times and asking them what they're doing or thinking at the moment (Hektner et al. 2007).

Purposive samples are particularly useful in the study of special and hard-to-find populations. Studies of injecting drug users, trial lawyers, shamans, or lacto-vegetarians require purposive samples.

Julie Barroso (1997) studied the experience of long-term survivors of AIDS. For her purposes, people eligible for the study had to have survived with AIDS for at least 3 years, be at least 18 years old, speak English, and live in the Tampa, Florida, area. To find participants, Barroso distributed 3,000 fliers to the offices of organizations that catered to the needs of people living with AIDS, and to health department offices, doctors' offices, and so on. She found that the stories about living with AIDS became redundant by the time she had interviewed 12 informants. However, she had mostly White men in that sample of 12, so she purposively selected women and minorities. In the end, she wound up with six women (including one African American) and 14 men (including one African American).

Kimberly Mahaffy (1996) was interested in how lesbian Christians deal with the cognitive dissonance that comes from being rejected by mainstream Christian churches. Mahaffy sent letters to gay Christian organizations, asking them to put an ad for potential respondents in their newsletters. She sent flyers to women's bookstores and to lesbian support groups, asking for potential respondents to get in touch with her. Mahaffy could not possibly have gotten an unbiased sample of lesbian Christians. Even a quota sample (so many of a particular age, so many of a particular occupational status) would be too much to ask for under the circumstances. The data that Mahaffy collected from her respondents, however, allowed her to answer her research question about cognitive dissonance.

Convenience Sampling

Convenience sampling is a step down from purposive sampling, in terms of reliability and representativeness. There are no predetermined criteria for inclusion in the sample (as in purposive sampling), and there is no sampling grid (as in quota sampling). You simply interview people who are available and who agree to be interviewed. Sometimes—in studies of the homeless, for example, or of children in hospitals, or of women in combat teams—this is the best you can do. All samples represent *something*. Understanding what a convenience sample represents turns it into an ex post facto purposive sample.

Hatton et al. (2006) studied the perceptions of health care and health problems among inmates of a county jail in the western United States. (As is customary in studies of prison populations, no information is published about the exact location of the facility.) Hatton et al. began by holding focus groups with women who had been inmates in the prison and were now living in the nearby community. There were 18 of these women, and they participated in a total of three focus groups. Then Hatton et al. recruited 60 women who were still in the prison. These women participated in a total of seven focus groups about perceived health problems in the prison. We wouldn't put much stock in the percentage of women who reported various health problems, but the list of problems reported is the basis for further research.

Network Sampling: The Snowball and RDS Methods

Snowball and respondent-driven sampling (RDS) are two methods for recruiting people from hard-to-find or hard-to-study populations. The methods are known, generically, as chain referral methods or network sampling. Populations can be hard to find and study for many reasons. Some populations are simply rare (think widowers in Canada with infant children). Some, like transgendered people, are stigmatized and reclusive. Some people—intravenous drug users, for example—try hard not to be found. Members of elite groups—like surgeons and professional athletes—aren't hiding, but they don't have time or interest in participating in studies. Chain referral helps you locate and interview all these kinds of people by introducing them to your study through a trusted member of their own network.

Snowball Sampling

Snowball sampling was the original chain referral method. You start with one or two people—starters—with whom you have a relationship. The relationship can be one of trust (key informants) or simply people who want to make some money by helping you find respondents for your study. Begin by asking the starters to list people they know who are like them in some detail (transgendered, practicing surgeon, young widowers) and to recommend one or two people from the list whom you might interview. You get handed from informant to informant, and the sampling frame grows with each interview. Eventually, the sampling frame becomes saturated—that is, no new names are offered (see Box 17.3).

Cara Rabe-Hemp (2008) used snowball sampling in her study of the resistance that women face in the United States when they become police officers and what accounts for the success of some women in overcoming that resistance. Rabe-Hemp asked a few women officers whom she knew to list other officers and asked those on the list to name other female officers. Some policewomen are hard to find—only 6% of sworn officers are women in rural police departments—but Rabe-Hemp was able to develop a sample of 26 female officers in the area of the U.S. Midwest where she was working, including 11 in large departments (over 100 sworn officers), seven in departments with 50–99 officers, and six in departments with less than 50 officers. All 26 had been on the job at least 10 years (this was Rabe-Hemp's criterion for having been successful in withstanding the harassment). She contacted all of them, and only two declined to participate in her study. (Further Reading: snowball sampling.)

> ### Box 17.3
>
> ### Snowball Sampling and Large Populations
>
> In a large population, people in a subpopulation who are well known have a better chance of being named in a snowball procedure than are people who are less well known, and people who have large networks name more people than do people who have small networks. Because every person does not have the same chance of being named under these conditions, snowball samples are generally not used in developing representative samples. Thomas Weisner, however, used snowball sampling in his longitudinal study of counterculture women and their families in California. He built the sample of 205 women in 1974 by recruiting women in their third trimester of pregnancy. To ensure that participants came from all over the state and represented various kinds of families, he used no more than two referrals from any one source (Weisner 2002b:277).
>
> Snowball sampling can, however, produce a representative sample of a relatively small group of people who are in contact with one another, like practitioners of alternative medicine in a small town. With such populations, the list of people in the population—the sampling frame—will become saturated quickly, with no new members appearing after the first handful of interviews. Once you have an exhaustive sampling frame, you can select people purposively or at random to interview, depending on your research question.

Respondent Driven Sampling

Respondent driven sampling (RDS) was developed by Douglas Heckathorn (1997). Like snowball sampling, RDS begins with a few key informants. The initial informants are interviewed and paid for their time. Then they are given coupons and are asked to recruit members of their networks into the study. Heckathorn ran his study out of a storefront. He told his informants that if the people they passed the coupons to came in for an interview, they (the first informants) would get paid. At the time, the rate was $10 for a male drug injector and $15 for a female drug injector (because women were harder to find than men in this population). The people who came in to be interviewed were paid for their time and then given more coupons, and so on.

This method deals with several problems in snowball sampling here. First, there's the ethical problem. In snowball sampling, you actually get the names of people's network members. Those people may not even want you to know they exist, much less want to be interviewed for your study. With the RDS method, informants don't come in for an interview unless they want to. Also, Heckathorn (1997, 2002) showed that RDS samples are less biased than are traditional snowball samples. (Further Reading: respondent driven sampling.)

Theoretical Sampling

Theoretical sampling is widely used by ethnographers. Bernard, for example, used theoretical sampling in his ethnographic study of Greek sponge divers (1987). When Bernard went to Kalymnos in 1964, one of the things he wanted to understand was how people on that island were reacting to what was then a relatively recent threat to the sponge industry on which Kalymnians depended for a living: the mass marketing of synthetic sponges.

Bernard knew he had to interview sponge merchants, boat owners, and divers—the three main actors in the Greek sponge industry—but his first interviews taught him that the industry went into decline partly because many young divers had recognized the threat of the synthetic sponge by the mid-1950s and had gone to Australia as labor migrants. This drove up the price of diving labor on the island, making natural sponges less competitive against the synthetics. By 1964, some of these labor migrants had accumulated money and had returned to the island. These men were no longer employed in the sponge industry, but their stories were important for understanding how and why the industry was changing. (It was very easy to find those returned migrants: Everyone on the island either had one in their family or knew people who did.)

In other words, Bernard changed his sampling procedure as he began to understand the theoretical importance of labor migration. By theoretical importance, we mean "something that helps explain why whatever-it-is-you're-studying happened at all." This method of chasing down leads as they turn up by interviewing people who have attributes germane to the emerging theory is typical of long-term ethnographic research.

Theoretical Sampling and Grounded Theory

Theoretical sampling is also an integral part of the original method of grounded theory. The idea was not only that coding and theory building would develop together but that researchers would select cases for study as concepts emerged (Glaser and A. Strauss 1967:45–77; A. Strauss and Corbin 1998:205–212).

Caron and Bowers (2003), for example, used theoretical sampling in their study of people who were caring for elderly family members. Their final sample comprised 16 participants: six men (who were taking care of their wives) and 10 women (who were taking care of either their husband or a parent or, in one case, a brother-in-law). Caron and Bowers knew they wanted to compare male and female caregivers, but, after a few interviews, they began selecting participants based on the presence or absence of Alzheimer's disease or other cognitive impairment; whether the caregiver and care recipient lived in the same house; and whether the caregiver was getting help from various services with housecleaning, cooking, and transportation (p. 1255).

Wilson et al. (2002) used a form of theoretical sampling in their grounded theory study of HIV-positive men and women in the San Francisco Bay area. At the start, the objective was to understand how people manage the symptoms associated with various stages of HIV infection. By coding and analyzing on the fly, however, the researchers quickly found that when they asked about symptoms, the "study participants talked about their stories of medication regimens and side effects" (p. 1310). Wilson et al. began asking people explicitly about adherence to anti-retroviral drug regimes, and this became a major focus of the study. (Further Reading: theoretical sampling in grounded theory.)

Key Informants

Across the social sciences, you'll see references to research participants as "respondents," or "subjects," or "informants." Respondents (the preferred term among quantitative sociologists) reply to survey questions; subjects (the preferred term among psychologists) are the focus of some experiment or observation; and informants (the preferred term among anthropologists and some qualitative sociologists) teach you about their culture.

Key informants are people who know a lot about their culture and are, for reasons of their own, willing to share all their knowledge with you. When you do long-term ethnography, you develop close relationships with a few key informants—relationships that can last a lifetime. You don't choose these people. They and you choose each other, over time (see Box 17.4).

Box 17.4

Specialized Informants

Specialized informants have particular competence in some cultural domain. If you want to know when to genuflect in a Roman Catholic Mass, or what herb tea to give children for diarrhea, or how to avoid being busted for streetwalking, you need to talk to people who can speak knowledgeably about those things.

Good key informants are people whom you can talk to easily, who understand the information you need, and who are glad to give it to you or get it for you. Pelto and Pelto (1978:72) advocate training informants "to conceptualize cultural data in the frame of reference" that you, the researcher, use.

In some cases, you may want to just listen. But when you run into a really great informant, there is no reason to hold back. Teach the informant about the analytic categories you're developing and ask whether the categories are correct. In other words, encourage the informant to become the ethnographer.

Bernard and Jesús Salinas have been working together since 1962. Bernard tells the following story about his work with this key informant:

In 1971, I was about to write an ethnography of his culture, the Ñähñu of central Mexico, when he mentioned that he'd be interested in writing an ethnography himself. I dropped my project and taught him to read and write Ñähñu. Over the next 15 years, Salinas produced four volumes about the Ñähñu people—volumes that I translated and from which I learned many things that I'd never have learned had I written the ethnography myself. For example, Ñähñu men engage in rhyming duels, much like the "dozens" of African Americans. I wouldn't have thought to ask about those duels because I had never witnessed one. (Bernard 2006:197; and see Bernard and Salinas Pedraza 1989:11–38)

Doc

One of the most famous key informants in the ethnographic literature is Doc in William Foote Whyte's *Street Corner Society* (1981 [1943]). Whyte studied "Cornerville," an Italian American neighborhood in a place he called "Eastern City." (Cornerville was the North End of Boston.) Whyte asked some social workers if they knew anyone who could help Whyte with his study. One social worker told Whyte to come to her office and meet a man whom she thought could do the job. When Whyte showed up, the social worker introduced him to Doc and then left the room. Whyte nervously explained his predicament, and Doc asked him "Do you want to see the high life or the low life?" (Whyte 1989:72).

Whyte couldn't believe his luck. He told Doc he wanted to see all he could, learn as much as possible about life in the neighborhood. Doc told him:

> Well, any nights you want to see anything, I'll take you around. I can take you to the joints—the gambling joints—I can take you around to the street corners. Just remember that you're my friend. That's all they need to know. I know these places and if I tell them you're my friend, nobody will bother you. You just tell me what you want to see, and we'll arrange it. . . . When you want some information, I'll ask for it, and you listen. When you want to find out their philosophy of life, I'll start an argument and get it for you. (Whyte 1989:72)

Doc was straight up; he told Whyte to rely on him and to ask him anything, and Doc was as good as his word all through Whyte's 3 years of fieldwork. Doc introduced Whyte to the boys on the corner; Doc hung out with Whyte and spoke up for Whyte when people questioned Whyte's presence. Doc was just spectacular (see Box 17.5).

Box 17.5

Informants Sometimes Lie

Boelen (1992) visited Cornerville 25 times between 1970 and 1989, sometimes for a few days, other times for several months. She tracked down and interviewed everyone she could find from *Street Corner Society*. Doc had died in 1967, but she interviewed his two sons in 1970 (then in their late teens and early 20s). She asked them what Doc's opinion of Whyte's book had been and reports the elder son saying: "My father considered the book untrue from the very beginning to the end, a total fantasy" (Boelen 1992:29).

Of course, Whyte (1996a, 1996b) refuted Boelen's report, but we'll never know the whole truth.

Doc may be famous, but he's not unique. He's not even rare. All successful ethnographers will tell you that they eventually came to rely on one or two key people in their fieldwork. What was rare about Doc is how quickly and easily Whyte teamed up with him—and that Whyte wrote clearly about all this.

Solid Insiders and Marginal Natives

In fact, the first informants with whom you develop a working relationship in the field may be somewhat deviant members of their culture. Agar (1980b:86) reports that during his fieldwork in India, he was taken on by the *naik*, or headman of the village. The *naik*, it turned out, had *inherited* the role, but he was not respected in the village and did not preside over village meetings. This did not mean that the *naik* knew nothing about village affairs and customs; he was what Agar called a "solid insider," and yet somewhat of an outcast—a "marginal native," just like the ethnographer was trying to be (Freilich 1977). If you think about it, Agar said, you should wonder about the kind of person who would befriend an ethnographer.

In all our fieldwork—at sea, in Mexican villages, on Greek islands, in rural Cameroon, in rural communities in the United States, and in modern American bureaucracies—we have consistently found the best informants to be people who are a bit cynical about their own culture. They may not be outcasts—in fact, they are always solid insiders—but they say they *feel* somewhat marginal to their culture, by virtue of their intellectualizing of and disenchantment with their culture. They are always observant, reflective, and articulate. In other words, they invariably have all the qualities that any ethnographer would like to have.

So Take Your Time

If you're doing long-term, participant observation ethnography, don't choose key ethnographic informants too quickly. Allow yourself to become flooded with data for a while and play the field. When you have several prospects, check on their roles and statuses in the community. Be sure that the key informants you select don't prevent you from gaining access to other important informants (i.e., people who won't talk to you when they find out you're so-and-so's friend).

When Jeffrey Johnson began fieldwork in a North Carolina fishing community, he went to the local marine extension agent (the equivalent of an agricultural extension agent) and asked for help. The agent, happy to oblige, told Johnson about a fisherman whom he thought could help Johnson get off on the right foot.

It turned out that the fisherman was a transplanted northerner; he had a pension from the Navy; he was an activist Republican in a thoroughly Democratic community; and he kept his fishing boat in an isolated moorage, far from the village harbor. He was, in fact, maximally different from the typical local fisherman. The agent had meant well, of course (J. C. Johnson 1990:56).

And because good ethnography is, at its best, a good story, find trustworthy informants who are observant, reflective, and articulate—who know how to tell good stories—and stay with them. In the end, ethnographic fieldwork stands or falls on building mutually supportive relations with a very small sample of informants.

Further Reading

♦ For an introduction to sampling theory, see Agresti and Franklin (2007). See Handwerker (2003) on sampling design.

♦ For more on the general problem of sampling in qualitative research, see Barroso and Sandelowski (2003), Curtis et al. (2000), Fielding and Lee (1996:253), Luborsky and Rubinstein (1995), Miles and Huberman (1994:27–34), Morse (2003, 2007), Onwuegbuzie and Leech (2007), and Patton (2002:230–246). For more on sample size in qualitative studies, see Crouch and McKenzie (2005), Kuzel (1999), Sandelowski (1995a), and Sobal (2001).

♦ For more on quota sampling, see Sudman (1967). In an important early experiment, Moser and Stuart (1953) showed that quota sampling can produce useful results, as did T. M. F. Smith (1983).

♦ For more on snowball sampling, see the important early work of Kadushin (1968). For a recent example, see Browne (2005).

♦ For more various kinds of chain referral sampling, including respondent-driven sampling, see Heckathorn and Jeffri (2001), Martin and Dean (1993), Penrod et al. (2003), Salganick and Heckathorn (2004), and Sudman and Kalton (1986), and see Carlson et al. (1994), Martsolf et al. (2006), and Peterson et al. (2008) for information on targeted sampling.

♦ For more on theoretical sampling in grounded theory, see Draucker et al. (2007). Some discussions of problems in theoretical sampling include Coyne (1997, Curtis et al. (2000), and Thompson (1999).

Appendix

Resources for Analyzing Qualitative Data

This appendix is online at www.qualquant.net/AQD.

Caution: Most software that runs on Windows will run on late-model Macs running Parallels (http://www.parallels.com/). However, not all software that runs on Windows will run on Vista 64. Be sure to check compatibility of any program before buying.

Transcription and Voice Recognition Software

Express Scribe (http://www.nch.com.au/scribe/) and Transcriber (http://trans.sourceforge.net/en/presentation.php) are free programs for transcribing audio files. The makers of the Express Scribe also sell a foot pedal.

Another program for transcribing is HyperTranscribe (http://www.researchware.com/ht/index.html). Many of the most widely used text analysis packages also support transcription.

Two widely used voice recognition programs are Dragon Naturally Speaking (http://www.nuance.com/naturallyspeaking/) and the built-in component in Windows Vista (http://www.consumersearch.com/voice-recognition-software/windows-vista).

See Itmar Even-Zohar's resource page for speech recognition (http://www.tau.ac.il/~itamarez/sr/).

A discussion forum on VRS and transcription hardware and software is here: http://www.knowbrainer.com/PubForum/index.cfm?page=forum

KWIC (Key Word in Context) and Semantic Network Analysis Software

Several programs are available free, including Simple Concordance Program (http://www.textworld.com/scp/).

For more, see Harald Klein's resource page for text analysis: http://www.textanalysis.info/ and click on "information retrieval" software in the section on Classification of Text Analysis Software.

WORDij is a program developed specifically for semantic network analysis (Danowski 1993) (http://wordij.net/). Semantic network analysis can also be done with UCINET (http://www.analytictech.com/) (Borgatti et al. 2004). DNA Discourse Network Analyzer (http://www.philipleifeld.de) produces matrices that can be analyzed with UCINET.

The Outline of Cultural Materials is available at The Human Relations Area Files (http://www.yale.edu/hraf/).

Text Analysis Software

For details about and demo versions of text analysis software, visit the program sites. You can get to many program sites through the text analysis site, maintained by Harald Klein: http://www.textanalysis.info/. Several programs for analyzing written text will also handle audio and video files, but there are also special-purpose programs, like f4 audio and f4 video, for transcribing audio and video files (http://www.audiotranskription.de/english).

More news at the CAQDAS site: http://caqdas.soc.surrey.ac.uk/. The CAQDAS (pronounced "cactus") networking project provides "practical support, training and information in the use of a range of software programs designed to assist qualitative data analysis."

CAQDAS stands for computer-assisted qualitative data analysis. For a review of major CAQDAS software packages, see the book, by Ann Lewins and Christina Silver: *Using Qualitative Software: A Step by Step Guide* (Sage 2007). For a review of how scholars use CAQDAS software, see Fielding and Lee (2002) and Mangabeira et al. (2004).

Content Analysis

For information resources for content analysis: http://www.content-analysis.de/.

Short courses on text analysis are offered at the following:

Essex Summer School in Social Science Data Analysis (http://www
.essex.ac.uk/methods/).

Summer Institute in Survey Research Techniques at the University of
Michigan (http://www.isr.umich.edu/src/si/).

European Consortium for Political Research at the University of Ljubljana
(http://www.essex.ac.uk/ecpr/events/summerschools/ljubljana/index.aspx).

The Qualitative Data Analysis Program (QDAP) at the University of
Pittsburgh has online tutorials and software for coding and managing text. The
main QDAP site is at http://www.qdap.pitt.edu/. An introduction to the coding
software, called CAT (Coding Analysis Toolkit), is at http://tinyurl.com/qs9h5n.

Cultural Domain Analysis

Software for cultural domain analysis includes ANTHROPAC and UCINET
(http://www.analytictech.com/). ANTHROPAC is particularly useful for
collecting cultural domain analysis data (free-lists, pile sorts, triad tests,
paired comparisons) and for getting those data into the computer for
analysis. Analysis chores for CDA data can be done in ANTHROPAC but are
better done in UCINET (which was originally developed for network analysis).

QCA: Qualitative Comparative Analysis

For computer programs and other resources for QCA, see the COMPASS
resource site for small-*n* research: www. compasss.org. Computer programs
for analyzing truth tables include FS/QCA (Ragin et al. 2006), Tosmana
(Cronqvist 2007), fuzzy (Longest and Vaisey 2008), and ANTHROPAC
(Borgatti 1996).

Journals

Increasingly, scholarly journals in the social sciences publish research
based on the collection and analysis of qualitative data. The following
journals, however, are devoted to publishing papers in the qualitative tradition.

Forum Qualitative Sozialforschung / Forum: *Qualitative Social Research*
(online only and free at http://www.qualitative-research.net/index.php/
fqs/index)

International Journal of Qualitative Studies in Education

Qualitative Health Research

Qualitative Inquiry

Qualitative Market Research

Qualitative Report

Qualitative Research

Qualitative Research in Accounting and Management

Qualitative Research in Organizations and Management

Qualitative Research Journal

Qualitative Research Reports in Communication

Qualitative Social Work

Qualitative Sociology

Qualitative Sociology Review

Qualitative Studies in Education

References

Abdul-Rahman, M. S. 2003. Islam: Questions and Answers. Vol. 4. London: MSA Publications.

Abelson, R. P. and A. Levi 1985. Decision making and decision theory. In: The Handbook of Social Psychology, Vol. 1, L. Gardener and E. Aronson, eds. New York: Random House. Pp. 231–309.

Addison, R. B. 1992. Grounded hermeneutic research. In: Doing Qualitative Research, B. F. Crabtree and W. L. Miller, eds. Newbury Park, CA: Sage Publications. Pp. 110–124.

Agar, M. 1973. Ripping and Running: A Formal Ethnography of Urban Heroin Addicts. New York: Seminar Press.

Agar, M. 1979. Themes revisited: Some problems in cognitive anthropology. Discourse Processes 2:11–31.

Agar, M. 1980a. Getting better quality stuff: Methodological competition in an interdisciplinary niche. Urban Life 9:34–50.

Agar, M. 1980b. The Professional Stranger. New York: Academic Press.

Agar, M. 1983. Political talk: Thematic analysis of a policy argument. Policy Studies Review 2:601–614.

Agar, M. 1996. The Professional Stranger: An Informal Introduction to Ethnography. 2nd ed. San Diego, CA: Academic Press.

Agar, M. and J. MacDonald 1995. Focus groups and ethnography. Human Organization 54:78–86.

Agresti, A. and C. Franklin 2007. Statistics: The Art and Science of Learning From Data. Upper Saddle River, NJ: Pearson Prentice Hall.

Alali, A. O. 1993. Management of death and grief in obituary and in memoriam pages of Nigerian newspapers. Psychological Reports 73:835–842.

Aldenderfer, M. S. and R. K. Blashfield 1984. Cluster Analysis. Beverly Hills, CA: Sage Publications.

Algase, D. L., B. Kupferschmid, C. A. Beel-Bates, and E. R. Beattie 1997. Estimates of stability of daily wandering behavior among cognitively impaired long-term care residents. Nursing Research 46:172–178.

Alkon, A. H. 2004. Place, stories, and consequences. Heritage narratives and the control of erosion on Lake County, California, vineyards. Organization and Environment 17:145–169.

Allan, C. 2007. Exploring natural resource management with metaphor analysis. Society and Natural Resources 20:351–362.

Allen, J. T. and G. Italie 1954. A Concordance to Euripides. Berkeley: University of California Press.

Alvarado, N. 1998. A reconsideration of the structure of the emotion lexicon. Motivation and Emotion 22:329–344.

Anderson, K. J. and C. Leaper 1998. Meta-analyses of gender effects on conversational interruption: Who, what, when, where, and how. Sex Roles 39:225–252.

Angrosino, M. V. 1989. Documents of Interaction: Biography, Autobiography, and Life History in Social Science Perspective. Gainesville: University of Florida Press.

Aquilino, W. S. 1993. Effects of spouse presence during the interview on survey responses concerning marriage. Public Opinion Quarterly 57:358–376.

Aquilino, W. S. 1994. Interview mode effects in surveys of drug and alcohol use: A field experiment. Public Opinion Quarterly 58:210–140.

Aquilino, W. S., D. L. Wright, and A. J. Supple 2000. Response effects due to bystander presence in CASI and paper-and-pencil surveys of drug use and alcohol use. Substance Use and Misuse 35:845–867.

Aristotle. Metaphysics. The Internet Classics Archive. Copyright (C) 1994–2000, D. C. Stevenson, Web Atomics. Online at http://classics.mit.edu/Aristotle/meta physics.html. Accessed 2-25-09.

Aristotle. Poetics. The Internet Classics Archive. Copyright (C) 1994–2000, D. C. Stevenson, Web Atomics. Online at http://classics.mit.edu/Aristotle/poetics .1.1.html. Accessed 3-24-09.

Aristotle. Rhetoric. The Internet Classics Archive. Copyright (C) 1994–2000, D. C. Stevenson, Web Atomics. Online at http://classics.mit.edu/Aristotle/rhetoric .html. Accessed 3-24-09.

Arthur, H., G. Johnson, and A. Young 2007. Gender differences and color: Content and emotion of written descriptions. Social Behavior and Personality 35:827–834.

Ascher, G. J. 2001. Sephardic songs, proverbs, and expressions: A continuing tradition. Shofar: An Interdisciplinary Journal of Jewish Studies 19:19–39.

Ashworth, G. J. 2004. Tourism and the heritage of atrocity: Managing the heritage of South African apartheid for entertainment. In: New Horizons in Tourism. Strange Experience and Stranger Practices, T. V. Singh, ed. Cambridge, MA: CABI Publishers. Pp. 95–108.

Atkinson, J. M. and J. Heritage, eds. 1984. Structures of Social Action: Studies in Conversation Analysis. New York: Cambridge University Press.

Atkinson, R. 1998. The Life Story Interview. Thousand Oaks, CA: Sage Publications.

Atkinson, R. 2002. The life story interview. In: Handbook of Interview Research, J. F. Gubrium and J. A. Holstein, eds. Thousand Oaks, CA: Sage Publications. Pp. 121–140.

Auer, P. 2005. A postscript: Code-switching and social identity. Journal of Pragmatics 37:403–410.

Auerbach, C. F. and L. B. Silverstein 2003. Qualitative Data: An Introduction to Coding and Analysis. New York: New York University Press.

Axinn, W. G. and L. D. Pearce 2006. Mixed Method Data Collection Strategies. New York: Cambridge University Press.

Ayres, B. 1973. Effects of infant carrying practices on rhythm in music. Ethos 1:387–404.

Ayres, C. E. 1978. The Theory of Economic Progress: A Study of the Fundamentals of Economic Development and Cultural Change. 3d ed. Kalamazoo: New Issues Press, Western Michigan University.

Bacon, F. 1864 [1620]. The Works of Francis Bacon, J. Spedding, R. L. Ellis, and D. D. Heath, eds. Vol. 3. New York: Hurd and Houghton. (Full text on books .google.com. Accessed 5-3-08.)

Badahdah, A. M. and K. A. Tiemann 2005. Mate selection criteria among Muslims living in America. Evolution and Human Behavior 26:432–440.

Bailey, J. 2008. First steps in qualitative data analysis: Transcribing. Family Practice 25:127–131.

Baker, R. 1996a. PRA with street children in Nepal. PLA Notes 25:56–60. London: International Institute for Environment and Development.

Baker, R. (with C. Panter-Brick and A. Todd) 1996b. Methods used in research with street children in Nepal. Childhood 3:171–193.

Baker-Ward, L. E., K. L. Eaton, and J. B. Banks 2005. Young soccer players' reports of a tournament win or loss: Different emotions, different narratives. Journal of Cognition and Development 6:507–527.

Baksh, M., C. G. Neumann, M. Paolisso, R. M. Trostle, and A. A. J. Jansen. 1994. The influence of reproductive status on rural Kenyan women's time use. Social Science and Medicine 39:345–354.

Barber, N. 1998. Ecological and psychosocial correlates of male homosexuality: A cross-cultural investigation. Journal of Cross-Cultural Psychology 29:387–401.

Barkin, S., G. W. Ryan, and L. Gelberg 1999. What pediatricians can do to further youth violence prevention—a qualitative study. Injury Prevention 5:53–58.

Barnes, J. H., B. F. Banahan, III, and K. E. Fish 1995. The response effect of question order in computer-administered questioning in the social sciences. Social Science Computer Review 13:47–63.

Barnett, G. and J. Danowski 1992. The structure of communication: A network analysis of the international communication association. Human Communication Research 19:164–285.

Barroso, J. 1997. Reconstructing my life: Becoming a long-term survivor of AIDS. Qualitative Health Research 7:57–74.

Barroso, J. and M. Sandelowski 2003. Sample reporting of qualitative studies of women with HIV infection. Field Methods 15:386–404.

Bartlett, F. 1964 [1932]. Remembering: A Study in Experimental and Social Psychology. Cambridge: Cambridge University Press.

Basturkman, H. 1999. A content analysis of ELT textbook blurbs: Reflections of theory in use. RELC Journal 30:18–38.

Bauer, M. and A. L. Wright 1996. Integrating qualitative and quantitative methods to model infant feeding behavior among Navajo mothers. Human Organization 55:183–192.

Bauman, R. 1984. Verbal Art as Performance. Prospect Heights, IL: Waveland Press.

Bauman, R. 1986. Story, Performance, and Event. Contextual Studies of Oral Narrative. New York: Cambridge University Press.

Beck, K. A. 2000. A Decision Making Model of Child Abuse Reporting. Ph.D. dissertation, University of British Columbia.

Becker, H. S. 1968. Social observation and social case studies. In: International Encyclopedia of the Social Sciences. Vol. 11. New York: Crowell.

Becker, H. S. 1993. How I learned what a crock was. Journal of Contemporary Ethnography 22:28–35.

Becker, H. S. 1998. Tricks of the Trade: How to Think About Your Research While You're Doing It. Chicago: University of Chicago Press.

Behar, R. 1990. Rage and redemption: Reading the life story of a Mexican marketing woman. Feminist Studies 16:223–258.

Bem, S. L. 1981. Gender schema theory: A cognitive account of sex typing. Psychological Review 88:354–364.

Bem, S. L. 1983. Gender schema theory and its implications for child development: Raising gender-aschematic children in a gender-schematic society. Signs 8:598–616.

Bem, S. L. 1985. Androgyny and gender schema theory: A conceptual and empirical integration. In: Psychology and Gender, T. B. Sonderegger, ed. Lincoln: University of Nebraska Press. Pp. 179–226.

Ben-Ari, A. and Y. Lavee 2007. Dyadic closeness in marriage: From the inside story to a conceptual model. Journal of Social and Personal Relationships 24:627–644.

Berelson, B. 1952. Content analysis in communication research. Glencoe, IL: Free Press.

Bernard, H. R. 1987. Sponge fishing and technological change in Greece. In: Technology and Social Change, H. R. Bernard and P. J. Pelto, eds. 2nd ed. Prospect Heights, IL: Waveland Press. Pp. 167–206.

Bernard, H. R. 1996. Qualitative data, quantitative analysis. Cultural Anthropology Methods Journal 8:9–11.

Bernard, H. R. 2006. Research Methods in Anthropology: Qualitative and Quantitative Approaches. 4th ed. Thousand Oaks, CA: Sage Publications.

Bernard, H. R., P. D. Killworth, L. Sailer, and D. Kronenfeld 1984. The problem of informant accuracy: The validity of retrospective data. Annual Review of Anthropology 13:495–517.

Bernard, H. R., P. Pelto, D. Romney, C. Ember, A. Johnson, O. Werner, J. Boster, et al. 1986. The construction of primary data in cultural anthropology. Current Anthropology 27:382–896.

Bernard, H. R., G. W. Ryan, and S. P. Borgatti 2009. Green cognition and behavior: A cultural domain analysis. In: Networks, Resources and Economic Action. Ethnographic Case Studies in Honor of Hartmut Lang, C. Greiner and W. Kokot, eds. Berlin, Dietrich Reimer Verlag. Pp. 189–215.

Bernard, H. R. and J. Salinas Pedraza 1989. Native Ethnography: A Mexican Indian Describes His Culture. Newbury Park, CA: Sage Publications.

Berra, Y. and J. Garagiola 1998. The Yogi Book: "I Really Didn't Say Everything I Said." New York: Workman Publishing.

Bessinger, J. B., ed. 1969. A Concordance to Beowulf. Ithaca, NY: Cornell University Press.

Best, D. L., A. S. House, A. E. Barnard, and B. S. Spicker 1994. Parent-child interactions in France, Germany, and Italy: The effects of gender and culture. Journal of Cross-Cultural Psychology 25:181–193.

Bialostok, S. 2002. Metaphors for literacy: A cultural model of White, middle-class parents. Linguistics and Education 13:347–371.

Biernacki, P. and D. Waldorf 1981. Snowball sampling: Problems and techniques of chain referral sampling. Sociological Methods and Research 10:141–163.

Blair, E. 1979. Interviewing in the presence of others. In: Improving Interview Method and Questionnaire Design: Response Effects to Threatening Questions in Survey Research, N. M. Bradburn and S. Sudman, eds. San Francisco: Jossey-Bass. Pp. 134–146.

Blair-Loy, M. 2003. Competing Devotions: Career and Family Among Women Executives. Cambridge, MA: Harvard University Press.

Blau, P. M. 1964. Exchange and Power in Social Life. New York: John Wiley and Sons.

Bletzer, K. and M. P. Koss 2006. After-rape among three populations in the Southwest. Violence Against Women 12:5–29.

Blommaert, J. 2006. Applied ethnopoetics. Narrative Inquiry 16:181–190.

Bloom, F. R. 2001. "New beginnings": A case study in gay men's changing perceptions of quality of life during the course of HIV infection. Medical Anthropology Quarterly 15:38–57.

Blum-Kulka, S. 1993. "You gotta know how to tell a story": Telling, tales, and tellers in American and Israeli narrative events at dinner. Language in Society 22:361–402.

Boas, F. 1901. Kathlamet Texts. Bureau of American Ethnology Bulletin 26. Washington, DC: U.S. Government Printing Office.

Boeije, H. R. 2002. A purposeful approach to the constant comparative method in the analysis of qualitative interviews. Quality and Quantity 36:391–409.

Boeije, H. R. 2004. And then there were three: Why third persons are present in interviews and the impact on the data. Field Methods 16:3–32.

Boelen, W. A. M. 1992. Street corner society. Cornerville revisited. Journal of Contemporary Ethnography 21:11–51.

Bogdan, R. 1972. Participant observation in organizational settings. Syracuse, NY: Syracuse University Press.

Bogdan, R. and S. K. Biklen 1982. Qualitative Research for Education: An Introduction to Theory and Methods. Boston: Allyn and Bacon.

Bogdan, R. and S. J. Taylor 1975. Introduction to Qualitative Research Methods. New York: John Wiley and Sons.

Bohenmeyer, J. 2003. Invisible time lines in the fabric of events: Temporal coherence in Yucatec narratives. Journal of Linguistic Anthropology 13:139–162.

Bondas, T. and K. Eriksson 2001. Women's lived experience of pregnancy: A tapestry of joy and suffering. Qualitative Health Research 11:824–840.

Borgatti, S. P. 1992. ANTHROPAC 4.98. Colombia, SC: Analytic Technologies. Online at http://www.analytictech.com/. Accessed 9-22-08.

Borgatti, S. P. 1994. How to explain hierarchical clustering. Connections 17:78–80.

Borgatti, S. P. 1996. ANTHROPAC 4.0 Methods Guide. Natick, MA: Analytic Technologies.

Borgatti, S. P. 1997. Multidimensional scaling. Online at http://www.analytictech .com/networks/mds.htm. Accessed 12-15-08.

Borgatti, S. P. 1999. Elicitation techniques for cultural domain analysis. In: Enhanced Ethnographic Methods: Audiovisual Techniques, Focused Group Interviews, and Elicitation Techniques, J. J. Schensul, M. D. LeCompte, B. K. Nastasi, and S. P. Borgatti, eds. (Ethnographer's Toolkit, Vol. 3). Walnut Creek, CA: AltaMira Press. Pp. 115–151.

Borgatti, S. P., M. G. Everett, and L. C. Freeman 2004. UCINET 6.69. Harvard, MA: Analytic Technologies.

Borges, S. and H. Waitzkin 1995. Women's narratives in primary care medical encounters. Women and Health 23:29–56.

Boster, J. S. and J. C. Johnson 1989. Form or function: A comparison of expert and novice judgments of similarity among fish. American Anthropologist 91:866–889.

Bourgois, P. I. 1990. Confronting anthropological ethics: Ethnographic lessons from Central America. Journal of Peace Research 27:43–54.

Bradburn, N. M. 1979. Interviewing in the presence of others. In: Improving Interview Method and Questionnaire Design, N. M. Bradburn and S. Sudman, eds. San Francisco: Jossey-Bass. Pp. 135–146.

Bradburn, N. M. 1983. Response effects. In: Handbook of Survey Research, P. H. Rossi, J. D. Wright, and A. B. Anderson, eds. New York: Academic Press. Pp. 289–328.

Bradburn, N. M. and S. Sudman and associates 1979. Improving interview method and questionnaire design: Response effects to threatening questions in survey research. San Francisco: Jossey-Bass.

Bradley, E. H., L. A. Curry, and K. J. Devers 2007. Qualitative data analysis for health services research: Developing taxonomy, themes, and theory. Health Service Research 42:1758–1772.

Bramley, N. and V. Eatough 2005. The experience of living with Parkinson's disease: An interpretative phenomenological analysis case study. Psychology and Health 20:223–235.

Brenneis, D. 1988. Telling troubles: Narrative, conflict, and experience. Anthropological Linguistics 30:279–291

Breslin, F. C., C. H. Gladwin, D. Borsoi, and J. A. Cunningham 2000. De facto client-treatment matching: How clinicians make referrals to outpatient treatments for substance use. Evaluation and Program Planning 23:281–291.

Brewer, D. D. 1995. Cognitive indicators of knowledge in semantic domains. Journal of Quantitative Anthropology 5:107–128.

Brewer, D. D. 2002. Supplementary interviewing techniques to maximize output in free listing tasks. Field Methods 14:108–118.

Brewer, D. D., S. B. Garrett, and G. Rinaldi 2002. Free-listed items are effective cues for eliciting additional items in semantic domains. Applied Cognitive Psychology 16:343–358.

Brewer, W. F. 2000. Bartlett's concept of the schema and its impact on theories of knowledge representation in contemporary cognitive psychology. In: Bartlett, Culture and Cognition, A. Saito, ed. Hove, UK: Psychology Press. Pp. 69–89.

Bridger, J. C. 1996. Community imagery and the built environment. The Sociological Quarterly 37:101–122.

Bridger, J. C. and D. R. Maines 1998. Narrative structures and the Catholic Church closings in Detroit. Qualitative Sociology 21:319–340.

Bridges, J. S. 1993. Pink or blue: Gender-stereotypic perceptions of infants as conveyed by birth congratulations cards. Psychology of Women Quarterly 17:193–206.

Browne, K. E. 2005. Snowball sampling: Using social networks to research non-heterosexual women. International Journal of Social Research Methodology 8:47–60.

Brudenell, I. 1996. A grounded theory of balancing alcohol recovery and pregnancy. Western Journal of Nursing Research 18:429–440.

Bryant, A. and K. Charmaz, eds. 2007. The Sage Handbook of Grounded Theory. London: Sage Publications.

Bucholtz, M. 2000. The politics of transcription. Journal of Pragmatics 32:1439–1465.

Buck, G. 1971 [1899]. The Metaphor: A Study in the Psychology of Rhetoric. Folcroft, PA: Folcroft Library Editions.

Bulmer, M. 1979. Concepts in the analysis of qualitative data. Sociological Review 27:651–677.

Burke, T. 1998. Cannibal margarine and reactionary Snapple: A comparative examination of rumors about commodities. International Journal of Cultural Studies 1:253–270.

Burton, L. 2007. Childhood adultification in economically disadvantaged families: A conceptual model. Family Relations 56:329–345.

Burton, M. L. 2003. Too many questions? The uses of incomplete cyclic designs for paired comparisons. Field Methods 15:115–130.

Busa, R. 1971. Concordances. In: Encyclopedia of Library and Information Science, A. Kent and H. Lancour, eds. Vol. 5. New York: Marcel Dekker. Pp. 592–604.

Buss, D. M. 1985. Human mate selection. American Scientist 73:47–51.

Butler-Smith, P., S. Cameron, and A. Collins 1998. Gender differences in mate search effort: an exploratory economic analysis of personal advertisements. Applied Economics 30:1277–1285.

Cachia, P. 2006. Pulp stories in the repertoire of Egyptian folk singers. British Journal of Middle Eastern Studies 33:117–129.

Calder, N. 1993. Studies in Early Muslim Jurisprudence. New York: Oxford University Press.

Callahan, L. 2005. "Talking both languages":20 perspectives on the use of Spanish and English inside and outside the workplace. Journal of Multilingual and Multicultural Development 26:275–295.

Cameron S. and A. Collins 1998. Sex differences in stipulated preferences in personal advertisements. Psychological Reports 82:119–123.

Campbell, D. T. 1988. Qualitative knowing in action research. In: Methodology and Epistemology for Social Science: Selected Papers, E. S. Overman, ed. Chicago: University of Chicago Press. Pp. 360–376.

Cannell, C. F. and R. L. Kahn 1968. Interviewing. In: The Handbook of Social Psychology, G. Lindzey and E. Aronson, eds. Vol. 2. Reading, MA: Addison-Wesley. Pp. 526–595.

Capello, M. 2005. Photo interviews: eliciting data through conversations with children. Field Methods 17:170–182.

Carballo-Diéguez, A. and J. Bauermeister 2004. "Barebacking": Intentional condomless anal sex in HIV-risk contexts. Reasons for and against it. Journal of Homosexuality 47:1–16.

Carey, J. W. and D. Gelaude 2008. Systematic methods for collecting and analyzing multidisciplinary team-based qualitative data. In: Handbook for Team-Based Qualitative Research, G. Guest and K. M. MacQueen, eds. Lanham, MD: AltaMira Press. Pp. 227–274.

Carey, J. W., M. Morgan, and M. Oxtoby 1996. Intercoder agreement in analysis of responses to open-ended interview questions: Examples from tuberculosis research. Cultural Anthropology Methods Journal 8:1–5.

Carley, K. 1988. Formalizing the social expert's knowledge. Sociological Methods and Research 17:165–232.

Carlson, R. G., J. Wang, H. A. Siegal, R. S. Falck, and J. Guo 1994. An ethnographic approach to targeted sampling: Problems and solutions in AIDS prevention research among injection drug and crack-cocaine users. Human Organization 53:279–286.

Carmichael, D. H. 2001. Parental behaviors in child anxiety. Unpublished Ph.D. dissertation, Florida International University, Miami.

Caron, C. D. and B. J. Bowers 2003. Deciding whether to continue, share or relinquish caregiving: Caregiver views. Qualitative Health Research 13:1252–1271.

Casagrande, J. B. and K. L. Hale 1967. Semantic relationships in Papago folk definitions. In: Studies in Southwestern Ethnolinguistics: Meaning and History in the Languages of the American Southwest, D. H. Hymes and W. E. Bittle, eds. Paris: Mouton. Pp. 165–193.

Casson, R. 1983. Schemata in cultural anthropology. Annual Review of Anthropology 12:429–462.

Catania, J. A., D. Binson, J. Canchola, L. M. Pollack, W. Hauck, and T. J. Coates 1996. Effects of interviewer gender, interviewer choice, and item wording on responses to questions concerning sexual behavior. Public Opinion Quarterly 60:345–375.

Caulkins, D. D. 2001. Consensus, clines, and edges in Celtic cultures. Cross-Cultural Research 35:109–126.

Cavanaugh, J. R. 2007. Making salami, producing Bergamo: The transformation of value. Ethnos 72:149–172.

Chaplin, E. 1994. Sociology and Visual Representation. London: Routledge.

Charmaz K. 1987. Struggling for a self: Identity levels of the chronically ill. In: The Experience and Management of Chronic Illness. Research in the Sociology of Health Care, J. A. Roth and P. Conrad, eds. Vol. 6. Greenwich, CT: JAI Press. Pp. 283–307.

Charmaz, K. 1990. "Discovering" chronic illness: Using grounded theory. Social Science and Medicine 30:1161–1172.

Charmaz, K. 1991. Good Days, Bad Days: The Self in Chronic Illness and Time. New Brunswick, NJ: Rutgers University Press.

Charmaz, K. 1995. Body, identity, and self: Adapting to impairment. Sociological Quarterly 36:657–680.

Charmaz, K. 2000. Grounded theory: Objectivist and constructivist methods. In: The Handbook of Qualitative Research, N. K. Denzin and Y. S. Lincoln, eds. Thousand Oaks, CA: Sage Publications. Pp. 507–535.

Charmaz, K. 2002. Qualitative interviewing and grounded theory analysis. In: Handbook of Interview Research, J. F. Gubrium and J. A. Holstein, eds. Thousand Oaks, CA: Sage Publications. Pp. 675–694.

Chatterjee, I. 2007. Packaging of identity and identifiable packages: A study of women-commodity negotiation through product packaging. Gender, Place and Culture 14:293–316.

Cho, G. E., T. L. Sandel, P. J. Miller, and S-h Wang 2005. What do grandmothers think about self-esteem? American and Taiwanese folk theories revisited. Social Development 14:701–721.

Chomsky, N. 1957. Syntactic Structures. Series Janua Linguarum, number 4. s-Gravenhage, Netherlands: Mouton.

Christopherson, N., M. Janning, and E. D. McConnell 2002. Two kicks forward, one kick back: A content analysis of media discourses on the 1999 women's World Cup Soccer Championship. Sociology of Sport Journal 19:170–188.

Churchill, S. L., V. L. Plano Clark, K. Prochaska-Cue, J. W. Creswell, and L. Ontai-Grzebik 2007. How rural low-income families have fun: A grounded theory study. Journal of Leisure Research 39:271–294.

Clark, G. K. 1967. The Critical Historian. London: Heinemann Educational Books.

Clark, L. and L. Zimmer 2001. What we learned from a photographic component in a study of Latino children's health. Field Methods 13:303–328.

Clover, C. J. 1992. Men, Women, and Chainsaws: Gender in the Modern Horror Film. Princeton, NJ: Princeton University Press.

Coffey, A. and P. Atkinson 1996. Making Sense of Qualitative Data: Complementary Research Strategies. Thousand Oaks, CA: Sage Publications.

Cohen, J. 1960. Coefficient of agreement for nominal scales. Educational and Psychological Measurement 20:37–46.

Cohen-Mansfield, J. and A. Libin 2004. Assessment of agitation in elderly patients with dementia: Correlations between informant rating and direct observation. International Journal of Geriatric Psychiatry 19:881–891.

Colby, B. N. 1966. The analysis of culture content and the patterning of narrative concern in texts. American Anthropologist 68:374–388.

Cole, A. L. and J. G. Knowles 2001. Lives in Context: The Art of Life History Research. Walnut Creek, CA: AltaMira Press.

Collaborative Group of Hormonal Factors in Breast Cancer 2002 (V. Beral, D. Bull, R. Doll, R. Peto, and G. Reeves). Breast cancer and breastfeeding: Collaborative reanalysis of individual data from 47 epidemiological studies in 30 countries, including 50 302 women with breast cancer and 96 973 women without the disease. The Lancet 360:187–195.

Collier, J., Jr. and M. Collier 1986. Visual Anthropology: Photography as a Research Method. Rev. and expanded ed. Albuquerque: University of New Mexico Press.

Collins, A. and D. Gentner 1987. How people construct mental models. In: Cultural Models in Language and Thought, D. Holland and N. Quinn, eds. Cambridge: Cambridge University Press. Pp. 243–265.

Collins, C. C. and W. W. Dressler 2008. Cultural models of domestic violence: Perspectives of social work and anthropology students. Journal of Social Work Education 44:53–73.

Conrad, C. F. 1978. A grounded theory of academic change. Sociology of Education 51:101–112.

Converse, J. M. and H. Schuman. 1974. Conversations at random: Survey research as the interviewers see it. New York: John Wiley.

Coombes, A. 1994. Reinventing Africa. Museums, Material Culture, and Popular Imagination in Late Victorian and Edwardian England. New Haven, CT: Yale University Press.

Corbin, J. and A. Strauss 2008. Basics of Qualitative Research: Techniques and Procedures for Developing Grounded Theory. 3rd ed. Thousand Oaks, CA: Sage Publications.

Cornell, L. L. 1984. Why are there no spinsters in Japan? Journal of Family History 9:326–339.

Corti, L. and G. Backhouse 2005. Acquiring qualitative data for secondary analysis. Forum: Qualitative Social Research 6: http://www.qualitative-research.net/index.php/fqs/article/view/459/980.

Côté-Arsenault, D., D. Bidlack, and A. Humm 2001. Women's emotions and concerns during pregnancy following perinatal loss. MCN: The American Journal of Maternal Child Nursing 26:128–134.

Cowan, G. and M. O'Brien 1990. Gender and survival vs. death in slasher films: A content analysis. Sex Roles 23:187–196.

Coyne, I. T. 1997. Sampling in qualitative research. Purposeful and theoretical sampling: merging or clear boundaries? Journal of Advanced Nursing 26:623–630.

Crabtree, B. F. and W. L. Miller, eds. 1999. Doing Qualitative Research. 2nd ed. Thousand Oaks, CA: Sage Publications.

Crane, D. and L. Bovone 2006. Approaches to material culture: The sociology of fashion and clothing. Poetics 34:319–333.

Cress, D. M. and D. A. Snow 2000. The outcomes of homeless mobilization: The influence of organization, disruption, political mediation, and framing. American Journal of Sociology 105:1063–1104.

Cressey, D. R. 1950. The criminal violation of financial trust. American Sociological Review 15:738–743.

Cressey, D. R. 1953. Other People's Money: A Study in the Social Psychology of Embezzlement. Glencoe, IL: Free Press.

Creswell, J. W. 1998. Qualitative Inquiry and Research Design: Choosing Among Five Traditions. Thousand Oaks, CA: Sage Publications.

Creswell, J. W. 2003. Research Design: Qualitative, Quantitative and Mixed Methods Approaches. Thousand Oaks, CA: Sage Publications.

Creswell, J. W. and V. L. Plano Clark 2007. Designing and Conducting Mixed Methods Research. Thousand Oaks, CA: Sage Publications.

Cronqvist, L. 2007. Tosmana—Tool for Small-N Analysis [Version 1.3]. Marburg. Online at http://www.tosmana.net. Accessed 9-22-08.

Crouch, M. and H. McKenzie 2006. The logic of small samples in interview-based qualitative research. Social Science Information 45:483–499.

Cunningham, G. B., M. Sagas, M. L. Sartore, M. L. Amsden, and A. Schellhase 2004. Gender representation in the NCAA News: Is the glass half or half empty? Sex Roles 50:861–870.

Curtis, S., W. Gesler, G. Smith, and S. Washburn 2000. Approaches to sampling and case selection in qualitative research: Examples in the geography of health. Social Science and Medicine 50:1001–1014.

Cutliffe, J. R. 2005. Adapt or adopt: Developing and transgressing the methodological boundaries of grounded theory. Journal of Advanced Nursing 51:421–428.

Dabelko, H. I. and J. A. Zimmerman 2008. Outcomes of adult day services for participants: A conceptual model. Journal of Applied Gerontology 27:78–92.

Daller, H, R. Van Hout, and J. Treffers-Daller 2003. Lexical richness in the spontaneous speech of bilinguals. Applied Linguistics 24:197–222.

D'Andrade, R. G. 1991. The identification of schemas in naturalistic data. In: Person Schemas and Maladaptive Interpersonal Patterns, M. J. Horowitz, ed. Chicago: University of Chicago Press. Pp. 279–301.

D'Andrade, R. G. 1995. The Development of Cognitive Anthropology. Cambridge: Cambridge University Press.

D'Andrade, R., N. Quinn, S, Nerlove, and A. K. Romney 1972. Categories of disease in American-English and Mexican-Spanish. In: Multidimensional Scaling: Theory and Applications in the Behavioral Sciences. Vol. 2, A. K. Romney et al., eds. New York: Seminar. Pp. 9–54.

D'Andrade, R. G. and C. Strauss, eds. 1992. Human Motives and Cultural Models. New York: Cambridge University Press.

Danielson, W. A. and D. L. Lasorsa 1997. Perceptions of social change: 100 years of frontpage content in The New York Times and the Los Angeles Times. In: Text Analysis for the Social Sciences: Methods for Drawing Statistical Inferences From Texts and Transcripts, C. W. Roberts, ed. Mahwah, NJ: Lawrence Erlbaum Associates. Pp. 103–115.

Daniulaityte, R. 2004. Making sense of diabetes: Cultural models, gender and individual adjustment to Type 2 diabetes in a Mexican community. Social Science & Medicine 59:1899–1912.

Danowski, J. 1982. Computer-mediated communication: A network-based content analysis using a CBBS conference. In: Communication Yearbook, R. Bostrom, ed. New Brunswick, NJ: Transaction Books. Pp. 905–925.

Danowski, J. 1993. Network analysis of message content. In: Progress in Communication Science, W. M. Richards and G. Barnett, eds. Progress in Communication Sciences XII. Norwood, NJ: Ablex. Pp. 197–222.

Dant, T. 2005. Materiality and Society. Maidenhead, Berks, UK: Open University Press.

Dant, T. 2006. Material civilization: Things and society. British Journal of Sociology 57:289–308.

Dardis, F. E. 2006. Marginalization devices in U.S. press coverage of Iraq war protest: A content analysis. Mass Communication and Society 9:117–135.

Davies, C. E. 2006. Gendered sense of humor as expressed through aesthetic typifications. Journal of Pragmatics 38:96–113.

De Fina, A. 1997. An analysis of Spanish bien as a marker of classroom management in teacher-student interaction. Journal of Pragmatics 28:337–354.

De Fina, A. 2007. Code-switching and the construction of ethnic identity in a community of practice. Language and Society 36:371–392.

DeJordy, R., S. P. Borgatti, and C. Roussin 2007. Visualizing proximity data. Field Methods 19:239–263.

Demarest, J. and J. Garner 1992. The representation of women's roles in women's magazines over the past 30 years. Journal of Psychology: Interdisciplinary and Applied 126:357–368.

de Munck, V., N. Dudley, and J. Cardinale 2002. Cultural models of gender in Sri Lanka and the United States. Ethnology 41:225–261.

Dennis, W. 1940. Does culture appreciably affect patterns of infant behavior? The Journal of Social Psychology 12:305–317.

Denzin, N. K. 1970. The Research Act. Englewood Cliffs, NJ: Prentice Hall.

DeRocher, J. E., M. S. Miron, S. M. Patton, and C. S. Pratt 1973. The Counting of Words: A Review of the History, and Theory of Word Counts With Annotated Bibliography. National Technical Information Service, Springfield, VA 22151. ERIC Document Number ED098814.

de Sola Pool, I. 1952. Symbols of Democracy (with the collaboration of H. Lasswell et al.). Stanford, CA: Stanford University Press.

de Sola Pool, I. 1959. Trends in content analysis today: A summary. In: Trends in Content Analysis, I. de Sola Pool, ed. Urbana: University of Illinois Press. Pp. 189–240.

de Sousa Campos, L. O. Emma, and J. de Oliveira Siqueira 2002. Sex differences in mate selection strategies: Content analyses and responses to personal advertisements in Brazil. Evolution and Human Behavior 23:395–406.

de Vreese, C. H. and H. G. Boomgaarden 2006. Media effects on public opinion about the enlargement of the European Union. Journal of Common Market Studies 44:419–436.

de Vries, B. and J. Rutherford 2004. Memorializing loved ones on The World Wide Web. Omega: Journal of Death and Dying 49:5–26.

DeWalt, B. R. 1979. Modernization in a Mexican Ejido. New York: Cambridge University Press.

DeWalt, K. M. and B. R. DeWalt 2002. Participant Observation: A Guide for Fieldworkers. Walnut Creek, CA: AltaMira Press.

Dey, I. 1993. Qualitative Data Analysis: A User Friendly Guide for Social Scientists. London: Routledge and Kegan Paul.

Dey, I. 1999. Grounding Grounded Theory: Guidelines for Qualitative Inquiry. San Diego, CA: Academic Press.

Díaz de Rada, V. 2005. The effect of follow-up mailings on the response rate and response quality in mail surveys. Quality and Quantity 39:1–18.

Dickson, D. B., J. Olsen, P. F. Dahm, and M. S. Wachtel 2005. Where do you go when you die? A cross-cultural test of the hypothesis that infrastructure predicts individual eschatology. Journal of Anthropological Research 61:53–79.

Dilthey, W. 1989. Introduction to the Human Sciences. R. A. Makkreel and F. Rodi, eds. Princeton, NJ: Princeton University Press.

Dilthey, W. 1996. Hermeneutics and the Study of History. R. A. Makkreel and F. Rodi, eds. Princeton, NJ: Princeton University Press.

Doerfel, M. L. 1998. What constitutes semantic network analysis? A comparison of research methodologies. Connections 21:16–26.

Doerfel, M. L. and G. A. Barnett 1999. A semantic network analysis of the International Communication Association. Human Communication Research 25:589–603.

Donnenworth, G. V. and U. G. Foa 1974. Effects of resource class on retaliation to injustice in interpersonal exchange. Journal of Personality and Social Psychology 29:785–793.

Doucet, L. and K. A. Jehn 1997. Analyzing harsh words in a sensitive setting: American expatriates in communist China. Journal of Organizational Behavior 18:559–582.

Doyle, K. O. 2001. Meanings of wealth in European and Chinese fairy tales. American Behavioral Scientist 45:191–204.

Draucker, C. B., D. S. Martsolf, R. Ross, and T. B. Rusk 2007. Theoretical sampling and category development in grounded theory. Qualitative Health Research 17:1137–1148.

Drazin, A. and D. Frolich 2007. Good intentions: Remembering through framing photographs in English homes. Ethnos 72:51–76.

Dressler, W. W., C. D. Borges, M. C. Balieiro, and M. C. Balieiro 2005. Measuring cultural consonance: Examples with special reference to measurement theory in anthropology. Field Methods 17:331–355.

Dressler, W. W., K. S. Oths, R. P. Ribeiro, M. C. Balieiro, and J. E. Dos Santos 2007. Cultural consensus and adult body composition in urban Brazil. American Journal of Human Biology 20:15–22.

Drew, P. and J. Heritage, eds. 2006. Conversation Analysis. Thousand Oaks, CA: Sage Publications.

Drury, C. C. 1990. Methods for direct observation of performance. In: Evaluation of Human Work: A Practical Ergonomics Methodology, J. R. Wilson and E. N. Corlett, eds. New York: Taylor & Francis. Pp. 35–57.

Du Bois, J. 1991. Transcription design principles for spoken discourse research. Pragmatics 1:71–106.

Dunbar, R. and L. Barrett, eds. 2007. Oxford Handbook of Evolutionary Psychology. Oxford: Oxford University Press.

Dundes, A. 1965. The Study of Folklore. Englewood Cliffs, NJ: Prentice-Hall.

Dundes, A. 1980. Interpreting Folklore. Bloomington: Indiana University Press.

Dundes, A. 1989. Folklore Matters. Knoxville: University of Tennessee Press.

Duranti, A. 2006. Transcripts, like shadows on a wall. Mind, Culture and Activity 13:301–310.

Durrenberger, E. P. 2003. Using paired comparisons to measure reciprocity. Field Methods 15:271–288.

Durrenberger, E. P. and S. Erem 2005. Checking for relationships across domains measured by triads and paired comparisons. Field Methods 17:150–169.

Dy, S. M., H. R. Rubin and H. P. Lehman 2005. Why do patients and families request transfers to tertiary care? A qualitative study. Social Science and Medicine 61:1846–1853.

Eastman K. L., R. Corona, G. W. Ryan, A. L. Warsofsky, and M. A. Schuster 2005. Worksite-based parenting programs to promote healthy adolescent sexual development: A qualitative study of feasibility and potential content. Perspectives on Sexual and Reproductive Health 37:62–69.

Ebbinghaus, H. 1913. Memory: A contribution to experimental psychology. H. A. Ruger and C. E. Bussenius, tr. New York: Teachers College, Columbia University.

Ecocultural Scale Project 2001. The Ecocultural Family Interview. Codebook. Final Version. UCLA Center for Culture and Health, 760 Westwood Plaza, Box 62, Los Angeles, CA 90024–1759.

Ekins, R. 1997. Male Femaling: A Grounded Theory Approach to Cross-Dressing and Sex-Changing. New York: Routledge.

Elahi, B. and G. Cos 2005. An immigrant's dream and the audacity of hope: The 2004 convention addresses of Barack Obama and Arnold Schwarzenneger. American Behavioral Scientist 49:454–465.

El Guindi, F. 2004. Visual Anthropology: Essential Method and Theory. Walnut Creek, CA: AltaMira Press.

Ember, C. R., M. Ember, A. Korotayev, and V. de Munck 2005. Valuing thinness or fatness in women. Reevaluating the effect of resources scarcity. Evolution and Human Behavior 26:257–270.

Emigh, R. J. 1997. The power of negative thinking: The use of negative case methodology in the development of sociological theory. Theory and Society 5:649–684.

Eyre, S. L. and S. G. Milstein 1999. What leads to sex? Adolescent preferred partners and reasons for sex. Journal of Research on Adolescence 9:277–307.

Fairclough, N. 1995. Critical discourse analysis: The critical study of language. London: Longman.

Fairweather, J. R. 1999. Understanding how farmers choose between organic and conventional production: Results from New Zealand and policy implications. Agriculture and Human Values 16:51–63.

Fan, D. P. and C. L. Shaffer 1990. Use of open-ended essays and computer content analysis to survey college students' knowledge of AIDS. College Health 38:221–229.

Fangman, T. D., J. P. Ogle, M. C. Bickle, and D. Rouner 2004. Promoting female weight management in 1920s print media: An analysis of Ladies' Home Journal and Vogue Magazines. Family and Consumer Sciences Research Journal 32:213–253.

Farmer, P. 1994. AIDS-talk and the constitution of cultural models. Social Science and Medicine 36:801–809.

Farringdon, J. M. and M. G. Farringdon, eds. 1980. A Concordance and Word-Lists to the Poems of Dylan Thomas. Swansea, UK: Ariel House.

Fenno, Richard 1990. Watching Politicians: Essays on Participant Observation. Berkeley: Institute of Governmental Studies, University of California at Berkeley.

Fernández, J. 1967. Revitalized words from "the parrot's egg" and "the bull that crashes in the kraal": African cult sermons. In: Essays on the Verbal and Visual Arts. Proceedings of the 1966 Annual Meeting of the American Ethnological Society. Seattle: University of Washington Press. Pp. 45–63.

Fielding, N. G. 2004. Getting the most from archived qualitative data: Epistemological, practical and professional obstacles. International Journal of Social Research Methodology: Theory and Practice 7:97–104.

Fielding, N. G. and R. M. Lee 1996. Diffusion of a methodological innovation: CAQDAS in the UK. Current Sociology 44:242–258.

Fielding, N. G. and R. M. Lee 2002. New patterns in the adoption and use of qualitative software. Field Methods 14:197–216.

Finkel, S. E., T. M. Guterbock, and M. J. Borg 1991. Race-of-interviewer effects in a pre-election poll: Virginia 1989. Public Opinion Quarterly 55:313–330.

Firth, J. R. 1957. A synopsis of linguistic theory, 1930–1955. In: Studies in Linguistic Analysis, Special Volume of the Philological Society. Oxford: Blackwell. Pp. 1–32.

Fjellman, S. M. and H. Gladwin 1985. Haitian family patterns of migration to South Florida. Human Organization 44:301–312.

Fleisher, M. 1998. Dead End Kids. Madison: University of Wisconsin Press.

Fleiss, J. L. 1971. Measuring nominal scale agreement among many raters. Psychological Bulletin 76:378–382.

Flick, U. 2002. An Introduction to Qualitative Research. 2nd ed. London: Sage Publications.

Ford, J. M., T. A. Stetz, M. M. Bott, and B. S. O'Leary 2000. Automated content analysis of multiple-choice test item banks. Social Science Computer Review 18:258–271.

Forgacs, D., ed. 2000. The Gramsci Reader: Selected Writings 1916–1935, 2000. New York: New York University Press.

Forster, M. 2008. Friedrich Daniel Ernst Schleiermacher. The Stanford Encyclopedia of Philosophy (Fall 2008 Edition), E. N. Zalta, ed. Online at http://plato.stanford .edu/archives/fall2008/entries/schleiermacher. Accessed 1-3-09.

Fox, C. 1989. A stop list for general text. ACM SIGIR Forum 24:19–35.

Frake, C. O. 1964. How to ask for a drink in Subanum. In: The Ethnography of Communication, J. Gumperz and D. Hymes, eds. American Anthropologist, Special issue 66 (6), part 2:127–132.

Freilich, M., ed. 1977. Marginal Natives at Work: Anthropologists in the Field. 2nd ed. Cambridge, MA: Schenkman.

Fung, L. and R. Carter 2007. Cantonese e-discourse: A new hybrid variety of English. Multilingua 26:35–66.

Furlow, C. 2003. Comparing indicators of knowledge within and between cultural domains. Field Methods 15:51–62.

Gafaranga, J. 2001. Linguistic identities in talk-in-interaction: Order in bilingual conversation. Journal of Pragmatics 33:1901–1925.

Gal, S. 1978. Peasant men can't get wives: Language change and sex roles in a bilingual community. Language in Society 7:1–16.

Gal, S. 1991. Between speech and silence: The problematics of research on language and gender. In: Gender at the Crossroads of Knowledge: Feminist Anthropology in the Postmodern Era, M. di Leonardo, ed. Berkeley: University of California Press. Pp. 175–203.

Gallimore R., J. Coots, T. S. Weisner, H. Garnier, and D. Guthrie 1996. Family responses to children with early developmental delays. II: Accommodation intensity and activity in early and middle childhood. American Journal of Mental Retardation 101:215–232.

Gallimore R., T. S. Weisner, S. Z. Kaufman, and L. P. Bernheimer 1989. The social construction of ecocultural niches: Family accommodation of developmentally delayed children. American Journal of Mental Retardation 94:216–230.

Gardner, R. 2001. When Listeners Talk. Response Tokens and Listener Stance. Philadelphia: John Benjamins Publishing.

Gardner, S. 1990. Images of family life over the family lifecycle. Sociological Quarterly 31:77–92.

Garot, R. 2004. "You're not a stone": Emotional sensitivity in a bureaucratic setting. Journal of Contemporary Ethnography 33:735–766.

Garrett, P. B. 2005. What a language is good for: Language socialization, language shift, and the persistence of code-specific genres in St. Lucia. Language in Society 34:327–361.

Garro, L. C. 1986. Intracultural variation in folk medical knowledge: A comparison between curers and non-curers. American Anthropologist 88:351–370.

Gatewood, J. B. 1983. Loose talk: Linguistic competence and recognition ability. American Anthropologist 85:378–387.

Gatewood, J. B. 1984. Familiarity, vocabulary size, and recognition ability in four semantic domains. American Ethnologist 11:507.

Gentner, D. and A. L. Stevens, eds. 1983. Mental Models. Hillsdale, NJ: Lawrence Erlbaum Associates.

Gerbner, G., O. R. Holsti, K. Krippendorff, W. J. Paisley, and P. J. Stone, eds. 1969. The Analysis of Communication Content. Developments in Scientific Theories and Computer Techniques. New York: Wiley and Sons.

Gilbreth, F. B. 1911. Motion Study. New York: D. Van Nostrand. (Reprinted 1972 by Hive Publishing Co., Easton, PA.)

Gil-Burman, C., F. Peláez, and S. Sánchez. 2002. Mate choice differences according to sex and age: An analysis of personal advertisements in Spanish newspapers. Human Nature 13:493–508.

Gilly, M. C. 1988. Sex roles in advertising: A comparison of television advertisements in Australia, Mexico, and the United States. Journal of Marketing 52:75–85.

Giorgi, A. 1986. Theoretical justification for the use of descriptions in psychological research. In: Qualitative Research in Psychology: Proceedings of the International Association for Qualitative Research, P. D. Ashworth, A. Giorgi, and J. J. de Koning, eds. Pittsburgh: Duquesne University Press. Pp. 6–46.

Giorgi, A. 2006. Concerning variations in the application of the phenomenological method. The Humanistic Psychologist 34:305–319.

Gladwin, C. H. 1989. Ethnographic Decision Tree Modeling. Newbury Park, CA: Sage Publications.

Gladwin, H. 1970. Decision Making in the Cape Coast (Fante) Fishing and Fish Marketing System. Ph.D. dissertation, Stanford University.

Glaser, B. 1965. The constant comparative method of qualitative analysis. Social Problems 12:436–445.

Glaser, B. G. 1978. Theoretical Sensitivity. Advances in the Methodology of Grounded Theory. Mill Valley, CA: Sociology Press.

Glaser B. G. 1992. Basics of grounded theory. Mill Valley, CA: Sociology Press.

Glaser, B. G. 1998. Doing Grounded Theory: Issues and Discussion. Mill Valley, CA: Sociology Press.

Glaser, B. G. 2001. Doing grounded theory. Grounded Theory Review 2:1–8.

Glaser, B. G. 2002. Constructivist grounded theory? FQS. Forum: Qualitative Social Research 3(3) September. Online at http://www.qualitative-research.net/index.php/fqs/index. Accessed 9-22-08.

Glaser, B. G. and A. Strauss 1967. The Discovery of Grounded Theory: Strategies for Qualitative Research. Chicago: Aldine.

Glover, T. D. 2003. The story of the Queen Anne Memorial Garden: Resisting a dominant cultural narrative. Journal of Leisure Research 35:190–212.

Gluckman, M. 1958 [1940]. The analysis of a social situation in modern Zululand. African Studies 14:1–30, 147–174. Reprinted as Rhodes-Livingston Paper No. 28. Manchester University Press, 1958.

Goffman, E. 1974. Frame Analysis. New York: Harper and Row.

Goffman, E. 1979. Gender Advertisements. New York: Harper and Row.

Goldsen, J. M. 1947. Analyzing the contents of mass communication: A step toward inter-group harmony. International Journal of Opinion & Attitude Research 1:81–92.

Gomes do Espirito Santo, M. E. and G. D. Etheredge 2002. How to reach clients of female sex workers: A survey "by surprise" in brothels in Dakar, Senegal. Bulletin of the World Health Organization 80:709–713.

Goode, E. 1996. Gender and courtship entitlement: Responses to personal ads. Sex Roles 34:141–169.

Goodwin, C. 1981. Conversational organization: Interaction between speakers and hearers. New York: Academic Press.

Goodwin, C. 1986. Gesture as a resource for the organization of mutual orientation. Semiotica 62:29–49.

Goodwin, C. 1994. Recording human interaction in natural settings. Pragmatics 4:181–209.

Goodwin, C. and J. Heritage 1990. Conversation analysis. Annual Review of Anthropology 19:283–307.

Gorden, R. L. 1987. Interviewing: Strategy, Techniques, and Tactics. 4th ed. Homewood, IL: Dorsey.

Gottschalk, L. A. and R. J. Bechtel 2005. Computerized content analysis of the writings of Mahatma Gandhi. The Journal of Nervous and Mental Disease 193:210–216.

Gottschalk, L. A. and G. C. Gleser 1969. The Measurement of Psychological States Through the Content Analysis of Verbal Behavior. Los Angeles: University of California Press.

Govrin, A. 2006. When the underdog schema dominates the we-ness schema: The case of radical leftist Jewish-Israelis. Psychoanalytic Review 93:623–654.

Gramsci, A. 1994. Letters From Prison. Frank Rosengarten, ed. Raymond Rosenthal, tr. New York: Columbia University Press.

Graves, T. D. and C. A. Lave. 1972. Determinants of urban migrant Indian wages. Human Organization 31:47–61.

Greckhamer, T. and M. Koro-Ljungberg 2005. The erosion of a method: Examples from grounded theory. International Journal of Qualitative Studies in Education 18:729–750.

Green, E. M. 2001. Can qualitative research produce reliable quantitative findings? Field Methods 13:3–19.

Green, J., M. Franquiz, and C. Dixon 1997. The myth of the objective transcript: Transcribing as a situated act. TESOL Quarterly 31:172–176.

Greenacre, M. 1984. Theory and Application of Correspondence Analysis. London: Harcourt Brace.

Greenacre, M. and J. Blasius 1994. Correspondence Analysis in the Social Sciences. London: Harcourt Brace.

Greene, J. C. and V. J. Caracelli, eds. 1997. Advances in Mixed-Method Evaluation: The Challenges and Benefits of Integrating Diverse Paradigms: New Directions for Evaluation, No. 74. San Francisco: Jossey-Bass.

Greenhalgh, S. 1994. De-orientalizing the Chinese family firm. American Ethnologist 21:746–775.

Gribble, J. N., H. G. Miller, and S. M. Rogers 1999. Interview mode and measurement of sexual behaviors: Methodological issues. Journal of Sex Research 36:16–24.

Groger, L. 1994. Decision as process: A conceptual model of black elders' nursing home placement. Journal of Aging Studies 8:77–94.

Groom, C. J. and J. W. Pennebaker 2005. The language of love: Sex, sexual orientation, and language use in online personal advertisements. Sex Roles: A Journal of Research 52:447–461.

Gross, D. R. 1984. Time allocation: A tool for the study of cultural behavior. Annual Review of Anthropology 13:519–558.

Guba, E. G. and Y. S. Lincoln 1981. Effective Evaluation. San Francisco: Jossey-Bass.

Guba, E. G. and Y. S. Lincoln 1994. Competing paradigms in qualitative research. In: Handbook of Qualitative Research, N. K. Denzin and Y. S. Lincoln, eds. Thousand Oaks, CA: Sage Publications. Pp. 105–117.

Gubrium, J. F. and J. A. Holstein 2002. Handbook of Interview Research: Context and Method. Thousand Oaks, CA: Sage Publications.

Gudelunas, D. 2005. Online personal ads: Community and sex, virtually. Journal of Homosexuality 49:1–33.

Guest, G., A. Bunce, and L. Johnson 2006. How many interviews are enough? An experiment with data saturation and variability. Field Methods 18:59–82.

Gummesson, E. 2000. Qualitative Methods in Management Research. 2nd ed. Thousand Oaks, CA: Sage Publications.

Gumperz, J. J. 1982. Discourse strategies. Cambridge: Cambridge University Press.

Guthrie, T. H. 2007. Good words: Chief Joseph and the production of Indian speech(es), texts, and subjects. Ethnohistory 54:509–546.

Hahn, C. 2008. Doing Qualitative Research Using Your Computer. London: Sage Publications.

Hak, T and T. Bernts 1996. Coder training: Theoretical training or practical socialization? Qualitative Sociology 19:235–257.

Haldrup, M. and J. Larsen 2006. Material cultures of tourism. Leisure Studies 25:275–289.

Hale, A. 2001. Representing the Cornish: Contesting heritage interpretation in Cornwall. Tourist Studies 1:185–196.

Halford, G. S. 1993. Childrens's Understanding: The Development of Mental Models. Hillsdale, NJ: L. Lawrence Erlbaum Associates.

Hamlet, J. D. 1994. Religious discourse as cultural narrative: A critical analysis of African-American sermons. Western Journal of Black Studies 18:11–17.

Hammersley, M. 1997. Qualitative data archiving: Some reflections on its prospects and problems. Sociology 31:131–142.

Hammersley, M. 2004. Towards a usable past for qualitative research. International Journal of Social Research Methodology 7:19–27

Handloff, R. 1982. Prayers, amulets and charms: Health and social control. African Studies Review 25:185–94.

Handwerker, W. P. 2001. Quick Ethnography. Walnut Creek, CA: AltaMira Press.

Handwerker, W. P. 2003. Sample design. In: Encyclopedia of Social Measurement, K. Kepf-Leonard, ed. San Diego, CA: Academic Press. Pp. 429–436.

Hardesty, J. L. and L. H. Ganong 2006. How women make custody decisions and manage co-parenting with abusive former husbands. Journal of Social and Personal Relationships 23:543–563.

Hardré, P. L. and D. W. Sullivan 2008. Teacher perceptions and individual differences: How they influence rural teachers' motivating strategies. Teaching and Teacher Education 24:2059–2075.

Hareven, T. 1982. Family Time and Industrial Time. Cambridge, UK: Cambridge University Press.

Harman, R. C. 2001. Activities of contemporary Mayan elders. Journal of Cross Cultural Gerontology 16:57–77.

Harris, R. 2005. Wang Luobin: Folk song king of the Northwest or song thief? Modern China 31:381–408.

Harrison, R. 1996. Bentham, Mill, and Sidgwick. In: The Blackwell Companion to Philosophy, N. Bunnin and E. P. Tsui-James, eds. Oxford: Blackwell. Pp. 627–642.

Hart, R. P. and J. P. Childers 2005. The evolution of candidate Bush: A rhetorical analysis. American Behavioral Scientist 49:180–197.

Hartmann, P. 1994. Interviewing when the spouse is present. International Journal of Public Opinion Research 6:298–306.

Harvey, S. M. and S. Thorburn Bird 2004. What makes women feel powerful? An exploratory study of relationship power and sexual decision-making with African Americans at risk for HIV/STDs. Women and Health 39:1–18.

Hatch, J. A. and R. Wisniewski, eds. 1995. Life History and Narrative. Washington, DC: Falmer Press.

Hatton, D. C., D. Kleffel, and A. A. Fisher 2006. Prisoners' perspectives of health problems and healthcare in a U.S. women's jail. Women and Health 44:119–136.

Haworth-Hoeppner, S. 2000. The critical shapes of body image: The role of culture and family in the production of eating disorders. Journal of Marriage and the Family 62:212–227.

Heath, C. 1989. Pain talk: The expression of suffering in the medical consultation. Social Psychology Quarterly 52:113–125.

Hebert, S. and N. Papadiuk 2008. University students' experience of nonmarital breakups: A grounded theory. Journal of College Student Development 49:1–14.

Heckathorn, D. D. 1997. Respondent-driven Sampling: A new approach to the study of hidden populations. Social Problems 44:174–199.

Heckathorn, D. D. 2002. Respondent-driven Sampling II: Deriving valid population estimates from chain-referral samples of hidden populations. Social Problems 49:11–34.

Heckathorn, D. D. and J. Jeffri 2001. Finding the beat: using respondent-driven sampling to study jazz musicians. Poetics 28:307–329.

Hedley, M. 2002. The geometry of gendered conflict in popular film:1986–2000. Sex Roles 47:201–217.

Heemskerk, M. 2000. Driving forces of small-scale gold mining among the Ndjuka Marroons: A cross-scale socioeconomic analysis of participation in gold mining in Suriname. Unpublished Ph.D. dissertation, University of Florida.

Hektner, J. M., J. A. Schmidt, and M. Csikszentmihalyi 2007. Experience Sampling Method: Measuring the Quality of Everyday Life. Thousand Oaks, CA: Sage Publications.

Henley, N. M. 1969. A psychological study of the semantics of animal terms. Journal of Verbal Learning and Verbal Behavior 8:176–184.

Henry, G. T. 1990. Practical Sampling. Applied Social Science Methods Series, Vol. 21.

Herbst, L. and S. Walker 2001. Language barriers in the delivery of police services: A study of police and Hispanic interactions in a Midwestern city. Journal of Criminal Justice 29:329–340.

Herzfeld, M. 1977. Ritual and textual structures: The advent of spring in rural Greece. In: Text and Context, R. K. Jain, ed. Philadelphia: Institute for the Study of Human Issues. Pp. 29–45.

Hewitt, M. 2002. Attitudes toward interview mode and comparability of reporting sexual behavior by personal interview and audio computer-assisted self-interviewing: Analyses of the 1995 National Survey of Family Growth. Sociological Methods and Research 31:3–26.

Hicks, A. 1994. Qualitative comparative analysis and analytic induction: The case of the emergence of the social security state. Sociological Methods and Research 23:86–113.

Hicks, A., J. Misra, and T. N. Ng 1995. The programmatic emergence of the social security state. American Sociological Review 60:329–349.

Hilden, P. P. and S. M. Huhndorf 1999. Performing 'Indian' in the national museum of the American Indian. Social Identities 5:161–183.

Hill, C. E. 1998. Decision modeling: Its use in medical anthropology. In: Using Methods in the Field: A Practical Introduction and Casebook, V. C. de Munck and E. J. Sobo, eds. Walnut Creek, CA: AltaMira Press. Pp. 137–159.

Hill, K. Q., S. Hanna, and S. Shafqat. 1997. The liberal-conservative ideology of U.S. senators: A new measure. American Journal of Political Science 41:1395–1413.

Hinck, S. 2004. The lived experience of oldest-old rural adults. Qualitative Health Research 14:779–791.

Hirschman, E. C. 1987. People as products: Analysis of a complex marketing exchange. Journal of Marketing 51:98–108.

Hockings, P. 2003. Principles of Visual Anthropology. 3rd ed. New York: Mouton de Gruyter.

Hodson, R. 1999. Analyzing Documentary Accounts. Thousand Oaks, CA: Sage Publications.

Hodson, R. 2004. A meta-analysis of workplace ethnographies: Race, gender, and employee attitudes and behaviors. Journal of Contemporary Ethnography 33:4–38.

Hoffman, K. E. 2002. Generational change in Berber women's Song of the Anti-Atlas Mountains, Morocco. Ethnomusicology 46:510–540.

Hoggett, P., P. Beedell, L. Jimenez, M. Mayo, and C. Miller 2006. Identity, life history and commitment to welfare. Journal of Social Policy 35:689–704.

Holland, D. 1985. From situation to impression: How Americans get to know themselves and one another. In: Directions in Cognitive Anthropology, J. Dougherty, ed. Urbana: University of Illinois Press. Pp. 389–412.

Holly, D. H., Jr., and C. E. Cordy 2007. What's in a coin? Reading the material culture of legend tripping and other activities. Journal of American Folklore 120:335–354.

Holmes, J. 2006. Sharing a laugh: Pragmatic aspects of humor and gender in the workplace. Journal of Pragmatics 38:26–50.

Holstein, J. A. and J. F. Gubrium 1995. The Active Interview. Thousand Oaks, CA: Sage Publications.

Holsti, O. R. 1969. Content Analysis for the Social Sciences and Humanities. Reading, MA: Addison-Wesley.

Homans, G. C. 1961. Social behavior as exchange. American Journal of Sociology 63:597–606.

Horizon Research Inc. 2001. September. 2001–2002 Local Systemic Change. 2001–2002 Core Evaluation Manual: Classroom Observation Protocol. Online at http://www.horizon-research.com/instruments/lsc/cop.pdf. Accessed 9-20-08.

Horowitz, D. M. 2007. Applying cultural consensus analysis to marketing. Unpublished Ph.D. dissertation, Florida State University.

Howard, D. C. P. 1994. Human-computer interactions: A phenomenological examination of the adult first-time computer experience. Qualitative Studies in Education 7:33–49.

Howe, K. R. 1988. Against the quantitative-qualitative incompatibility thesis or dogmas die hard. Educational Researcher 17:10–16.

Hruschka, D. J., D. Schwartz, D. C. St. John, E. Picone-Decaro, R. A. Jenkins, and J. W. Carey 2004. Field Methods 16:307–331.

Hudak, M. A. 1993. Gender schema theory revisited: Men's stereotypes of American women. Sex Roles: A Journal of Research 28:279–293.

Huddy, L., J. Billig, J. Bracciodieta, L. Hoeffler, P. J. Moynihan, and P. Pugliani 1997. The effect of interviewer gender on the survey response. Political Behavior 19:197–220.

Husserl, E. 1964 [1907]. The Idea of Phenomenology. W. P. Alston and G. Nakhnikian, tr. The Hague: Nijhoff.

Husserl, E. 1989 [1913]. Ideas Pertaining to a Pure Phenomenology and to a Phenomenological Philosophy. R. Rojcewicz and A. Schuwer, tr. Dordrecht, Netherlands: Kluwer Academic.

Hutcheon, L. 1989. The Politics of Postmodernism. New York: Routledge.

Hutchins, E. 1995. Cognition in the Wild. Cambridge, MA: MIT Press.

Hyman, H. H. (with W. J. Cobb et al.). 1975. Interviewing in Social Research. Chicago: University of Chicago Press.

Hymes, D. 1976. Louis Simpson's "The Deserted Boy." Poetics 5:119–155.

Hymes, D. 1977. Discovering oral performance and measured verse in American Indian narrative. New Literary History 8:431–457.

Hymes, D. 1980a. Verse Analysis of a Wasco Text: Hiram Smith's "At'unaqa." International Journal of American Linguistics 46:65–77.

Hymes, D. 1980b. Particle, pause, and pattern in American Indian narrative verse. American Indian Culture and Research Journal 4:7–51.

Hymes, D. 1981. In Vain I Tried to Tell You: Essays in Ethnopetics. Philadelphia: University of Pennsylvania Press.

Hymes, D. 1985. Language, memory, and selective performance: Cultee's "Salmon's Myth" as twice told to Boas. The Journal of American Folklore 98:391–434.

Hymes, D. 2003. Now I Know Only So Far: Essays in Ethnopoetics. Lincoln: University of Nebraska Press.

Hymes, V. 1987. Warm Springs Sahaptin narrative analysis. In: Native American Discourse: Poetics and Rhetoric, J. Sherzer and A. Woodbury, eds. Cambridge: Cambridge University Press. Pp. 62–102.

Ignatow, G. 2004. Speaking together, thinking together? Exploring metaphor and cognition in a shipyard union dispute. Sociological Forum 19:405–433.

Jacobs, B. A. 2004. A typology of street criminal retaliation. Journal of Research in Crime and Delinquency 41:295–323.

Jacobs, J. K., H. Hollingsworth, and K. B. Givvin 2007. Video-based research made "easy": Methodological lessons learned from the TIMSS video studies. Field Methods 19:284–299.

Jacobs, L. 1995. The Jewish Religion: A Companion. New York: Oxford University Press.

James, D. and S. Clarke 1993. Women, men and interruptions: A critical review of research. In: Gender and Conversational Interaction, D. Tannen, ed. New York: Oxford University Press. Pp. 281–312.

Jang, H-Y. 1995. Cultural differences in organizational communication and interorganizational networks: A semantic network analysis. Unpublished Ph.D. dissertation, State University of New York at Buffalo.

Jang, H-Y. and G. A. Barnett 1994. Cultural differences in organizational communication: A semantic network analysis. Bulletin de Methodologie Sociologique 44:31–59.

Janis, M. 1965. The problem of validating content analysis. In: Language of Politics: Studies in Quantiative Semantics, H. D. Lasswell, N. Leites, and associates, eds. Cambridge, MA: MIT Press. Pp. 55–82.

Jasienski, M. 2006. Letter to the editor. Nature 440:1112.

Jaskyte, K. and W. W. Dressler 2004. Studying culture as an integral aggregate variable: Organizational culture and innovation in a group of nonprofit organizations. Field Methods 16:265–284.

Javeline, D. 1999. Response effects in polite cultures. Public Opinion Quarterly 63:1–28.

Javidi, M. N. and L. W. Long 1989. Teachers' use of humor, self-disclosure, and narrative activity as a function of experience. Communications Research Reports 6:47–52.

Jefferson, G. 1973. A case of precision timing in ordinary conversation: Overlapped tag-positioned address terms in closing sequences. Semiotica 9:47–96.

Jefferson, G. 1983. Issues in the transcription of naturally-occurring talk. Caricature versus capturing pronunciation particulars. Tilburg Papers on Language and Literature. Tilburg, Netherlands: University of Tilburg.

Jefferson, G. 2004. Glossary of transcript symbols with an introduction. In: Conversation Analysis: Studies From the First Generation, G. H. Lerner, ed. Philadelphia: John Benjamins Publishing. Pp. 43–59.

Jehn, K. A. and L. Doucet 1996. Developing categories from interview data: Text analysis and multidimensional scaling. Part I. Cultural Anthropology Methods Journal 8:15–16.

Jehn, K. A. and L. Doucet 1997. Developing categories for interview data: Consequences of different coding and analysis strategies in understanding text. Part II. Cultural Anthropology Methods Journal 9:1–7.

Jobe, J. B., D. M. Keler, and A. F. Smith 1996. Cognitive techniques in interviewing older people. In: Answering Questions: Methodology for Determining Cognitive and Communicative Processes in Survey Research, N. Schwarz and S. Sudman, eds. San Francisco: Jossey-Bass. Pp. 197–219.

Johnson, A. 1975. Time allocation in a Machiguenga community. Ethnology 14:301–310.

Johnson, E. 1996. Word lengths, authorship, and four-letter words. TEXT Technology 6:15–23.

Johnson, J. C. 1990. Selecting Ethnographic Informants. Newbury Park, CA: Sage Publications.

Johnson, J. C., D. C. Griffith, and J. D. Murray 1987. Encouraging the use of underutilized marine fishes by southeastern U.S. anglers. Part I. Marine Fisheries Review 49:122–137.

Johnson, R. B., ed. 2006. New Directions in Mixed Methods Research. Special Issue of Research in the Schools. Spring. Online at http://www.msera.org/rits_131.htm. Accessed 9-22-08.

Johnson, R. B. and A. J. Onwuegbuzie 2004. Mixed methods research: A research paradigm whose time has come. Educational Researcher 33:14–26.

Johnson-Laird, P. N. 1983. Mental Models: Toward a Cognitive Science of Language, Inference, and Consciousness. Cambridge, MA: Harvard University Press.

Johnston, J. and C. Walton 1995. Reducing response effects for sensitive questions: A computer-assisted self-interview with audio. Social Science Computer Review 13:304–319.

Joinson, A. N., C. Paine, T. Buchanan, and U-D. Reips 2008. Measuring self-disclosure online: Blurring and non-response to sensitive items in web-based surveys. Computers in Human Behavior 24:2158–2171.

Jones, D. 2003. The generative psychology of kinship: Part 2. Generating variation from universal building blocks with optimality theory. Evolution and Human Behavior 24:320–350.

Jones, D. 2004. The universal psychology of kinship: Evidence from language. Trends in Cognitive Science 18:211–215.

Jones, P. 1996. Hume. In: The Blackwell Companion to Philosophy, N. Bunnin and E. P Tsui-James, eds. Oxford: Blackwell. Pp. 555–570.

Juzwik, M. M. 2004. What rhetoric can contribute to an ethnopoetics of narrative performance in teaching: The significance of parallelism in one teacher's narrative. Linguistics and Education 15:359–386.

Kadushin, C. 1968. Power, influence, and social circles: A new methodology for studying opinion-makers. American Sociological Review 33:685–699.

Kahn, R. L. and C. F. Cannell. 1957. The dynamics of interviewing. New York: John Wiley.

Kane, E. W. and L. J. Macaulay 1993. Interviewer gender and gender attitudes. Public Opinion Quarterly 57:1–28.

Kang, N., A. Kara, H. A. Laskey, and F. B. Seaton 1993. A SAS MACRO for calculating intercoder agreement in content analysis. Journal of Advertising 23:17–28.

Kaplan, A. 1964. The Conduct of Inquiry: Methodology for Behavioral Science. San Francisco, CA: Chandler.

Kassis, H. 1983. A Concordance of the Qur'an. Berkeley: University of California Press.

Kaufman, G. and P. Voon Chin 2003. Is ageism alive in date selection among men? Age requests among gay and straight men in Internet personal ads. Journal of Men's Studies 11:225–235.

Kearney, M. H. 1996. Reclaiming normal life: Women's experiences of quitting drugs. Journal of Obstetric, Gynecologic, and Neonatal Nursing 25:761–768.

Kearney, M. H. 1998. Truthful self-nurturing: A grounded formal theory of women's addiction recovery. Qualitative Health Research 8:495–512.

Kearney, M. H., S. Murphy, K. Irwin, and M. Rosenbaum 1995. Salvaging self: A grounded theory of pregnancy on crack cocaine. Nursing Research 44:208–213.

Kelly, E. F. and P. J. Stone 1975. Computer Recognition of English Word Senses. Amsterdam: North-Holland Publishing Company.

Kempton, W. 1987. Two theories of home heat control. In: Cultural Models in Language and Thought, D. Holland and N. Quinn, eds. Cambridge: Cambridge University Press. Pp. 222–242.

Kendall, S. and D. Tannen 2001. Discourse and gender. In: The Handbook of Discourse Analysis, D. Schiffrin, D. Tannen, and H. E. Hamilton, eds. Oxford: Blackwell. Pp. 548–567.

Kennedy, C. W. and C. Camden 1983. A new look at interruptions. Western Journal of Speech Communication 47:45–58.

Khaw, L. and J. L. Hardesty 2007. Theorizing the process of leaving: Turning points and trajectories in the stages of change. Family Relations 56:413–425.

Kidwell, M. 2005. Gaze as social control: How very young children differentiate "the look" from a "mere look" by their adult caregivers. Research on Language and Social Interaction 38:417–449.

Kilburn, H. W. 2004. Explaining U. S. urban regimes: A qualitative comparative analysis. Urban Affairs Review 39:633–651.

Kim, A. I. 1985. Korean color terms: An aspect of semantic fields and related phenomena. Anthropological Linguistics 27:425–436.

King, A. 1996. The fining of Vinnie Jones. International Review for the Sociology of Sport 31:119–134.

Kirchler, E. 1992. Adorable woman, expert man: Changing gender images of women and men in management. European Journal of Social Psychology 22:363–373.

Kirk, J. and M. Miller 1986. Reliability and Validity in Qualitative Research. Beverly Hills, CA: Sage Publications.

Klecka, W. R. 1980. Discriminant Analysis. Beverly Hills, CA: Sage Publications.

Koven, M. 2002. An analysis of speaker role inhabitance in narratives of personal experience. Journal of Pragmatics 34:167–217.

Koven, M. 2004. Getting "emotional" in two languages: Bilinguals' verbal performance of affect in narratives of personal experience. Text 24:471–515.

Krippendorff, K. 1980. Content Analysis: An Introduction to Its Methodology. Beverly Hills, CA: Sage Publications.

Krippendorff, K. 2004a. Content Analysis: An Introduction to Its Methodology. 2nd ed. Thousand Oaks, CA: Sage Publications.

Krippendorff, K. 2004b. Reliability in content analysis. Some common misconceptions and recommendations. Human Communication Research 30:411–433.

Kroeber, A. L. 1919. On the principle of order in civilization as exemplified by changes in women's fashions. American Anthropologist 21:235–263.

Krueger, R. A. 1994. Focus groups: A practical guide for applied research. 2nd ed. Thousand Oaks, CA: Sage Publications.

Krueger, R. A. and M. A. Casey 2000. Focus Groups: A Practical Guide for Applied Research. Thousand Oaks, CA: Sage Publications.

Kruskal, J. B. and M. Wish 1978. Multidimensional Scaling. Beverly Hills, CA: Sage Publications.

Kurasaki, K. S. 1997. Ethnic identify and its development among third-generation Japanese Americans. Unpublished Ph.D. dissertation, DePaul University.

Kurasaki, K. S. 2000. Intercoder reliability for validating conclusions drawn from open-ended interview data. Field Methods 12:179–194.

Kuzel, A. J. 1999. Sampling in qualitative inquiry. In: Doing Qualitative Research, B. F. Crabtree and W. L. Miller, eds. 2nd ed. Thousand Oaks, CA: Sage Publications. Pp. 33–45.

Kvale, S. 1996. Interview: An Introduction to Qualitative Interviewing. Thousand Oaks, CA: Sage Publications.

Labov, W. J. and J. Waletzky 1997. Narrative analysis: Oral versions of personal experience. Journal of Narrative and Life History 7:3–38.

Lakoff, G. and M. Johnson 2003 [1980]. Metaphors We Live By. Chicago: University of Chicago Press.

Lakoff, G. and Z. Kövecses 1987. The cognitive model of anger in American English. In: Cultural Models in Language and Thought, D. Holland and N. Quinn, eds. Cambridge: Cambridge University Press. Pp. 195–221.

Lampert, M. D. and S. M. Ervin-Trip 2006. Risky laughter: Teasing and self-directed joking among male and female friends. Journal of Pragmatics 38:51–72.

Lance, L. M. 1998. Gender differences in heterosexual dating: A content analysis of personal ads. Journal of Men's Studies 6:297–305.

Landauer, T. K. and J. W. M. Whiting. 1964. Infantile stimulation and adult stature of human males. American Anthropologist 66:1007–1028.

Landis, J. R. and G. G. Koch 1977. The measurement of observer agreement for categorical data. Biometrics 33:159–174.

LaRossa, R., C. Jaret, M. Gadgil, and R. G. Wynn 2000. The changing culture of fatherhood in comic-strip families: A six-decade analysis. Journal of Marriage and the Family 62:375–387.

Lasswell, H. D. 1949. Why be quantitative? In: Language of Politics: Studies in Quantitative Semantics, H. D. Lasswell, N. Leites, and associates, eds. New York: George Stewart. Pp. 40–52. [Reprinted 1965, Cambridge, MA: MIT Press.]

Laubach, M. 2005. Consent, informal organization and job rewards: A mixed methods analysis. Social Forces 83:1535–1565.

Laver, M. and J. Garry 2000. Estimating policy positions from political texts. American Journal of Political Science 44:619–634.

Lea, K. L. 1980. Francis Bacon. Encyclopaedia Britannica. Vol. 2. Chicago: Encyclopaedia Britannica.

Ledema, R., A. Flabouris, S. Grant, and C. Jorm 2006. Narrativizing errors of care: Critical incident reporting in clinical practice. Social Science and Medicine 62:134–144.

Leighton Dawson, B. and W. D. McIntosh 2006. Sexual strategies theory and Internet personal advertisements. CyberPsychology and Behavior 9:614–617.

Lévi-Strauss, C. 1963. Structural Anthropology. New York: Basic Books.

Levy, R., and D. Hollan. 1998. Person-centered interviewing and observation. In: Handbook of Methods in Cultural Anthropology, H. R. Bernard, ed. Walnut Creek, CA: AltaMira Press. Pp. 333–364.

Levy, V. 1999. Protective steering: A grounded theory study of the processes by which midwives facilitate informed choices during pregnancy. Journal of Advanced Nursing 29:104–112.

Lewins, A. and C. Silver 2007. Using Qualitative Software: A Step by Step Guide. London: Sage Publications.

Li, J. 2004. Parental expectations of Chinese immigrants: A folk theory about children's school achievement. Race, Ethnicity and Education 7:167–183.

Lieberson, Stanley 1991. Small N's and big conclusions: An evaluation of the reasoning in comparative studies based on a small number of cases. Social Forces 70:307–320.

Lincoln, Y. S. and E. G. Guba 1985. Naturalistic Inquiry. Newbury Park, CA: Sage Publications.

Linnekin, J. 1987. Categorize, cannibalize? Humanistic quantification in anthropological research. American Anthropologist 89:920–926.

Lofland, J., L. Anderson, D. Snow, and L. H. Lofland 2006. Analyzing Social Settings. A Guide to Qualitative Observation and Analysis. Belmont, CA: Wadsworth/Thompson Learning.

Loftus, E. F. and W. Marburger 1983. Since the eruption of Mt. St. Helens, has anyone beaten you up? Improving the accuracy of retrospective reports with landmark events. Memory and Cognition 11:114–120.

Lomax. A. 1968. Folk Song Style and Culture. Washington, DC: American Association for the Advancement of Science, Publication number 88.

Lomax, A. 1977. A stylistic analysis of speaking. Language in Society 6:15–36.

Lomax, A. 2003. Alan Lomax. Selected Writings. R. D. Cohen, ed. New York: Routledge.

Lombard, M., J. Snyder-Duch, and C. Campanella Bracken 2004. A call for standardization in content analysis reliability. Human Communications Research 30:434–437.

Lombard, M., J. Snyder-Duch, and C. Campanella Bracken 2005. Practical resources for assessing and reporting intercoder reliability in content analysis research projects. Online at http://www.temple.edu/sct/mmc/reliability/. Accessed 3-31-08.

Longest, K. C. and S. Vaisey 2008. fuzzy: A program for performing qualitative comparative analysis in Stata. Stata Journal 8:79–104.

Longfield, K. 2004. Rich fools, spare tyres, and boyfriends: Partner categories, relationship dynamics and Ivorian women's risk for STIs and HIV. Culture, Health and Sexuality 66:483–500.

Luborsky, M. R. and R. L. Rubinstein 1995. Sampling in qualitative research: Rationale, issues, and methods. Research on Aging 17:89–113.

Lueptow, L. B., S. L. Moser, and B. F. Pendleton 1990. Gender and response effects in telephone interviews about gender characteristics. Sex Roles 22:29–42.

Luhn, H. P. 1960. Keyword-in-context index for technical literature. American Documentation 11:288–295.

MacQueen, K. M., E. McLellan, K. Kelly, and B. Milstein 1998. Code book development for team-based qualitative analysis. Cultural Anthropology Methods Journal 10:31–36.

MacQueen, K. M., E. McLellan, K. Kelly, and B. Milstein 2008. Team-based codebook development: Structure, process, and agreement. In: Handbook for Team-Based Qualitative Research, G. Guest and K. M. MacQueen, eds. Lanham, MD: AltaMira Press. Pp 119–135.

Mahaffey, K. A. 1996. Cognitive dissonance and its resolution: A study of lesbian Christians. Journal for the Scientific Study of Religion 35:392–402.

Malimabe-Ramagoshi, R. M., J. G. Maree, D. Alexander, and M. M. Molepo 2007. Child abuse in Setswana folktales. Early Child Development and Care 177:433–448.

Malkin, A. R., K. Wornian, and J. C. Chrisler 1999. Women and weight: Gendered messages on magazine covers. Sex Roles 40:647–655.

Maloney, R. S., and M. Paolisso 2001. What can digital audio data do for you? Field Methods 13:88–96.

Mandler, J. M. 1984. Stories, Scripts, and Scenes: Aspects of Schema Theory. Hillsdale, NJ: Lawrence Erlbaum Associates.

Mangabeira, W. C., R. M. Lee, and N. G. Fielding 2004. Computers and qualitative research: Adoption, use, and representation. Social Science Computer Review 22:167–178.

Mann, S. 2007. Understanding farm succession by the objective hermeneutics method. Sociologia Ruralis 47:369–383.

Manning, P. K. 1971. Fixing what you feared: Notes on the campus abortion search. In: The Sociology of Sex, J. Henslin, ed. New York: Appleton-Century-Crofts. Pp. 137–163.

Manning, P. K.1982. Analytic induction. In: Handbook of Social Science Methods, R. Smith and P. K. Manning, eds. Vol. 2. New York: Harper. Pp. 273–302.

Manzo, J. 1996. Taking turns and taking sides: Opening scenes from two jury deliberations. Social Psychology Quarterly 59:107–125.

Margolis, M. 1984. Mothers and Such. Berkeley: University of California Press.

Markovic, M. 2006. Analyzing qualitative data: health care experiences of women with gynecological cancer. Field Methods 18:413–429.

Markovic, M., L. Manderson, N. Wray, and M. Quinn 2004. "He's telling us something." Women's experiences of cancer disclosure and treatment decision-making in Australia. Anthropology and Medicine 3:327–341.

Martin, C. L. and S. Parker 1995. Folk theories about race and sex differences. Personality and Social Psychology Bulletin 21:45–57.

Martin, J. L. and L. Dean 1993. Developing a community sample of gay men for an epidemiological study of AIDS. In: Researching Sensitive Topics, C. M. Renzetti and R. M. Lee, eds. Newbury Park, CA: Sage Publications. Pp. 82–100.

Martindale, C. and D. McKenzie 1995. On the utility of content analysis in author attribution: The Federalist. Computers and the Humanities 29:259–270.

Martsolf, D. S., T. J. Courey, T. R. Chapman, C. B. Draucker, and B. L. Mims 2006. Adaptive sampling: Recruiting a diverse community sample of survivors of sexual violence. Journal of Community Health Nursing 23:169–182.

Mastin, T., A. Coe, S. Hamilton, and S. Tarr 2004. Product purchase decision-making behavior and gender role stereotypes: A content analysis of advertisements in Essence and Ladies' Home Journal, 1990–1999. Howard Journal of Communications 15:229–243.

Matarazzo, J. 1964. Interviewer mm-humm and interviewee speech duration. Psychotherapy: Theory, Research and Practice 1:109–114.

Matheson, J. L. 2007. The voice transcription technique: Use of voice recognition software to transcribe digital interview data in qualitative research. The Qualitative Report 12:547–560. Online at http://www.nova.edu/ssss/QR/QR12-4/matheson.pdf. Accessed 12-24-08.

Mathews, H. F. 1992. The directive force of morality tales in a Mexican community. In: Human Motives and Cultural Models, R. G. D'Andrade and C. Strauss, eds. New York: Cambridge University Press. Pp. 127–162.

Mathews, H. F. and C. Hill 1990. Applying cognitive decision theory to the study of regional patterns of illness treatment choice. American Anthropologist 91:155–170.

Mattei, L. R. W. 1998. Gender and power in American legislative discourse. The Journal of Politics 60:440–461.

Maxwell, J. A. 2005. Qualitative Research Design: An Interactive Approach. 2nd ed. Thousand Oaks, CA: Sage Publications.

Maynard, D. W. 1991. Interaction and asymmetry in clinical discourse. American Journal of Sociology 97:448–495.

Maynard, D. W. and J. Heritage 2005. Conversation analysis, doctor-patient interaction, and medical communication. Medical Education 39:428–435.

McCarty, C., M. House, J. Harman, and S. Richards 2006. Effort in phone survey response rates: The effects of vendor and client controlled factors. Field Methods 18:172–188.

McColl, R. W. 1982. Personal icons and amulets: Reflections of culture values and human/land relationships. The Professional Geographer 34:447–450.

McHoul A. and R. Rapley 2005. A case of attention-deficit/hyperactivity disorder diagnosis: Sir Karl and Francis B. slug it out on the consulting room floor. Discourse and Society 16:419–449.

McLaughlin, T. and N. Goulet 1999. Gender advertisements in magazines aimed at African Americans: A comparison to their occurrence in magazines aimed at Caucasians. Sex Roles 40:61–71.

McLellan, E., K. M. MacQueen, and J. L. Neidig 2003. Beyond the qualitative interview: Data preparation and transcription. Field Methods 15:63–84.

McNamara, M. S. 2005. Knowing and doing phenomenology: The implications of the critique of 'nursing phenomenology' for a phenomenological inquiry: A discussion paper. International Journal of Nursing Studies 42:695–704.

McVee, M. B., K. Dunsmore, and J. R. Gavelek 2005. Schema theory revisited. Review of Educational Research 75:531–566.

Means, B., A. Nigam, M. Zarrow, E. F. Loftus, and M. S. Donaldson 1989. Autobiographical memory for health-related events. National Center for Health Statistics, Vital and Health Statistics, ser. 6, no. 2, pub. no. 89-1077. Washington, DC: U.S. Government Printing Office.

Meh, C. C. 1996. SOCRATES streamlines lesson observations. Educational Leadership 53:76–78.

Mele, M. M. and B. M. Bello 2007. Coaxing and coercion in roadblock encounters on Nigerian highways. Discourse and Society 18:437–452.

Merriam, S. B. 1998. Qualitative Research and Case Study Applications in Education: Revised and Expanded. San Francisco: Jossey-Bass.

Mertens, D. M. 2005. Research and Evaluation in Education and Psychology: Integrating Diversity With Quantitative, Qualitative, and Mixed Methods. Thousand Oaks, CA: Sage Publications.

Merton, R. K., M. Fiske, and P. L. Kendall 1956. The focused interview: A manual of problems and procedures. Glencoe, IL: Free Press.

Messer, E. and M. Bloch 1985. Women's and children's activity profiles: A comparison of time allocation and time allocation methods. Journal of Comparative Family Studies 16:329–343.

Messner, B. A., A. Jipson, P. J. Becker, and B. Byers 2007. The hardest hate: A sociological analysis of country hate music. Popular Music and Society 30:513–531.

Metzger, D. and G. Williams. 1966. Some procedures and results in the categories: Tzeltal "firewood." American Anthropologist 68:389–407.

Miles, M. B. 1979. Qualitative data as an attractive nuisance: The problem of analysis. Administrative Science Quarterly 24:590–601.

Miles, M. B. and A. M. Huberman 1994. Qualitative Data Analysis: An Expanded Sourcebook. Thousand Oaks, CA: Sage Publications.

Mill, J. S. 1898. A system of logic, ratiocinative and inductive: Being a connected view of the principles of evidence and the methods of scientific investigation. People's edition. London: Longmans, Green and Co.

Miller, D. 1987. Material Culture and Mass Consumption. Oxford: Blackwell.

Miller, M., J. Kaneko, P. Bartram, J. Marks, and D. D. Brewer 2004. Cultural consensus analysis and environmental anthropology: Yellowfin tuna fishery management in Hawaii. Cross-Cultural Research 38:289–314.

Miller, S. I. 1982. Quality and quantity: Another view of analytic induction as a research technique. Quality and Quantity 16:281–295.

Mingers, J. 1989a. An empirical comparison of pruning methods for decision tree induction. Machine Learning 4:227–243.

Mingers, J. 1989b. An empirical comparison of selection measures for decision-tree induction. Machine Learning 3:319–342.

Mishler, E. G. 1986. Research Interviewing: Context and Narrative. Cambridge, MA: Harvard University Press.

Mitchell, R. 1965. Survey materials collected in the developing countries: Sampling, measurement, and interviewing obstacles to intra- and international comparisons. International Social Science Journal 17:665–685.

Montbriand, M. J. 1994. Decision Heuristics of Patients with Cancer: Alternative and Biomedical Choices. Ph.D. dissertation, University of Saskatchewan.

Moore, N. 2007. (Re)using qualitative data? Sociological Research Online 12(3). Online at http://www.socresonline.org.uk/12/3/1.html. Accessed 1-30-09.

Moran, D. 2000. Introduction to Phenomenology. London: Routledge.

Morera, M. C. and C. H. Gladwin 2006. Does off-farm work discourage soil conservation? Incentives and disincentives throughout two Honduran hillside communities. Human Ecology 34:355–378.

Moret, M., R. Reuzel, G. J. Van Der Wilt, and J. Grin 2007. Validity and reliability of qualitative data analysis: Interobserver agreement in reconstructing interpretative frames. Field Methods 19:24–39.

Morgan, D. L. 1997. Focus Groups as Qualitative Research. 2nd ed. Thousand Oaks, CA: Sage Publications.

Morgan, D. L., and R. Krueger 1998. The Focus Group Kit, 6 vols. Thousand Oaks, CA: Sage Publications.

Morgan, M. G., B. Fischoff, A. Bostrom, and C. J. Atman 2002. Risk Communication: A Mental Models Approach. New York: Cambridge University Press.

Morgan, T. F. and W. M. Ammentorp 1993. Practical creativity in the corporate world: Capturing expert judgment with qualitative models. American Behavioral Scientist 37:102–111.

Morine-Dershimer, G. 2006. Classroom management and classroom discourse. In: Handbook of Classroom Management: Research, Practice, and Contemporary Issues, C. M. Evertson and C. S. Weinstein, eds. Mahwah, NJ: Lawrence Erlbaum Associates. Pp. 127–156.

Morse, J. M. 1994. Designing funded qualitative research. In: Handbook of Qualitative Research, N. K. Denzin and Y. S. Lincoln, eds. Thousand Oaks, CA: Sage Publications. Pp. 220–235.

Morse, J. M. 2003. Biased reflections: Principles of sampling and analysis in qualitative inquiry. In: Moving Beyond Effectiveness in Evidence Synthesis. Methodological Issues in the Synthesis of Diverse Sources of Evidence, J. Popay, ed. London: National Institute for Health and Clinical Excellence. Online at http://www.nice.org.uk/nicemedia/docs/Moving_beyond_effectiveness_in_evidence_synthesis2.pdf. Accessed 4-18-09.

Morse, J. M. 2007. Sampling in grounded theory research. In: The Sage Handbook of Grounded Theory, T. Bryant and K. Charmaz, eds. London: Sage Publications. Pp. 229–244.

Morse, J. M. and C. Pooler 2002. Analysis of videotaped data: Methodological considerations. International Journal of Qualitative Methods 1(4):1–19. Online at http://ejournals.library.ualberta.ca/index.php/IJQM/index, accessed 4-12-09.

Moser, C. A. and A. Stuart 1953. An experimental study of quota sampling. Journal of the Royal Statistical Society, Series A (General), 116:349–405.

Moss, B. J. 1994. Creating a community: Literacy events in African American churches. In: Literacy Across Communities, B. Moss, ed. Cresskill, NJ: Hampton Press. Pp. 147–178.

Mosteller, F. and D. L. Wallace 1964. Inference and Disputed Authorship: The Federalist Papers. Reading, MA: Addison-Wesley.

Moustakas, C. 1994. Phenomenological Research Methods. Thousand Oaks, CA: Sage Publications.

Mugavin, M. E. 2008. Multidimensional scaling: A brief overview. Nursing Research 57:64–68.

Muñoz Leiva, F., F. J. Montoro Ríos, and T. L. Martínez 2006. Assessment of interjudge reliability in the open-ended questions coding process. Quality and Quantity 40:519–537.

Murdock, G. P., C. S., Ford, A. E. Hudson, R. Kennedy, L. W. Simmons, and J. W. Whiting 2004 [1961]. Outline of Cultural Materials. 5th ed., with modifications. New Haven, CT: HRAF Press.

Murphy, J. M. and M. E. Stuckey 2002. Never cared to say goodbye: Presidential legacies and vice presidential campaigns. Presidential Studies Quarterly 32:46–66.

Murray, N. M. and S. B. Murray 1996. Music and lyrics in commercials: a cross-cultural comparison between commercials run in the Dominican Republic and in the United States. Journal of Advertising 25:51–63.

Nagata, J. 1974. What is Malay? Situational selection of ethnic identity in a plural society. American Ethnologist 1:331–350.

Namenwith, J. and R. P. Weber 1987. Dynamics of Culture. Winchester, MA: Allen and Unwin.

Necheles, J. E., E. Q. Chung, J. Hawes-Dawson, G. W. Ryan, L. B. Williams, H. N. Holmes, K. B. Wells, M. E. Vaiana, and M. A. Schuster 2007. The teen photovoice project: A pilot study to promote health through advocacy. Progress in Community Health Partnerships: Research, Education, and Action 1:221–229.

Negrón, R. 2007. Switching of ethnic identification among New York City Latinos. Unpublished Ph.D. dissertation, University of Florida.

Neto, F. and A. Furnham 2005. Gender-role portrayals in children's television advertisements. International Journal of Adolescence and Youth 12:69–90.

Neuendorf, K. A. 2002. The Content Analysis Guidebook. Thousand Oaks, CA: Sage Publications.

Nevile, M. 2007. Talking without overlap in the airline cockpit: Precision timing at work. Text and Talk 27:225–249.

Niebel, B. W. 1982. Motion and Time Study. 7th ed. Homewood, IL: Irwin.

Nikitina, S. 2003. Stories that stayed "under the skin." Qualitative Studies in Education 16:251–265.

Nolan, J. M. and G. W. Ryan 2000. Fear and loathing at the cineplex: Gender differences in descriptions and perceptions of slasher films. Sex Roles 42:39–56.

Norrick, N. R. 2001. On the conversational performance of narrative jokes: Toward and account of timing. Humor 14:255–274.

Nyamongo, I. K. 1999. Home case management of malaria: An ethnographic study of lay people's classification of drugs in Suneka division, Kenya. Tropical Medicine and International Health 4:736–743.

Nyamongo, I. K. 2002. Assessing intracultural variability statistically using data on malaria perceptions in Gusii, Kena. Field Methods 14:148–160.

Ochs, E. 1979. Transcription as theory. In: Developmental Pragmatics, E. Ochs and B. Schieffelin, eds. New York: Academic Press. Pp. 43–72.

Ochs, E. and L. Capps 2001. Living Narrative: Creating Lives in Everyday Storytelling. Cambridge, MA: Harvard University Press.

Ogilvie, D. M., P. J. Stone, and E. S. Schneidman 1966. Some characteristics of genuine versus simulated suicide notes. In: The General Inquirer: A Computer Approach to Content Analysis, P. J. Stone, D. C. Dunphy, M. S. Smith, D. M. Ogilvie, and associates, eds. Cambridge, MA: MIT Press. Pp. 527–535.

O'Halloran, S. 2005. Symmetry in interaction in meetings of Alcoholics Anonymous: The management of conflict. Discourse and Society 16:535–560.

Okamoto, D. G., L. S. Rashotte, and L. Smith-Lovin 2002. Measuring interruption: Syntactic and contextual methods of coding conversation. Social Psychology Quarterly 65:38–55.

Okamura, J. Y. 1981. Situational ethnicity. Ethnic and Racial Studies 4:452–465.

Onwuegbuzie, A. J. and N. L. Leech 2007. Sampling designs in qualitative research: Making the sampling process more public. The Qualitative Report 12:238–254. Online at http://www.nova.edu/ssss/QR/QR12-2/onwuegbuzie1.pdf. Accessed 12-24-08.

Opler, M. E. 1945. Themes as dynamic forces in culture. American Journal of Sociology 51:198–206.

Osgood, C. 1959. The representational model and relevant research methods. In: Trends in Content Analysis, I. de Sola Pool, ed. Urbana: University of Illinois Press. Pp. 33–88.

Otterbein, K. F. 1969. Basic steps in conducting a cross-cultural study. Behavior Science Notes 4:221–236.

Otterbein, K. F. 1986. The Ultimate Coercive Sanction: A Cross-Cultural Study of Capital Punishment. New Haven, CT: HRAF Press.

Öztürkmen, A. 2003. Remembering through material culture: Local knowledge of past communities in a Turkish Black Sea town. Middle Eastern Studies 39:179–193.

Panchanadeswaran, S. and C. Koverola 2005. The voices of battered women in India. Violence Against Women 11:736–758.

Parekh, R., and E. V. Beresin. 2001. Looking for love? Take a cross-cultural walk through the personals. Academic Psychiatry 25:223–233.

Parmelee, J. H., S. C. Perkins, and J. J. Sayre 2007. "What about people our age?" Applying qualitative and quantitative methods to uncover how political ads alienate college students. Journal of Mixed Methods 1:183–199.

Parr, M. G. and B. D. Lashua 2004. What is leisure. The perceptions of recreation practitioners and others. Leisure Sciences 26:1–17.

Parsons, T. 1951. The Social System. Glencoe, IL: Free Press.

Patterson, B. R, L. Bettini, and J. F. Nussbaum 1993. The meaning of friendship across the life-span: Two studies. Communication Quarterly 41:145–160.

Patton, M. Q. 1987. Creative Evaluation. Newbury Park, CA: Sage Publications.

Patton, M. Q. 2002. Qualitative Research and Evaluation Methods. 3rd ed. Thousand Oaks, CA: Sage Publications.

Pawlowski, B. and G. Jasienska 2008. Women's body morphology and preferences for sexual partners' characteristics. Evolution and Human Behavior 29:19–25.

Pelto, P. J. and G. H. Pelto 1978. Anthropological Research: The Structure of Inquiry. Cambridge: Cambridge University Press.

Penrod, J., D. B. Preston, R. E. Cain, and M. T. Starks 2003. A discussion of chain referral as a method of sampling hard-to-reach populations. Journal of Transcultural Nursing 14:100–107.

Peterson, J. A., H. S. Reisinger, R. P. Schwartz, S. G. Mitchell, S. M. Kelly, B. S. Brown, and M. H. Agar 2008. Targeted sampling in drug abuse research: A review and case study. Field Methods 20:155–170.

Phua, V. C. 2002. Sex and sexuality in men's personal advertisements. Men and Masculinities 5:178–191.

Pink, S. 2007. Doing Visual Ethnography: Images, Media, and Representation in Research. Thousand Oaks, CA: Sage Publications.

Pinkley, R. L., M. J. Gelfand, and L. Duan 2005. Where, when and how: The use of multidimensional scaling methods in the study of negotiation and social conflict. International Negotiation 10:79–96.

Polanyi, M. and E. Tompa 2004. Rethinking work-health models for the new global economy: A qualitative analysis of emerging dimensions of work. Work 23:3–18.

Polletta, F. 1998. "It was like a fever. . . ." Narrative and identity in social protest. Social Problems 45:137–159.

Pollner, M. and R. E Adams 1997. The effect of spouse presence on appraisals of emotional support and household strain. Public Opinion Quarterly 61:615–626.

Poortman, A-R. and T. van Tilburg 2005. Past experiences and older adults' attitudes: A lifecourse perspective. Ageing and Society 25:19–39.

Poveda, D. 2002. Quico's story: An ethnopoetic analysis of a Gypsy boy's narratives at school. Text 22:269–300.

Presser, L. 2004. Violent offenders, moral selves: Constructing identities and accounts in the research interview. Social Problems 51:82–101.

Pressman, S. D. and S. Cohen 2007. Use of social words in autobiographies and longevity. Psychosomatic Medicine 69:262–269.

Price, L. 1987. Ecuadorian illness stories: Cultural knowledge in natural discourse. In: Cultural Models in Language and Thought, D. Holland and N. Quinn, eds. Cambridge: Cambridge University Press. Pp. 313–342.

Propp, V. 1990. Morphology of the Folktale. Austin: University of Texas Press.

Psathas, G., ed. 1979. Everyday Language. New York: Irvington Publishers.

Psathas, G. 1995. Conversation Analysis: The Study of Talk in Interaction. Thousand Oaks, CA: Sage Publications.

Puchta, C. and J. Potter 2004. Focus Group Practice. Thousand Oaks, CA: Sage Publications.

Quinlan, M. 2005. Considerations for collecting freelists in the field: Examples from ethnobotany. Field Methods 17:219–234.

Quinn, N. 1982. Commitment in American marriage: A cultural analysis. American Ethnologist 9:775–798.

Quinn, N. 1987. Convergent evidence for a cultural model of American marriage. In: Cultural Models in Language and Thought, D. Holland and N. Quinn, eds. Cambridge: Cambridge University Press. Pp. 173–192.

Quinn, N. 1992. The motivational force of self-understanding: Evidence from wives' inner conflicts. In: Human Motives and Cultural Models, R. D'Andrade and C. Strauss, eds. New York: Cambridge University Press. Pp. 90–126.

Quinn, N. 1996. Culture and contradiction: The case of Americans reasoning about marriage. Ethos 24:391–425.

Quinn, N. 1997. Research on shared task solutions. In: A Cognitive Theory of Cultural Meaning, C. Strauss and N. Quinn, eds. New York: Cambridge University Press. Pp. 137–188.

Quinn, N., ed. 2005a. Finding Culture in Talk: A Collection of Methods. New York: Palgrave Macmillan.

Quinn, N. 2005b. How to reconstruct schemas people share, from what they say. In: Finding Culture in Talk: A Collection of Methods, N. Quinn, ed. New York: Palgrave Macmillan. Pp. 35–81.

Rabe-Hemp, C. 2008. Survival in an "all boys club": Policewomen and their fight for acceptance. Policing: An International Journal of Police Strategies and Management 31:251–270.

Raby, D. 2007. The cave-dweller's treasure: Folktales, morality, and gender in a Nahua community in Mexico. Journal of American Folklore 120:401–444.

Radnofsky, M. L. 1996. Qualitative models: Visually representing complex data in an image/text balance. Qualitative Inquiry 2:386–410.

Ragin, C. C. 1987. The comparative method. Moving beyond qualitative and quantitative strategies. Berkeley: University of California Press.

Ragin, C. C. 1994. Introduction to qualitative comparative analysis. In: The Comparative Political Economy of the Welfare State, T. Janowski and A. M. Hicks, eds. New York: Cambridge University Press. Pp. 299–319.

Ragin, C. C., K. A. Drass, and S. Davey 2006. Fuzzy-Set/Qualitative Comparative Analysis 2.0. Tucson: Department of Sociology, University of Arizona.

Rantala, K. and E. Hellström 2001. Qualtiative comparative analysis and a hermeneutic approach to interview data. International Journal of Social Research Methodology 4:87–100.

Rathje, W. L. and C. Murphy 1992. Garbage demographics. American Demographics 14:50–54.

Reed, T. W. and R. J. Stimson, eds. 1985. Survey Interviewing: Theory and Techniques. Boston: Allen & Unwin.

Rees, C. E., L. V. Knight, and C. E. Wilkinson 2007. Doctors being up there and we being down here: A metaphorical analysis of talk about student/doctor–patient relationships. Social Science and Medicine 65:725–737.

Reid, B. V. and J. Valsiner 1986. Consistency, praise, and love: Folk theories of American parents. Ethos 14:282–304.

Reimer, M. and B. Mathes 2007. Collecting event histories with true tales: Techniques to improve autobiographical recall problems in standardized interviews. Quality and Quantity 41:711–735.

Reyes-García, V., E. Byron, V. Vadez, R. Godoy, L. Apaza, E. Pérez-Limache, W. R. Leonard, and D. Wilkie 2004. Measuring culture as shared knowledge: Do data collection formats matter? Cultural knowledge of plant uses among Tsimane' Amerindians, Bolivia. Field Methods 16:135–156.

Ricci, J. A., N. W. Jerome, N. Megally, and O. Galal 1995. Assessing the validity of information recall: Results of a time-use pilot study in peri-urban Egypt. Human Organization 54:304–308.

Rice, E. 1980. On cultural schemata. American Ethnologist 7:152–171.

Rice, R. E. and J. A. Danowski 1993. Is it really just like a fancy answering machine? Comparing semantic networks of different types of voice mail users. Journal of Business Communication 4:369–397.

Rich, E. 1977. Sex-related differences in colour vocabulary. Language and Speech 20:404–409.

Rich, E. 2005. Young women, feminist identities, and neo-liberalism. Women's Studies International Forum 28:495–508.

Richards, L. 2002. Qualitative computing—a methods revolution? International Journal of Social Research Methodology 5:263–276.

Richards, L. 2005. Handling Qualitative Data: A Practical Guide. Thousand Oaks, CA: Sage Publications.

Richards, L. and T. Richards 1995. Using hierarchical categories in qualitative data analysis. In: Computer-Aided Qualitative Data Analysis: Theory, Methods and Practice, U. Kelle, ed. London: Sage Publications. Pp. 80–95.

Richards, T. 2002. An intellectual history of NUD*IST and NVivo. International Journal of Social Research Methodology 5:199–214.

Richardson, S. A., B. S. Dohrenwend, and D. Klein 1965. Interviewing: Its Forms and Functions. New York: Basic Books.

Ricoeur, P. 1981. Hermeneutics and the Human Sciences: Essays on Language, Action, and Interpretation. J. B. Thompson, tr. and ed. New York: Cambridge University Press.

Ricoeur, P. 1991. From text to action. Evanston, IL: Northwestern University Press.

Riffe, D., L. Stephen, and F. G. Fico 2005. Analyzing Media Messages: Using Quantitative Content Analysis in Research. 2nd ed. Mahwah, NJ: Lawrence Erlbaum Associates.

Rihoux, B. 2003. Bridging the gap between the qualitative and quantitative worlds? A retrospective and prospective view on qualitative and comparative analysis. Field Methods 15:351–365.

Rihoux, B. 2006. Qualitative comparative analysis and related systematic comparative methods. International Sociology 21:679–706.

Rihoux, B. and C. C. Ragin, eds. 2008. Configurational Comparative Methods. Thousand Oaks, CA: Sage Publications.

Robbins, M. and J. M. Nolan 1997. A measure of dichotomous category bias in free listing tasks. Cultural Anthropology Methods Journal 9:8–12.

Robbins, M. and J. M. Nolan 2000. A measure of semantic category clustering in free-listing tasks. Field Methods 12:18–28.

Roberts, C. W., ed. 1997. Text Analysis for the Social Sciences: Methods for Drawing Statistical Inferences from Texts and Transcripts. Mahwah, NJ: Lawrence Erlbaum Associates.

Robinson, J. D. 1998. Getting down to business—Talk, gaze, and body orientation during openings of doctor-patient consultations. Human Communication Research 25:97–123.

Robinson, J. D. and J. Heritage 2005. The structure of patients' presenting concerns: The completion relevance of current symptoms. Social Science and Medicine 61:481–493.

Robinson, W. S. 1951. The logical structure of analytic induction. American Sociological Review 16:812–818.

Romme, A. G. 1995. Boolean comparative analysis of qualitative data: A methodological note. Quality and Quantity 29:317–329.

Romney, A. K., S. C. Weller, and W. H. Batchelder 1986. Culture as consensus: A theory of culture and informant accuracy. American Anthropologist 88:313–338.

Rosch, E. 1975. Cognitive representations of semantic categories. Journal of Experimental Psychology 104:192–233.

Rosch, E. and C. B. Mervis 1975. Family resemblances: Studies in the internal structure of categories. Cognitive Psychology 5:573–605.

Rosenberg, S. D., P. P. Schnurr, and T. E. Oxman 1990. Content analysis: A comparison of manual and computerized systems. Journal of Personality Assessment 54:298–310.

Ross, J. L., S. L. Laston, P. J. Pelto, and L. Muna 2002. Exploring explanatory models of women's reproductive health in rural Bangladesh. Culture, Health, and Sexuality 4:173–190.

Ross, N., T. Barrientos, and A. Esquit-Choy 2005. Triad tasks, a multipurpose tool to elicit similarity judgments: The case of Tzotzil Maya plant taxonomy. Field Methods 17:269–282.

Rossi, P. H. 1994. The war between the quals and the quants: Is a lasting peace possible? In: The Qualitative-Quantitative Debate: New Perspectives, C. S. Reichardt and S. F. Rallis, eds. San Francisco: Jossey-Bass. Pp. 23–36.

Rossi, P. H. and S. L. Noch 1982. Measuring Social Judgments: The Factorial Survey Approach. Beverly Hills, CA: Sage Publications.

Roy, K. 2006. Father stories: A life course examination of paternal identity among low-income African American men. Journal of Family Issues 27:31–54.

Royal Anthropology Institute 1951 [1971]. Notes and Queries on Anthropology. 6th ed., revised and rewritten. London: Routledge and Kegan Paul.

Rubin, H. J. and I. S. Rubin 2005. Qualitative Interviewing: The Art of Hearing Data. Thousand Oaks, CA: Sage Publications.

Rubinstein, R. L. 1995. Narratives of elder parental death: A structural and cultural analysis. Medical Anthropology Quarterly 9:257–276.

Rumelhart, D. E. 1975. Notes on a schema for stories. In: Representation and Understanding: Studies in Cognitive Science, D. Bobrow and A. Collins, eds. New York: Academic Press. Pp. 211–236.

Rumelhart, D. E. 1980. Schemata: The building blocks of cognition. In: Theoretical Issues in Reading Comprehension: Perspectives from Cognitive Psychology, Linguistics, Artificial Intelligence, and Education, R. J. Spiro, B. C. Bruce and W. B. Brewer, eds. Hillsdale, NJ: Lawrence Erlbaum Associates. Pp. 38–58.

Ryan, G. W. 1995. Medical Decision Making Among the Kom of Cameroon: Modeling How Characteristics of Illnesses, Patients, Caretakers, and Compounds Affect Treatment Choice in a Rural Community. Unpublished Ph.D. dissertation, University of Florida.

Ryan, G. W. 1998. Modeling home case management of acute illness in a rural Cameroonian village. Social Science and Medicine 4:209–225.

Ryan, G. W. 1999. Measuring the typicality of text: Using multiple coders for more than just reliability and validity checks. Human Organization 58:313–322.

Ryan, G. W. and H. R. Bernard 2003. Techniques to identify themes. Field Methods 15:85–109.

Ryan, G. W. and H. R. Bernard 2006. Testing an ethnographic decision tree model on a national sample: Recycling beverage cans. Human Organization 65:103–115.

Ryan, G. W. and H. Martínez 1996. Can we predict what mothers do? Modeling childhood diarrhea in rural Mexico. Human Organization 55:47–57.

Ryan, G. W., J. M. Nolan, and P. S. Yoder 2000. Successive free listing: Using free lists to generate explanatory models. Field Methods 12:83–107.

Ryan, G. W. and T. Weisner 1996. Analyzing words in brief descriptions: Fathers and mothers describe their children. Cultural Anthropology Methods Journal 8:13–16.

Saban, A., B. N. Kocbecker, and A. Saban 2007. Prospective teachers' conceptions of teaching and learning revealed through metaphor analysis. Learning and Instruction 17:123–139.

Sacks, H. 1992. Lectures on Conversation. Cambridge, MA: Basil Blackwell.

Sacks, H., E. A. Schegloff, and G. Jefferson. 1974. A Simplest Systematics for the Organization of Turn-Taking Conversation. Language 50:696–735.

Saito, A., ed. 2000. Bartlett, Culture and Cognition. Hove, UK: Psychology Press.

Saks, M. and J. Allsop, eds. 2007. Researching Health: Qualitative, Quantitative and Mixed Methods. Thousand Oaks, CA: Sage Publications.

Salganik, M. J. and D. D. Heckathorn 2004. Sampling and estimation in hidden populations using respondent-driven sampling. Sociological Methodology 34:193–239.

Sammons, K. and J. Sherzer, eds. 2000. Translating Native American Verbal Art: Ethnopoetics and Ethnography of Speaking. Washington, DC: Smithsonian Institution Press.

Sandelowski, M. 1995a. Qualitative analysis: What it is and how to begin. Research in Nursing and Health 18:371–375.

Sandelowski, M. 1995b. Sample size in qualitative research. Research in Nursing and Health 18:179–183.

Sayles, J. N., G. W. Ryan, J. S. Silver, and W. E. Cunningham 2007. Experiences of social stigma and implications for healthcare among a diverse population of HIV positive adults. Journal of Urban Health 84:814–828.

Schank, R. and R. Abelson. 1977. Scripts, Plans, Goals and Understanding: An Inquiry into Human Knowledge Structures. Hillsdale, NJ: Lawrence Erlbaum Associates.

Schegloff, E. A. 1968. Sequencing in conversational openings. American Anthropologist 70:1075–1095.

Schegloff, E. A. 1979. Identification and recognition in telephone conversation openings. In: G. Psathas, ed. Everyday Language: Studies in Ethnomethodology. New York: Irvington. Pp. 23–78.

Schegloff, E. A. 2007. Sequence Organization in Interaction. A Primer in Conversation Analysis. New York: Cambridge University Press.

Schegloff, E. A. and H. Sacks. 1973. Opening up closings. Semiotica 7:289–327.

Schifflett, B. and R. Revelle 1994. Gender equity in sports and media coverage: A review of the NCAA News. Journal of Sport and Social Issues 18:144–150.

Schiffren, D., D. Tannen, and H. E. Hamilton 2001. Introduction. In: The Handbook of Discourse Analysis, D. Schiffren, D. Tannen, and H. E. Hamilton, eds. Malden, MA: Blackwell. Pp. 1–10.

Schlau, J. 2004. I did not die, I just can't hear—A grounded theory study of acquired deafness. Unpublished Ph.D. dissertation, Hofstra University.

Schleiermacher, F. 1998. Hermeneutics and Criticism: And Other Writings. Friedrich Schleiermacher. A. Bowie, tr. and ed. Cambridge: Cambridge University Press.

Schmitt, R. 2005. Systematic metaphor analysis as a method of qualitative research. Qualitative Report 10:358–394.

Schnegg, M. and H. R. Bernard 1996. Words as actors: A method for doing semantic network analysis. Cultural Anthropology Methods Journal 8:7–10.

Schonhardt-Bailey, C. 2008. The Congressional debate on partial-birth abortion: Constitutional gravitas and moral passion. British Journal of Political Science 38:383–410.

Schraw, G., T. Wadkins, L. Olafson 2007. Doing the things we do: A grounded theory of academic procrastination. Journal of Educational Psychology 99:12–25.

Schuster, M. A., N. Halfon, and D. L. Wood 1998. African American mothers in south central Los Angeles. Their fears for their newborn's future. Archives of Pediatric and Adolescent Medicine 152:264–268.

Schuster, M. A., N. Duan, M. Regalado, and D. J. Klein 2000. Anticipatory guidance: What information do parents receive? What information do they want? Archives of Pediatric and Adolescent Medicine 154:1191–1198.

Schweizer, T. 1996. Actor and event orderings across time: Lattice representation and Boolean analysis of the political disputes in Chen Village, China. Social Networks 18:247–266.

Scott, S. 1991. The History and Philosophy of Social Science. London: Routledge.

Scott, S. B., C. S. Bergeman, A. Verney, S. Logenbaker, M. A. Markey, and T. L. Bosconti 2007. Social support in widowhood: A mixed methods study. Journal of Mixed Methods Research 1:242–266.

Scotton, C. M. and W. Ury 1977. Bilingual strategies: The social functions of code-switching. International Journal of the Sociology of Language 13:5–20.

Seale, C., J. Charteris-Black, C. Dumelow, L. Locock, and S. Ziebland 2008. The effect of joint interviewing on the performance of gender. Field Methods 20:107–128.

Sefcek, J. A., B. H. Brumbach, and G. Vasquez, 2007. The evolutionary psychology of human mate choice: How ecology, genes, fertility, and fashion influence mating strategies. Journal of Psychology and Human Sexuality 18:125–182.

Shanahan, E. A., M. K. McBeth, P. L. Hathaway, and R. J. Arnell 2008. Conduit or contributor? The role of media in policy change theory. Policy Sciences 41:115–138.

Shapiro, G. 1997. The future of coders: Human judgments in a world of sophisticated software. In: Text Analysis for the Social Sciences: Methods for Drawing Statistical Inferences From Texts and Transcripts, C. W. Roberts, ed. Mahwah, NJ: Lawrence Erlbaum Associates. Pp. 225–238.

Shapiro, G. and J. Markoff 1997. A matter of definition. In: Text Analysis for the Social Sciences: Methods for Drawing Statistical Inferences From Texts and Transcripts, C. W. Roberts, ed. Mahwah, NJ: Lawrence Erlbaum Associates. Pp. 9–34.

Shelley, G. A. 1992. The social networks of people with end-stage renal disease: Comparing hemodialysis and peritoneal dialysis patients. Unpublished Ph.D. dissertation, University of Florida.

Shepard, R. N., A. K. Romney, and S. B. Nerlove, eds. 1972. Multidimensional Scaling: Theory and Applications in the Behavioral Sciences. New York: Seminar Press.

Sherzer, J. 1994. The Kuna and Columbus: Encounters and confrontations of discourse. American Anthropologist 96:902–25.

Silva, E. 2007. What's [yet] to be seen? Re-using qualitative data. Sociological Research Online 12(3). Online at http://www.socresonline.org.uk/12/3/4.html. Accessed 1-30-09.

Silverman, D. 1993. Interpreting Qualitative Data: Methods of Analyzing Talk, Text, and Interaction. Thousands Oaks, CA: Sage Publications.

Silverman, D. 1998. Harvey Sacks: Social Science and Conversation Analysis. New York: Oxford University Press.

Silverman, E., S. Woolshin, L. M. Schwartz, S. J. Byram, H. G. Welch, and B. Fischoff 2001. Women's views on breast cancer risk and screening mammography: A qualitative interview study. Medical Decision Making 21:231–240.

Silverman, M., M. A. Terry, R. K. Zimmerman, J. F. Nutini, and E. M. Ricci 2004. Tailoring interventions: Understanding medical practice culture. Journal of Cross-Cultural Gerontology 19:47–76.

Sin, C. H. 2007. Using software to open up the "black box" of qualitative data analysis in evaluations: The experience of a multi-site team using NUD*IST Version 6. Evaluation: The International Journal of Theory, Research and Practice 13:110–120.

Slaughter, V. 2005. Young children's understanding of death. Australian Psychologist 40:179–186.

Smilde, D. 2005. A qualitative comparative analysis of conversion to Venezuelan evangelicism: How networks matter. American Journal of Sociology 111:757–796.

Smith, A. 2000. "Safety" in gay men's personal ads, 1985–1996. Journal of Homosexuality 39:43–48.

Smith, C. A. and S. Stillman 2002a. Butch/femme in the personal advertisements of lesbians. Journal of Lesbian Studies 6:45–51.

Smith, C. A. and S. Stillman 2002b. What Do Women Want? The Effects of Gender and Sexual Orientation on the Desirability of Physical Attributes in the Personal Ads of Women. Sex Roles 46:337–342

Smith, C. D. and W. Kornblum 1996. In the Field. Readings on the Research Experience. New York: Praeger.

Smith, J. J. 1993. Using ANTHROPAC 3.5 and a spreadsheet to compute a freelist salience index. Cultural Anthropology Methods Newsletter 5:1–3.

Smith, J. J. and S. P. Borgatti 1997. Salience counts—and so does accuracy: Correcting and updating a measure for free-list item salience. Journal of Linguistic Anthropology 7:208–209.

Smith, T. M. F. 1983. On the validity of inferences from non-random samples. Journal of the Royal Statistical Society, Series A (General) 146:394–403.

Smith, T. W. 1997. The impact of the presence of others on a respondent's answers to questions. International Journal of Public Opinion Research 9:33–47.

Smith-Lovin, L. and C. Brody 1989. Interruptions in group discussions: The effect of gender and group composition. American Sociological Review 54:424–435.

Sobal, J. 2001. Sample extensiveness in qualitative nutrition education research. Journal of Nutrition Education 33:184–193.

Sokolowski, R. 2000. Introduction to Phenomenology. New York: Cambridge University Press.

Spiegelberg, H. 1980. Phenomenology. Encyclopaedia Brittanica. 15th ed., Vol. 14. Chicago: Encyclopaedia Brittanica.

Spradley, J. P. 1972. Culture and Cognition: Rules, Maps, and Plans. New York: Chandler Publishing Company.

Spradley, J. P. 1979. The Ethnographic Interview. New York: Holt, Rinehart and Winston.

Spradley, J. P. 1980. Participant Observation. New York: Holt, Rinehart and Winston.

Sproull, L. S. 1981. Managing education programs: A micro-behavioral analysis. Human Organization 40:113–122.

Stalp, M. C. and L. Grant 2001. Teaching qualitative coding in undergraduate field method classes: An exercise based on personal ads. Teaching Sociology 29:209–218.

Stefflre, V. J. 1972. Some applications of multidimensional scaling to social science problems. In: Multidimensional Scaling: Theory and Applications in the Behavioral Sciences, R. N. Shephard, A. K. Romney, and S. B. Nerlove, eds. Vol. 2. New York: Seminar Press. Pp. 211–243.

Steger, T. 2007. The stories metaphors tell: Metaphors as a tool to decipher tacit aspects in narratives. Field Methods 19:3–23.

Stein, R. H. 1987. The synoptic problem. Grand Rapids, MI: Baker Book House.

Stewart, D. W. and P. N. Shamdasani 1990. Focus Groups: Theory and Practice. Newbury Park, CA: Sage Publications.

Stewart, P. J. and A. Strathern 2002. Gender, Song, and Sensibility. Folktales and Folksongs in the Highlands of New Guinea. Westport, CT: Praeger.

Stigler, J. W., P. A. Gonzales, T. Kawanka, S. Knoll, and A. Serrano 1999. The TIMSS Videotape Classroom Study: Methods and Findings from an Exploratory Research Project on Eighth-Grade Mathematics Instruction in Germany, Japan, and the United States. National Center for Education Statistics. NCES 99–074.

Washington, DC: U.S. Government Printing Office. Online at http://nces.ed.gov/pubs99/1999074.pdf. Accessed 8-22-08.

Stokke, O. S. 2007. Qualitative comparative analysis, shaming, and international regime effectiveness. Journal of Business Research 60:501–511.

Stone, P. J., D. C. Dunphy, M. S. Smith, and D. M. Ogilvie, eds. 1966. The General Inquirer: A Computer Approach to Content Analysis. Cambridge, MA: MIT Press.

Strauss, A. 1987. Qualitative Analysis for Social Scientists. Cambridge: Cambridge University Press.

Strauss, A. and J. Corbin 1990. Basics of Qualitative Research: Grounded Theory Procedures and Techniques. Newbury Park, CA: Sage Publications.

Strauss, A. and J. Corbin, eds. 1997. Grounded Theory in Practice. Thousand Oaks, CA: Sage Publications.

Strauss, A. and J. Corbin 1998. Basics of Qualitative Research: Grounded Theory Procedures and Techniques. 2nd ed. Thousand Oaks, CA: Sage Publications.

Strauss, C. 1992. What makes Tony run? Schemas as motive reconsideration. In: Human Motives and Cultural Models, R. D'Andrade and C. Strauss, eds. Cambridge: Cambridge University Press. Pp. 191–224.

Strauss, C. 1997. Research on cultural discontinuities. In: A Cognitive Theory of Cultural Meaning. C. Strauss and N. Quinn, eds. Cambridge: Cambridge University Press. Pp. 210–251.

Strauss, C. and N. Quinn 1997. A Cognitive Theory of Cultural Meaning. Cambridge: Cambridge University Press.

Sudman, S. 1967. Reducing the Cost of Surveys. Chicago: Aldine.

Sudman, S. and N. M. Bradburn. 1974. Response effects in surveys: Review and synthesis. Chicago: Aldine.

Sudman, S. and G. Kalton 1986. New developments in the sampling of special populations. Annual Review of Sociology 12:401–429.

Suedfeld, P., S. Bluck, and E. J. Ballard 1990. Canadian federal elections: Motive profiles and integrative complexity in political speeches and popular media. Canadian Journal of Behavioural Science 22:26–36.

Sutrop, U. 2001. List task and a cognitive salience index. Field Methods13:263–276.

Swora, M. G. 2003. Using cultural consensus analysis to study sexual risk perception: A report on a pilot study. Culture, Health, and Sexuality 5:339–352

Sykes, R. E. and E. E. Brent 1983. Policing: A Social Behaviorist Perspective. New Brunswick, NJ: Rutgers University Press.

Sykes, W. 1990. Validity and reliability in qualitative market research: A review of the literature. Journal of the Market Research Society 32:289–328.

Sykes, W. 1991. Taking stock; Issues from the literature on validity and reliability in qualitative research. Journal of the Market Research Society 33:3–12.

SYSTAT 12 2008. Systat Software Inc., 225 W. Washington St., Suite 425, Chicago, IL 60606. Online at http://www.systat.com. Accessed on 9-22-08.

Tabenkin, H., M. A. Goodwin, S. J. Zyzanski, K. C. Stange, and J. H. Medalie 2004. Gender differences in time spent during direct observation of doctor-patient encounters. Journal of Women's Health 13:341–349.

Tacq, J. 2007. Znaniecki's analytical induction as a method of sociological research. Polish Sociological Review 2:187–208.

Tan, K. P. 2007. Singapore's National Day rally speech: A site of ideological negotiation. Journal of Contemporary Asia 37:292–308.

Tang, E. and H. Nesi 2003. Teaching vocabulary in two Chinese classrooms: Schoolchildren's exposure to English words in Hong Kong and Guangzhou. Language Teaching Research 7:65–97.

Tang, Z., L. Weavwind, J. Mazabob, E. J. Thomas, M. Y. L. Chu-Weininger, and T. R. Johnson 2007. Workflow in intensive care unit remote monitoring: A time-and-motion study. Critical Care Medicine 35:2057–2063.

Tannen, D. 1984. Conversational Style: Analyzing Talk Among Friends. Norwood, NJ: Ablex.

Tannen, D. 1994. Gender and Discourse. New York: Oxford University Press.

Tashakkori, A. and C. Teddlie 1998. Mixed Methodology: Combining Qualitative and Quantitative Approaches. Thousand Oaks, CA: Sage Publications.

Tashakkori, A. and C. Teddlie, eds. 2003. Handbook of Mixed Methods in Social and Behavioral Research. Thousand Oaks, CA: Sage Publications.

Taylor, P. M. 1995. Collecting icons of power and identity: Transformation of Indonesian material culture in the museum context. Cultural Dynamics 7:101–124.

Taylor, W. K., L. Magnussen, and M. J. Amundon 2001. The lived experience of battered women. Violence Against Women 7:563–585.

ten Have, P. 1991. Talk and institution: A reconsideration of the "asymmetry" of doctor-patient interaction. In: Talk and Social Structure. Studies in Ethnomethodology and Conversation Analysis, D. Boden and Z. H. Zimmerman, eds. Berkeley: University of California Press. Pp. 138–163.

Tesch, R. 1990. Qualitative Research: Analysis Types and Software Tools. New York: The Falmer Press.

Therkelsen, A. and M. Gram 2008. The meaning of holiday consumption: Construction of self among mature couples. Journal of Consumer Culture 8:269–292.

Thomas, J. S. 1981. The economic determinants of leadership in a Tojalabal Maya community. American Ethnologist 8:127–138.

Thompson, C. 1999. Qualitative research into nurse decision making: Factors for consideration in theoretical sampling. Qualitative Health Research 9:815–828.

Thompson, C., D. McCaughan, N. Cullum, T. A. Sheldon, and P. Raynor 2004. Increasing the visibility of coding decisions in team-based qualitative research in nursing. International Journal of Nursing Studies 41:15–20.

Thompson, E. C. and Z. Juan 2006. Comparative cultural salience: Measures using free-list data. Field Methods 18:398–412.

Thompson, S. 1932–1936. Motif-Index of Folk-Literature. A Classification of Narrative Elements in Folktales, Ballads, Myths, Fables, Mediaeval Romances, Exempla, Fabliaux, Jest-Books, and Local Legends. Bloomington: Indiana University Press.

Thornberg, R. 2008. "It's not fair!"—Voicing pupils' criticism of school rules. Children and Society 22:418–428.

Timm, J. R., ed. 1992. Texts in Context. Traditional Hermeneutics in South Asia. Albany: State University of New York Press.

Tourangeau, R. and T.Yan. 2007. Sensitive questions in surveys. Psychological Bulletin 133:859–883.

Toyokawa, N. 2006. The function of the social network formed by Japanese sojourners' wives in the United States. International Journal of Intercultural Relations 30:185–193.

Trotter, R. T., III, and J. M. Potter 1993. Pile sorts, a cognitive anthropological model of drug and AIDS risks for Navajo teenagers: Assessment of a new evaluation tool. Drugs and Society 7:23–39.

Tsang, W. K. and M. Wong 2004. Constructing a shared "Hong Kong identity" in comic discourses. Discourse and Society 15:767–785.

Tufte, E. R. 1997. Visual Explanations: Images and Quantities, Evidence and Narrative. Cheshire, CT: Graphics Press.

Turner, L. H. and R. Shuter 2004. African American and European American women's visions of workplace conflict: A metaphorical analysis. The Howard Journal of Communications 15:169–183.

Turner, R. 1953. The quest for universals in sociological research. American Sociological Review 18:604–611.

United States v. Pelley; *Same v. Brown*; *Same v. Fellowship Press, Inc.* Nos. 8086-8088. United States Court of Appeals for the Seventh Circuit. 132 F.2d 170; 1942 U.S. App. LEXIS 2559. December 17, 1942.

Van Boeschoten, R. 2006. Code-switching, linguistic jokes and ethnic identity: Reading hidden transcripts in a cross-cultural context. Journal of Modern Greek Studies 24:347–377.

Van Der Vaart, W. and T. Glasner 2007. Applying a timeline as a recall aid in a telephone survey: A record check study. Applied Cognitive Psychology 21:227–238.

Van Leeuwen, T. and C. Jewitt, eds. 2001. Handbook of Visual Analysis. London: Sage.

Van Maanen, J., M. Miller, and J. C. Johnson 1982. An occupation in transition: Traditional and modern forms of commercial fishing. Work and Occupations 9:193–216.

van Manen, M. 1990. Researching Lived Experience. Human Science for an Action Sensitive Pedagogy. Albany: State University of New York Press.

Van Vliet, K. J. 2008. Shame and resilience in adulthood: A grounded theory study. Journal of Counseling Psychology 55:233–245.

Vaughn, S., J. S. Schumm, and J. M. Sinagub 1996. Focus Group Interviews in Education and Psychology. Thousand Oaks, CA: Sage Publications.

Viney, L. L. 1983. Assessment of psychological states through content analysis of verbal communications. Psychological Bulletin 94:542–563.

Waitzkin, H., T. Britt, and C. Williams 1994. Narratives of aging and social problems in medical encounters with older persons. Journal of Health and Social Behavior 35:322–348.

Wansink, B., K. V. Ittersum, and J. E. Painter 2006. Ice cream illusions: Bowls, spoons, and self-served portion sizes. American Journal of Preventive Medicine 31:240–242.

Ward, W. and D. Spennemann 2000. Meeting local needs? Case study of a communication project in the Pacific islands. Public Administration and Development 20:185–195.

Warwick, D. P. and C. A. Lininger 1975. The sample survey: Theory and practice. New York: McGraw-Hill.

Watts, D. D. 1997. Correspondence analysis—A graphical technique for examining categorical data. Nursing Research 46:235–239.

Watts, L. K. and S. E. Gutierres 1997. A Native American-based cultural model of substance dependency and recovery. Human Organization 56:9–18.

Weaver, S. E. and M. Coleman 2005. A mothering but not a mother role: A grounded theory study of the nonresidential stepmother role. Journal of Social and Personal Relationships 22:477–497.

Weber, R. P. 1990. Basic Content Analysis. 2nd ed. Newbury Park, CA: Sage Publications.

Wei, L. and L. Milroy 1995. Conversational code-switching in a Chinese community in Britain: A sequential analysis. Journal of Pragmatics 23:281–299.

Weine, S., K. Knafl, S. Feetham, Y. Kulauzovic, A. Klebic, S. Sclove, S. Besic, A. Mujagic, J. Muzurovic, and D. Spahovic 2005. A mixed methods study of refugee families engaging in multiple-family groups. Family Relations 54:558–568.

Weisner, T. S. 2002a. Ecocultural understanding of children's developmental pathways. Human Development 45:275–281.

Weisner, T. S. 2002b. The American dependency conflict: Continuities and discontinuities in behavior and values of countercultural parents and their children. Ethos 29:271–295.

Weisner, T. S. 2008. Well being and sustainability of the daily routine of life. In: The Good Life: Well-Being in Anthropological Perspective, G. Mathews and C. Izquerdo, eds. New York: Berghahn Press. Pp. 349–380.

Weisner, T. S., L. Beizer, and L. Stolze 1991. Religion and families of children with developmental delays. American Journal of Mental Retardation 95:647–662.

Weller, S. C. 2007. The cultural consensus model. Field Methods 19:339–368.

Weller, S. C. and A. K. Romney 1988. Systematic Data Collection. Newbury Park, CA: Sage Publications.

Weller, S. C. and A. K. Romney 1990. Metric Scaling: Correspondence Analysis. Newbury Park, CA: Sage Publications.

Weller, S. C., T. K. Ruebush II, and R. E. Klein 1997. Predicting treatment-seeking behavior in Guatemala: A comparison of the health services research and decision-theoretic approaches. Medical Anthropology Quarterly 11:224–245.

Wennerstrom, A. 2001. The Music of Everyday Speech. Prosody and Discourse Analysis. New York: Oxford University Press.

Werner, O. 1972. Ethnoscience 1972. Annual Review of Anthropology 1:271–308.

Werner, O. 1992. How to record activities. Cultural Anthropology Methods Journal 4:1–3.

West, C. 1984. Routine Complications: Troubles with Talk Between Doctors and Patients. Bloomington: University of Indiana Press.

West, C. 1995. Women's competence in conversation. Discourse and Society 6:107–131.

West, C. and D. Zimmerman 1983. Small insults: A study of interruptions in cross-sex conversations between unacquainted persons. In: Language, Gender, and

Society, B. Thorne, C. Kramarae, and N. Henley, eds. Rowley, MA: Newbury House Publishers. Pp. 102–117.

Weston, C., T. Gandell, J. Beauchamp, L. McAlpine, C. Wiseman, and C. Beauchamp 2001. Analyzing interview data: The development and evolution of a coding system. Qualitative Sociology 24:381–400.

White, S. B. 2006. Telling the story: Kansas City mayor and United Methodist pastor Emmanuel Cleaver's use of storytelling to transcend racial barriers. Journal of African American Studies 9:32–44.

Whiting, B. W., J. W. M. Whiting (with R. Longabaugh) 1975. Children of six cultures: A psycho-cultural analysis. Cambridge, MA: Harvard University Press.

Whiting, J. B. and R. E. Lee III 2003. Voices from the system: A qualitative study of foster children's stories. Family Relations 52:288–295.

Whorf, B. L. 1945. Grammatical categories. Language 21:1–11.

Whyte, W. F. 1960. Interviewing in field research. In: Human Organization Research, by R. W. Adams and J. J. Preiss, eds. Homewood, IL: Dorsey. Pp. 299–314.

Whyte, W. F. 1981 [1943]. Street Corner Society: The Social Structure of an Italian Slum. 3rd ed. Chicago: University of Chicago Press.

Whyte, W. F. 1989. Doing research in Cornerville. In: In the Field: Readings on the Field Research Experience, C. D. Smith and W. Kornblum, eds. New York: Praeger. Pp. 69–82.

Whyte, W. F. 1996a. Qualitative sociology and deconstructionism. Qualitative Inquiry 2:220–226.

Whyte, W. F. 1996b. Facts, interpretations, and ethics in qualitative inquiry. Qualitative Inquiry 2:242–244.

Whyte, W. F. and K. A. Whyte 1984. Learning from the field: A guide from experience. Beverly Hills, CA: Sage Publications.

Wickham-Crowley, T. P. 1991. A qualitative comparative approach to Latin American Revolutions. International Journal of Comparative Sociology 32:82–109.

Wiederman, M. W. 1993. Evolved gender differences in mate preferences—Evidence from personal advertisements. Ethology and Sociobiology 14:331–351.

Wiederman, M. W., D. Weis, and E. Algeier 1994. The effect of question preface on response rates in a telephone survey of sexual experience. Archives of Sexual Behavior 23:203–215.

Wierzbicka, A. 2004. The English expression good boy and good girl and cultural models of child rearing. Culture and Psychology 10:251–278.

Wilcox, F. D. 1900. The American newspaper: A study in social psychology. Annals of the American Academy of Political and Social Science 16:56–92.

Williams, L. M. and R. A. Farrell 1990. Legal responses to child sexual abuse in day care. Criminal Justice and Behavior 17:284–302.

Willis, F. N. and R. A. Carlson 1993. Singles ads—Gender, social class, and time. Sex Roles 29:387–404.

Wilson, H. S., S. A. Hutchinson, and W. H. Holzemer 2002. Reconciling incompatibilities: a grounded theory of HIV medication adherence and symptom management. Qualitative Health Research 12:1309–1322.

Witavaara, B., B. Lundman, M. Barnekow-Bergkvist, and C. Brulin 2007. Striking a balance—health experience of male ambulance personnel with musculoskeletal symptoms: A grounded theory. International Journal of Nursing Studies 44:770–779.

Wodak, R. 1992. Strategies in text production and text comprehension: A new perspective. In: Cooperating With Written Texts, D. Stein, ed. New York: Mouton de Gruyter. Pp. 493–528.

Wodak, R. and M. Reisig 1999. Discourse and Discrimination. The Rhetoic of Racism and Antisemitism. London: Routledge.

Wolcott, H. F. 1992. Posturing in qualitative inquiry. In: The Handbook of Qualitative Research in Education, M. D. LeCompte, W. L. Millroy, and J. Preissle, eds. New York: Academic Press. Pp. 3–52.

Wolcott, H. F. 2005. The Art of Fieldwork. 2nd ed. Walnut Creek, CA: AltaMira Press.

Woodward, J. L. and R. Franzen 1948. A study of coding reliability. Public Opinion Quarterly 12:253–257.

Wright, J. 1997. Deconstructing development theory: feminism, the public/private dichotomoy, and the Mexican maquiladoras. Canadian Journal of Sociology and Anthropology 34:71–91.

Wutich, A., T. Lant, D. D. White, K. L. Larson, and M. Gartin 2009. Comparing focus group and individual responses on sensitive topics: A study of water decision-makers in a desert city. Field Methods 21: in press.

Wysoker, A. 2002. A conceptual model of weight loss and weight regain: An intervention for change. Journal of the American Psychiatric Nurses Association 8:168–173.

Yakali-Çamoglu, D. 2007. Turkish family narratives: The relationships between mothers- and daughters-in-law. Journal of Family History 32:161–178.

Yancey G. A. and S. W. Yancey 1997. Black-white differences in the use of personal advertisements for individuals seeking interracial relationships. Journal of Black Studies 27:650–667.

Yang, Y. 2001. Sex and language proficiency level in color naming performance: An ESL/EFL perspective. International Journal of Applied Linguistics 11:238–256.

Yeh, C. J. and A. G. Inman 2007. Qualitative data analysis and interpretation in counseling psychology: Strategies for best practices. Counseling Psychologist 35:369–403.

Yin, R. K. 2008. Case Study Research: Design and Methods. 4th ed. London: Sage Publications.

Yodanis, C. 2006. A place in town: Doing class in a coffee shop. Journal of Contemporary Ethnography 35:341–366.

Young, J. C. 1981. Non-use of physicians: Methodological approaches, policy implications, and the utility of decision models. Social Science and Medicine 15:499–507.

Young, J. C. and L. C. Garro 1994 [1981]. Medical Choice in a Mexican Village. Prospect Heights, IL: Waveland Press.

Yule, G. U. 1968 [1944]. The Statistical Study of Literary Vocabulary. Hamden, CT: Archon.

Zakrzewski, R. F. and M. A. Hector 2004. The lived experiences of alcohol addiction: Men of Alcoholics Anonymous. Issues in Mental Health Nursing 25:61–77.

Zeitlyn, D. 2004. The gift of the gab: Anthropology and conversation analysis. Anthropos 99:452–468.

Zimmerman, D. H. and C. West 1975. Sex roles, interruptions, and silences in conversation. In: Language and Sex: Difference and Dominance, B. Thorne and N. Henley, eds. Rowley, MA: Newbury House. Pp. 105–129.

Zipp, J. F. and J. Toth 2002. She said, he said, they said: The impact of spousal presence in survey research. Public Opinion Quarterly 66:177–208.

Znaniecki, F. 1934. The Method of Sociology. New York: Farrar and Rinehart.

Author Index

Subject Index

About the Authors

H. Russell Bernard is Professor Emeritus of Anthropology at the University of Florida. He served as editor of the *American Anthropologist* and *Human Organization*, and is currently editor of *Field Methods*. The four editions of his text *Research Methods in Anthropology* (AltaMira 2006) and his text *Social Research Methods* (Sage 2000), have been used by many students. Bernard co-founded (with Pertti Pelto) and co-directed (with Pelto and Stephen Borgatti) the National Science Foundation's Institute on Research Methods in Cultural Anthropology and has done fieldwork in Greece, Mexico, and the United States. His publications include (with Jesús Salinas Pedraza) *Native Ethnography: An Otomí Indian Describes His Culture* (Sage 1989), which won special mention in the Chicago Folklore Prize.

Gery W. Ryan is a senior behavioral scientist at RAND and an adjunct assistant professor in the Department of Psychiatry and Biobehavioral Sciences at UCLA. He specializes in applying systematic methods to qualitative research, and designing tools to evaluate attitudes and beliefs about health and education topics. Ryan received his Ph.D. in cultural anthropology from the University of Florida. He has taught graduate courses in advanced ethnographic methods and text analysis and has run workshops on qualitative methods—sponsored by the National Science Foundation, the National Institutes of Health, and the Centers for Disease Control and Prevention—in the United States, Europe, Latin America, Asia, and Africa. Ryan is on the editorial boards of *Field Methods* and the *Journal of Public Policy & Marketing*.

Supporting researchers for more than 40 years

Research methods have always been at the core of SAGE's publishing program. Founder Sara Miller McCune published SAGE's first methods book, *Public Policy Evaluation*, in 1970. Soon after, she launched the *Quantitative Applications in the Social Sciences* series—affectionately known as the "little green books."

Always at the forefront of developing and supporting new approaches in methods, SAGE published early groundbreaking texts and journals in the fields of qualitative methods and evaluation.

Today, more than 40 years and two million little green books later, SAGE continues to push the boundaries with a growing list of more than 1,200 research methods books, journals, and reference works across the social, behavioral, and health sciences. Its imprints—Pine Forge Press, home of innovative textbooks in sociology, and Corwin, publisher of PreK–12 resources for teachers and administrators—broaden SAGE's range of offerings in methods. SAGE further extended its impact in 2008 when it acquired CQ Press and its best-selling and highly respected political science research methods list.

From qualitative, quantitative, and mixed methods to evaluation, SAGE is the essential resource for academics and practitioners looking for the latest methods by leading scholars.

For more information, visit **www.sagepub.com**.